Classical Monologues

Women

Volume 3: From Aeschylus to Racine

CLASSICAL MONOLOGUES

Women

Volume 3: From Aeschylus to Racine

Edited with introductions by
Leon Katz

with the assistance of Georgi Iliev

APPLAUSE THEATRE *&* CINEMA BOOKS

NEW YORK

Classical Monologues: Women
Volume 3: From Aeschylus to Racine
edited with introductions by Leon Katz

ISBN 1-55783-614-0

Library of Congress Cataloging-in-Publication Data:
Classical monologues from Aeschylus to Bernard Shaw / edited with introductions by Leon Katz with the assistance of Georgi Iliev.
   p. cm.
   ISBN 1-55783-575-6
1. Monologues.
2. Drama—Collections.
3. Young men—Drama.
I. Katz, Leon, 1919–
   PN2080.C58 2002
808.82'45—dc21
2002004863

British Library Cataloging-in-Publication Data:
A catalog record of this book is available from the British Library

Applause Theatre & Cinema Books
151 West 46th Street, 8th Floor
New York, NY 10036
Phone: (212) 575-9265
Fax: (646) 562-5852
Email: info@applausepub.com
Internet: www.applausepub.com
Applause books are available through your local bookstore, or you may order at www.applausepub.com or call Music Dispatch at 800-637-2852.

SALES & DISTRIBUTION
North America:
Hal Leonard Corp.
7777 West Bluemound Road
P. O. Box 13819
Milwaukee, WI 53213
Phone: (414) 774-3630
Fax: (414) 774-3259
Email: halinfo@halleonard.com
Internet: www.halleonard.com

Europe:
Roundhouse Publishing Ltd.
Millstone, Limers Lane
Northam, North Devon EX39 2RG
Phone: (0) 1237-474-474
Fax: (0) 1237-474-774
Email: roundhouse.group@ukgateway.net

CONTENTS

* Y=young, O=older; T=tragedy/drama, C=comedy

ROMAN

ITALIAN RENAISSANCE

ELIZABETHAN AND JACOBEAN

SIXTEENTH- AND
SEVENTEENTH-CENTURY SPANISH

SEVENTEENTH-CENTURY FRENCH

PRELIMINARY NOTE ON THE CHARACTERIZATION OF WOMEN IN WESTERN DRAMA

There's no getting away from it; most of it is damning testimony. The portrayals of women; the ideologies behind those portrayals; the characteristics attributed to them; the constrictions of situation in which they appear; the extraordinary psychology, morality, and causality, which are shown to govern their behavior; and the systematized rewards and punishments visited on them by the conventions of drama's structures might properly be said to belong to fantasy, if they were not reflections as in a partially shattered mirror of the same beliefs in reality. There's also no getting away from the fact that the portrayals of men suffer from the same fatalities. The difference, in effect, is enormous. There's implicit flattery in the portrayals of men even at their most "vicious": they're enlarged, after all, by manliness. There is implicit, at best, condescension and, at worst, condemnation in the portrayals of women even at their most "courageous" or "brilliant" or "virtuous": they're diminished, after all, by womanliness. For most of the development of Western drama, the basic assumption is that women are natively rudderless and that all of them—whether wise or foolish, virtuous or vicious, sane or insane—need guidance, constraint, and authority. Miraculously, with the exception of the most foolish and the most vicious, women characters themselves subscribe universally to that same set of beliefs.

To this extent: One of the extraordinary anomalies in our dramatic literature is the gusto with which women characters who are discovered to have committed moral transgressions volunteer to submit to or, if possible, anticipate the grimmest punishments of themselves they can imagine. They disgust themselves, verbally lash themselves, lay hands on themselves, starve themselves, and, if none of these are efficacious enough, they deliberately damn themselves to perdition with knives, swords, poisons, pistols, rivers, wells, or passing trains.

Or take the opposite case. There are the extraordinary number of women characters who take pride and pleasure in being models of servility, weakness, and helplessness. Listen to them carefully: they pride themselves on their abject surrender of themselves, their utter self-negation, and their proud admission that they don't have either the desire or the nature to exceed the handicap of womanhood; they flatter themselves on their perfect accommodations to subservience. The light they bathe in is shed by father, lover, or husband; the rule they live by is his, whether its substance is generous thought or private whim or worse. And the severity with which they live by this code is generally based on the demands father, lover, husband, or anyone makes on them. But that's the plus of the highest virtue: nobody asked and yet they give. Yet these apparent opposites are the same. Both are sworn to the principles of technical virtue and perfect obedience, and whether they are successful negotiators or fallen angels, they praise or blame themselves according to the same book of moral etiquette.

It's been observed before and it's observed here again that, as a consequence, the depiction of women as dramatic characters is made up of nothing but a small collection of cultural attributions. When we imagine we're discerning in that repository of fixed didacticisms characters' inner depth, meaning, or reality, we are not being blessed with unique powers of observation or intuition, but only with the delusionary comfort of self-flattery. Ingenuity can make anything of anything. It has recourse, after all, to a range of sophisticated vocabularies from the wisdom of street talk to the more formal packagings of words in professional psychology.

Sadly, apart from recreative pleasure, knowing all this helps not at all. No one—neither critics, dramaturgs, directors, spectators, nor (imagine) even playwrights—will voluntarily surrender their own moral and psychological idolatries for the small gain of admitting that, with respect to the realities of human beings, they're determinedly avoiding them and sticking to familiar pretense. Liars? No. We have no other filters for screening the truth of being, and the misfiltering of that truth is permanent. Characters—most particularly women characters as depicted in Western drama—are illusionary constructs, better or worse depending on the investment of illusionary perceptions with which the naked banality of their fixed didactic types is camouflaged and decorated.

The types are four—sometimes as is, sometimes qualified, sometimes mixed and matched: 1) helpless virtue (the patient Griselda); 2) sinister seductress (*la belle dame sans merci*); 3) Mother of Us All (Virgin Mary); 4) virago ("unwomanly" woman). Why these? For their implicit sermon, and for their fixity of reference, which is entirely toward their physical, moral, and psychological value to men. Two are "positive," two are "negative" models. The sermonizing may vary, as it does in our enlightened time, tolerating what was negative as positive and converting what was positive into negative; it makes no difference. The fundamental banality and unreality persist.

Then why bother? Why study to perform? Why pay attention at all? Habitually, it's done for the ingenuity of the construct. For the subtleties to be leeched out of the fixed pattern, for the game of intensifying a make-believe conviction, for the sheer force of, or the ingenious heaping of meaning onto, that make-believe. In fact, the only possible pleasure in all this:

creating artifice that exceeds the reach of banality. To be sure, the ingredients that go into the construction of that make-believe are themselves artificial constructs. Well, so it is in painting, so it is in music. And in those arts too the sheerest artifice can be converted into an illusion of representation. But when anyone wallows in that simple pleasure in those arts, we laugh, because we know better. We know that paint is paint and notes are notes, and that they refer more to themselves than to another referent. But in drama alone—well, in fiction too—we domesticate constructs and convert them into the real. As critics, we judge them, reason with them, correct their faults, and approve their good behavior; as audience, we fall in love with them, hate them, advise them, give up on them, and give them tenancy in the house next door. All of which is stupid, but relatively harmless. Real harm is done when constructs are divested of their decorative camouflage and revert to their original banality: to sermon, when we, their spectators, are asked to emulate artifice, the non-existent, and walk into a forest of mirrors in which the unreal reflects itself twice over and calls itself real. The illusion is costly; the emulation is impossible; the lunacy is rampant within the culture's ideological prisonhouse. That's where the defining nature of women characters is persistently lodged—within the confines of that ideological prisonhouse. Outside of which are real women.

In these pages—which catalogue a fair sampling of women characters in Western drama —something else becomes depressingly clear. With almost no exceptions, every woman depicted lives in only one relation: to men, and in only a very few postures toward them. In comedy, the push and pull of love, marriage, and adultery, with recourse to forgiveness and reconciliation; in tragedy, drama, and melodrama, the push and pull of love, hate, and adultery, with recourse to suicide and murder. The tempering of these relations and these recourses may be great or small, but until a slight modicum of fresh air was breathed into Western drama in the last hundred or so years, the fortunes of women in drama confronted almost nothing but the beneficence or the castigation of men. But make no mistake: as already pointed out above, reversing the moral understandings and preferences among these options opens no wide doors. The fundamental banality persists, and its unreality, and the tininess of the enclosure within which its morality has been renovated.

It's a depressing landscape. If you can find a way to adorn it with a bit of reality, a bit of truth, a bit of genuine conviction, more power to you. Of course, you'll only be decorating a corrupt body, but corrupt or not, illusionary or not, there is still the possibility in performance of that decoration bringing illusion and cliché closer to a semblance of reality, as close as transforming acting genius has done it many times over laboring in the lists of performance for the last more than two thousand years.

PREFACE

This anthology consists of more than five hundred entries in four volumes, the first two of men's monologues, the other two of women's.

The initial question is of course: what is "classic" and what is "classical?" "Classic" is more easily defined: every movie more than a year old. "Classical" as it pertains to plays is necessarily more difficult to pin down. For practical purposes, it involves some sort of separation from "modern," and the guidelines for that separation might be these: 1) texts that are "classical" are restricted by date to those that are roughly a century away (with a few exceptions which conscience did not permit to be excluded), and 2) texts that are recognizably at a distance from contemporary speech, and that demand a reasonable, sometimes considerable, stretch from an actor's normal rhetorical habits. Under these guidelines, it seems reasonable to include, for example, some nineteenth-century texts from farce and melodrama that have currently unfamiliar dialectal twists (see, for example, Sailor William in *Black-Ey'd Susan*, in Men's Volumes), as well as translations that though friendly to contemporary ears are still sufficiently distant from current speech to qualify. These demarcations may be a bit porous, but for practical purposes of audition and workshop, they should hold.

Similarly, the division between "younger" and "older" is also porous. What's young? Before our own age of lengthening longevity, right through the nineteenth century, it was more or less the rule that "young" hardly extended beyond the twenties—for men possibly to the very early thirties, for women at the very best to the early twenties. But not to be too harsh or doctrinaire, there is added here another, more malleable criterion: the weight of authority, the weight of experience, and the dignity of title. Between the two, the decision regarding the age of characters remains of course subjective, but the harm to characters' standing or reputation, in whatever category they find themselves, is at most, slight.

Emotion is the beginning, the wellspring, from which we naïvely suppose actors channel and shape their performances and bring them to life. Well, in a way, yes. But consider. A sequence of thoughts can conceivably be expressed with no particular emotion and be understood and accepted as rational communication. Try it the other way around—expressing emotion with no particular thought—and you'd be certifiable. Emotion is the ephemera of thought. And the actor's performance begins inside the line of logical—not emotional—connections of a text's moment to moment.

This anthology is devoted to the proposition that intelligent textual analysis is the primary instrument of performance, and it gives the occasion, in a large number of instances, for the actor to draw significantly on intellectual acuity preceding any emotional urges. To put it another way, a speech's emotional progression is its logical progression at a second remove. And the particularity and finesse of emotional performance corresponds precisely to the particularity and finesse of its intellectual perception.

With that proposition in mind, the headnotes preceding each of the monologues are of three kinds (sometimes featured individually, sometimes all in one): a description of the speech's strategy; a breakdown of its logical progression; a description of its context. Let's go over them one at a time:

STRATEGY

1. The speaker's strategy (his/her intention): Sometimes it's uniform throughout the speech, and in the labor of defining it, I've seen many actors stuck trying to articulate what that uniform intention might be. ("I want love"; no, says the mentor, that's not specific. All right, "I want to get her into bed"; no, says the mentor, that's not the motive behind the motive. Okay, "I want to dominate"; well, let's talk further about this.) But articulated precisely or not, it is as likely as not that initial intent may not stay fixed throughout the speech. When it doesn't, the vagaries of the character's mind may dance through a jungle of intents (see Lorenzaccio's remarkable speech when he's getting ready to murder de Medici in de Musset's *Lorenzaccio*) or the speaker taking cues from his listener's silent or spoken reaction, or his own, may alter its direction, qualify it, or change it altogether. The tendency in classically structured soliloquy is to stay doggedly on track, because the private conference with the self is usually intended to work toward the resolution of a dilemma, to process the likely obstacles to a plan of action, or—and these are the most interesting ones—to battle conscience whose fixed ideals and unspoken beliefs overwhelm practical intent. Whatever the case may be, the tracking of the "intent's" progress is one task assumed in these headnotes.

2. The playwright's strategies: They're not formulas but habits. Major speeches tend to fall into distinguishable kinds and tend to be shaped, by both habit and tradition, into certain formal patterns that have remained fairly fixed throughout the course of Western drama. Some of the most powerful speeches, in for example, Euripides, Seneca, Schiller, Büchner, or Shaw, are almost identical in their rhetorical structure. Some examples of the most usual ones (it might be helpful if we gave them names): the Speech of Justification (among the greatest, the Emperor Augustus in Corneille's *Cinna*); the Speech of Persuasion (among the most moving, Jocasta in Seneca's *Phoenician Women*); the Speech of Denunciation, in which the

decibels run from wrath (Theseus in Euripides' *Hippolytus*) to barely audible contempt (Mr. O'Connell's great speech in Granville-Barker's *Waste*); the formal narrative speech (Messengers' recitations of offstage catastrophes in Greek tragedy, or Rodrigue's recounting of his battlefield triumph in *Le Cid*). All have formally shaped addresses, in which over and above their dramatic function and emotional investment (sometimes enormous and sometimes nil) the actor has also to catch the sheer display involved in the music and the epic scaling of their rhetoric. The playwright's strategy in these passages usually comes as close to aria as it does to flat speech, and not to honor that dimension is like muttering song lyrics under your breath instead of singing them out loud.

Logical (sometimes alogical) Progression

Whether rational or deranged, the mind is moving from one notion to the next in a chain of changing assertions that link. Figuring out the exact continuity of those links can be easy in narratives or in expositions that merely detail a sequence of ordered events. But when the connections are either muffled or random, the work of the actor begins. The headnotes try particularly hard to be helpful in this respect: at the risk of being accused of childishness, they sometimes enumerate unashamedly and naively the steps of these progressions, sometimes—can you believe it?—by the numbers. Why such silliness? Because it is precisely these progressions of linked-but-sometimes-difficult-to-grasp sense that provide the basis for the emotional progressions that then become the sustaining life of soliloquies.

Context

Obviously, there's the plot, the character, the situation just before, and the surrounding situation, that provide the immediate context for individual monologues. The headnotes provide necessary information concerning these facts. But there's the larger, enormously significant perspective—the mindset and the beliefs and assumptions which the plays inevitably reflect—that the headnotes dwell on too. It's within these structures of belief that plays and speeches harbor their ultimate meanings, and their exploration, certainly in the greatest performances I've been privileged to see, give the ultimate richness of meaning and effect to actors' interpretations.

On the question of translation, Voltaire still, I think, has the last word. It's discouraging. How close can translation get—to meaning, to tone, to deftness of statement, in translatorese? Voltaire in the eighteenth century had this to say, and nobody has yet spoken the bad news better:

> It is impossible to convey through any modern language, all
> the power of Greek expressions; they describe, with one
> stroke, what costs us a whole sentence... That language had
> not only the advantage of filling the imagination with a word,

but every word, we know, had its peculiar melody, which charmed the ear while it displayed the finest pictures to the mind; and for this reason all our translations from the Greek poets are weak, dry, and poor; it is imitating palaces of porphyry with bricks and pebbles.

What's true for Greek remains as true for modern language translation as well: no language can give up its peculiar music/sense to equivalents in another language. What Molière, for example, suffers in transit from French to English is possibly an exceptionally grim instance of bricks and pebbles making believe they're porphyry. When imitated precisely in English, his clarity, his ease, his perfect accommodation of plain sense to the straitjacket of hexameter couplets convert into deadly banality, insufferable in expression, and plainly laughable in sense. (Goethe, another victim, this editor felt it best to sidestep altogether. *Faust* in English sometimes marches to the tune and sense of Jack and Jill.)

What to do? Without hoping for true equivalence, for the purposes of actors speaking texts intended to stand in for some of the greatest dramatic passages in other languages, the uneasy solution is simply to avoid the unspeakable, in both senses. No rigid policy was followed: for example, of using only up-to-date, "relevant"—and sometimes hopelessly removed from the original—translations on the one hand, or scrupulously "faithful"—and sometimes hopelessly unspeakable—versions on the other. Compromises, of course, abound—some for reasons of availability, others in the interest of sampling different tacks to a single author's texts when multiple selections from the same author are included. The criterion was roughly this: how comfortably can the text sit on the actor's tongue, and how far can it reach toward the overall effect, admittedly very approximate, of the original? And admittedly, you can't win.

GREEK

1.

IO, TORMENTED BY A GADFLY, CLAMORS FOR AN END TO HER SUFFERING (YT)

(468+ BC) AESCHYLUS, *PROMETHEUS BOUND*, TR. DAVID GRENE

Io, horns embedded in her forehead, fleeing from the stinging gadfly and the terrifying ghost of the hundred-eyed Argus, condemned to run and never rest, stumbles in her endless flight on the other great sufferer of Zeus's omnipotence, the prisoner Prometheus, who is fixed, motionless, and chained to a rock. So paired and contrasted by Aeschylus, the two mirror the alpha and omega of Zeus's punishing reign.

Io's plight: Zeus had lusted and then raped the beautiful nymph and—to conceal his transgression from his lynx-eyed, quickly-approaching wife, Hera—instantly converted Io into a heifer. Hera, not deceived, assigned the hundred-eyed Argus to imprison and watch over the transformed Io. Zeus's messenger Hermes killed Argus, but his ghost pursued Io all over the ancient world together with the monstrous gadfly Hera had also sent to torment her.

The Titan Prometheus [see in Men's volumes: "Prometheus Cries Out Against His Sufferings"] no such passive victim, defied the king of the gods, Zeus—who had determined to destroy mankind—by stealing forbidden fire to advance humanity's struggle toward civilized life. One—Io—laments, screams in unbearable pain, begs each moment to be free of her physical suffering; the other—Prometheus—makes no lamentation over physical suffering, makes no gesture to be free of it, only cries aloud, unrelentingly, his defiance of the god.

Two victims' postures: one, inadvertently so, is passive, helpless, conscious only of her innocence and pain; the other, an intentional transgressor, remains vigorously, unabatingly, morally defiant. The ultimate distinction between their opposite responses to their plights has to do with the limit of human foreknowledge. Io has no more than human foreknowing, that is, none at all. Her screams respond to each immediate instant of suffering. The Titan Prometheus, who has the gift of prophecy, responds only to the certainty of his eventual and triumphant redemption. But confronted by Io, his compassion moves him once again to pity a human plight. After her plea, he subsequently shares with her his knowledge of her destiny. It will involve long and bitter suffering, he tells her, but its end is glorious. So reassuring an end might well win her forbearance. It doesn't. Her suffering of the moment remains unendurable. Io, after hearing Prometheus' prophecy, is again, and immediately, stung by the gadfly, and tormented as before, runs off screaming, and uncomforted.

Io

What land is this? What race of men? Who is it
I see here tortured in this rocky bondage?
What is the sin he's paying for? Oh tell me
to what part of the world my wanderings have brought me.
O, O, O,
there it is again, there again—it stings me,
the gadfly, the ghost of earth-born Argus:
keep it away, keep it away, earth!
I'm frightened when I see the shape of Argus,
Argus the herdsman with ten thousand eyes.
He stalks me with his crafty eyes: he died,
but the earth didn't hide him; still he comes
even from the depths of the Underworld to hunt me:
he drives me starving by the sands of the sea.

The reed-woven pipe drones on in a hum
and drones and drones its sleep-giving strain:
O, O, O,
Where are you bringing me, my far-wandering wanderings?
Son of Kronos, what fault, what fault
did you find in me that you should yoke me
to a harness of misery like this,

that you should torture me so to madness
driven in fear of the gadfly?

Burn me with fire: hide me in earth: cast me away
to monsters of the deep for food: but do not
grudge me the granting of this prayer, King.
Enough have my much wandering wanderings
exercised me: I cannot find
a way to escape my troubles.
Do you hear the voice of the cow-horned maid?

Tell me, who are you? Who are you? Oh
who are you that so exactly accosts me by name?
You have spoken of the disease that the gods have sent to me
which wastes me away, pricking with goads,
so that I am moving always
tortured and hungry, wild bounding,
quick sped I come,
a victim of jealous plots.
Some have been wretched
before me, but who of these
suffered as I do?
But declare to me clearly
what I have still to suffer: what would avail
against my sickness, what drug would cure it:
Tell me, if you know:
tell me, declare it to the unlucky, wandering maid.

REED-WOVEN PIPE: Hermes' flute was known to induce sleep. Here, Io longs for sleep's relief denied to her by the incessant attacks of the gadfly. SON OF KRONOS: Zeus

2.

CLYTEMNESTRA HAILS THE NEWS OF AGAMEMNON'S HOMECOMING (OT)

(458 BC) AESCHYLUS, *Agamemnon*, TR. LEON KATZ

Concealed within Clytemnestra's speech is its whole intent, which is precisely the opposite of what it avows. The grimness of its ironies and the irony of all her words spoken before her murder of Agamemnon, are blatantly evident only after that event. She has been waiting for ten years to revenge his sacrifice of their daughter Iphigenia for the sake of his advancing the war against Troy, and she has taken his mortal enemy, Aegisthus, as her paramour in anticipation of their murdering him together. The revelation of her intent is the action of the tragedy, and its triumph provides its climax.

Her first small victory: her announcing the news that beacon signals reported the fall of Troy was met with skepticism by the citizenry (the chorus of old men) who questioned her credibility as a woman who reads "signs." But a herald arrives who confirms the news, and announces the imminent arrival of Agamemnon. Clytemnestra, with joy and scorn, reminds the old men of their snickering behind their hands at a mere woman "beguiled."

Her concealments: the sacrifices and the chants of thanksgiving before the holy shrines, the "sweetness in her eyes" when she will welcome Agamemnon home will be gratitude not for his safe return, but for the certainty, now that he will be safely home, of his assassination. The message the Herald is to return to Agamemnon is not only blatant, but meant to be as contemptuous a lie as possible: that her husband will be received as her lover, that she has been the shield and watchdog of his house against his enemies, and—most blatant of all—that she has for ten long years been chaste ("the holy seal...unbroken") his house and kingdom untouched by scandal.

The enormity of the lie is matched by the zest and joy in the telling. Clytemnestra, unlike almost all other vengeful murderesses in Western drama, is moved only by the fitness, the propriety, the moral rightness of her intent. There is no qualifying feeling or thought, because it is not merely, or hardly, the zest for murder alone that moves her, and there is not the shadow of a sense of guilt; it is justice. The appeal to justice, and *of* justice, follows Clytemnestra's action through the whole of the *Oresteia* trilogy of which *Agamemnon* is Part One. The drama of the entire trilogy centers on the issue of justice, which, from its simple aspect here of barbarously meted-out revenge, moves to the complexity of understanding symbolized and dramatized in the last play.

Clytemnestra throws open the palace doors (as she is to do again later to reveal the murdered bodies of Agamemnon and his paramour, Cassandra, and as her son Orestes is to do subsequently when he reveals the murdered bodies of Clytemnestra and her paramour, Aegisthus,) when the herald's news is brought, and at once, she exhibits the towering authority with which she humbles the stature of everyone else. Her certainty, her will, and inner strength, are one.

CLYTEMNESTRA

Old men, I shouted triumph when the first bright
Messenger of fire arrived at night,
And signaled news that Ilium was doomed.
But there were those of you who smiled
And shook your heads and said:
"Mere beacon flames—do they persuade you
That the war is won?
So like a woman's heart to be beguiled,"
And snickered behind your hands
As though my wits were gone.
But still I made my sacrifice,
And in one quarter, then another,
Women, as is their way, sang chants of praise,
While in their holy shrines, the gods of Argos banked
The aromatic fires fed on incense.
Why do I need to hear the whole long story now
Of Troy's destruction?
My husband when he comes will tell the tale,
And I, to welcome him most perfectly—
For what is sweeter in a woman's eyes
Than, throwing wide the door, to see her man
Whom god has brought back safely home from war?
Bring him this word from me:
Come quickly, Argos' lover, come!
And find your woman as you left her,
Faithful, loyal, watchdog of your house,
Enemy of those who wish you ill,
And in these many years,
The holy seal you set on her unbroken,
As ignorant of shame with other men,
Or shame of scandal, as she is ignorant
Of how to temper bronze.
This is my boast, a boast confirmed by truth,
And fitting for the honor of a noble wife.

MESSENGER OF FIRE: the news of the fall of Troy reached Agamemnon's Argos by a line of signal fires that stretched from the fallen city to Hellas. ARGOS: the city of Agamemnon, and, by extension, the whole surrounding region of ARGOLIS: (In myth, it alternated with Mycenae as the city of Agamemnon.) Argos is located in the northeastern Peloponnesus.

3.

CLYTEMNESTRA GREETS FULSOMELY HER HUSBAND RETURNED FROM TROY (OT)

(458 BC) AESCHYLUS, *AGAMEMNON*, TR. LEON KATZ

[See No. 2, above] A pattern of expanding light hovers over the action of *Agamemnon,* from the darkness of the lonely Watchman's scene before dawn that opens the play, to the blaze of the light of day when Agamemnon arrives in his splendid warrior's chariot with his attendant soldiers and his captive-concubine Cassandra, and Clytemnestra's women hold the great carpet they are preparing to spread for Agamemnon's step. It parallels the gradual illumination of hidden motive and meaning in the tragedy's progression, and the waiting revelation of its fated action.

Clytemnestra once again throws open the palace doors and stands regally before her lord, welcoming him, praising him, exalting him, and, increasingly as she does so, diminishing him. More openly than before [as in No. 2], the mockery underlying her expressions of joy at Agamemnon's return is in evidence. The catalogue of woes she endured during his absence—her terror of sitting home alone "while this man slept beneath the walls of Troy"; the rumors she endured of "disaster"; her dreaming of his being "hacked and wounded"; of his wounds "riddled through with gashes like a net"; her fears that his death in Troy would lead to rebellion at home; all of these can be read, as she mockingly intends for only herself to read them, as her real fears that he would die before her revenge could strike, and her real pleasure is anticipating the wounds, the gashes, the "net" he will suffer in his destruction at her hands. All these complaints of woe are followed by the adulation that genuinely belittles. Finally, the spreading of the carpet—one of the most celebrated moments in Greek tragedy—challenges him under cover of that same praise to commit the act of pride that would condemn him before the gods.

Agamemnon's response to her suspect welcome is tempered, cautious, even suspicious, but Clytemnestra's prowess in argument and her unremitting insistence on his stepping sacrilegiously on the carpet, will symbolically prefigure his doom. The irony of her prayer that "true justice" guide him to his "home," that is, his destiny, where her own "care and vigilance shall manage, fittingly" poses perfect double meaning.

*(Clytemnestra enters, attended by
servants carrying purple tapestries.)*

CLYTEMNESTRA

Citizens of Argos, Elders of this state,
I feel no shame in speaking of
The love I bear my husband.
Modesty, in time, wears thin.
The suffering I speak of now
I did not learn from others;
It was my own, while this man slept
Beneath the walls of Troy.
A terror it is for warrior's wife
To sit alone at home,
Hearing new rumors every day,
Each messenger with tidings of disaster
Worse than the last.
And as for wounds, if my dear lord
Had borne as many as false rumor carried home,
He would be riddled through with gashes like a net.
And had he died each time that rumor spoke him dead,
He must have been some triple-bodied Geryon,
Killed three times, three times returned to life,
And three times over buried in the earth.
Because of rumors such as these,
More than once they freed my throat
Against my will,
When the noose was already knotted around my neck.
And if our son Orestes, pledge and seal
Of your devotion and of mine,
Does not stand here to greet you.
Do not be alarmed. He is in
The care of Strophius of Phocis,
Your ally and faithful friend,
Who warned me of danger on two counts:
Your own beneath the walls of Troy,
And here, rebellion and
The Council's overthrow.
For men are quick to trample on
A man already fallen.
This is my excuse to you, without deceit.

As for myself, the gushing fountains of my tears
Are dry; no drop is left in them.
My eyes are sore with weeping, holding vigil
Through the night, waiting for beacon lights
That never flared. The buzzing of a gnat
Could wake me from my dreams, in which
I saw you hacked and wounded more often
Than the time through which I slept could hold.
But my suffering is past. My heart is free
Of torment and of pain. My love is home!

I long to hail his prowess and his strength
Great lord! The watch-dog of our fold!
The strength that keeps our ship of state afloat;
The lofty pillar that sustains our home
Like a doting father's treasured only son;
What bliss, what happiness compares with this?
Ah yes: when land is seen by sailors after hope is gone;
Or a daybreak's splendor after a night of storm;
A gushing spring to thirsty travelers;
A sweet escape from hard necessity!

So do I praise and greet you, as you well deserve.
Let none, not god, not man, be envious!
I've borne my fill of sorrow for years past.
My husband, Agamemnon, now step down!
Step down from this, your conqueror's chariot!
But let your foot not touch the common earth,
My lord and king, who trampled Ilium!
Women, no more delay! Your task it is
To strew the ground below his feet with tapestries.
Quickly, let his path be spread with purple,
And let true Justice guide him
To the home he never hoped to see!
The rest my care and vigilance
Shall manage fittingly, as fate ordained.

(*The handmaidens spread the tapestries
from the chariot to the door.*)

GERYON: In Greek mythology, the strongest man alive. Geryon was born with three heads, six hands, and three bodies joined together at the waist. STROPHIUS: King of Phocis, married to Agamemnon's sister, and a firm ally of the House of Atreus. His son, Pylades, with whom Orestes grew up, became Orestes' closest friend and ally.

4.

CASSANDRA RECALLS THE CURSE
ON THE HOUSE OF ATREUS (YT)

(458 BC) AESCHYLUS, *AGAMEMNON*, TR. LEON KATZ

Cassandra, silent, watches Agamemnon step on the blood-red carpet spread for him by his wife, Clytemnestra, at his homecoming; waits in the chariot that brought him, the king, and her, his Trojan captive, to Argos after the Greeks' destruction of her city. She is silent, makes no response to Clytemnestra's determined plea for her to follow Agamemnon into the palace, none to the chorus' anxious song of foreboding, until, with a great tormented scream, she sees, in the instant, the entire curse-ridden pageant of the House of Atreus from its initiating crime to its current moment of doom. The chorus of old men do not understand, cannot follow.

The prophetess Cassandra is herself cursed. She was the fairest of the Trojan princesses, and Apollo yearned for her promising her the gift of prophecy (in fact, a sharing with him of his own prophetic power) if she would surrender to him. The gift was granted; the surrender was not. Apollo, in retaliation, punished Cassandra by letting her retain her prophetic gift, but depriving her of power to be believed. Apollo speaks through her, she is his medium, but, unlike the god himself, she suffers the double torment of both experiencing prophetic visions as though they were immediate and their effect emotionally and almost physically penetrating, and being neither believed nor understood.

It is the concomitant of pain that gives to Cassandra's visionary outbursts their chilling power. Each perceived horror is vivid, and the degree of its vividness induces in her rhythms of excruciating pain followed by debility and exhaustion, just as her mad, screaming utterances are followed by relative calm, relative clarity. Apollo's gift is her unbearable curse, and more than the horror of envisioning her own imminent murder at Clytemnestra's hands, is the torment of these unbidden, Apollo-induced revelations that at the end provoke her futile attempt to abandon her priestess' role and escape Apollo's "gift" altogether.

In the three passages from the episode of Cassandra quoted here, we follow the painful rhythms of tension and release through which she suffers, as well as the terrifying images she evokes of the horrors of the past in the House of Atreus, those hovering and those to come.

a) *("Ototoi! Papai! Da!")* In her first frenzied outburst, Apollo the "Destroyer" seizes her, and Cassandra mingles images of the crime of Atreus (who, in revenge against his brother, fed Thyestes his own slaughtered children) and the crime born out of that one and pending at this very moment, Clytemnestra's coming deed (when she and her paramour, Aegisthus, will murder Agamemnon in his bath). "She [Clytemnestra] purposes, she intends." And added to the horror of the coming deed is the absence of those who might forestall it. Gradually,

b) *("Oh lovely song of nightingale…")* her pain and frenzy subside, and more calmly, she recognizes and mourns her own coming murder at their hands, and, because of the abduction of the Greek Helen by her brother Paris, the destruction of her beloved Troy.

Cassandra

Ototoi! Papai! Da!
Apollo, shame upon the earth, Apollo!
Apollo, there! Beside the palace door!
God of Wanderers, destruction, ruin!
Utterly destroys! Once more, once more!
Apollo, God of Wanderers, of Roads!
What road, Destroyer? Where? What house is this?
House loathed of god; butchery of kin;
Slaughter-house; floor washed in blood!
Witnesses beside the door; the screams
Of children; slaughter; father eats
The roasted flesh.
She who purposes, she who intends.
What horror? Monstrous!
Evil plotted in this house!
Evil to them, the lovers of this house,
Beyond endurance, beyond remedy!
And they, the mighty who can stop her hand,
So far away!
Woman, poised, the coming act!
Partner of her bed
Washed, cheered, comfortable bath;
She sees the end. Vile!
One hand raised high; the other stretching toward!
Vision! Net of death!
She, snare and net, who shared his bed,

Shares his guilt, his murder!
And they, the Furies, watch in glee,
Shout: Stone her! Stone her!
Stone the avenger-victim, bind the net!
Look there! The bull is gored!
Save it from its mate!
She folds him in his robe
And with her black horn strikes.
He sinks below the waters of his bath.
Hear me! Understand!
I cry his doom by guile, by murder!

Sorrow, sorrow, agony of fate!
My own affliction crowns the cup.
Why here? What end is here
For me and for my destiny?
Nothing but death and death,
To die and share his death.
Oh, lovely song of nightingale!
The fate of Procne, slayer of her child!
The gods gave her winged form
And a sweet, lamenting song
Without the curse of tears, and free from pain.
To me, they gave a different end:
Murder by a two-edged sword.

Wedding of Paris, death for those he loved!
Oh, my dear Scamander,
River beside my home,
Nurtured at your banks,
Happy until this sad,
This fateful womanhood,
Soon by the banks of the river
Of the shadowy Underworld,
I'll chant my songs to the dead.
My city, oh my city, utterly destroyed!
My father's offerings, the beasts he sacrificed
To save our home!
No remedy, no cure: the city fell
And I too, soon, my soul in flames,
Blood seeping to the ground!

APOLLO, GOD OF WANDERERS, OF ROADS: Among many functions attributed to
Apollo, one (in Athens in particular) is that of god of streets and highways, "whose
rude symbol…stood by street doors and in courtyards…to let in good and keep out

evil." In this context, he is the protector of travelers. Cassandra, seeing the god's image at the palace door, cries out against her "destroyer...once more!" first in Troy, when she was mocked for her prophecies, and now, when she is a captive. THE MURDER OF AGAMEMNON: After entering the palace, Clytemnestra threw a net over him in his bath, Aegisthus struck him with a sword, and Clytemnestra beheaded him with an ax. FURIES: or Erynyes, the goddesses of vengeance who punish without mercy. "They are the avengers of every transgression of natural order, especially those touching the foundation of human society." THE BULL IS GORED...HER BLACK HORN: Agamemnon "gored" by Clytemnestra's ax. THE FATE OF PROCNE: Procne is the wife of the king of Thrace, Tereus. The gods, to spare her the vengeance of her husband for the murder of their son, turned her into a nightingale. SCAMANDER: river in Asia Minor, adjoined ancient Troy. RIVER OF THE SHADOWY UNDERWORLD: the river Lethe, which the souls of the dead crossed in order to enter the Underworld (Hades).

5.

CASSANDRA, FRENZIED, ENVISIONS AGAMEMNON'S FATE AND HER OWN (YT)

(458 BC) AESCHYLUS, *AGAMEMNON*, TR. LEON KATZ

[Continues No. 4, above] After a short, quietly spoken colloquy with the old men of the chorus ("ah, nothing, nothing do you understand!"):

a) ("I will speak now...") Cassandra determines to be understood, and explains in an even tone how she can "scent" the avenging Furies, who have hung over the House of Atreus ever since the crime, which provoked Atreus' crime against his brother—the "primal sin" of Thyestes, who abducted Atreus' wife. And there is pride in her claim that like "an archer," she has struck with precision at the heart of the secret crimes that have foredoomed this House. But an instant later,

b) (Torment! Again! The twisting pain!) she is again seized by her "Destroyer" Apollo, again screams her pain at the even more vivid, even more terrible image of Thyestes' horrifying feast, the recalled tableau vivant she had already suffered. But this time, it is the sight of the children being ripped apart, and then "warm and cooked for the father's feast." And once again, there is the immediate connection between that first image and this last—the crime about to happen: the paramour Aegisthus, the "lion" waiting on Agamemnon's couch to murder him; and "the bitch" Clytemnestra, the serpent, the treacherous, avenging Ate, "breathing death/But screaming out her joy at his return." From this painful outcry,

c) (*All one; believe or not believe…*) she falls into exhausted apathy, cares little whether she is believed or not, only forewarns.

Cassandra

I will speak now, speak with calm,
And my prophecies will no more
Come from behind a veil
Like a frightened, newly-wedded bride,
But rush like a wind blowing fresh
Up to the rising sun,
And figure against its rays
Like a mighty, upended wave,
A sorrow far greater than mine.
No. I will riddle no more.
Witness how I can scent
The track of brutal crimes
Buried here long ago.
For over the roof of this house,
An unmelodious choir,
Together with reveling kin
Haunting the house's halls,
Reveling Furies who,
Drunk on human blood,
Chant forever their chant
Of a brother's primal sin.
And each of the Furies shrieks
With rage at the spouse's bed
Defiled by a lusting brother.
An archer I am, am I not?
Who strikes to the heart of the quarry,
And no beggar prophet of lies
Babbling from door to door.
Witness, old men, on oath,
That I know the deed and the sin,
Old, and whispered among you,
Locked in the walls of this house.

Torment! Again! The twisting pain!
Mouth of prophecy! Again!
Children sitting before the house,
Young ones mangled by their kin,
Their hands molding mounds of flesh

Torn from themselves, warm and cooked
For the father's feast.
For this, for this, the lion wallows
On his couch and plots revenge
Watching the house against
My master's coming home—
My master, master, I, the captive
Trapped beneath his yoke—
The ships' commander, Ilium's ruin
Does not recognize the bitch's tongue
That licked his hand,
The bitch that bent her ear, like treacherous Ate,
Female daring murder of the male.
Her name is Amphisbaena,
Serpent moving backwards, forwards,
At each end a poisonous sting,
And her name is Scylla, crouching over rocks,
Raging, breathing death,
But screaming out her joy at his return.

All one; believe or not believe;
What comes will come.
But you who stand and gape,
Will soon, in pity, cry:
The prophetess spoke true.

SPOUSE'S BED DEFILED BY A LUSTING BROTHER: Thyestes' seduction of Aerope, Atreus' wife. ATE: personifies the infatuation that "has guilt as its cause and evil as its consequence;" by extension, an Avenger. AMPHISBAENA: a venomous serpent with a head at each end and able to move in either direction. SCYLLA: a female monster dangerous to mariners, inhabiting the cave opposite Charybdis in the Sicilian Strait.

6.

CASSANDRA SPEAKS HER FINAL PROPHECY AND GOES TO HER DOOM (YT)

(458 BC) AESCHYLUS, *AGAMEMNON*, TR. LEON KATZ

[Continues No. 5, above] Again failing in her attempt to forewarn the chorus of old men ("and yet I speak the language that you speak"), Cassandra is once again seized by the pain of prophecy,

a) *("Fire! The twisting flame...")* and suffers the most excruciating prevision of all: of herself and Agamemnon together being hacked to death by the "lioness" and the "wolf" she couples with. But now desperate to block out forever the terrible visions inflicted by Apollo,

b) *("No more! No more!)* she throws off the wreath and staff of Apollo's priestess, and cries out in rebellion against her tormenting god ("the god who saw me mocked and spit upon"), but confronts clear-eyed, she confronts the reality of her coming death. Comforted in her last prediction, that an "avenger" (Orestes, Agamemnon's son) is to come, Cassandra with great dignity and utter acceptance of death's imminence ("there's no escape; none but delaying the hour,") prepares to enter the palace gate. But once more, for an instant,

c) *("The palace wreaks of slaughter...")* the vision, the very stench of the slaughter to come, overwhelms her as it instantly subsides, and

d) *("I'll go within...I will not shrink in terror from my death")* what ensues is certainly one of the greatest passages in Western literature epitomizing the tragedy and the acceptance of the leaving of life: Cassandra asks those left (the chorus of old men) to "bear witness" to her memory when, in the future, the moment of retribution comes, because that memory will be, in effect, the only hostage taken against life's vanishing into non-existence.

CASSANDRA

Fire! The twisting flame!
Apollo! Ah!
Two-footed lioness, her noble lion gone
Couples with the wolf,
Cuts and hacks. I, lost, under her flailing arm!
Brews a drug, cup of her wrath
Mixed for our lips, mine and her lion-spouse.
And whets the sword for spilling the blood
Of her man who carried a concubine home!

No more! No more!
Why do I need these mockeries.
This staff, this prophet's wreath
Around my neck?
Let them be torn and trampled
Before my coming death.
Let them be destroyed
For what they've done to me.
Let him bestow on others
The blessing of these gifts.

For me no more!
It's he who strips me of my prophet's art
The god who saw me mocked and spit upon
By those I loved at home
Through all the years I wore his cursed gifts.
And I, among them, like a beggar
Called by those who once were friends
A fool, a liar, lunatic.
And now this prophet god undoes his prophetess
And brings her to her end
Not at her father's altar
But at a sacrificial block
Running with blood from victims' butcheries.

Ah, but my death will not go unrevenged.
One comes, an exile, wanderer,
A lion who will set the crowning stone
Upon the evils of this house,
Kill the one who bore him,
And revenge his father's blood.
For the gods have sworn an oath
That the murdered father's corpse shall bring him home.
Then why do I weep in pity for myself?
From the first I saw the city that I loved
Brought to ruin by fate, and visioned, for its conquerors,
The doom ordained for them.
Now I too will bow before my fate,
Enter these palace gates to meet my end.
I pray that I be dealt one mortal blow,
Close my eyes without a struggle,
And let my life-blood ebb away in easy death.

I'll go within,
And there I will lament
My own and Agamemnon's fate.
My life is done,
I will not shrink in terror from my death
Like a fluttering bird
Afraid to light on a trembling bush.
I ask another oath: when I am gone,
When death lays claim because of me
On another woman's life, and when for him,
Ill-wedded man, another man is slain,
That you will bear me witness, and remember me.
This one favor, on your oath.

It is the last that I shall ever ask.

One thing remains, but not my elegy.
A prayer to the sun in its last fading light:
That when the avengers come,
And the guilty pay their bloody penalty,
They pay in blood as well for the slave who died,
So easy a victim, so easily destroyed.
Poor human destiny!
Even in prosperity men's lives are only shadows,
But when life falls to ruin,
A wet sponge in one stroke wipes it out.
And that is the most bitter fate of all.

(She enters the palace.)

EXILE, WANDERER…LION: Orestes, Agamemnon's son, who will return to Argos and avenge his father's murder. DEATH LAYS CLAIM…ANOTHER WOMAN'S LIFE…ANOTHER MAN IS SLAIN: Clytemnestra's and Aegisthus' deaths when Orestes will in time execute his revenge.

7.

CLYTEMNESTRA EXULTS OVER THE BODIES OF AGAMEMNON AND CASSANDRA (ot)

(458 BC) AESCHYLUS, *AGAMEMNON*, TR. LEON KATZ

[See in Men's volumes "Orestes is Jubilant and Uncertain over His Revenge."] The "net" Clytemnestra throws over the bodies of her victims Agamemnon and Cassandra is the sustaining image of the entire *Oresteia* trilogy. It enlarges into the "net" that binds all the events and all their victims and perpetrators, including Clytemnestra, into the unbroken sequence of murder and counter-murder that constitutes the fate of the House of Atreus from the generations before Agamemnon's to the generation following. Clytemnestra's heroic exultation while she stands over the bodies of her victims at the palace's open doors, her detailed, triumphant recounting of the vengeful murder itself, and her forceful accusations of Agamemnon's double guilt of daughter-murder and concubinage as justifications for her act, begin to shrivel, at speech's end into a longing to be unbound, taken out of the "net." "There the matter stands," she concludes, in effect writing "finis" to the "work well and truly done." But with the onset of exhaustion detectable at the speech's close, she hopes to effect a bargain with Fate itself. If He "quits this house," she will take an oath to live in peace "with what is already done," even to remain content "with the smallest part of our wealth"—if only the house were rid of "the terrible fury that goads it to the shedding of blood." The hope is heartfelt but feeble, even meaningless. She herself has goaded "the curse of the murder of kin by kin" to be replicated. For closure to come, the meaning of "justice" itself would have to be transmuted.

Two distinctive themes of the many that weave through the trilogy and build its multiple meanings register here. One is the territorial divide between male and female: the strengths, the inherent combat, the prerogatives, the definitions of either. Clytemnestra's powerful and bitter contention for the woman's claim to justice as equal to the male's is to be reinforced immensely in the following two plays by the introduction of the Erinnyes, the female Furies aroused by unavenged crimes against women. The second theme is the opposite: the cosmic reconciliation to come foreshadowed at the most gruesome moment of slaughter. As Clytemnestra hacked at Agamemnon's body and the blood gushed out of him in streams, it spattered her face and body. The thick, dark blood did so, as Aeschylus has Clytemnestra report, falling "like heaven's rain/On fields in summer giving birth/To flowering buds." The image, born out of the mouth of the murderess glorying in its pleasurable evocation of death and vengeance, harbors also its opposite meaning, as the harbinger of the cosmic reconciliation to come. It is an inadvertent evocation of the Greek myth of creation: the "raining" of the male Uranus in the sky on the earth-goddess Gaia, which in the myth gives birth, precisely as Aeschylus puts it here, to "flowering buds" and the beginning of life.

Matching the strength and power of assertion with which she had bespoke the love of her husband, her chastity awaiting his return and the obeisance to his glory at this arrival by spreading the purple carpet for him to walk on to the palace doors shaming him, as he recognizes, into hopeless and demeaning protest at her forcing him into the sacrilegious posture of, he protests, "an oriental potentate." She now, with equal strength and power of assertion, "unsay[s] it all." Hate, not love, waited for ten long years; and pride, not guilt, moves her now to unburden herself of the whole so long concealed truth.

CLYTEMNESTRA

Much did I say before to bide my time;
Now without shame I will unsay it all.
With hate I planned against my hated enemy
Whom I pretended was so much a friend.
How else was I to snare the victim but to raise up
Snares too high for him to overleap?
This is the end of an ancient feud
Long thought and dreamed and brooded over,
And its finish long delayed. Here and now I've dealt
The final blow. The feud is done.
I confess to the bloody deed with pride.
There was no way he could escape his doom,
Or ward it off. Throwing over him
A web of robes, impenetrable nets,
As though I were a fisherman
Hauling in a shoal of fish,
I struck him twice, and twice he groaned,
And crumpled at my feet.
And lying dead, another stroke, a third,
In gratitude to the God of Hades,
Gatherer of the dead.
As he was dying, breathing out his life,
Great spurts of blood gushed out of him
Which spattered me with thick, dark drops
Of bloody dew, and I rejoiced in them
As though, like heaven's rain, they fell
On fields in summer giving birth
To flowering buds.
So it stands, old men; and if you can,
Rejoice. Myself, I glory in the deed.
Had it been fitting to pour wine
In gleeful celebration over corpses,
I would have done it, and with justice,
More than justice.
It was he himself who filled our cup with evil,
And he himself has drained it to the dregs.

You rail at me as though
I were a weak and foolish woman.
But my heart is not unmanned by you.
I say to you, old men, who know it well:
Whether you praise or blame, it's one to me.
There lies Agamemnon, murdered,

The precious work of this right hand,
Work well and truly done,
And there the matter ends.

So it is with this wretched house.
For myself, I would willingly swear an oath
To the Fiend who caused our bloody destiny
To live at peace with what is already done,
Hard though it is to live with its memory,
So long as he quits this house,
And carries the curse of his plague to another,
The curse of the murder of kin by kin.
And more than willingly I would remain
Content with the smallest part of our wealth,
Could I rid this house of the terrible fury
That goads it to the shedding of blood.

THE BLOODY DEED: an alternate account to the one Clytemnestra offers here: when Agamemnon had washed himself and set foot out of the bath, Clytemnestra came forward as if to wrap a towel about him, but instead threw over his head a garment of net, woven by herself, without either neck or sleeve holes. Then Aegisthus struck him twice with a sword, and finally Clytemnestra beheaded the king with an ax. It is the version used by Seneca, in his tragedy *Agamemnon.* THE FIEND: the daimon, here; the malignant spirit attached to the House of Atreus

8.

CLYTEMNESTRA BITTERLY DEFENDS HER ACT OF REVENGE (OT)

(458 BC) AESCHYLUS, *AGAMEMNON*, TR. LEON KATZ

[See No. 7, above] Revenge accomplished, Clytemnestra confronts a hostile, muttering, accusing populace (the chorus of old men) threatening to banish her from Argos. Her defense is forthright, as bold and unblushing as her pretense before the murder had been bold and unblushing. But she argues the genuine power of her case, the very argument that will level the contest between the two opposing principles—the male, the female—that more and more becomes the central social/political/moral contention of the *Oresteia*. Just as Apollo in the last play, *The Eumenides,* will argue the male's higher claim to justice and so, his control of law, so Clytemnestra argues here the greater strength of the woman's claim to that same final justice: the superficiality of the male's blood tie compared to the woman's ("the child he seeded only for his pleasure" as opposed to "the child I bore with terrible pain"); the slight reason for the father's murdering his daughter ("to woo the winds to hurry him to war") as opposed to her reason of blood revenge for a murdered daughter.

But in the midst of her soldier-like bantering of threats with the men, a new irony emerges: her defensive power against these men, she boasts, will be Aegisthus—already understood by the Old Men to be "the woman" skulking behind the virility of Clytemnestra. Her revelation adds to the foredoom already hinted at [see No. 3 above] in her having sent the child Orestes "to safety"—but in fact to distance him from the revenge he might seek in maturity against his mother for her father-murder. The stage is set for her later vulnerability, even though she ends here with the brag of her continuing revenge against Agamemnon even after his death: he will have no other burial than a mean one by her hand alone, there will be no mourning for his demise, there will only be the moment she happily anticipates when he meets his daughter Iphigenia in the Underworld, where surely she will reward her assassin with "a daughter's loving kiss."

CLYTEMNESTRA

You curse me now, and threaten me with exile.
Why did you not doom him to banishment,
This butcher at my feet,
When he used his child for sacrifice
As though she were a beast,
Used and butchered his own child,
Although his camp was filled with sacrificial beasts?
It was the child he seeded only for his pleasure;
But it was the child I bore with terrible pain.
And why was she, my daughter, murdered?
To woo the winds to hurry him to war!
It's he you should have banished
To scourge him for his sin.
But no! No judgment's visited on him, the male,
But only on the woman's deed.
This is the even justice meted out by men!
I warn you, citizens of Argos:
If you threaten me, and if then you win in equal fight,
Yes, I shall submit, and you shall be my judge,

And you shall rule.
But if the gods grant me the victory,
Then you will learn a bitter lesson,
Bitter, though you will learn it late.

Listen well, old men: this is my solemn oath!
I swear by Justice, that avenged my child,
By Ate and the Furies, Spirits of Revenge
To whom I sacrificed this man,
My hope of coming good fortune
Will never walk in fear
As long as he, my loyal friend, Aegisthus,
Loyal to me now and over many years,
Lights the fire of my hearth
And serves, with no weak arm, to shield my daring.
My husband, he now lying at my feet
Who played the lover of each captive girl
Below the walls of Ilium; and she entangled with him,
His captive prophetess, his harlot,
Whose back knew well the sailors' roving benches,
They have the honor they deserved.
The sight of her, Cassandra, who swanlike sang her last
lament,
Is lying beside him now, wrapped in death.
The sight of them gives added relish to my bed's delight!

Go now, old men; do nothing more.
The care for his burial rites is mine, not yours.
By my hand did he fall, by mine he died,
And by my hand will he be entombed.
There will be no tears at his burial.
When he comes to the river Lethe,
The river that flows to the ghostly dead,
Let him meet with the one whose life he cut.
Iphigenia surely will smile with pleasure,
And open her arms in gratitude,
And offer her father a daughter's loving kiss.

ATE: the Greek goddess who blinded men to their actions when they committed the sin of hubris, or overweening pride. SWANLIKE SANG HER LAST LAMENT: Cassandra's "swan song" was the prediction of her own death.

9.

THE MOTHER OF RHESUS, HOLDING THE BODY OF HER SON, MOURNS HIS DEATH IN WAR (OT)

(455–441 BC) EURIPIDES, *RHESUS*, TR. LEON KATZ

It is still a question whether *Rhesus* was in fact written by Euripides. The play centers on battlefield action in the dead of night, where Greeks and Trojans, and war in general, are seen at their unheroic worst. Spies from either army are silently infiltrating one another's camps, scouting for needed information, and incidentally doing a bit of casual killing. Rhesus—a Thracian king, under obligation to the Trojan leader, Hector—arrives at night and is shown by his host to a quiet spot where he might sleep in safety until the morning. Odysseus and Diomedes, scouting for the Greeks, stumble on the sleeping Rhesus and kill him.

The play resembles an unusually cynical war movie more than it does a Greek tragedy but at least one episode, the mother of Rhesus—a divinity, one of the nine Muses—confronting the Greek camp bearing her dead son in her arms, rises to the anger of Euripides' similar texts on the moral iniquities of war. The Muse's speech is, on the face of it, a lamentation, but hardly a passive one. Her bitter intent is to accuse the Greeks and their patron goddess, Athene, of committing cowardly murder, depicting the two Greek warriors as silently sneaking up on the sleeping Rhesus and hacking him to death. This is in a shaming contrast to her picture of her royal son at home in the Thracian mountains, where in battle his "bloody helmet flashed" and where, by implication, he fought with courage and honor among like warriors, so that she had no cause before his entanglement with Greeks and Trojans to fear for her son's life. It's the ignoble Greeks, the cunning Odysseus in particular, whom she feared, in anticipation of her son's arrival. Her fears are now borne out by their acting less like warriors than like common assassins. The mother of Rhesus is mourning, but she is also crying bitterly: "shame and vengeance."

MUSE

Hear me, you Trojans! It is I,

The Muse of many sisters,
The Muse revered by men of wisdom,
Who bears now in her arms
The murdered body of her son.
I come to you to mourn, to mourn the death
Of my most injured, my beloved son,
To mourn his death, and curse his murderers,
The Greek Odysseus and Diomedes,
Who stole upon him sleeping,
Crawled to him in silence,
And stabbed him where he lay.
Vengeance on them, vengeance!
They shall pay.
I mourn, I mourn for you, my son.
I sing your funeral song, a dirge
Sung first in Thracian mountains, in your home.
A mother's song of tears, a song of weeping
For the launching of the ships
That brought you to the evil shores of Troy,
Weeping for the evil spirits watching,
Weeping for the mother's warning,
But you rose and went,
Weeping for the father's premonition,
But angrily, my son, King Rhesus, went.

Cursed be Diomedes, cursed be he,
And cursed be vile Odysseus!
They have left me childless,
Left me bereft forever
Of the flower of all sons.
And cursed, yes, cursed be Helen,
Who wrapped in the arms of her lover
Feared neither ships nor sea,
And called you, my son, to die
For her thieving, sinful lover,
And emptied a thousand cities
Calling on their good men.

I bore you, child, to him, to Strymon,
Thracian river god,
Bore you in shame before my sisterhood,
In shame for dear virginity,
Then stood again upon your father's shore,
And cast you deep into your father's stream,
And he enfolded you, and gave you to

The water nymphs who nurtured you,
And nursed you to a king, the first of Thrace,
The first in war, whose bloody chariot passed
On Thracian hills, and bloody helmet flashed,
But never did I, your mother, know such fear
As when the cry of Hector charged you go
To Troy to battle for his friends,
Never did I know such fear
As when my son was sailing
On an embassy of death, sailing
To the Trojan's battle, not his own,
And to his death.
Athene, goddess, yours the guilt,
Not Diomede's, nor his, the vile Odysseus,
Yours the guilt, yours the cruel hand
That through those Grecians did this monstrous deed.
And yet the Muses, sisters, smiled on you
And on your city, Athens,
Sang its praise above all others,
Filled it with our love.
And for this kindly love,
This is the gift you pay.

I fold him in my arms; I weep alone,
I ask no other mourner's song.
My son shall not be laid in any grave.
He will not lie in darkness, no.
I ask Persephone, the Queen of Tartarus,
One gift: to set this one soul free.
He will be dead to me, he will not see
His mother's face. But may he live in light
As Orpheus lives, a man, yet spirit,
Still hid from all men's sight.

Oh fleshly love of sad mortality,
Oh bitter motherhood of those who die,
She that has wisdom will endure her doom,
The days of emptiness, the fruitless womb.
But in her sorrow may she never again
Bear her love's children to their tomb.

MUSE OF MANY SISTERS: the nine Muses were goddesses of song, intellectual creation, and poetic and musical inspiration. STRYMON: a river god, the father of Rhesus; the river Strymon runs through Bulgaria, Macedonia and Greece. HECTOR: the hero who led the Trojan army in the war. ATHENE: the warrior goddess, patron of the Greeks in the Trojan War, and protector of Odysseus. **PERSEPHONE:** the daughter of Demeter, the goddess of agriculture; abducted by Tartarus (Hades), ruler of the underworld, where she remained as queen. **ORPHEUS:** so magical a singer "that wild beasts followed him and trees bent to hear him." In death, he was permitted in Elysium to remain forever with his love, Eurydice.

10.

TECMESSA PLEADS WITH AJAX TO SPARE HER THE GRIEF OF HIS DEATH (OT)

(450–440 BC) SOPHOCLES, *AJAX*, TR. JOHN MOORE

[See in Men's volumes, "Ajax Pretends to be Reconciled to His Shame" and "Ajax Bids Farewell to the Gods and to Athens, and Falls on His Sword."] "Don't give me up to bear the harsh speech/Of your enemies," pleads Tecmessa, "and bow to it, their bondslave." Once a Trojan princess "born of a free father," she's now the captive-concubine of the Greek warrior Ajax. Having fully accepted her lot and borne him a son, Eurysaces, suddenly, after a night of terror and shame for her husband, she—as much as or perhaps more than he—has become cruelly vulnerable.

The shame of Ajax is the shame of a warrior who loses honor, is in fact "annihilated" by loss of face. Because he was passed over by Menelaus and Agamemnon in favor of Odysseus in awarding the arms of the dead Achilles, he planned to kill the Greek chieftains in the dead of night. But the goddess Athena caused madness to possess him. Imagining the army's cattle to be warriors, he captured and slaughtered them, and the following morning—at play's opening—having recovered his reason, he is bowed down with shame at what he has done. He asks to see his young son, Eurysaces, bids him farewell as though he is intent on suicide: "Nobly to live, or else nobly to die befits proud birth." But Tecmessa, who also knew "proud birth," is nevertheless exempt from claiming such private privilege. Unlike Ajax, who feels obligation wholly to his own honor, Tecmessa's is considerably more inclusive, and in her pleading with Ajax to recognize the multiplicity of obligation that should define his very being, she defines her own as well.

His voluntary death, noble in his sense, would be entirely ignoble in hers. First, her instant and certain enslavement and humiliation after his suicide "will be," she argues, "a reproach to you and all your race." Further reproach to his honor: his suicide betrays the reverence owing to his father and mother, leaving them childless "in the misery of old age." And his son, "reft of you," will be left to the mercies of strangers and "wretchedness." Finally, the destruction of alternatives he has already accomplished for her: he and the Greeks have destroyed her country, killed her mother and father, and so left her with only one safe harbor, himself. That safety taken from her—and this, her last argument, is the ultimate undercutting of his idea of "nobility"—signifies that he has answered kindness with forgetfulness, a fundamental ingredient of obligation, and therefore, in her sense, an undercutting of "nobility."

In *Ajax,* Sophocles famously poses the fading concept of external, warrior's honor (Ajax) against a more internalized, more rationally driven concept of honor (Odysseus), and in the main action of the play accomplishes the reconciliation of these two models. But Tecmessa's plea and argument pose the contrast differently: the "noble" as defined by the conduct and bearing of the self toward the self as opposed to the "noble" as defined by the conduct and bearing of the self toward the fullest extensions of the self—that is, toward the fullest extent of human obligation.

Tecmessa's argument and desperate situation go altogether unheeded by Ajax, and quickly fade from the rest of the play's memory, but her clear and rational assertion of principle—transcending the posture of captive-slave begging for personal safety—bears very much the echo of the former princess of "proud birth."

TECMESSA

Ajax, my master, life knows no harder thing
Than to be at the mercy of compelling fortune.
I, for example, was born of a free father;
If any man in Phrygia was lordly and prosperous, he was.
Now I'm a slave. Such, it seems, was the gods' will,
And the will of your strong hand. But since I've come
To share your bed with you, my thoughts are loyal
To you and yours. And I beg you
In the holy name of Zeus who guards your hearth-fire,
And by your bed, in which you have known peace with me,
Don't give me up to hear the harsh speech
Of your enemies and bow to it, their bondslave.

For this is certain: the day you die
And by your death desert me, that same day
Will see me outraged too, forcibly dragged
By the Greeks, together with your boy, to lead a slave's life.
And then someone of the lord class,
With a lashing word, will make his hateful comment:
"There she is, Ajax' woman;
He was the greatest man in the whole army.
How enviable her life was then, and now how slavish!"
Some speech in that style. And my ill fate
Will be driving me before it, but these words
Will be a reproach to you and all your race.

Ajax, revere your father; do not leave him
In the misery of his old age—and your mother,
Shareholder in many years, revere her too!
She prays the gods for your safe return, how often!
And last, dear lord, show pity to your child.
Robbed of his infant nurture, reft of you,
To live his life out under the rule of guardians
Not kind nor kindred—what a wretchedness
You by your death will deal to him and me!

And I no longer have anywhere to look for help,
If not to you. My country was destroyed
Utterly by your spear, and another fate
Brought down my mother and my father too,
To dwell in death with Hades. Then what fatherland
Shall I ever have but you? Or what prosperity?
You are my only safety. O my lord,
Remember even me. A man ought to remember
If he has experienced any gentle thing.
Kindness it is that brings forth kindness always.
But when a man forgets good done to him
And the recollection of it slips away,
How shall I any longer call him noble?

REFT: from reave, to deprive forcibly, strip or rob.

11.
ANTIGONE DEFENDS HER BURIAL
OF HER BROTHER (YT)

(441 BC) SOPHOCLES, *ANTIGONE*, TR. PETER ARNOTT

[See in Men's volumes, "Oedipus Bids Farewell to His Daughters."] After Oedipus' demise, the battle of his two sons for the rule of Thebes leaves both dead, and their uncle, Creon, supplants both as the new king. He buries Eteocles, the defender of the city, with honors, but the "traitor" Polyneices, who laid siege to the city, is forbidden burial by anyone under pain of death. Antigone, Oedipus' daughter and Polyneices' sister, refuses to obey Creon's injunction, performs the burial rite, is arrested and brought before Creon. In perhaps the most famous confrontation in Greek tragedy, she poses her allegiance to the unwritten sacred law of tie-of-blood against Creon's commitment to the supremacy of the laws of the state.

The most celebrated analysis of this confrontation—and for decades, the most influential—was the philosopher Hegel's, who understood the "principle" defended by Creon and the one defended by Antigone to be on a par. Both absolutes, both equal in their moral force, their opposition is subject to ultimate reconciliation only at the cost of the human agents'—Creon's and Antigone's—demise. The dialectic underlying such "world-historical struggles" of antithetical principles such as these inevitably ends in the sacrifice of the protagonists to and by that eventual reconciliation.

But just as it can be argued that the character underlying the dicta of Creon, who lives comfortably within his narrowness of soul, a narrowness which makes possible the emanations of his dicta and the eventual tragedy of his acts [for which argument, see in Men's volumes "Tiresias Violently Condemns Creon's Stubbornness and Folly"], so, it is arguable, it is the inflexibility in Antigone's "character," and possibly a similar narrowness of soul, not of a credo, that is on par with Creon's. Unquestionably, and unlike Hegel's assumption, there is a distinct moral preference discernible between their two positions; ironically, there may be none between their characters. If that is so, there's an interesting disconnect between the virtue of argument and the virtue of person. As Ibsen ruefully explores in *The Wild Duck*, the virtue of argument may be altogether undone by the practical burdens placed on it by the misguided or overguided underlying intentions of the person. In other words, the motive behind argument may be altogether in bad faith, yet the argument not at all, and the effect of argument may be altogether destroyed by the irrelevant or compromising urgencies advancing it.

Noticeably in Creon, the purity of his principle was sabotaged in every way by the personal urgencies of his idea of women and his mystique of self. It was the force and the direction in which he privately reconceived and manipulated his principle —not it itself—that led to the tragic consequence for himself, Antigone, and his son Haemon. Unlike Creon's, the core of Antigone's argument, given abiding cultural norms and preferences of belief, is unanswerable. Does she, as does Creon, impulsively and propulsively subvert it?

Antigone argues that she is beyond argument. The proof of the virtue of her belief is not that it contradicts Creon's, but that it has altogether no relation to it. They have, she insists, no common ground. "My laws," she explains, "are meaningless to you," and "If what I do is foolish in your sight/It may be that a fool condemns my folly." In another way, too, they have no common ground. Creon threatens her with taking her life for disobedience to his "law." Not only is his law no law to her, but the threat of taking her life has no sting. "I know that I must die even without your edict." In any case, the value of life is small indeed "when a person lives as I do in the midst of evils."

She cannot be touched by argument; she cannot be touched by threat. Her deed and her defiance will gain for her something greater than debased life: "the world's renown," and beyond its praise (merely, praise from all those cowards who remain alive and uncomplaining in so debased a world), the approval of the gods.

That certainty—the certainty of a law beyond the laws of men mired in the world's contingencies—is the argument and defense of all the world's proud and willful martyrs. Given Antigone's perfect assurance of being at one with perfect principle, there is indeed no argument against her. But person so thoroughly self-enwrapped in perfect accord with divinity, is, as a person at a distance from the humility and self-abnegation that, in principle, adheres to that certainty itself. And so martyrs to that law above laws can conceivably exemplify for us the "commands" of divinity. They can also be hell on earth.

Antigone is replying to Creon's "Did you know there was an order forbidding this?… And yet you dared to go against the law?"

ANTIGONE

Why not? It was not Zeus who gave the order,
And justice living with the dead below
Has never given men a law like this.
Nor did I think that your pronouncements were
So powerful that mere man could override
The unwritten and unfailing laws of heaven.
These live, not for today and yesterday
But for all time; they came, no man knows whence.
There is no man's resolve I fear enough
To answer to the gods for breaking these.
I knew that I must die—how could I help it?
Even without your edict; but if I die
Before my time is up, I count it gain.
For when a person lives as I do, in the midst
Of evils what can death be but gain?
And so for me to happen on this fate
Is grief not worth a thought; but if I had left
My mother's son to lie a homeless corpse,
Then had I grieved. I do not grieve for this.
If what I do seems foolish in your sight
It may be that a fool condemns my folly.

What more would you take from me than my life?
Then what are you waiting for? Your arguments
Fall on deaf ears; I pray they always will.
My loyalties are meaningless to you.
Yet, in the world's eyes, what could I have done
To earn me greater glory, than to give
My brother burial? Everybody here
Would cheer me, if they were not dumb with fear.
But royalty, among so many blessings,
Has power to say and do whatever it likes.

12.

ANTIGONE LAMENTS HER
ENTOMBMENT AND COMING DEATH (YT)

(441 BC) SOPHOCLES, *ANTIGONE*, TR. PETER ARNOTT

[See No. 11, above] Antigone is condemned to death, and on her way to her entombment (she is to die by her own hand or in the course of time in rock-bound imprisonment), she mourns her fate. But the Chorus offers its double judgment of her acts: "You go," they tell her, "with honor and praise/Below to the caverns of the dead…a law unto yourself." It is the "honor and praise" for her allegiance to that very law that Antigone herself had anticipated. But they add, "Your own willful temper has destroyed you." The two judgments are posed in perfect and mutual contradiction: the greatness of her principle praised; the "willfulness" of her person condemned.

As "the Bride of Death," she is marching in a "wedding procession," so to speak, with the bridegroom Hades. But it's a vastly different Antigone who goes to her death from the one who so briskly dismissed the value of life in her confrontation with Creon. In her lamentation, she mourns the loss of the worldly blessings that signify for her (certainly for Greek culture, and apparently too for Sophocles) a woman's life fulfillment: marriage, motherhood, friendship, and, with those blessings, a long life. Deprived now of all of them, she regards those dispossessions as her punishment. And arguing backwards from the cruelty of this punishment, she wonders: What must have been her sin? Explicitly, Antigone expected two signs of reward: one, her welcome in Hades by the family she so stalwartly defended; and two, by the gods, who rightfully should have bestowed on her worldly blessings. She goes to her death baffled. "Why should I look to the gods any longer/After this? To whom am I to turn for help/When doing right has branded me a sinner?" Antigone, in effect, demands that "doing no less than heaven bids us do" should be rewarded by the gods through the very "hands" on earth whose ways she has transgressed. The narrowness of her insistent personal demand—whether one sees it as justified or not—in terms of "character" is a match for Creon's narrowness of soul.

ANTIGONE

Friendless, unwept, without a wedding song,
They call for me, and I must tread my road.
Eye of heaven, light of the holy sun,
I may look on you no longer.
There is no friend to lament my fate,
No one to shed a tear for me.

Tomb, bridal-chamber, my eternal home
Hewn from the rock, where I must go to meet
My own, those many who have died, and been
Made welcome by Persephone in the shadow-world.
I am the last, my death the worst of all
Before my allotted span of years has run.
But as I go I have this hope in heart,
That my coming may be welcome to my father,
My mother; welcome, dearest brother, to you.
For when you died, with my own hands I washed
And robed your bodies, and poured offerings
Over your graves. Now this is my reward,
Polyneices, for rendering such services to you.
Yet wisdom would approve my honoring you.
Such was the principle by which I chose
To honor you; and for this Creon judges me guilty
Of outrage and transgression, brother mine!
And now he seizes me to lead me off,
Robbed of my bride-bed and my marriage song.
I shall never marry, never be a mother.
And so, in misery, without a friend,
I go still living to the pit of death.
Which one of heaven's commandments have I broken?
Why should I look to the gods any longer
After this? To whom am I to turn for help
When doing right has branded me a sinner?
If the gods approve what is happening to me,
After the punishment I shall know my fault,
But if my judges are wrong, I wish them no worse
Than what they have unjustly done to me.

PERSEPHONE: queen of the Underworld. TOMB...HEWN FROM THE ROCK: Creon had
ordered Antigone locked alive inside her brother's burial chamber

13.

ALCESTIS, BIDDING FAREWELL TO ADMETUS, RECONCILES HIM TO HER LIFE'S SACRIFICE (YT)

(438 BC) EURIPIDES, *ALCESTIS*, TR. MOSES HADAS AND JOHN H. MACLEAN

It was the god Apollo who won from his sister Artemis the promise that when the day appointed for Admetus' death came, he would be spared on condition that a member of his family died voluntarily for love of him. Neither his father nor his mother is willing to offer their life for their son; there is still pleasure, argues his father, to be found in living it to its end. Only Alcestis, Admetus' wife, volunteers her life for her husband's, a sacrifice mournfully but nevertheless gratefully accepted by him.

Although Admetus is represented in the drama as a pious and altogether decent man and king, ever since the play has been known in Western tradition, he has been condemned for accepting such a sacrifice, his parents for a selfishness shocking to tender notions of parental devotion, and the exchange itself, of Alcestis for her husband, warranting shudders of disgust for being morally monstrous. Euripides, if anything, exploits these moral incongruities by treating the family more as middle-class Athenians than as figures of royalty seen from the salving distance of myth. Even though the grave figures of Apollo and Death and the broadly comic figure of Heracles set the terms of and control the play's action, the world and setting of the family itself are distinctly domestic. And the relations among the family—particularly in the no-holds-barred quarrel between Admetus and his father—are observed with frank and even brutal objectivity.

But given the story's assumptions, the condemnation of Admetus is altogether beside the point. Like Apollo's gift to Cassandra [see No. 4, above], his gift of life to Admetus is a blessing wrapped in a curse. Once the gift is given by the god, it is not Admetus' prerogative to choose whether to accept it or not; he can choose only his surrogate in death. And that choice is somewhat constricted. Like the Everyman of the medieval morality play, he can find neither willing friend nor kin, and must accede to the sacrifice of the very one he least desires to lose, the wife he deeply loves. Their mutual mourning as she is fading into death and the grief he suffers afterwards are meant as testimonial not to his hypocrisy, but to his decency (at one point in their mutual lamentation, he yearns ironically for the one thing that is no longer possible for him: that they enter death together.)

Although the chorus holds Alcestis in the greatest esteem ("the greatest of women"), and though her praises are sung extravagantly by Heracles, husband, children, and servants, she does not see herself as either sentimentally or romantically heroic, but as making what she sees—given her role and duty—as a hard, necessary, and appropriate choice. That she regrets the necessity for it is clear—she has hard words to say about Admetus' parents—but in her code of matrimonial honor, she's bound to do it. And so, while her life is ebbing away, while she is being held in her weeping husband's arms, while her children are clutching at her and clamoring for their mother to stay alive (Euripides, when exploiting pathos, knew no shame), Alcestis, in the midst of these universal tears, still rallies determinedly to recite, in effect, her last will and testament for the continuing well-being of husband and children. She warns first and foremost that, for the good of the children and for the honor of her husband, there must be no second wife, no cruel stepmother for her children. She is quite literally leaving everything in pat order before she goes.

When she is borne onstage, in her last moments, in her husband's arms, she is imagining that she is already on the final journey of mortal death, being carried in the ferryman Charon's boat across the river Lethe to the realms of Hades.

ALCESTIS

I see the two-oared boat, I see it upon the lake. The ferryman
of the dead has his hand upon the pole, Charon is already
calling me: "Why do you linger? Hasten! You are delaying us."
So is he hurrying me, brusquely. He is wagging me, someone
is dragging me—do you not see?—to the court of the dead.
Under his dark brows he is gazing at me; he has wings. It is
Hades. What will you do? Let go of me! What a road, what a
luckless road I am entering upon!

Let me go, let me go now, lay me down: my feet have no
strength. Hades is near. Dark night is creeping over my eyes.
Children, my children, your mother is dying, dying. Farewell,
my children, and look long upon the light.

Admetus, I want to declare my wishes before I die. For your

sake I die, though I could have lived and married any
Thessalian I wished and lived in a house happy with kinship.
He that begot you and she that bore you betrayed you, though
they had come to a time of life fitting for death, fitting to save
their son and die glorious. You were their only child, and they
had no hope of getting other children if you were dead. Then I
should have lived, and you too, the rest of our time, and you
would not be groaning at the loss of your wife, and would not
have to bring up your children motherless.

So be it. But do you remember to render me gratitude for
these things. I do not seek an equal return. That is impossible,
for nothing is so precious as life. What I ask is only fair, as you
yourself will admit.
These children you love no less than I, if you are right-
minded: let them be masters of my house. Do not marry a
stepmother over these children, a woman who will love them
less than I, who will, out of envy, lay hands upon your children
and mine. For a stepmother that comes later hates the children
that were there before she came; she is no gentler than a viper.
A boy has his father as a tower of strength; but how, my
daughter, how will you find your father's wife? You will have
no mother to deck you for your marriage, nor be present to
hearten you in your childbearing, dear child, when nothing is
so kindly as a mother. I must die. This evil is coming upon
me, not tomorrow or the next day, but in a moment they will
be speaking of me as dead. Farewell and be happy.

Admetus, receive these children from my hand. Be now a
mother to these children in my stead. My eyes are dimmed
and grow heavy. Speak of me as dead, dead and gone. Farewell,
my children! I die. Farewell.

TWO-OARED BOAT…CHARON…HADES…LUCKLESS BOAT: Alcestis imagines she is
already undergoing her journey toward death, borne by Charon's ferryboat across
the river Lethe and entering Hades. THESSALIAN: from Thessaly, northern Greece;
Alcestis' original home. HE THAT BEGOT YOU…BETRAYED YOU: Admetus' mother
and father.

14.

MEDEA REVILES THE FATE
OF WOMEN IN MARRIAGE (OT)

(431 BC) EURIPIDES, *MEDEA*, TR. FREDERIC PROKOSCH

Medea, enraged, weeps and broods on revenge. For love of Jason, she had helped him to steal the Golden Fleece using her skills in magic, murdered her own brother to effect his escape from Colchis, and caused the death of Jason's uncle Pelias, who had deprived him of his rightful throne in Iolchus. Now living in exile in Corinth with her husband and two sons, she learns that he is abandoning her to marry King Creon's daughter, and that she herself is being banished from the kingdom.

But characteristic of Euripides, Medea does not complain merely for, or as, herself alone, but as an "instance" an example first, of the humiliation of the foreigner unfamiliar to the citizenry, and then as example of the universal humiliation of women. The isolated foreigner is hated for his "pride," the woman, once married, is many times over humiliated and abased. The catalogue of her humiliations is long, and ranges beyond Medea's personal plight. Women must buy husbands with a dowry; the husband is chosen for her, without her knowing whether he will be kind or a perpetual tyrant; she has no option of refusing marriage and loses honor if divorced; she must learn the delicate subtlety and tact of "how to manage a man"; and whether she can or not, he has easy escape to friends from an unhappy household, but she has none, her world circumscribed "by him and him alone." As for the protection and freedom from danger the husband offers (his protection of hearth and home on the battlefield), "I'd rather be sent three times over to the battlefront than give birth to a single child."

Whatever the women of the chorus may know of comfort, family, fellowship, and native country, Medea (at last speaking only of her own plight) has no such refuges "in a sea of disaster" having lost them all through her love and labors for Jason. She sees no escape, and imagines no other satisfaction than revenge—against the husband, the father, the bride. Why? Because "when things go wrong in this thing of love, no heart is so fearless as a woman's; no heart so filled with the thought of blood."

It's a theme and motive Euripides pursues throughout the tragedy of *Medea*: the only option for a love turned to hate "for all that he has done to me" is the satisfaction of revenge. Subsequently, when another clear option does appear—escape to the protection of Aegeus in Athens—it alters neither the direction nor the force of her revenge; in fact, it gives it practical sanction. Then the questions of moral justification or condemnation of Medea's acts—Is she sufficiently aggrieved? Can she conceivably in any instance be justified?— become irrelevant. There is a code operating which lives by psychological, not ethical sanction: the balance of wrong by wrong. The balancing or overbalancing of the wrongs Medea feels is so powerful, so controlling a need, that even her own moral persuasion against herself is powerless to overcome it. Euripides explores in Medea the limits of her exultation, her deep, thrilled pleasure when that need is satisfied—and the limits of her unbearable anxiety when it is yet to be satisfied. The need is beyond pain; the repletion is orgasmic.

(Medea enters from the house.)

MEDEA

Ladies of Corinth, I have come forth from my house; lest you should feel bitterness toward me; for I know that men often acquire a bad name for their pride—not only the pride they show in public, but also the pride of retirement; those who live in solitude, as I do, are frequently thought to be proud. For there is no justice in the view one man takes of another; often hating him before he has suffered wrong, hating him even before he has seen his true character. Therefore, a foreigner above all should fit into the ways of a city. Not even a native citizen, I think, should risk offending his neighbors by rudeness or pride.

But this new thing has fallen upon me so unexpectedly, my strength is broken. O my friends, my life is shattered; my heart no longer longs for the blessings of life, but only for death! There was one man through whom I came to see the world's whole beauty: and that was my husband; and he has turned out utterly evil. O women, of all creatures that live and reflect, certainly it is we who are the most luckless. First of all, we pay a great price to purchase a husband; and thus submit our bodies to a perpetual tyrant. And everything depends on whether our choice is good or bad—for divorce is not an honorable thing, and we may not refuse to be married. And then a wife is plunged into a way of life and behavior entirely new to her; and must learn what she never learned at home— she must learn by a kind of subtle intuition how to manage the man who lies beside her. And if we have the luck to handle all these things with tact and success, and if the husband is willing to live at our side without resentment, then life can become happy indeed. But if not, I'd rather be dead. A man who is disgusted with what he finds at home, goes forth to put an end to his boredom, and turns to a friend or companion of his own age; while we at home continue to think of him and him only.

And yet people say that we live in security at home, while the men go forth to war. How wrong they are! Listen: I'd rather be sent three times over to the battlefront than give birth to a single child.

Still, my friends, I realize that all this applies not to you but to me; you after all have a city of your own, and a family home, and a certain pleasure in life, and the company of your friends. But I am utterly lonely, an exile, cast off by my own husband—nothing but a captive brought here from a foreign land—without a mother or brother, without a single kinsman who can give me refuge in this sea of disasters. Therefore, my ladies, I ask only one thing of you: promise me silence. If I can find some way, some cunning scheme of revenge against my husband for all that he has done to me, and against the man who gave away his daughter, and against the daughter who is now my husband's wife: then please be silent. For though a woman is timid in everything else, and weak, and terrified at the sight of a sword, still when things go wrong in this thing of love, no heart is so fearless as a woman's; no heart is so filled with the thought of blood.

THE MAN WHO GAVE AWAY...WIFE: Jason divorced Medea and married Glauce, daughter of the king of Thebes, Creon.

15.

MEDEA DELIBERATES ON HER PLANS FOR REVENGE (OT)

(431 BC) EURIPIDES, *MEDEA*, TR. FREDERIC PROKOSCH

Like many complex characters in literature, Medea speaks in several voices. In her interview with King Creon, she is outraged at his insistence that she leave immediately with her two children, since, as he tells her frankly, he fears her resentment and her cunning, to do mischief. She quickly finds the right register for that cunning and wrings sufficient compassion out of him to grant her a single day's reprieve before exile. The moment he leaves, she takes a moment to congratulate herself on her triumph over his suspicions. Then immediately, in a distinctly practical register, she begins to calculate her best use of that newfound day. The objective is clear: revenge against the three—the bridegroom, the bride, the father—by murder; and the balance and overbalance of their wrong against her [see No. 14, above]. How? There are two considerations: the repletion of her satisfaction and her safety. Fire? Sword? Both entail her presence in the palace, where she would certainly be caught and killed. Therefore, her more familiar and more practiced way: poison from a distance. Even then, what of her safety? With no certain safe harbor afterward, best to delay until she finds one. Still, revenge, now her absolutely fixed intent, must be accomplished even if it entails her own death.

Then, invocation: the manner of revenge set, she steels herself to her purpose, weighing the wrong done to her against the stature of the woman to whom it was done—she who is at one with the witch-goddess Hecate's dark powers, she who boasts divine lineage—and once again, the moral component has no bearing, is nothing; the appropriateness of the weapon alone—"mischief"—is everything.

MEDEA

Everything has gone wrong. None can deny it. But not quite
everything is lost; don't give up hope, my friends! There still
are troubles in store for the young bride, and for the
bridegroom too. Do you think I would have fawned on that
old man without some plan and purpose? Certainly not. I
would never have touched him with my hands. But now,
although he could have crushed all my plans by instant exile,

he has made a fatal error; he has given me one day's reprieve. One day in which I can bring death to the three creatures that I loathe: the father, the bride, my husband. There are many manners of death which I might use; I don't quite know yet which to try. Shall I set fire to the bridal mansion? Or shall I sharpen a sword and steal into the chamber to the wedding bed and plunge it into their hearts? One thing stands in my way. If I am caught making my way into the bridal room on such an errand, I shall surely be put to death; and my foes will end up triumphing over me. Better to take the shortest way, the way I am best trained in: better to bring them down with poison. That I will do, then. And after that? Suppose them dead. What city will take me in then? What friend will offer me shelter in his land, and safety, and a home? None. Then best to wait a little longer; perhaps some sure defense will appear, and I can set about the murder in stealth and stillness. And if no help should come from fate, and even if death is certain, still I can take at last the sword in my own hand, and go forth boldly to the crime, and kill. Yes, by that dark Queen whom I revere above all others, and whom I now invoke to help me, by Hecate who dwells in my most secret chamber: I swear no man shall injure me and not regret it. I will turn their marriage into sorrow and anguish! Go now, go forward to this dangerous deed! The time has come for courage. Remember the suffering they caused you! Never shall you be mocked because of this wedding of Jason's, you who are sprung from a noble father and whose grandfather was the Sun-God himself! You have the skill; what is more, you are a woman: and it's always a woman who is incapable of a noble deed, yet expert in every kind of mischief!

THE BRIDE AND THE BRIDEGROOM: Jason and his new bride, Glauce. POISON: Medea was trained in the art of poisoning by her aunt, the witch Circe. HECATE: a confusing divinity, identified with the Moon, Artemis (the goddess of the hunt) and Persephone (the queen of the Underworld). Invoked by sorcerers, she is the great sender of visions, of madness, and of sudden terror. Medea was her witch-priestess before falling in love with Jason. SUN-GOD: Helios. Medea is the daughter of King Aeetes of Colchis and granddaughter of Helios.

16.

MEDEA VENTS HER ANGER AGAINST JASON (OT)

(431 BC) EURIPIDES, *MEDEA*, TR. FREDERIC PROKOSCH

Like a man behind an office desk being polite to an impolitic colleague who's just been fired, Jason visits Medea after he's heard the news that Creon has banished her, offers her a measure of comfort. He points out where she made a strategic error in dealing with Creon and even volunteers a small stipend against her suffering poverty when she's gone. Jason, in the very act of justifying himself [see in Men's volumes: "Jason Defends His Abandonment of Medea"], is unaware that he's condemning himself by the spuriousness and irrelevance of his arguments. It is not merely the arguments themselves that revolt Medea, but the make-believe behind them. She is enraged as much by his blatant emotional indifference as by his betrayal of her. That is his cowardice, that is the shamelessness that is "the worst of all human vices": the careful skirting of the emotional depths genuinely belonging to the moment, and on his part, genuinely owing to the "friend" he has injured. Her intention in her response is to drag him into her level of emotional pain, so that "I can ease my heart in reviling you: and perhaps you too will suffer as you listen."

Her strategy is to remind him first of the incredible sacrifices—the courageous acts, the outright crimes—she had committed for him "when my love was stronger than my reason," and the shameful ingratitude and betrayal with which he rewarded them. Then she exacerbates his guilt for winning the profit of his new marriage at the expense of the exile and misery of his former wife and children. It has little effect. He answers glibly with the "clever phrases and specious arguments" Medea feels deserve the worst punishment of all, the punishment earned by "the man who speaks brilliantly for an evil cause, the man who knows he can make an evil thing sound plausible."

MEDEA

You filthy coward! That is the only name I can find for you,
you and your utter lack of manliness! And now you, who are
the worst of my enemies, now you too have chosen to come to

me! No; it isn't courage which brings you; not recklessness in facing the friends you have injured; it is worse than that, it is the worst of all human vices: shamelessness. Still, you did well to come to me, for now I can ease my heart by reviling you: and perhaps you too will suffer as you listen.

Let me begin, then, at the very beginning. I saved your life; every Greek who sailed with you on the Argo knows I saved you, when you were sent to tame the fire-breathing bulls and to yoke them, and to sow the deadly fields. Yes, and I killed the many-folded serpent who lay guarding the Golden Fleece, forever wakeful, coil upon coil. And I raised a beacon of lights to bring you to safety. Freely I deserted my own father and my own home; and followed you to Iolcos, to the hills of Pelion; and all this time my love was stronger than my reason. And I brought death to Pelias by his own daughters' hands; I utterly destroyed the household. All of these things I did for you, traitor! And you forsook me, and took another wife, even though I had borne your children. Had you been childless, one might have pardoned your wish for a second wedding. But now all my faith in your vows has vanished. I do not know whether you imagine that the gods by whom you swore have disappeared, or that new rules are now in vogue in such matters; for you must be aware that you have broken your vows to me. Oh this poor right hand, which you so often pressed! These knees, which you so often used to embrace! And all in vain, for it was an evil man that touched me! How wildly all my hopes have fallen through!...

Come, Jason, I shall speak to you quite frankly, as though we still were friends. Can I possibly expect any kindness from someone like you? Still, let us assume that I can: it will only make you appear still more ignoble. Very well. Where shall I go? Home to my father? Home to him and the land I betrayed when I followed you? Or back to the pitiful daughters of Pelias? What a fine welcome they would give me, who arranged the death of their own father! So this is how it now stands with me. I am loathed by my friends at home; and for your sake I made enemies of others whom I need never have harmed. And now, to reward me for all this, look, look, how doubly happy you've made me among the women of Hellas! Look what a fine, trustworthy husband I have had in you! And now I am to be cast forth into exile, in utter misery, alone with my children and without a single friend! Oh, this will be a shameful shadow upon you, as you lie in your wedding bed!

That your own children and their mother, who saved your life,
should go wandering around the world like beggars!…O Zeus,
why have you given us a way to tell true gold from the
counterfeit, but no way, no emblem branded on a man's body
whereby we can tell the true man from the false?

I SAVED YOUR LIFE: several times during the Argonauts' expedition, she warned Jason
about plots to kill him, cured his wounds, and cast spells on monsters he was supposed to fight. THE FIRE-BREATHING BULLS: when Jason had to subdue two fire-
breathing bulls in order to gain the Golden Fleece, Medea gave him a flask of magical
lotion that preserved his body from the flames. SOW THE DEADLY FIELDS: another
task of Jason's was to plough the Field of Ares (the god of war) and sow it with a serpent's teeth, from which armed men grew. MANY-FOLDED SERPENT: a loathsome and
immortal dragon of a thousand coils that was larger than the Argo itself. Born from
the blood of the monster Typhon, which was destroyed by Zeus, it guarded the
Fleece. According to the legend, Medea didn't kill him but only soothed him with
incantations, and then sprinkled soporific drops on his eyelids. I RAISED A BEACON
OF LIGHT: while Jason was away with Argo, Pelias usurped his father's throne. Upon
return of the expedition, Medea persuaded Pelias that he can become younger if his
daughters cut him to pieces and then magically re-assemble him. Part of the ritual
required the daughters to go on the roof with blazing torches and pray to the
Moon—the signal for Jason that Pelias was dead.

17.

MEDEA, EMBRACING HER CHILDREN, DEBATES HER RESOLVE (OT)

(431 BC) EURIPIDES, *MEDEA*, TR. FREDERIC PROKOSCH

[See No. 14, No. 15 and No. 16, above] Medea, after receiving Aegeus'
promise of shelter in his city of Athens, has no further reason for
delay. She prepares at once for her "hour of triumph," for executing
her revenge on the ones she hates. Her plans are swift and deadly:
First, conciliatory words to Jason, and as a stratagem, she begs him to
let their children remain with him. This, so that they can bring gifts,
a poisoned dress and diadem, to Jason's bride. The dress will effect
the bride's death and cause her father, when he touches her, to die in
anguish as well. But the next step "sets her weeping": her determination to kill her own children, to make Jason's ruin complete.

The gift is sent and accepted, and the children return with the boon of having been reprieved from exile. Instead of exulting that her plan is succeeding, she is terrified. Knowing that once the bride and king are poisoned, her children will be put to death, she recognizes that—over and above her original determination to murder them as part of her own revenge—she must forestall the Corinthians from killing them on her own. She must perform the act herself: murder her own sons. Now her "passion," as she understands it, must struggle with her "reason." But in the instance of Medea, the great question is, what is her "passion?" Which of her motives underlies it and which counter that passion—or passions—with "reason?" And what, for Medea, represents the sobriety and constraint of "reason?" In her struggle with her decision as she holds her children in her arms, the complexity of motive, passion, and rational deliberation in Medea is revealed.

And revealed to herself as well. As each consideration confronts her, each seems to her unarguable, but each in turn is supplanted by a contradictory consideration equally unarguable. At the end of this monologue, her decision is firm: she has been led astray by "passion" and recognizes, now that "reason" prevails, that she could not conceivably murder the children she loves. (Nevertheless, subsequently, she is to "consider" again, and murders them.)

The sequence:

a) *("O my children, my children")* Having just agreed ostensibly to surrender her children to Jason, since they are reprieved from exile, she gathers them to her to bid them a heartfelt farewell. But considering her lonely future in exile, where she will not know the pleasures of raising her children, she forgets the intended generosity of her farewell to them, and instead mourns her own plight. But an even stronger argument than her despair at losing them to a life without her is their loving looks and smiles as they regard her. It is that that kills her resolve to give them up.

b) *("O women, I cannot do it! Farewell to all my plans")* New decision—to take her children with her. But to what "plans" is she saying "farewell?" We realize suddenly that the plan—hidden beneath the ostensible plan generously to give them up—was the one to kill them. And firmly, she says goodbye to *that* plan "to hurt their father by hurting them." In other words, she had still been planning to murder them while ostensibly saving them for Jason.

c) *("And yet—O what is wrong with me?)* Immediately, her revulsion at the thought of her "enemies go[ing] unpunished" moves her to rebel against *that* decision. And this is possibly the deepest "passion" of all for Medea—her powerful demand for the justice of that balance of wrong with wrong [see No. 14, above] the demand she cannot withstand, and that in the end determines her choice. But at the moment as she sends the children out of her sight so that her determination will remain firm, even proud, even challenging ("if anyone prefers not to witness my sacrifice, let him do as he wishes!"), at the same moment her "heart" again contradicts:

d) (*"my poor heart, have pity on them"*) And she determines to take them with her into exile where "they'll bring cheer to you." But instantly,

e) (*"No, by all the avenging Furies, this shall not be!"*): Why not? Because it will induce the "insolence and mockery of my enemies." What will? Her taking them into exile with herself? Clearly not. What enemies are lying in wait in Athens? Again, the underlying image she's rejecting, hidden beneath the rejection of the plan to take the children with her, is the one of giving them up to her husband and the Corinthians—her fixed enemies. Thought piled on top of thought, one image of defeat (taking the children with her) simultaneously evokes the apparently contrary image of defeat (leaving them with Jason.) Why are these opposites unconsciously so equated? Because neither satisfies Medea's fundamental need, her internal—whether rational or not—emotionally demanded, feeling for "justice": that balancing of wrong with wrong.

f) (*"It is settled. I have made my decision. They must die. Their mother must kill them"*): With that firm decision, she will once again say farewell to her children, now for the last time. But again seeing and embracing them destroys her resolution. Keeping them in her sight, and remembering her (now seen as) barbaric resolution, appalls her. She sends them away, heaves a great sigh of relief, thankful for her escape from the murder of her children, and reflects,

g) (*"At last I see how my passion is stronger than my reason"*): But this moment's "reason" is no proof against the passion for righting the balance with revenge that governs her far more profoundly, and will govern her entirely in the end.

*(The attendant goes into the house,
and Medea turns to her children.)*

MEDEA

O my children, my children, you will still have a city, you will still have a home where you can dwell forever, far away from me, far forever from your mother! But I am doomed to go in exile to another land, before I can see you grow up and be happy, before I can take pride in you, before I can wait on your brides and make your marriage beds, or hold the torch at your wedding ceremony! What a victim I am of my own self-will! It was all in vain, my children, that I reared you! It was all in vain that I grew weary and worn, and suffered the anguish and pangs of childbirth! Oh pity me! Once I had great hopes for you; I had hopes that you'd look after me in my old age, and that you'd lovingly deck my body with your own hands when I died, as all men hope and desire. But now my lovely dreams are over. I shall love you both. I shall spend my life in grief and solitude. And never again will you see your mother with your own dear eyes; now you will pass into another kind of life. Ah, my dear children, why do you look at me like this? Why are you smiling your sweet little smiles at me? O children, what can I do? My heart gives way when I see the joy shining in my children's eyes. O women, I cannot do it!…Farewell to all my plans! I will take my babies away with me: from this. Why should I hurt their father by hurting them? Why should I hurt myself doubly? No: I cannot do it. I shall say good-bye to my plans. And yet—O, what is wrong with me? Am I willing to see my enemies go unpunished? Am I willing to be insulted and laughed at? I shall follow this thing to the end. How weak I am! How weak to let my heart be touched by these soft sentiments! Go back into the house, my children…And if anyone prefers not to witness my sacrifice, let him do as he wishes! My poor heart—do not do this thing! My poor heart, have pity on them, let them go, the little children! They'll bring cheer to you, if you let them live with you in exile!…No, by all the avenging Furies, this shall not be! Never shall I surrender any children to the insolence and mockery of my enemies! It is settled. I have made my decision. And since they must die, it is their mother who must kill them. Now there is no escape for the young bride! Already the crown is on her head; already the dress is hanging from her body; the royal bride, the princess is dying! This I know. And now—since I am about to follow a dreadful path, and am sending them on a path still more terrible—I will simply say this: I want to speak to my children.

> *(She calls and the children come back;
> she takes them in her arms.)*

Come, come, give me your hands, my babies, let your mother kiss you both. O dear little hands, dear little lips: how I have loved them! How fresh and young your eyes look! How straight you stand! I wish you joy with all my heart; but not here; not in this land. All that you had here your father has stolen from you…How good it is to hold you, to feel your soft, young cheeks, the warm young sweetness of your breath…Go now; leave me. I cannot look at you any longer…I am overcome…

> *(The children go into the house again.)*

Now at last I understand the full evil of what I have planned. At last I see how my passion is stronger than my reason: passion, which brings the worst of woes to mortal man.

18.

THE MESSENGER (NURSE) REPORTS THE OUTCOME OF MEDEA'S REVENGE (OT)

(431 BC) EURIPIDES, *MEDEA*, TR. FREDERIC PROKOSCH

It's become customary in modern productions of *Medea* to give the Nurse the Messenger's speech that describes in gruesome detail the deaths of King Creon and his daughter by Medea's gifts of the poisoned robe and diadem. The change adds considerably to the dramatic power of the scene, as the Nurse struggles with her compassion for the victims, her revulsion at the scene that she is forced to describe, and most particularly, her compassion for the plight of Medea now that her crime is accomplished. It is customary in performance too—although not a plus when the speech is given as a monologue—for the focus to be not on the Nurse, but on Medea's response to her recital. It is a great deal more than her satisfaction at the outcome; it is something resembling almost orgasmic pleasure as she listens to the details of the Nurse's account.

Messenger's speeches in classical drama were understood to be anything but neutral reports of an event. They were its present-tense realization in words, just as a film sequence of a battle or murder or suicide is their present-tense realization in image; both are expected to have the same evocative power, with the difference that the Messenger on stage is humanly invested in the event's recapitulation.

Some of the greatest actor's moments in Greek drama are in these speeches. 'So far as words can serve, you shall see it,' [one of the Messengers] promises, and makes good his promise. The *seeing* of the event currently is the occasion for the Messenger's immersion in its progress—as though it is currently happening and currently being felt exactly as at first.

It is the Nurse who brought the children and their gifts to Creon's palace, and in this alteration of roles, it is she who runs in terror from the palace with the warning on her lips for Medea to escape. "Fly, Medea, fly," she cries, as she runs to her. But what begins as breathless warning becomes the horrified and at the same time compassionate reliving of the event; it concludes as strength and breath abated, with rueful, resigned calm. The speech offers careful admonition, not pointed enough to provoke, but general enough to fit all sufferers: there is a way to avoid the deepest suffering, by not probing too deeply.

(Messenger rushes in.)

MESSENGER (NURSE)

Fly, Medea, fly! You have done a terrible thing, a thing breaking all human laws: fly, and take with you a ship for the seas, or a chariot for the plains!

She lies dead! The royal princess, and her father Creon, too! They have died: they have been slain by your poisons! You have done an outrage to the royal house: does it make you happy to hear it? Can you hear of this dreadful thing without horror?

When those two children, your own babies, Medea, came with their father and entered the palace of the bride, it gave joy to all of us, the servants who have suffered with you; for instantly all through the house we whispered that you had made up your quarrel with your husband. One of us kissed your children's hands, and another their golden hair, and I myself was so overjoyed that I followed them in person to the women's chambers. And there stood our mistress, whom we now serve instead of you; and she kept her eyes fixed longingly on Jason. When she caught sight of your children, she covered up her eyes, and her face grew pale, and she turned away, filled with petulance at their coming. But your husband tried to soothe the bride's ill humor, and said: "Do not look so unkindly at your friends! Do not feel angry: turn your head to me once more, and think of your husband's friends as your own friends! Accept these gifts, and do this for my sake: beg of your father not to let these children be exiled!" And then, when she saw the dress, she grew mild and yielded, and gave in to her husband. And before the father and the children had gone far from her rooms, she took the gorgeous robe and put it on; and she put the golden crown on her curly head, and arranged her hair in the shining mirror, smiling as she saw herself reflected. And then she rose from her chair and walked across the room, stepping softly and delicately on her small white feet, filled with delight at the gift, and glancing again and again at the delicate turn of her ankles. And after that it was a thing of horror we saw. For suddenly her face changed its color, and she staggered back, and began to tremble as she ran, and reached a chair just as she was about to fall to the ground. An old woman servant, thinking no doubt that this was some kind of seizure, a fit sent by Pan, or some other god, cried out a prayer: and then, as she prayed, she saw the flakes of foam flow from her mouth, and her eyeballs rolling, and the blood fade from her face. And then it was a different prayer she uttered, a terrible scream, and one of the women ran to the house of the King, and another to the newly wedded groom to tell him what had happened to the bride; and the whole house echoed as they ran to and fro.

Let me tell you, time enough for a man to walk two hundred yards past before the poor lady awoke from her trance, with a dreadful scream, and opened her eyes again. A twofold torment was creeping over her. The golden diadem on her head was sending forth a violent stream of flame, and the finely woven dress which your children gave her was beginning to eat into the poor girl's snowy soft flesh. And she leapt from her chair, all on fire, and started to run, shaking her head to and fro, trying to shake off the diadem; but the gold still clung firmly, and as she shook her hair the fire blazed forth with double fury. And then she sank to the ground, helpless, overcome; and past all recognition except to the eye of a father—for her eyes had lost their normal expression, and the familiar look had fled from her face, and from the top of her head a mingled stream of blood and fire was pouring. And it was like the drops falling from the bark of a pine tree when the flesh dropped away from her bones, torn loose by the secret fangs of the poison. And terror kept all of us from touching the corpse; for we were warned by what had happened.

But then her poor father, who knew nothing of her death, came suddenly into the house and stumbled over her body, and cried out as he folded his arms about her, and kissed her, and said: "O my child, my poor child, which of the gods has so cruelly killed you? Who has robbed me of you, who am old and close to the grave? O my child, let me die with you!" And he grew silent and tried to rise to his feet again, but found himself fastened to the finely spun dress, like vine clinging to a laurel bough, and there was a fearful struggle. And still he tried to lift his knees, and she writhed and clung to him; and as he tugged, he tore the withered flesh from his bones. And at last he could no longer master the pain, and surrendered, and gave up the ghost. So there they are lying together: and it is a sight to send us weeping…

As for you, Medea, I will say nothing of your own problems: you yourself must discover an escape from punishment. I think, and I have always thought, the life of men is a shadow; and I say without fear that those who are wisest among all men, and probe most deeply into the cause of things—they are the ones who suffer most deeply! For, believe me, no man among mortals is happy; if wealth comes to a man, he may be luckier than the rest; but happy—never.

(Exit Messenger.)

PAN: Originally an Arcadian god of the wilderness, a god of flocks and shepherds. He was known for producing sudden fears and panics.

19.

PHAEDRA, TORMENTED BY SHAME, LONGS FOR DEATH (OT)

(428 BC) EURIPIDES, *HIPPOLYTUS*, TR. DAVID GRENE

Phaedra is ill. One moment her body is slack and willess; then suddenly she is taut, shrill, and raving. Too weak to move on her own, she is borne in on a couch by servants, and her settling into it is helped by their holding her "beautiful hands." Then they must see to her hat, which she complains is too heavy to be tolerated, too imprisoning of her flowing hair. She eats nothing, she is shriveling, she longs to sink into death.

The mystery of Phaedra's illness, about which she refuses to offer a hint, is hardly unveiled by her ravings: she longs, cries madly to join the huntsmen in the mountains, to break young colts for the goddess Artemis, to hurl the javelin for sport as the young huntsmen do who follow Hippolytus. All this, with her body taut, her voice shrill, acting out these longings.

Though no one—neither her nurse nor the chorus of women—understands why these images and longings so exercise her, once they are uttered, she realizes why they've burst out of her, and overwhelmed with shame, she begs the nurse, who is standing over her wringing her hands in bewilderment and terror, to cover her face in order to hide the shame of her speaking in madness of the secret she must never reveal. And then, once again limp, weeping, desperate, Phaedra wants only to die "and know no more of anything," to be free of the criminal reason for her self-inflicted suffering.

The motives operating in *Hippolytus* [as spelled out in Men's volumes: "Hippolytus Curses Women and Adultery…"] are absolute and unqualified. Just as Hippolytus' devotion to his chastity is accompanied by his equally absolute detestation of women, so Phaedra's incestuous love for him (her husband is Theseus' son by the Amazon Queen Hippolyta) is an uncontrollable desire so overwhelming that she believes death is its only possible constraint. The secret is later gotten out of her by the Nurse, but Phaedra's powerful yearning for it never to be known is motivated by another devotion—to *aidos,* the constraint of shame. More than shame: *aidos* personifies the modesty and honor that is harnessed to a sense of shame. In Phaedra, it is a devotion as overwhelming, as powerful as her yearning for Hippolytus.

PHAEDRA

(To the servants)
Lift me up! Lift my head up! All the muscles
are slack and useless. Here, you, take my hands.
They're beautiful, my hands and arms!
Take away this hat! It is too heavy to wear.
Take it away! Let my hair fall free on my shoulders.

O, if I could only draw from the dewy spring
a draught of fresh spring water!
If I could only lie beneath the poplars,
in the tufted meadow and find my rest there!

Bring me to the mountains! I *will* go to the mountains!
Among the pine trees where the huntsmen's pack
trails spotted stags and hangs upon their heels.
God, how I long to set the hounds on, shouting!
And poise the Thessalian javelin drawing it back—
here where my fair hair hangs above the ear—
I would hold in my hand a spear with a steel point!

Artemis Mistress of the Salty Lake,
mistress of the ring echoing to the racers' hoofs,
if only I could gallop your level stretches,
and break Venetian colts!

O, I am miserable! What is this I've done?
Where have I strayed from the highway of good sense?
I was mad. It was the madness sent from some god
that caused my fall.
I am unhappy, so unhappy! Nurse,
cover my face again. I am ashamed
of what I said. Cover me up. The tears
are flowing and my face is turned to shame.
Rightness of judgment is bitterness to the heart.
Madness is terrible. It is better then,
that I should die and know no more of anything.

THESSALIAN JAVELIN: a spear made in Thessaly, in northern Greece. ARTEMIS: goddess of the hunt and of chastity.

20.

CREUSA RECALLS WITH BITTERNESS APOLLO'S RAPE AND ITS TRAGIC OUTCOME (OT)

(421–408 BC) EURIPIDES, *ION*, TR. MOSES HADAS AND JOHN H. MCLEAN

Rape is the crime from which Creusa suffered years ago, first with shame and anger at the god Apollo who perpetrated it, then with the shame and sorrow of her child's secret birth and exposure. That past event is unknown to her husband Xuthus, with whom she's come to the oracle of Apollo to consult about their childlessness. Creusa, alone with Ion, the shrine's attendant, tells him of a "friend" who suffered rape and babe's exposure and who now wants to learn whether the child is still alive. But Ion gives her no comfort. "If he were proven a villain in his own temple, [Apollo] would justly inflict some calamity on him who passed the judgment. Desist then, lady," he advises her. But when she's gone, he passes private judgment: "He ravishes girls and betrays them! Begets children by stealth and callously leaves them to die!…If the day ever comes…when you have to make amends for your rapings and whorings,…you will bankrupt your temples to pay for your sins." And as for blaming men "for imitating the splendid conduct of the gods, blame those who set us the example."

The question of Apollo's guilt toward Creusa, or the possible divine virtue of his conduct in the context of the entire play, is a heavily debated one. Those who lean toward piety with respect to gods in general find complicated justifications for him. Those others—like Creusa; and early in the play, Ion; and very possibly Euripides himself—tally his gross acts and find them outrageous. Creusa's sorrow, for example, turns to rage against Apollo when she learns of her husband's remarkable good luck with Apollo's oracle: the first person he will see on leaving the temple will be his own son, the oracle assured him; Ion is that person. Creusa, believing her husband had in fact known of this bastard son's existence and is planning to seat him on the throne of Athens (Creusa and he are Athens' rulers), decides to revenge herself on Apollo by poisoning Ion in the god's own temple. "My soul is in anguish; gods and men have conspired against me." Her new complaint against her "vile seducer": "To my husband who has done you no kindness, you have given a son and heir; but my child, yes and yours (where is your heart?) is gone, the prey of the birds." The Creusa who was greeted by Ion at their first meeting with, "You have nobility, lady, whoever you are; and your bearing indicates your character," in her jealousy and chagrin loses her nobility and the marks of "character." She becomes a potential murderess of the Ion who is in fact the son whom she bore for the god Apollo.

The plot, perhaps the most complicated in extant Greek tragedy, is made up of a labyrinth of misunderstandings cleared up a moment before they threaten to end in disaster. For Creusa, the pleasure of the ultimate outcome [see No. 21, below] barely compensates for the bitterness of the experience she endures before it materializes.

CREUSA

O my soul, how can I keep silence? Yet how unveil that dark amour and lose the name of honor? But what is left to stop me? Why strive any longer for virtue? Has not my husband proved false? And I am robbed of home, robbed of children: gone are the fair hopes which I tried to realize by keeping my union secret, keeping secret that lamentable birth, but I could not. No! By the starry throne of Zeus, by the goddess that haunts our mountains, by the holy shore of the waters of Triton's lake, no longer will I hide my lover. When the load is lifted from my breast I shall be easier. My eyes drop tears, my soul is in anguish; gods and men have conspired against me. But I shall expose them, ingrates and seducers of women.

You that make music from the seven voices of the lyre, drawing from the lifeless horns of oxen strains of lovely music—yours is the reproach, son of Leto, that I will publish to the bright light of day. You came to me with the sunlight in your golden hair when I was gathering the yellow flowers in the folds of my robe, the flowers that shone like golden suns. You caught the white wrists of my hands and drew me screaming "Mother, Mother" to the bed in that cave. Divine seducer, you drew me there and shamelessly you worked the pleasure of Cypris. And I bore you a son—O Misery!—and in fear of my mother I cast him upon your bed, upon the cruel couch where cruelly you ravished me, the hapless girl. Woe is me, woe! And now my boy is gone, fowls of the air have torn and devoured him, my boy—and yours, cruel god. But you only play your lyre and sing songs of triumph!

Ho, son of Leto, you I call, you who sit on your throne of gold
and give holy answers from earth's center: I will shut a word
into your ear. Vile seducer! To my husband, who has done you
no kindness, you have given a son and heir, but my child, yes
and yours (where is your heart?) is gone, the prey of the birds,
reft from his mother's swaddling clothes. Delos hates you, the
young laurels hate you, beside the soft-leaved palm, where
Leto bore you in a holy birth by the seed of Zeus.

(Creusa collapses.)

THE GODDESS THAT HAUNTS OUR MOUNTAINS: Artemis, twin sister of Apollo and the
virgin goddess of the hunt, is also associated with the moon. Protectress of animals
and especially of their young, Artemis was also thought to preside over human childbirth. TRITON'S LAKE: Triton was a sea divinity; named after him were a river and
lake in Libya. THE SON OF LETO: Apollo, god of light, the sun, and music which he
played on his seven-string lyre. CYPRIS: Aphrodite, the Goddess of Love, who rose out
of the sea to the island shore of Cyprus; hence, she is called in Greek "Kypris," the
Cyprian. DELOS: a small island in the Aegean Sea and birthplace of Apollo and
Artemis.

21.
ATHENA, THE GODDESS OUT OF
THE MACHINE, JUSTIFIES APOLLO,
COMFORTS CREUSA AND ION,
AND FORETELLS GOOD FORTUNE (OT)

(421–408 BC) EURIPIDES, *ION*, TR. MOSES HADAS AND
JOHN H. MCLEAN

[See No. 20, above] Athena is careful from the moment she appears
rising behind the *skene,* the scene building, to reassure the overwhelmed humans that she is no enemy, that she means them well,
and that she has none but pleasant and reassuring messages for them.
Euripides, who more than the other tragedians rationalizes, psychol-
ogizes, and generally domesticates the mythic content of his
tragedies, paradoxically in the epilogue of *Ion,* when Athena, the *deus
ex machina,* appears, restores to the myth its lofty eteological func-

tion, in which is explained the origins of cults of worship or of races or city-states or institutions (such as the institution of justice at the end of Aeschylus' *Oresteia*). Athena not only clears up the plot misunderstandings that still remain, but validates the mythical origins of all Greeks: Ion, she predicts, will become the ancestor of the Ionians, and Creusa and Xuthus will become the parents of two sons who will found the races of the Dorians and Achaeans.

Nevertheless, there's a lurking irony. Added to the list of the divine Apollo's all-too-human frailties is, as Athena confesses, his sending his sister to so to speak cover for him to avoid the embarrassment of his having to confront accusations from Creusa and Ion concerning his past behavior. How bad was it? Euripides is ambiguous, probably intentionally. The god had raped Creusa, he had robbed her of knowing her child, and he had treated Xuthus to the thumping lie that he was in fact Ion's father, giving additional pain to his original victim, Creusa. On the other hand, the argument has been made, "mortal misapprehensions and suspicions," according to one critic, "are skillfully brought to enlightenment [by Apollo], and the stupidities and selfish aims of the human beings are guided to a happy conclusion by the wisdom and kindliness of the god." He might be thought, then, of as implementing, with divine serenity, justice, and aesthetic symmetry, an ending to the tale that leaves all matters revealed and all participants happy.

But are they? Or will they remain so? Creusa and Ion are sworn to keep secret the real paternity of Ion, and Xuthus is left with the illusion that Ion is in fact his own son. The god hasn't written *finis* to their tale; he's left it patched together by a lie, to which he has sworn two accomplices—not really commendable divine behavior after all.

ATHENA

Do not flee. I am no enemy that you should flee from me, but gracious toward you, both in Athens, and here. I am Pallas that come to you, the namesake of your land. I hurry here to represent Apollo; he did not see fit to face you two, lest upbraidings about bygones be bandied about. So he sent me to you to recite his message: that this woman is your mother and Apollo your father; that he bestowed you as he did, not because that man was your father, but so that you might be brought into a noble house. But when the truth came out and Creusa was informed, he was afraid you would die by your mother's devices, or she be murdered by you, and so he schemed to save you. King Apollo meant to hush the matter up till you were in Athens, and then inform you that this woman is your mother and that you are her son, and Apollo's.

Now let me finish my task. Hear, both of you, the god's oracles which I harnessed my chariot to bring you.

Take this boy and go to the land of Cecrops, Creusa, and set him on the royal throne. He is sprung from the sons of Erechtheus and is worthy to rule over my land; he shall be famous throughout Hellas. The sons born to him, four out of a single stock, will give their names to the tribal peoples of the land, who dwell upon my cliff. To Xuthus and you shall be born sons: Dorus, from whom shall spring the fame and glory of the Dorian state; the second, Achaeus, who will be ruler of the seacoast by Rhion.

Apollo has managed all things well. First he gave you an easy birth, so that your friends knew nothing. And when you had given birth to this boy and had wrapped him in his swaddling clothes, he bade Hermes snatch the infant in his arms and transport him here; and he fed him, and did not allow his life to expire. Now be quiet about his child being your own; let Xuthus cherish his pleasant fancy, and you your blessings. Farewell. After this respite from troubles I proclaim a happy lot for you.

Praise Phoebus. Praise the god. Ay, the gods act late perhaps, but at the last the good attain their deserts.

PALLAS: Athens was named after and protected by Pallas Athena, warrior-goddess and patroness of wisdom. CECROPS: the first king of Attica (called after him Cecropia) in central Greece and of Athens. ERECHTHEUS: king of Athens. The Athenians were often called his sons (Erechtheidae). FOUR OUT OF A SINGLE STOCK...: From the four sons attributed to Ion are descended the four Ionic tribes. DORIAN STATE: in central Greece. RHION: the Gulf of Corinth. PHOEBUS: "shining," epithet of Apollo.

22.

CLYTEMNESTRA CONFRONTS ELECTRA AND DEFENDS HER ACTS (OT)

(418–410 BC) SOPHOCLES, *ELECTRA*, TR. DAVID GRENE

For years, Electra has been living a virtual captive in the palace of her mother, Clytemnestra, and the paramour Aegisthus, dreaming of revenge for their murder of her father, Agamemnon. For years, she has been waiting for the return of her brother, Orestes, whom she spirited away the night of the murder so that one day he might return to effect that revenge. But after so long wait, she's lost almost all hope for his return. She lives, bitter and desperate, smoldering with hate.

In the absence of the watchful Aegisthus, Electra's wandered outside the palace walls for a rare moment of relative freedom. Clytemnestra, on her way to the shrine of Apollo, meets her daughter. She has suffered a frightful dream of her dead husband's resumption of rule and power, and terrified, she is on her way to propitiate his spirit.

All the meetings of mother and daughter quickly disintegrate into sessions of mutual recrimination. So habituated is Clytemnestra to this certainty that, anticipating Electra's customary outburst, she defends herself against the usual, but, at the moment, still unspoken accusations—the wanton assassination of Agamemnon and the complicity of her bedmate Aegisthus—with the usual justifications. But in this version of Sophocles', it is a far different Clytemnestra from Aeschylus' [see No. 4, above], who confronts accusers not with the proud assertion of her revenge, but with querulous justification. "There is no insolence in myself," she maintains, "but being accused by you so constantly, I give abuse again." It is Electra who holds the high moral and argumentative ground here, and Clytemnestra's so-to-speak preemptive defense has more the intention of avoiding any further descent into their usual recriminations. But it's of course impossible. The battle between them will inevitably revive and flare once again. [See No. 23, below.]

CLYTEMNESTRA

It seems you are loose again, wandering about.
Aegisthus isn't here, who always restrains you
from going abroad and disgracing your family.

But now that he is away you pay no heed
to me, although there's many a one you have told
at length how brutally and how unjustly
I lord it over you, insulting
you and yours.
    There is no insolence in myself,
but being abused by you so constantly
I give abuse again.
    Your father, yes,
always your father. Nothing else is your pretext—
the death he got from me. From me. I know it,
well. There is no denial in me. Justice,
Justice it was that took him, not I alone.
You would have served the cause of Justice if
you had been right-minded.
For this your father whom you always mourn,
alone of all the Greeks, had the brutality
to sacrifice your sister to the Gods,
although he had not toiled for her as I did,
the mother that bore her, he the begetter only.
Tell me, now, why he sacrificed her. Was it
for the sake of the Greeks?

They had no share in my daughter to let them kill her.
Was it for Menelaus' sake, his brother,
that he killed my child? And shall he not then pay for it?
Had not this Menelaus two children who
ought to have died rather than mine? It was their parents
for whose sake all the Greeks set sail for Troy.
Or had the God of Death some longing to feast
on my children rather than hers? Or had
that accursed father lost the love of mine
and felt it still for Menelaus' children?
This was the act of a father thoughtless
or with bad thoughts. That is how I see it
even if you differ with me.
    The dead girl,
if she could speak, would bear me out.
I am not dismayed by all that has happened.
If you think me wicked, keep your righteous judgment
and blame your neighbors.

TO SACRIFICE YOUR SISTER TO THE GODS: Iphigenia, Agamemnon's other daughter.
FOR MENELAUS' SAKE: Agamemnon's brother Menelaus, the husband of Helen. To
avenge her abduction, the Trojan War was fought.

23.

ELECTRA REFUTES HER MOTHER'S DEFENSE OF HER CRIME (YT)

(418–410 BC) SOPHOCLES, *ELECTRA*, TR. DAVID GRENE

[Continues No. 22, above] Surprisingly, Electra, apparently as weary of their familiar arguments as Clytemnestra is, asks with unaccustomed restraint if she might answer her mother this once calmly and truthfully. Clytemnestra is more than willing: "If you had always begun our conversations so, you would not have been so painful to listen to." Electra obliges and begins her defense of her father's act—the sacrifice of his daughter Iphigenia demanded by the goddess Artemis—calmly, restrainedly, and truthfully.

It doesn't last. The speech shifts quickly into emotionally charged accusations impelled by Electra's underlying rage, which willy-nilly quickly overwhelms her effort to be reasonable. Their confrontation eventually descends into its customary bout of mutual vituperation, but halts this time on a weary note of truce.

Electra's accusations tumble over one another. Her mother's claim of "justice" in avenging Iphigenia's sacrifice? A sham; in reality, it was for the seduction of Aegisthus. Her father's sacrifice of his daughter for the sake of his brother, Menelaus? It was only in response to the angry demand of the goddess, which could in no way be thwarted. Her mother merely obeyed the law of revenge? Then Clytemnestra is subject to the same law, and by that law, she should be executed by her legitimate children—Electra and Orestes—whom she had thrust aside in favor of the illegitimate children she bore for Aegisthus. And most infuriating: Clytemnestra's offering the opportunity for Electra to speak her mind, and then accusing her of the sin of "reviling a mother." Electra's parting shot: it is the shameful mother who provokes the shamefulness in the daughter.

As in the comparable scene in Euripides' *Electra* [see No. 27, above], the battle between them is bare-knuckled; little of the "nobility" usually attributed to Sophocles' Electra is evident here, any more than it is in Euripides.

ELECTRA

You say you killed my father. What claim more shameful

than that, whether with justice or without it?
But I'll maintain that it was not with justice
you killed him, but the seduction of that bad man,
with whom you now are living, drew you to it.
Ask Artemis the Huntress what made her hold
the many winds in check at Aulis. Or
I'll tell you this. *You* dare not learn from her.

My father, as I hear, when at his sport,
started from his feet a horned dappled stag
within the Goddess' sanctuary. He
let fly and hit the deer and uttered some boast
about his killing of it. The daughter of Leto
was angry at this and therefore stayed the Greeks
in order that my father, to compensate
for the beast killed, might sacrifice his daughter.

Thus was her sacrifice—no other deliverance
for the army either homeward or toward Ilium.
He struggled and fought against it. Finally,
constrained, he killed her—not for Menelaus.
But if—I will plead in your own words—he had done so
for his brother's sake, is that any reason
why he should die at your hands? By what law?
If this is the law you lay down for men, take heed
you do not lay down for yourself ruin and repentance.
If we shall kill one in another's requital,
you would be the first to die, if you met with justice.
No. Think if the whole is not a mere excuse.
Please tell me for what cause you now commit
the ugliest of acts in sleeping with him,
the murderer with whom you first conspired
to kill my father, and breed children to him, and
your former honorable children born
of honorable wedlock you drive out.
What grounds for praise shall I find in this? Will you say
that this, too, is retribution for your daughter?
If you say it, still your act is scandalous.
It isn't decent to marry with your enemies
even for a daughter's sake.

But I may not
even rebuke you! What you always say
is that it is my mother I am reviling.
Mother! I do not count you mother of mine,

but rather a mistress. My life is wretched
because I live with multitudes of sufferings,
inflicted by yourself and your bedfellow.
But the other, he is away, he has escaped
your hand, though barely. Sad Orestes now
wears out his life in misery and exile.
Many a time you have accused me
of rearing him to be your murderer.
I would have done it if I could. Know that.
As far as that goes, you may publicly
proclaim me what you like—traitor, reviler,
a creature full of shamelessness.
If I am
naturally skilled as such, I do no shame
to the nature of the mother that brought me forth.

ARTEMIS THE HUNTRESS: Artemis, protectress of animals sacred to her, kept the
Greek fleet blockaded at Aulis until Agamemnon sacrificed his daughter Iphigenia to
propitiate the goddess' anger against him for his sacrilege in killing a deer in her
sacred precincts and boasting of it. (Aeschylus' Agamemnon uses another version of
Agamemnon's transgression.) LETO: mother of Apollo and Artemis by Zeus.
MENELAUS: Agamemnon's brother and husband of the abducted Helen, for whose
return the Trojan War was fought. Clytemnestra had argued that, since the war was
fought on his behalf, his children, not hers, should have been offered by Agamemnon
as sacrifice to Artemis.

24.

HERMIONE, JEALOUS, BEGRUDGES
HOSPITALITY TO ANDROMACHE (YT)

(417–415 BC?) EURIPIDES, *ANDROMACHE*,
TR. MOSES HADAS AND JOHN H. MCLEAN

The chorus commiserates with Andromache's "hard trials that have
engaged you and Hermione in a poisonous feud." The "feud" is worse
than unequal. Andromache, once the wife of the Trojan Hector, is
now, after the fall of Troy, the concubine of the Greek Neoptolemus
(the son of Achilles, the very Greek who killed Hector on the battlefield) and has delivered him a son, Molossus. But Neoptolemus has
also married Hermione, the daughter of Menelaus and Helen, and it

is Hermione's intense jealousy of Andromache that moves her and her father to plan the death of both the concubine and her son.

Euripides' portraits of both the Spartan princess Hermione and King Menelaus are clearly colored by the current war Athens was waging against Sparta. Beyond their villainy, the Spartans have become insensitive boors who with no vestige of shame flaunt their power, wealth, and privilege. Hermione, from the moment of her arrival, demonstrates the quintessence of vulgarity. "I'm covered with gold," she says in effect, "which gives me the right to do and say anything I like." Her first "liking" is to attack her helpless rival Andromache, who, anticipating her arrival, has taken refuge in the Temple of Thetis, from whose throne it would be sacrilege to wrest her.

Hermione's verbal assault on the helpless Andromache is a fairly complete catalogue of the gross insults the mighty can visit with abandon on the weak. You're a slave, a witch, she accuses Andromache. If I don't succeed in killing you now, you'll remain my slave and scrub my floors on your knees. And—the standard insult hurled by ensconced patriots at refugees—you barbarian (i.e., foreign) slaves are all alike: lawless and given to immorality, incest, and murder, habits you'd better not practice here.

Consumed by jealousy and plotting murder, Hermione nevertheless sees herself as a model so to speak gated-community suburbanite shocked by the moral transgressions of the low.

HERMIONE

(To the Chorus) These gorgeous golden ornaments on my
head, these elaborate robes that clothe my body, these are no
gifts from the stores of Achilles or Peleus. No, I brought them
here with me from Laconia, the land of the Spartans, them
and all the rest of my dowry, given me by my father Menelaus.
So I have the right to speak freely.

(To Andromache) As for you, you slave, won in war, you want
to drive me out of this house and take possession yourself.
Thanks to your spells, my husband hates me. Thanks to you,
my womb is barren and dead. You are all very clever at that
sort of thing, you continental women. But I'll put a stop to
your tricks. The house of the Nereid here will do you no good,
nor the altar, nor the temple. You will die. But if it be that
some god or mortal consents to rescue you, you must give up
the high notions of the dignity you once enjoyed. You will
have to crouch low and fall at my feet; you will have to sweep

my floors and with your own hands sprinkle the house with river water from vessels of beaten gold; in short, you will have to learn just where in the world you are. This is not Hector, you know, or Priam and his gold. This is a Greek city. But you, poor wretch, have so little sensibility that you can stoop to sleep with the son of the man who slew your husband, and have children by his murderer. The whole tribe of barbarians is like that. Fathers have intercourse with daughters, sons with mothers, brothers with sisters. Kinsman slaughters closest kinsman, no law preventing. Don't introduce these practices here. It's a bad thing for one man to hold the reins over two women. The man who wants a happy home is content to confine his attention to one woman's bed.

ACHILLES AND HIS FATHER PELEUS: the Greek heroes who were the father and grandfather of Neoptolemus. Hermione is asserting that none of her splendor comes from her husband Neoptolemus' family, but from her dowry, and so is free of obligation. CONTINENTAL WOMEN: Andromache's home, Troy, was in Asia Minor. THE HOUSE OF NEREID: the shrine of Thetis, the sea goddess. Of the fifty daughters of Nereus the sea-divinity, the foremost was Thetis, the mother of Achilles by Peleus. Priam, the defeated king of Troy. BARBARIANS: non-Greeks.

25.

ANDROMACHE RESPONDS TO HERMIONE'S CRUEL ATTACK (YT)

(417–415 BC?) EURIPIDES, *ANDROMACHE*, TR. MOSES HADAS AND JOHN H. MCLEAN

[Continues No. 24, above] Andromache, herself once a princess of Troy, responds to Hermione's attack with remarkable *amour propre*. There is bitter irony in her denigrating herself as a mere slave, inferior to "the great," and no longer possessing "a fresh, young body." But there is also her painful recognition that it is true, that as a slave, she is in danger by responding, and conceivably besting, "the great" Hermione in argument. But those facts are the very assurances that her defense is unassailable, arguing as she does the implausibility of winning the contest for Neoptolemus' love and esteem from the vantagepoint of all her incapacities. What is left then of plausible reasons for Neoptolemus' preference? Only Hermione's own incapacities: her congenital incompatibility, her mere beauty rather than genuine virtue, and her violent jealousy growing out of her sexual incontinence (like her notorious mother, Helen's.)

Andromache's final thrust, demonstrating her superior appeal as a woman and her superior nobility as a wife, is that she not only tolerated but even "offered her breast" to her Trojan husband Hector's bastards "to avoid causing [him] offense." Here is perhaps the most telling evidence of not only Euripides', but of the Greeks' view generally of the ideal of womanhood: their pride in themselves, like that of Andromache's and Alcestis' [see No. 13, above] earned by their perfect accommodation to subservience. This is the inherent misogyny for which Aristophanes enjoyed attacking Euripides, although he shared it.

ANDROMACHE

Alas! youth is the world's plague, youth and its injustice. For my part, I am afraid that my being a slave may deny me the right to reply to you, though I have many truths to utter; or that if I speak and win, my victory may be to my cost. The great ones of the world resent being beaten in argument by their inferiors. Still, nobody will accuse me of scamping my own case.

Tell me, young woman, what considerations could have made me so confident of expelling you from your legitimate marriage? Is the city of Sparta less important than Phrygia? Does my fortune exceed yours? Are you looking at a free woman? Or is it youthfulness, or a fresh, young body, or great wealth, or a multitude of friends, that encouraged me to seek to supplant you in this house? And why? In order that I, in your place, may give birth to slaves, to hang to my skirts in wretchedness? Will any man tolerate my children as kings of Phthia, if you have no children? I suppose the Greeks love me and Hector's line.

It is not because of any spells of mine that your husband hates you. No! it's your incompatibility. There is your philtre; it is not our beauty, woman, but our virtues that delight our husbands.

You are rich in a poor country. In your eyes Menelaus is greater than Achilles. This is what your husband hates in you. Even if she gets a humble husband, a woman ought to be content and not start a competition of pretensions. If you had married a prince somewhere in Thrace, land of blizzards, where one husband shares his bed with many wives in turn, would you have slain these others? Then the sexual incontinence, manifest in you, would have been extended to all womankind. A shameful imputation, and yet we do suffer worse than men from that disease; though we hide it beautifully.

O dear, dear Hector, I at least for your sake actually joined you in loving the occasional objects of your roaming fancy. Many a time in the past did I offer my breasts to your bastards, to avoid causing you any offence. And so doing I attached myself to my husband and was a good wife to him. But you are so full of fears, you would not suffer even a drop of heaven's rain to visit your husband's face. Woman, do not seek to outdo your mother Helen's amorousness.

SCAMPING: performing carelessly or hastily. PHRYGIA: interior section of western Asia Minor, embracing Troy. PHTHIA: a city in Thessaly (northern Greece), where the play's action takes place, and of which Neoptolemus is king. PHILTRE: philter, love potion. THRACE: a region in northeastern Greece, northwestern Turkey, and southern Bulgaria.

26.

HECUBA PLEADS WITH AGAMEMNON TO AVENGE HER BETRAYAL (OT)

(417–415 BC?) EURIPIDES, *HECUBA*,
TR. JANET LEMBKE AND KENNETH L. RECKFORD

Hecuba may well be Euripides' bitterest antiwar play against victors. They are free to use power unchecked, and so what if their implicitly uncivilized, not to say bestial, nature surfaces, flourishes, and triumphs? Worse, it enrages its victims so far that in their seeking vengeance, they sink to the same level of bestiality. Hecuba, the noble Trojan queen now a helpless Greek captive, enraged by the violent injustice visited on her, outdoes the bestiality of her conquerors.

In captivity, Hecuba has only the consolation that two of her children, Polyxena and Polydorus, are still alive and still with her. Before the defeat of Troy, King Priam sent their son, Polydorus, to King Polymester with treasure, so that should Troy fall, his sons would be provided for. But learning of Troy's fall, Polymester kills the defeated prince, who no longer has the protection of allies, for his gold. Hecuba is ignorant of this deed when the Greeks, as a sacrifice to the dead Achilles, decide to put Polyxena to death. Hecuba's entreaties to Odysseus count for nothing; her appeals to the justice of his returning her kindness in saving his life before Troy's fall for her daughter's life now is countered by warrior's justice: the hero Achilles' ghost demands the sacrifice of an enemy. When the shroud of a dead body is brought to Hecuba, thinking it is her daughter, she removes the shroud and discovers to her horror the body of Polydorus. She then prevails on Agamemnon, the Greek leader, to allow her to be revenged against the treachery of Polymester.

Her plea to Agamemnon shows an already altered Hecuba. "Once a queen, but now I am your slave," she confesses, pleading her helplessness to an initially indifferent Agamemnon. The arguments that do not move him are these: she is bereft of everything, and her life and fortune are destroyed. The vengeance she seeks is against a man who committed the most ungodly of crimes—premeditated murder of her son and the sacrilege of non-burial—this, by a man to whom she had offered friendship and hospitality. But the most telling argument, the one she assumes will be most persuasive is that if justice (*nomos*), the law of custom that "confirms our faith in gods," is transgressed and if murderers and the plunderers of the holy are not punished, "then no justice—none—exists for humankind." For Agamemnon to implement that law, she argues, requires two things: his sense of shame and his compassion.

There's considerable profundity in Euripides' linking of two factors: the majesty of "law," and the appeal of the otherwise helpless to that law. Its majesty somehow diminishes when the helpless appeal to its purveyors. And when Agamemnon turns away from this suppliant, it in effect disappears altogether.

"Oh, helpless," cries Hecuba, and suddenly realizes the only practical strategy of appeal for the powerless: not to the sanctity of justice, but to the trickery of persuasion. "Without that art, how may anyone [such as herself, 'a captive ugly in my shame'] hope to come out well?" That's the lesson to be learned before all others: the chicanery of Persuasion. And she tries it. How about "Love's divine name?" Agamemnon has already taken her daughter, Cassandra, for his captive concubine. Pressing her against your body, Hecuba whispers like an old bawd, acknowledging his nights of "love's delights," how about a little fee for the girl's mother? And at the same time, you'll be honoring the dead boy lying there, your concubine's brother.

Then, she's at a loss for more of the same: "One thought still looks for words." But she can't find the words. In mild panic, she prays to Daedalus, or any god, to give voice to every part of her body, and then "all would clasp your knees," and plead for her. But she stoops at last to a common resource for persuasion: gross flattery ("My master, most shining light among the Greeks"), together with appeal to his pity ("Lend your hand to an old woman"). Although her dignity is gone, she gets her way.

The vengeance of a now-altered Hecuba will outdo Polymester's crime: she will kill his two sons and blind the king.

HECUBA

I am destroyed. No further suffering is left.
Could any woman be less fortunate?
None, except Misfortune herself.
But now, the reason that I grasp your knees—
please hear me.
And if you think the gods approve my suffering,
I'll accept that. But if you think otherwise,
avenge me on that mate, that most ungodly friend.
Fearing neither those below nor those on high,
he has done the most ungodly crime.
A man who often shared my food, a man I counted
first among my friends, to whom I gave
every courtesy—he did premeditated
murder. Yet, the murder planned, he gave no thought
to decent burial but made the sea his rubbish pit.
True, I am a slave without strength. But the gods
are strong and so is that which forms their power—
the law of custom. For, this age-old law confirms our faith in
gods
and gives us lives that can distinguish right from wrong.
Keeping the law depends on you. If it's transgressed,
and if no punishment is dealt to those who murder
friends or plunder the gods' holy places,
then no justice—none—exists for humankind.
Let your sense of shame give you compassion.
Have pity. Like a painter, stand back,
look at me and see my sorrows whole.

Once a queen, but now I am your slave,
once blessed with sons, now old, without my sons,
without a home, alone, struggling to the utmost,
helpless—

(Agamemnon tries to pull away.)
No! Where are you going?
I'll accomplish nothing. Oh helpless.
Why do we spend our short lives straining,
craving after knowledge of all sorts but one—
Persuasion, who alone is mankind's queen?
Why no zeal in us to hire a teacher
and learn the art so perfectly
that we persuade and we obtain?
Without that art, how may anyone hope to come out well?
Those who were my sons are mine no more,
and I, a captive ugly in my shame, am lost.
I see the smoke still rolling up from Troy.
Perhaps it is pointless for me to put forward
Love's divine name. But I shall do it.
Pressed against your ribs, my daughter sleeps,
my child possessed by prophecy, Cassandra.
How, my lord, will you acknowledge love's delights?
Or for the loveliest embraces in your bed,
what thanks, what fee will my child gain, and I for her?
For out of darkness, out of night's enchantments comes
the strongest drive toward thanks that flesh can know.
Listen to me. Do you see that dead boy?
Do him honor, and you honor kin, your bedmate's brother.
One thought still looks for words.
If only Daedalus could work his wonders,
or some god, to give my arms a voice,
my hands a voice, and my hair and feet,
then all would clasp your knees in concert
crying out my plea in all possible ways.
My master, most shining light among the Greeks,
be moved. Lend your hand to an old woman, a hand
for vengeance, though it come to nothing. Be fair.
For the man born noble and good always serves justice
and finds fit consequences for a crime.

UNGODLY FRIEND: Odysseus, with whom Hecuba pleaded in vain to spare her daughter Polyxena. DAEDALUS...HIS WONDERS: the inventor, who with his son, escaped Minos on the wings he fashioned of feathers and fastened with wax. He was for the Greeks, especially the Athenians, the mystical representative of all handiwork. A cult of worship was established for him by the artists' guilds of Attica. Here, the desperate Hecuba appeals to him for a hypothetical craftsman's miracle: giving "voice" to hands, arms, feet, and hair.

27.

ELECTRA CASTIGATES CLYTEMNESTRA'S LIFE OF MURDER AND ADULTERY (YT)

(417–408 BC?) EURIPIDES, *ELECTRA*,
TR. MOSES HADAS AND JOHN H. MCLEAN

Sophocles famously observed that Euripides wrote of men as they are, and he of men as they ought to be. But [See No. 23, above] there is little difference in the confrontations between Electra and her mother Clytemnestra in the two playwrights' respective *Electra*s. The blunt realism of the one is much like that of the other, and both monologues follow much the same arguments to much the same effect. But Euripides scores a cynical note or two that is beyond Sophocles' slightly more decorous Electra.

For one, Euripides' Electra remembers her mother's primping before the mirror the moment her husband, Agamemnon, was off to war, at once ready to satisfy the "wantonness" she notes in both her mother and her mother's sister, Helen—both women who shamelessly exploited their beauty and sexuality. Electra draws a quick portrait too of Clytemnestra struck with glee whenever the news from the Trojan battlefront was bad, praying her husband would never return. And so little is Clytemnestra, notes her daughter, attuned to loyalty as wife and mother that she's committed the unpardonable sin of "marrying with her [husband's] enemy," the Aegisthus who was her ally in revenge against Agamemnon.

There is one notable difference in the dramatic situations of the two Electras, however, that colors importantly the effect of their confrontations with their hated mothers. Sophocles' Electra, a miserable prisoner with little hope of redemption, is not yet aware that Orestes, her avenger, has arrived; her hate has no relief or hope. Euripides' Electra is meeting with her mother before the peasant's hut in which Orestes is already waiting to murder her. Clytemnestra has been gulled into visiting the hut, where Electra has pretended to have given birth to a son with the peasant, to whom Electra has been humiliatingly wedded. As her mother, directly after their confrontation, enters the hut to see the "baby," Electra intones with satisfaction: "The sacrificial basket is in proper order, the knife is whetted…Do you [by your death] give me vengeance for my father."

ELECTRA

You plead justice, but your plea is shameful. I will speak, and my preface will be this: I wish you had a better heart, my mother. Your beauty deserves praise, yours and Helen's, two true sisters, both wantons, both unworthy of Castor. She was kidnapped and lost her virtue gladly. Then you destroyed the bravest man of Hellas; and you hold out the pretense that you killed your husband for the sake of your child! People do not know you as well as I. Why, even before your daughter's sacrifice had been determined, when your husband had but newly left home, you were already training the golden clusters of your hair before a mirror. Any woman that cultivates her beauty when her husband is far from home you can write down as a wanton. There is no need for her to display a face made fair unless she is looking for some mischief. You were the only Hellene woman, I know you were, who was happy when the Trojan side prospered, and when they were getting the worse of it your eyes were all clouded. You did not want Agamemnon to come back from Troy. And yet it was so easy for you to be chaste. You had a husband who was at least as good as Aegisthus; Hellas chose him to be her general. After your sister Helen had done what she did, you had a chance to win great glory. Evil deeds afford precept and example to the good.

And even if, as you say, my father killed your daughter, how did I or my brother injure you? Why, when you killed your husband, did you not give us our ancestral home? You brought an outsider into it; you bought his love at that price. Your lover was not exiled, though your son was. Your lover was not slain. I was. Yes, though I am alive, he has inflicted on me double my sister's death. If blood for blood is the law, then must I and your son, Orestes, kill you to avenge our father. If your conduct was right then this must be right. [The man who marries a bad woman, unable to see beyond wealth or noble birth, is a fool. A humble and chaste wife is better in a house than a high and mighty one.]

You sigh too late, when you have no cure. My father is dead. I say no more.

CASTOR: Helen's and Clytemnestra's brother, was a demigod, protector of sailors.
BRAVEST MAN IN HELLAS: Agamemnon, leader of the Greek armies against Troy.

28.

ELECTRA WITH HATRED EULOGIZES OVER THE BODY OF AEGISTHUS (YT)

(417–408 BC?) EURIPIDES, *ELECTRA*,
TR. MOSES HADAS AND JOHN H. MCLEAN

[See No. 27, above] Electra, over the murdered body of Aegisthus, is not so much eulogizing as sentencing to perdition her father's abhorred assassin, her mother's paramour, and the tyrant over herself. "What beginning shall I make of my reproaches against you?" She can hardly imagine their beginning, middle, and end, so much unalloyed hatred has for years accumulated in her soul.

The body arrived with her brother, Orestes, and his companion, Pylades, who waylaid Aegisthus at the altar of the nymphs where he had gone to conduct a sacrificial feast. A messenger had already reported that after Aegisthus invited the "strangers" to assist him, the "strangers" made Aegisthus himself the "sacrifice."

Electra welcomes the news ecstatically. "I lift up my eyes in freedom!" she cries. And when the assassins return, she crowns both of them with diadems of victory. Orestes, in similar euphoria, suggests they throw the corpse to wild beasts or impale it on a high stake for the birds to consume. But suddenly, their mood changes. In a remarkably telling psychological twist, Electra's feeling swings in an instant from euphoria to dread. Urged by her brother to speak, since now she has nothing to fear, she responds: "I am ashamed to insult the dead." If there was ever any felt grandeur in their deed of "justice" before the murder, there is none now. Not in triumph, but in bitter accusation and, by implication, anxious self-justification, does she rail against the dead Aegisthus. She condemns, excoriates, and musters many reasons for the deed of justice. But soon, with the murder of their mother, Clytemnestra, both brother and sister will be loathing their own deed.

The contrast with Aeschylus' *Libation Bearers* [see, in Men's volumes "Orestes Is Jubilant, Then Uncertain, Over His Revenge"], in which the same event occurs, could hardly be greater. There, Orestes proclaims his triumph in full consciousness of justice done over the bodies of Aegisthus and Clytemnestra. There is no demurrer; both brother and sister have done, they feel, a wholly righteous deed. Only later do the Furies, an external punishing force, begin Orestes' retribution. In Euripides, the retribution is self-administered, internalized, self-inflicted. The punishment of the Furies is to arrive later, as though in belated obedience to the received myth. The torment of their ineradicable guilt is already accomplished by the perpetrators themselves, without divine assistance.

ELECTRA

What beginning shall I make of my reproaches against you? What shall be the end? What shall occupy the middle place in my argument? Morning by morning, I have never left off rehearsing what I wished to say to your face if ever I should be free of the fear I once felt. Now I am free, and I shall pay you out with hard words I wished to say when you were alive. You ruined me; you orphaned me of my dear father, me and Orestes, though we had done you no wrong. You married my mother, shamefully, and you slew her husband; though you never marched to Troy, you slew the commander of the Greek army. To such a depth of folly did you sink that you expected my mother, my father's wife whom you seduced, to be a true wife to you. If a man corrupts another's wife with secret dalliance and then is forced to marry her, let him know that he is a poor fool if he thinks she will possess chastity in his house when she did not with her first husband.

Your life was most wretched, though you thought it quite happy. You knew you had made an unholy marriage; my mother knew she had a scoundrel to husband. Both of you were wicked, and each was infected with the other's evil; she took your lot and you took her sin. Among all the Argives it was said, "Clytemnestra's husband," not "Aegisthus' wife." It is disgraceful when the woman and not the man rules the household. I loathe it too when children are called in the city not by the name of their father, the man, but of their mother. When a man makes a match with a woman of distinguished station, higher than his own, no one takes any account of the husband, but only of the wife.

In this especially you were deceived and did not realize it: you boasted you were somebody, relying on your wealth. But wealth does nothing more than keep you company for a short time. Character, not money, is the stable thing. For character abides forever, and banishes evil. But wealth is unjust and keeps company with boors, and it flits out of the house when it has bloomed for a short while.

As to your women, I say nothing, for it is not a nice subject for a maiden; but I shall hint, not darkly. You were conceited because you possessed a royal house and because you were endued with beauty. But my wish would be not for a girl-faced husband, but for one of a more manly sort. The children of such men cleave to Ares, but comeliness is only an ornament for the dance.

Be damned, unsuspecting fool; for your sins, which time has discovered, you have paid the penalty. Let no evil-doer think, if he has run the first lap well, that he has outrun justice; let him first come to the final mark and round the goal of life.

Very well. We must take this man's body in and put it out of sight, slaves, so that, when my mother comes, she may not see it before she dies.

29.

HELEN, CONDEMNED TO DEATH, PLEADS HER DEFENSE BEFORE MENELAUS (YT)

(415 BC) EURIPIDES, *THE TROJAN WOMEN*, JEAN-PAUL SARTRE VERSION, TR. RONALD DUNCAN

Euripides' text is in this instance filtered through a double screen: Jean-Paul Sartre's fairly free French adaptation of the original, and the English poet Ronald Duncan's translation of the French. But just as Sartre's adaptation is devastatingly close to the bone of the play's intent, his prefatory statement of that intent is also close and down-right accurate: "It was colonial imperialism into Asia Minor [where Troy had been situated in legend and in fact, and where Athens' war of colonial expansion was currently being conducted] that Euripides denounced.… [The play] is an explicit condemnation of war in general, and of imperial expeditions in particular… The play demonstrates this fact precisely: that war is a defeat to humanity. The Greeks destroy Troy but they receive no benefit from their victory. The gods punish their belligerence by making them punish themselves… It is sufficient to leave the final statement to Poseidon [in fact, Sartre's final statement in his adaptation, with nuclear war in mind]: 'Can't you see war will kill you, all of you?'"

The Trojan Women is by common consent the most powerful attack on war's justification in Western literature, and its portrayal of human brutality and human suffering mirrors in anticipation the wanton brutality and suffering that's become casually familiar to us in the twentieth—and now twenty-first—century. The tragedy's effect and relevance have not dimmed, but it has also not noticeably impinged on civilization's behavior.

What is a telling irony in the excerpted scene of Helen's defense becomes in the context of the entire play a genuinely sickening one. Helen's transgression, her willing abduction from her husband Menelaus' home by the Trojan Prince Paris, was the initiating act that generated the ten-year havoc of the Trojan War. Hers is the act, but whose is the culpability? Euripides, in the text of Helen's defense, sets the model for all later defendants of generating crimes who, after centuries of sophistical demonstration, have perfected the arguments that easily elude punishment—not by their logic, but by their pertinence to the time, the place, the judges. Logically, Helen's defense is a model of absurdity; practically, given the nature of her judge (Menelaus) it is knowing and deft. Her defense:

She, herself free of blame, can name the culprits: Hecuba, for giving Paris birth; Aphrodite, for making Helen victim of her own beauty; Menelaus, for not protecting her against adulterers; the Greek guards after Troy's defeat, for preventing her immediate escape to her husband; destiny itself, for forcing her captivity by a loathed lover in his loathed city (which sacrifice she endured for the sake of her country); the gods, whose "sin" in so forcing her fate can be redeemed by her return to her husband's bed.

Tradition has it, however, that the telling argument for Menelaus was none of these, but early in her defense, her baring her breasts to demonstrate for him his potential loss.

(Helen comes out of her tent and
confronts Menelaus and Hecuba.)

HELEN

You need not have used force to have me brought to you.
The instant I saw you, I wanted to run to you.
For though you hate me, I still love you.
I have wanted you. I have waited for you.

Let me ask you one question:
I will never ask another: What do you want to do to me?
To kill me? If you, my love, want my death,
Then I, my love, want my own death too.
No, do not turn away. Look at me.
Have the courage to look at me for the last time.
Look on every part, then know what it is you are killing.
You hate me? I do not hate you.
If only you knew...Yes, there are some things you should know.
Oh, I know the sort of things I've been accused of.
But I have an explanation for each.
I don't know whether you'll believe me or not,
But let me speak, and have the courage to listen.

Do you know who is really to blame for all this misery?
She is—that old woman there—Hecuba—
She was the start of it all.
It was she who gave birth to Paris.
The Gods themselves were alarmed.
They foresaw that that scoundrel would foment a war—
And what a war!
They ordered her to smother him. And did she do it?
No. And King Priam was too weak to make her.
All of this stems from that; that was the beginning of it all.
Paris was only twenty when three Goddesses
Competed for his favors.
Pallas herself offered him the whole of Greece
If he'd choose her. And with her behind him
He'd have overrun it in no time.
And what was Hera's bribe?
She offered him Asia Minor. And the whole of Europe.

But Aphrodite offered nothing. Nothing except me.
She merely described me. She won.
Paris chose her for his Goddess, then worshipped me.
You were lucky then.
For if he'd chosen either of the other two,
He would have conquered Greece.
If it were not for his body
Which your soldiers have so misused,
You yourself would be a subject of that barbarian.
But your luck was my misfortune.
That you might escape, I became the victim:
Aphrodite sacrificed me. And my beauty,
My beauty became my shame.

And darling, it was you, not I, who left.
You were a careless husband when you went off to Crete,
And left me alone with your lecherous guest.
And I, a mere mortal, resist the Goddess Aphrodite?
Could you do that? A pity you cannot punish her
For what she did to me. If you could
You'd be stronger than Zeus himself,
For even the King of the Gods
Is as much her slave as everybody else.
Why did I go? That's a question I've often asked myself.
And the answer is always the same: It was not I who left
But somebody who was not me.
Aphrodite was an unseen guest in your palace,
Like an invisible shadow to Paris; and as you know,
Aphrodite had made a bargain with Paris
To give me to him as long as he lived.
There was nothing I could do
To break the odious but sacred tie.
But the moment Paris was dead, I was free.
Immediately I did everything, everything I could
To get back to you.
At night, I climbed up on the city walls,
Tied ropes together to carry me to the ground
Where I might run to you. Your own guards can prove it
Because they always caught me.
That's all I have to say; that's my story.
I am the victim of circumstance;
Destiny's plaything; abducted;
Married against my will to a man I loathed;
Forced to live in a foreign city I despised.
All this I endured to save my country.

My own chastity was my contribution;
And there is nothing more precious
To a woman than that.
Yet in spite of this sacrifice,
They are wanting to stone me to death.
I am hated by the Greeks, detested by the Trojans,
Alone in the world, understood by none.
Do you think it is right to put me to death
When it was the Gods, not I, who sinned?
If you don't, then take me where I belong;
In your bed, on your throne;
To do less would be to insult the Gods
Who, for all their mistakes, do not err in justice.

PARIS: son of Priam, the king of Troy, who "stole" Helen from her marriage with Menelaus and caused the Trojan War. THREE GODDESSES COMPETED FOR HIS FAVORS: Hera (Zeus' wife), Athena Pallas (goddess of wisdom), and Aphrodite (goddess of love) appeared before the handsome Paris and asked him to determine which one was the most beautiful. Aphrodite promised him Helen if he picked her, which he did. YOU WERE…GUEST: Paris was a guest at Menelaus' home when the host sailed away to Crete and left his wife Helen to entertain their guests and run the country in his absence.

30.

HECUBA REPLIES CONTEMPTUOUSLY TO HELEN'S DEFENSE OF HER CONDUCT (OT)

(415 BC) EURIPIDES, *THE TROJAN WOMEN*,
TR. MOSES HADAS AND JOHN H. McLEAN

[Continues No. 29, above] Quoting from Men's volumes "Jason Defends His Abandonment of Medea": "Euripides' characters…tend to argue their 'case' like lawyers in a courtroom or logicians in a debating society. His characteristic speeches of self-justification (or in this instance a rebuttal of such a defense) are rationally structured and logically argued: firstly, secondly, thirdly, etc. And frequently his actors address and clarify for their auditors the shape of the argument they are about to offer: 'I will begin with this thesis, go on to examples,'"

Hecuba's rebuttal treats Helen's brief as self-evident silliness, but beneath her mockery is, of course, her rage at the—to her—despicable Helen who caused the horror of the war now ended in Troy's destruction. But characteristic of Euripides' speeches-as–legal briefs, the speaker Hecuba is more revealing of herself than of the target of her argument. The ease and assurance with which she dismisses Helen's lame justifications reflect her missing the point altogether. It was not Helen's arguments that were calculated to persuade Menelaus to spare her life, but her enticing presence—the irrefutable argument, and Menelaus' warm reception of it—that made such bitter mockery of the entire ten-year war of vengeance against Paris' abduction and Helen's willing flight.

HECUBA

Eloquence allied to wickedness, it is a fearful combination.

First of all I shall come to the defense of the goddesses and
show that her charges against them are unjust. For my part I
do not believe that Hera and virgin Pallas were ever so silly
that the one was ready to barter away Argos to the barbarian,
and the other to make her Athens the slave of Phrygia, and all
for a childish whim that took them to Ida to quarrel about
their beauty. For why should goddess Hera have conceived
such a passion for beauty? Did she hope to get a better
husband than Zeus? Was Athena laying her lines for a match
with one of the gods, Athena who shuns wedlock and begged
the Father to let her remain virgin? Don't make the gods silly
to cover up your own wickedness. You'll find you cannot
convince the wise. And Cypris—this is very funny—you say
she came with my son to the home of Menelaus. Could she
not have stayed quietly in heaven and brought you to Ilium?
My son was of surpassing beauty; at the sight of him your
heart transformed itself into Cypris. Every lewd impulse in
man passes for Aphrodite. Rightly does her name begin like
the word Aphrosyne—lewdness. So when you saw my son in
the splendor of gold and barbaric raiment, mad desire took
possession of your heart. In Argos you were used to a small
retinue; having got rid of the Spartan city, you looked forward
to a deluge of extravagance in Phrygia with its rivers of gold.
The halls of Menelaus weren't large enough for your luxury to
wanton in. You say you were *forced* to go with my son. Did
anybody in Sparta hear anything? What sort of outcry did you
make? Yet Castor was there, a strong young man, and his
brother, not yet translated to the stars. Then when you had

come to Troy with the Argives at your heels and the deadly
jousting of spears had started, whenever a success of Menelaus
was announced to you, you would praise him, just to torment
my son with the reminder that he had a formidable rival in
the lists of love. But if ever the Trojans were successful,
Menelaus here was nobody. You kept an eye on Fortune and
made it your practice to stick to her side. You had no taste for
Virtue's side. Furthermore, you speak of trying to escape by
stealth, of letting ropes down from the towers, as if you were
there against your will. When, tell me, were you ever caught
fixing a noose for your neck or whetting a sword? Yet that's
what a noble woman would do who yearned for her former
husband. In any case, I was constantly at you, remonstrating
with you. "Go away, my daughter. My sons will find other
brides, and I will have you conveyed out secretly to the
Achaean ships. Stop this fighting between the Greeks and us."
But you didn't like that. Why? Because you gloried and
revelled in the palace of Alexander, because it gave you
pleasure to receive the adoration of barbarians. (That, to you,
was greatness.) And after all this you titivate yourself and
come out here and brave the light of day beside your husband.
O you abomination! You should have come crawling out in
rags and tatters, in fear and trembling, your hair cropped to
the scalp; modesty would become your guilty past better than
impudence.

Menelaus, crown Greece with honor, and do yourself justice,
by killing this woman. There are also your allies whom she
slew; do not betray them. On behalf of them and their
children I entreat you, do not let her on board the same ship
with you. No lover ever loses all his liking.

A CHILDISH WHIM: the "whim" initially responsible for the tragedy of the Trojan War.
Hera promised Paris power, Athena promised him wisdom, and Aphrodite promised
the love of the most beautiful woman on earth. The barbarian is Paris because as a
Trojan (Phrygian) he is non-Greek. IDA: the mountain near Troy where the contest
took place. CYPRIS: Aphrodite, who led Paris to the house of Menelaus, where she
caused Helen to fall in love with him. Helen, originally from austere Sparta, married
Argos' Prince Menelaus, who inherited the Spartan throne. CASTOR AND POLY-
DEUCES: demi-gods and brothers of Helen. After Polydeuces refused to go to heaven
without his brother, Zeus put them both halfway between heaven and earth as the
constellation The Twins. ARGIVES: Greeks. ESCAPE BY STEALTH: Helen assured
Menelaus that she tried many times unsuccessfully to escape Troy by climbing down
the city walls. ACHAEAN: Greek. ALEXANDER: another name for Paris. TITIVATE: to
make oneself smart or spruce.

31.

HECUBA PREPARES THE BODY OF HER GRANDSON FOR BURIAL (OT)

(415 BC) EURIPIDES, *THE TROJAN WOMEN*, TR. GILBERT MURRAY

It is probably the case that no figure in Western drama suffers such tragic finality as does Hecuba in *The Trojan Women*. She, in legend "the garden of fifty sons," has witnessed the destruction of all her sons in the fall of Troy and her daughters by enslavement and death as well. There's still, however, a slender hope that prevents her from falling into ultimate despair: her infant grandson Astyanax will be with her in captivity. Her hope, slight though it is, is that he might grow to manhood and redeem the legacy of Troy. The Greeks, as aware as she is of that distant possibility, carefully destroy that hope: the body of the young Astyanax—the son of the greatest of Troy's heroes, Hector, who might well have been Troy's redemption—is brought to Hecuba on his father's shield, having been thrown from the ramparts to his death by the Greeks.

One of the most overwhelmingly moving moments in Greek tragedy is this scene, in which Hecuba binds the wounds of the body of her grandson, preparing him for the remnant still available to her of ritual burial. Toneless, calm, she begins her task, rises to unbearable emotional pitch, swoons, recovers, and reaches, finally the fullest expression, possibly at the limit of human lamentation, of a despair that has no redemption: the great climactic moment toward which the meaning of the play has been tending from its beginning, when Hecuba raises her cry of bitter revelation: "O women, I have seen the open hand of God, and in it, nothing." But, "all is well," she concludes. There's a splendor that remains, a splendor offered by this "ruin"—the eternal song of sorrow, the gift these women can bring to heaven and earth: the "everlasting music" of sorrow itself.

The ritual is done, Astyanax is prepared for burial, and the flames of the doomed city shoot up. As the women are moving toward the Greek ships that will take them to their permanent captivity, Hecuba, but for the restraint of the Greek soldiers, rushes toward the flames of Troy, crying, "Take me to die with thee!"

HECUBA

Set the great orb of Hector's shield to lie
Here on the ground. 'Tis bitter that mine eye
Should see it... O ye Argives, was your spear
Keen, and your hearts so low and cold, to fear
This babe? 'Twas a strange murder for brave men!
For fear this babe might one day raise again
His fallen land! Had ye so little pride?
While Hector fought, and thousands at his side,
Ye smote us, and we perished; and now, now,
When all are dead and Ilion lieth low,
Ye dread this innocent! I deem it not
Wisdom, that rage of fear that had no thought...
Ah, what a death hath found thee, little one!
Hadst thou but fallen fighting, hadst thou known
Strong youth and love and all the majesty
Of godlike kings, then had we spoken of thee
As of one blessed...could in any wise
These days know blessedness. But now thine eyes
Have seen, thy lips have tasted, but thy soul
No knowledge had nor usage of the whole
Rich life that lapt thee round... Poor little child!
Was it our ancient wall, the circuit piled
By loving Gods, so savagely hath rent
Thy curls, these little flowers innocent
That were thy mother's garden, where she laid
Her kisses; here, just where the bone-edge frayed
Grins white above—Ah heaven, I will not see!
Ye tender arms, the same dear mould have ye
As his; how from the shoulder loose ye drop
And weak! And dear proud lips, so full of hope
And closed for ever! What false words ye said
At daybreak, when he crept into my bed,
Called me kind names, and promised: "Grandmother,
When thou art dead, I will cut close my hair
And lead out all the captains to ride by
Thy tomb." Why didst thou cheat me so? 'Tis I,
Old, homeless, childless, that for thee must shed
Cold tears, so young, so miserably dead.

Dear God, the pattering welcomes of thy feet,
The nursing in my lap; and O, the sweet
Falling asleep together! All is gone.
How should a poet carve the funeral stone

To tell thy story true? "There lieth here
A babe whom the Greeks feared, and in their fear
Slew him." Aye, Greece will bless the tale it tells!

Child, they have left thee beggared of all else
In Hector's house; but one thing shalt thou keep,
This war-shield, bronze-barred, wherein to sleep.
Alas, thou guardian true of Hector's fair
Left arm, how art thou masterless! And there
I see the handgrip printed on thy hold;
And deep stains of the precious sweat, that rolled
In battle from the brows and beard of him,
Drop after drop, are writ about thy rim.

Go, bring them—such poor garments hazardous
As these days leave. God hath not granted us
Wherewith to make much pride. But all I can,
I give thee, Child of Troy. O vain is man,
Who glorieth in his joy and hath no fears:
While to and fro the chances of the years
Dance like an idiot in the wind! And none
By any strength hath his own fortune won.

> (During these lines Hecuba, kneeling by
> the body, has been performing a funeral
> rite, symbolically staunching the dead
> child's wounds.)

I make thee whole;
I bind thy wounds, O little vanished soul.
This wound and this I heal with linen white:
O emptiness of aid!…Yet let the rite
Be spoken. This and…Nay, not I, but he,
Thy father far away shall comfort thee!

> (She bows her head to the ground and
> remains motionless and unseeing.)

O Women! Ye mine own…

> (She rises.)

Lo, I have seen the open hand of God;
And in it nothing, nothing, save the rod
Of mine affliction, and the eternal hate,
Beyond all lands, chosen and lifted great
For Troy! Vain, vain were prayer and incense-swell
And bulls' blood on the altars!…All is well.

Had He not turned us in His hand, and thrust
Our high things low and shook our hills as dust,
We had not been this splendor, and our wrong
An everlasting music for the song
Of earth and heaven!

Go, women: lay our dead
In his low sepulchre. He hath his meed
Of robing. And, methinks, but little care
Toucheth the tomb, if they that moulder there
Have rich encerement. 'Tis we, 'tis we,
That dream, we living and our vanity!

> *(The women bear out the dead child
> upon the shield, singing, when presently
> flames of fire and dim forms are seen
> among the ruins of the city.)*

Ah, me! and is it come, the end of all,
The very crest and summit of my days?
I go forth from my land, and all its ways
Are filled with fire! Bear me, O aged feet,
A little nearer: I must gaze, and greet
My poor town ere she fall.
Farewell, farewell!
O thou whose breath was mighty on the swell
Of orient winds, my Troy! Even thy name
Shall soon be taken from thee. Lo, the flame
Hath thee, and we, thy children, pass away
To slavery... God! O God of mercy!... Nay:
Why call I on the Gods? They know, they know,
My prayers, and would not hear them long ago.
Quick, to the flames! O, in thine agony,
My Troy, mine own, take me to die with thee!

> *(She springs toward the flames, but is
> seized and held by the soldiers.)*

ORB: circular, circle. THE SHIELD OF HECTOR: Hector is the Trojan hero and son of Hecuba. His shield was made by Hephaestus, the blacksmith god of arms, and had the entire world, in peace and in war, engraved on it. ARGIVES: Greeks. ILION: Troy. THE CIRCUIT PILED BY LOVING GODS: the walls of Troy were built by Poseidon and Apollo. BONE-EDGE FRAYED GRINS WHITE ABOVE: a jagged, broken bone exposed through the skin. SAME DEAR WOULD...AS HIS: as Hector's, Astyanax's father. HOW ART THOU MASTERLESS: without Hector, who bore the shield on his left arm. HIS MEED OF ROBING: his recompense or reward of clothing (meant ironically). ENCEREMENT: grave-clothes.

32.

LYSISTRATA SPELLS OUT HER PLAN FOR PEACE THROUGH A SEX STRIKE AGAINST MEN (OC)

(411 BC) ARISTOPHANES, *LYSISTRATA*, TR. LEON KATZ

The most famous woman political activist in Western literature is most famously fed up with the political stupidities of men in resorting to war. Aristophanes wrote his comedy—his third agitating for peace—when the Athenians, in their endless war with the Spartan League, were fresh from the total disaster of their expedition to Sicily; when the Athenian constitution, under the exigencies of the war, had been alarmingly set aside; and when Athens was altogether on the verge of total defeat. Lysistrata, in these near catastrophic circumstances, puts in motion her radical remedy for war.

Lysistrata (her name means "Disband the Army") is waiting impatiently before her house. She's called together women from both sides in the war and from all parts of Greece, and explains: she has a plan to end it. Emphatically, the women are delighted with the prospect. When she tells them what it is, they groan, they turn their backs, and they're ready to leave. Lysistrata, rising to wrath, cows them, and they listen. She explains the practical application of her plan: the crossing of the legs; the lying under, if pushed to that, like a lump; the absent hands for putting the thing straight in.

She moves on to defensive strategy: the old will secure the treasury up on the Acropolis to prevent any more funding for armament, and the rest will stay below. All will take an oath. Aristophanes irresistibly makes the stale joke of Grecian women's love of imbibing. They're solemn about their oath of allegiance, and delighted with the cup endorsing it.

LYSISTRATA

I've called this council of women together, because I have wonderful news. But first you must answer one question. Doesn't it make you miserable that the fathers of your children are in the army, far from home? I'll bet not one of you has a husband at home with her right now. And not even the memory of a lover! Since the day the Milesians betrayed us, I haven't seen so much as an eight-inch dildo, which is at least a leather consolation for us poor war-widows. Now if I've figured out a way to end this stupid war, will you help me? If you will, then I'll let you in on my wonderful secret.

Women, sisters! If you want to force your husbands to make peace, you'll have to—ah, but will you do it?—you'll have to refrain from having sex with them altogether. Why are you turning your backs on me? Where are you going? Why are you biting your lips and shaking your heads? Oh, these pained looks! And tears?—Come on, ladies! Will you do it, yes or no? Ah, you abandoned, whorish creatures! The poets are right to sneer at us in their tragedies. Are we good for nothing but wallowing in bed and making babies? Ladies! I swear by the two Goddesses, all you have to do is sit in your houses beautifully made up, wearing lovely, thin, see-through, hardly-there gowns of Amorgos silk, everywhere depilated perfectly smooth, and when your husbands come in, they'll meet you penis erect, wild to jump on top, and that's the moment when you cross your legs and say, No!

Believe me, they'll make peace. You can be sure. And if they try in their agony to drag you to the bedroom, grab the doorpost and hold on to it for dear life. But if they beat you and try to rape you, then yield, to be sure, but be sluggish, lumpish, cold—lie there without moving,—as though you didn't notice. There's no pleasure in it for them if they just wham, bam, and that's it. Besides, there are so many ways of driving them mad. They can't stay hard forever, and how much fun can it be for them if we don't squirm and wrestle a lot before, and then with loving hands aim the thing straight in.

I have no doubt that we can do this. Yes, we can persuade our husbands to make a decent peace. The question is, though, what about the rest of the Athenian population? They're patriotic lunatics, they love this war. How do we cure *them*? We have to make them listen to reason. They won't, of course, so long as they have their trusty navy and that bulging national treasury stored up in the temple of Athena on top of the Acropolis. So I've seen to that. This very day, we're taking over the Acropolis. But it's a job I'm leaving to the older women. While we stay here working out strategy, they'll march up the hill, and under cover of offering sacrifices to the Goddess, they'll secure the citadel. So come, ladies, quick!

We'll bind ourselves to an inviolable oath! Lampito, set a great bowl on the ground, and get a great skin of Thasian wine to sacrifice in the bowl. Dip your cups in this blood red sacrifice, ladies, and pray: Almighty Goddess called Persuasion, receive this our delicious offering, and show kindness and mercy to us poor women, and to this, our noble cause.

SINCE THE DAY THE MILESIANS BETRAYED US: in 412 BC, the year before *Lysistrata* was performed, the port city of Milesia defected from the Delian League, which Athens dominated. Lysistrata's complaint may signify that commodities imported from Milesia, like dildoes, were now in critically short supply. AMORGOS SILK: from the neighboring island of Samos in the Aegean Sea. DEPILATED: hair removed, particularly from the sexually engaged body parts

33.
LYSISTRATA ARGUES THE CASE FOR WOMEN TAKING OVER THE NATION'S POLITICS ENTIRELY (OC)

(411 BC) ARISTOPHANES, *LYSISTRATA*, TR. LEON KATZ

[Continues No. 32, above] Lysistrata's troops rendezvous on the Acropolis, where they're attacked by the chorus of old men who come carrying faggots and firebrands to smoke the women out. But the women douse their fire with buckets of water, winning their first engagement. When a Magistrate, determined to break open the treasury for money to recruit rowers for the war galleys, arrives with four policemen, the women storm the cops, who retire trembling and defecating, leaving the Magistrate alone to deal with his formidable adversary, the leader of the revolt. He takes umbrage against the women "meddling in matters of state." In Lysistrata's reply lies the core of the play's argument.

LYSISTRATA

Why, you ask, Magistrate, Your Honor, are women meddling in matters of state, and bothering their heads with questions of war and peace? I'll tell you. All these years the war's been dragging on, we women have been sitting by quietly, saying nothing, suffering in silence whatever it was you men were doing. We didn't open our mouths; our lips were sealed, even though we knew very well how things were going. And we would listen to you men at home talking politics and discussing events and yelling your heads off, and we, sitting silently, our hearts sinking, would smile even so, and ask demurely, "What did you all do in the Assembly today? Did you, by any chance, vote for peace?" And you would answer, so politely: Shut up! Hold your tongue! If you can't be quiet, out! Well—I held my tongue. I said nothing. I sat in the house, miserable, hearing the news—every day more great decisions, every day more stupid, more killing, than the day before. So I'd venture: Darling, dearest, husband dear, tell me, why are we behaving like lunatics, why are we trying so hard to kill ourselves? And he would curl his lip and look at me out of the corner of his eye, and sneer: Stick to your weaving, woman! Any more out of you, and I'll smack your mouth! War is a man's business.

Not letting us say a word against your madness was bad enough, but when we heard you yourselves out in the open, in the streets, in the marketplace, crying out loud: Isn't there anyone, a real man, a commander, a hero, who can save us? And when the answer came back: No, no one. There's no one left. We knew. We knew then what had to be done. We called together all the women of Hellas to unite in common cause—to do what? To force our lunatic husbands to get back their common sense, and save Greece for all of us.

So now you'll listen to us; now you'll hold your tongues! Sh! Quiet. Not a word! It will bother you, will it, to take orders from one of us, from one of us women creatures who wears a veil? If that's all that bothers you, Magistrate, Your Honor, here, take it, I'll wrap it around your head, and see?—oh, beautiful!—it looks lovely on you. And now, take this, this basket, and here's a spindle, and your wool, and this nice tight girdle, and you'll sit at home, and munch beans, and card the wool, and not a peep out of you! Because now war, you understand, has become woman's business.

Oh, help us, Aphrodite, Cyprian Queen! Bathe our women's breasts and thighs in your lascivious charms, and stir our men to so much lecherous feeling that when they meet us, they'll stand stiff as sticks, and then we'll win the name of peace-makers for all of Greece!

APHRODITE, CYPRIAN QUEEN: the Goddess of Love who emerged from the sea at the island of Cyprus (or Cypris).

34.

THE FIRST WOMAN ANGRILY RECITES HER INDICTMENT AGAINST EURIPIDES FOR HIS INSULTS TO WOMEN (OC)

(411 BC) ARISTOPHANES, *THESMOPHORIAZUSAE*, TR. LEON KATZ

It was a joke Aristophanes couldn't let die—that Euripides hated women and denigrated them in his plays. Said often enough by Aristophanes, it's become a mantra, even for posterity and even in the face of all the other tragedies with not dissimilar portrayals of women. Still, one of Aristophanes' funniest plays is given to this premise, in which, quoting from Men's volumes, "Mnesilochus in Drag at the Women's Festival…," "Euripides is terrified that the women in their Assembly at the festival of Thesmaphoria will condemn him to death for the insults to their sex in his plays, he whom they loathe for his misogyny. When Agathon, the effeminate poet, refuses the favor of defending him at the Festival in convincing drag, Euripides' burly father-in-law, Mnesilochus, volunteers. He is shaved above and below, dressed in a lady's wardrobe loaned by Agathon, and goes to the Festival. Sure enough, there's a motion made to put Euripides to death," and the First Woman rises to voice the indictment.

FIRST WOMAN

I did not ask to speak, ladies, just to show off, but because I'm furious. I'm furious about the way Euripides, that miserable son of a green-grocer, insults us women in his tragedies, and leaves us without a shred of dignity. He leaves us covered, ladies, with shame. There isn't a theatre in all of Greece, wherever there are spectators, actors or choruses, where he hasn't attacked us, slandered us, called us every name—liars, lechers, drunks, deceivers, braggers, betrayers—every calumny, every vile name. We're rotten, we're evil, we're the plague of our husbands, we're the absolute curse, can you believe it? of all men. And what's the result? Whenever our husbands come home, the minute they step inside the door, they narrow their eyes, they stare at us, and wonder. Then they run to the closets, they go through every corner of the house, looking. Lovers? Hiding? We can't do anything anymore, nothing we used to do. The husbands, the lovers, the brothers, the fathers, they've become ridiculous. You're weaving a wreath for your own head? Who's that for? Your lover? Your lover! On the way home from the market, you drop a pitcher on the ground. Accidentally. Aha! Who did you buy that for? That Corinthian? That good-looking Corinthian? That "friend?" Or this little girl is ill—sick to her stomach. So her brother shakes his head: M-mm! Pale. Her complexion's green. Aha! Or a barren woman wants to get hold of a baby and palm it off as her own. Not a chance! All her neighbors are sitting around the bed, waiting. And watching. Do you remember how old men, rich old men, loved to marry young girls? Not any more. Euripides says: "An old man marries a tyrant and a shrew, not a wife." Ah, well! Euripides says it! So they shy away. Poor girls! They can't even catch rich old men anymore. And sisters, sisters! You know how they watch us now like hawks! They lock us up, they bolt the doors with iron bars, and outside the door, they chain up those great big Molossian dogs to scare off all the beautiful young men.

It's all, every bit of it, his doing. Well, we might even put up with all that. But oh, sisters! The other things! All the things that matter most! Who has the keys now? Us? No! To get to the wine, to the oil, the corn, the flour, in the storerooms—out of our reach, all of it, gone! They had those keys made, the ones from Sparta, with the three rows of filed teeth, and there's no getting around them. Remember when we only had to jiggle the lock with a cheap little ring, and the storeroom doors would fly open? Well—no more.

So, ladies, my proposal is: kill him. By poison, or any old way. But finish him. There are other charges, other crimes he's accused us of, but actually, I'd rather not air those in public. I'll give the list to the secretary, and she can insert them into the minutes. You can read them there in private, ladies.

35.

ANTIGONE LAMENTS OVER THE BODIES OF HER MOTHER AND BROTHERS (YT)

(409 BC) EURIPIDES, *THE PHOENICIAN WOMEN*, TR. LEON KATZ

"I dance, wild, in the train of death," Antigone cries out or sings, as she follows the corpses of her two brothers and her mother Jocasta. Her dance is wild, her cries are wrenching, but they accord with the customary practice of mourners in funeral processions, given the urgencies of both ritual expectation and private grief.

Antigone had run with her mother to the battlefield to stop the single combat of brother against brother, which was to settle the war between them: Eteocles defending the city of Thebes, his brother, Polyneices. attacking. Mother and daughter arrive too late and find both brothers dead, each having killed the other. At the sight of her dead sons, Jocasta stabs herself to death.

In *The Phoenician Women,* Euripides compacts much of the Oedipus saga into a single play. Briefly, Oedipus' unknowing double crime of parricide and incest led, on his discovery of it, to his self-blinding and his loss of rule over Thebes. His sons agreed to alternate rule each year, but Eteocles banished his brother to prevent his reigning in turn. Polyneices gathered an army and laid siege to the city.

But in Euripides' version, Oedipus had not been banished; he remained a virtual prisoner in the palace, solitary and outcast. Nor was Jocasta dead, but still lived in the city, solaced by her daughter. Antigone's lamentation turns first to Polyneices ("Your name [meaning 'much strife'] was your fate"). Then to the futility of the brothers' struggle since the House of Oedipus was destroyed, she says, "In that very hour…when cunning Oedipus slew the cunning Sphinx." That is, from the moment Oedipus answered the Sphinx's riddle and won the kingship of the city, house and city were already marked for destruction. Finally, she laments for her father's and her own suffering, and for the futility of the life that remains for her.

The procession arrested, she ritually offers clumps of her hair as funeral offerings before the burning of the bodies on a funeral pyre. At last, she calls out her blind father from his dark house into "the light," to share with him the terrible news of their doom.

ANTIGONE

There's no veil, no shroud, can cover my pain,
No shame, no modesty can hide the pulse
Of hot blood pounding in my head,
The crimson flush burning my face,
While I dance, wild, in the train of death,
Tearing the band from my hair,
Letting my robe, my saffron robe,
Fly loose, and so escorting my dead.

Woe, Polyneices, brother, woe!
Your name was your fate:
"The one forever embattled."
And woe to our city, to Thebes.
Your war did not end war, my brother. No.
The murder of brother fed only the murder of brother,
And brought the house of Oedipus to ruin.

My home, my sacred home!
What chanter can I raise from the dead
To sing the song of our house's terrible fate,
Of these three corpses,
Of my mother and her two sons,
For him alone a welcome sight,
For him alone, the avenging fiend,
Who destroyed the house of Oedipus, root and branch.
Destroyed it in that hour, the very hour
When cunning Oedipus slew the cunning Sphinx.

My father, what Theban, what man beyond our world,
What other noble soul in all the worlds beyond our world,
Suffered, or knew, or saw such suffering?

Pitiful Antigone, no one will ever match,
No bird will ever sing, from the leaves of oaks,
From the branches of olive trees,
The pitiful song of Antigone, alone,
Her mother dead, her maidenhood left
With nothing but lamentation,
With nothing but tears of mourning
Streaming forever for sorrow that never ends.
Pluck the hairs out of your head.
Throw them as funeral offerings on these,
The dead. Which first?
On the breasts of my mother who fed me?

On the wide wounds of my brothers' corpses?

Miserable Oedipus, blind old man,
Come out of the dark house
Where you suffer life
In pain, in bitterness.
Listen, you who are stumbling your way
Across the courtyard. Listen.
Your sons are no more, they are dead,
Out of the light.
Your wife, the staff who led
Your blind footsteps, no more.

She found her sons at the Electran gate
Where they had fought their duel like lions
In their lair, their blood already congealed,
And seizing a sword that lay between,
She plunged it into her flesh
And fell with her arms around them.
Today, my father, the God whose work this is
Summed up and gathered to a head
All the sufferings of our house.

SAFFRON: the color variously known as orange-yellow or orange-red. THE CUNNING SPHINX: the Sphinx was a monster with a woman's head, a lion's body, a snake's tail, and an eagle's wings who sang the riddle: "What is it that has one voice, can have two, three, or four legs, and is the weakest when it has the most?" Whoever couldn't answer the riddle was killed. Oedipus replied, "Man, because he crawls on all fours when he's an infant, then walks on two legs, and leans on a stick in his old age." The Sphinx, defeated, killed herself, and the citizens of Thebes made Oedipus their king in gratitude, bringing about the curse of his marrying his own mother. THE ELECTRAN GATE: one of the seven gates surrounding the city of Thebes, all of which had been besieged; the gate at which the brothers fought.

36.

AGAVE, COMING OUT OF TRANCE, RECOGNIZES THE BODY SHE DISMEMBERED AS HER SON'S (OT)

(CA. 405 BC) EURIPIDES, *THE BACCHAE*, TR. LEON KATZ

[For more on *The Bacchae*, see in Men's volumes "Tiresias Heatedly Defends the God Dionysus..." and "The Herdsman Reports to Pentheus the Magical Feats of the Bacchants...."] Agave's transformation from the delusion that she has successfully hunted a lion and is triumphantly carrying the trophy of its severed head in her arms, to her gradual recognition that she holds instead the severed head of her son Pentheus, is generally conceded to be one of the most gripping, possibly the most horrifying moment in extant Greek tragedy.

It's the god Dionysus who has driven the women of Thebes into a frenzy, in which they continuously celebrate his rites on the mountain slopes of Cithaera. This, in punishment for their initially denying his godhead. But the mysterious god's punishment of Pentheus, their rational, skeptical, even puritanical king, is the most savage of all. Pentheus, enraged at what he imagines is the drunkenness and sexual license of the women's revels on the mountain, is put under a spell by Dionysus, which awakens in him the desire to spy on the celebrants, dressed—so that he might not be detected—as a woman. He takes shelter in the branches of a pine tree, and the women, prompted by the god, tear the tree out by its roots, pull Pentheus to the ground, and tear him to pieces. It is his mother, Agave, the leader of the women in trance, who, cradling her son's head in her arms, returns triumphantly to the city.

The power of the women to execute such a savage deed, and the explanation of their power for savagery, is close to the heart of explaining the play's central mystery: the meaning of Dionysus. A herdsman has reported to Pentheus—to his disbelief—that the women on awakening share entirely the god's power and perform benign acts exhibiting that power with perfect serenity. But when they are jarred by intrusion or threat, and are brought down a single notch from the height of pure ecstasy and benignity, their power—still equal in force to the god's—becomes savage.

There's further transformation: a god-willed distortion of self-image in his victims that underlines the slippery identity of the god himself, and the slippery nature of godly effect ("There be many shapes of mystery,/And many things god makes to be,/Past hope or fear," sings the Chorus at the play's conclusion). For just as Pentheus, who had mocked the god's effeminacy in his earthly appearance, was made to emulate the woman, so Agave, in her triumphant celebration of her prowess, emulates the man.

AGAVE

Men of Thebes! Men of our city
With its shining towers,
Come! Come quick! And see
This prey, this beast, which we,
The daughters of the house of Cadmus,
Hunted down!
Not with spears, and not with javelins,
But with our hands, our women's hands,
We tore this mighty animal limb from limb!

Where is my father? Where is he?
Bring him to me, quick! And where is he,
My son, my darling Pentheus! Tell him to come,
And bring with him a great step-ladder
He will set against the house,
And on its triglyphs, nail this head,
This lion's head that I have conquered,
Killed, and earned my glory,
I, the daughter of Cadmus, even I!

> (Cadmus enters with servants bearing
> the headless body of Pentheus on a
> bier.)

My father! Now it's yours to brag,
Yours to boast that you begot these daughters,
Daughters who are proud and valiant,
Mightier than men; and of your daughters,
I, Agave, mightiest of all!
No more for me the shuttle and the loom,
No more of women's work!
I go to greater, manly things,
To hunt and kill wild beasts with my white hands.

Here in my arms, you see this bloody prize?
Take it, my father, hang it above our door

To show the men what grit your daughters have!
Take it, and call a feast, and shout the blessings
We, your daughters, bring to Cadmus' house!

You frown. You have a grieving look.
What is it that shrivels courage in old men?
May Pentheus, my son, be like his mother,
And be as lucky in the hunt when he,
Together with his comrades, men of Thebes,
Hunt for mighty animals in the woods.
Ah, no, my son is thoughtful, quarrels with the gods,
And doesn't hunt and kill like other men.
Teach him, father! Admonish him,
And call him to my sight
To see his mother's joy, her strength, her happiness!
You grieve. What is there to mourn?
My father, what? Look up? To see the sky?
I see it, brighter than before.
My soul's unrest? Unrest? I do not know.
My thoughts—? You said—? The thoughts I had are gone.
The head I carry in my arms?
A lion's—so the women said with whom I hunted.
I turn it. Yes, I see—

O god! It is the head—O god!
His head, it's drenched in blood!
Who murdered him? Why am I holding this—
My son's—? My son's—?
Answer me! My heart's in dread of what's to come!

I! I and my sisters killed my son!
Agave! Misery!
Betrayer Dionysus murdered him!
I see it. Now I see it.
With his mother's arm!

CADMUS' DAUGHTERS: the women of Thebes (Cadmus founded Thebes). TRIGLYPH:
an architectural ornamental detail, a short column.

37.

IPHIGENIA ASSENTS TO HER FATHER'S EDICT OF DEATH (YT)

(CA. 406 BC) EURIPIDES, *IPHIGENIA IN AULIS*, TR. LEON KATZ

"Is life so dear, so sweet, that it is worth /The loss of what is more than life?" Iphigenia's remarkable speech is fixed on settling nothing less than the question of the ultimate value of life. Incidentally she must prevent her mother from interfering with her decision to be sacrificed—to forestall her mother's passionate argument for what has become for Iphigenia a meaningless, "familial" idea of justice.

The dilemma that is resolved so transcendently by Iphigenia is Agamemnon's. The Greek expedition to Troy under his command is becalmed at Aulis. Because of his transgression against the sacred province of Artemis (there are conflicting versions of precisely what that transgression was), no favorable winds will blow until Agamemnon sacrifices his daughter Iphigenia to relieve the goddess's distress. Agamemnon wavers: must he satisfy first the blood-lust of his near-mutinous men to get to Troy and the war, or must he succumb to the natural feeling of a father—augmented by the violent appeals of his wife, Clytemnestra—and forego so savage and unnatural a murder? Thought of in normal moral or psychological terms, his wavering and his later decision to sacrifice his daughter brand him as a man of weak will and small ambition, fearful of the immediate consequences of his army's anger more than for his daughter's life. But Agamemnon's dilemma can be put differently: whether to satisfy the demands of the goddess (an incontrovertible absolute) or to satisfy the demands of the blood-tie of father and daughter (an equally incontrovertible absolute.) So considered—from the perspective of conflicting irreconcilable absolutes—there is no resolution of the dilemma itself, both alternatives being on the one hand, absolutely right, and on the other, absolutely wrong.

It is Iphigenia who cuts the Gordian knot. Weighing the fear of losing life against the fear of losing the ultimate value of life, she decides for the latter. To the question: what *is* its ultimate value? her answer is the one most applauded and most revered before her time and since: its greatest value lies in its surrender, its free offering, for something greater than itself—the nation, the people, the cause, God, flag, grail—the offer of the self to one of these signifying the greatest good the self can do, both for itself and for one or another of these relevant abstractions.

Like all volunteered martyrdoms, Iphigenia's is, from one point of view, folly; from another, glory. Whether she or any other soldier wedded to a cause accomplishes their intent cannot be known in hindsight either. (For that lesson—that its inevitable failure can be known only too well and invariably—see de Musset's Lorenzacchio's meditation on the same question, in Men's volumes "Lorenzacchio Deliberates: Am I Satan?'") But either way, the gesture itself, and the cost of the gesture, is awesome and Iphigenia's clear-eyed faith in the absolute value for the future of the Greeks in what she is doing is at least poetically redemptive, regardless of the consequences we in hindsight know of the Trojan War, and those that Euripides himself spelled out so devastatingly in *The Trojan Women* [for which spelling out, see No. 29, above].

In the scene, Iphigenia interrupts the frantic efforts of her mother and of Achilles to keep her safe from the advancing soldiers, who are ready to pull her toward the sacrificial altar and her waiting executioner, Agamemnon. With a word, she stops the labors of her would-be saviors and explains calmly, with happy composure, that death, not rescue, is her choice. Having silenced her mother, forestalled rescue, having explained why "Grecians' victory over Troy shall be/My husband and my children—and my fame," she asks with unalloyed joy to be led, not funereally to a sacrifice, but in celebration of the victory of her eagerly offered death.

IPHIGENIA

Hear me, Mother. Let me speak.
There's little use in being angry with my father,
Little use in bringing force against his men.
We cannot win.
This brave Achilles here, I thank his courage,
But he must not raise his sword against my father.
It does us little good, and ruins him.
I know what I must do now, Mother. Listen.
Of my own free will, I've chosen death—no, hear me.
It is my will. My death will be my honor.

My love is for our country, for our Hellas.
It looks to me to save it from destruction,
To save its fleet for victory over Troy.

It is my woman's way to honor, the renown
Of freeing Hellas, to win that blessedness.
Is life so dear, so sweet, that it is worth
The loss of what is more than life?
Did you bear your child, myself, for you alone,
Or for a greater love, a greater good?
For Hellas, surely—a greater than yourself.
Look, Mother, there! A sea of soldiers, waiting,
Ready to sail, and all afire to punish
The outrage to their country, die for Hellas!
Have I the right to cripple their resolve?
The right to hold Achilles to his vow
To save one woman's life against ten thousand?
Artemis, goddess, asks my life; shall I refuse?
No. Grecians' victory over Troy shall be
My husband and my children—and my fame.
Barbarians and slaves will never triumph
Over our freedom and our sacred land.

Sh! Mother! No more weeping. No.
After my death, I want no mourning, no.
No cutting of the hair, no blackened robes,
No tomb. The sacrificial altar is my tomb.
My death is good; it's fitting, what I do.
I do not hate my father, and your husband.
He sacrifices me against his will.

Who will lead me to the place of sacrifice?
Forestall those who would drag me by the hair?
No, mother! It is not for you to go.
One of my father's soldiers, Agamemnon's man,
Must bring me to the field of Artemis,
Must bring me to her arms, where I must die.
No tears, no tears, my mother, shed no tears!

Sing hosannas, women, for my destiny!
Let Grecian soldiers hear your song of praise
For her, the child of Zeus, for Artemis!
Raise baskets, light the fire, fling the barley!
Father Agamemnon, touch the altar
Where Iphigenia, daughter, brings to you
Victory and triumph for all Greece!

38.

SIMAETHA IN THE THROES OF EROTIC PASSION COMPOUNDS LOVE-CHARMS TO BRING HER LOVER HOME (YT)

(CA. 270+ BC) THEOCRITUS, *IDYLLS NO. 2, "THE SORCERESS"*, TR. LEON KATZ

Wooing the moon and "blood-bathed Hecate," the great demon of witchery, bringing to her door the terrifying Artemis who sets off howling dogs, turning the wheel that holds the magic brew, tying the blood-red string to the rim of the bowl, tossing into it the bay leaves, the heap of barley, the corn husks and the tassel of her lover's robe, setting these magic charms on fire, burning them to ashes, sending her girl Thestylis to the very door of the absent one, the lover Delphis, to smear ashes on his threshold, begging and threatening him in a single breath, Simaetha, in the dead of night, with Moon, Hecate, Artemis and howling dogs outside for companionship, longs, remembers, anticipates, knows for certain he will come, suffers despair that he will not, nurses hope, and bears her infinite pain.

In North Africa, in the cosmopolitan city of third century BC, Alexandria, in a culture which had become "aware of itself," a highly self-conscious literary form evolved, the literary mime. It was intended for recitation more than for dramatic performance and developed a realism that was both external and psychological, one that is instantly recognizable to us. All too recognizable: the hidden preoccupations of urban sophisticates, their emotional stresses, their fantasy remedies, on which personal, very private life could devolve. Simaetha, deserted by her lover, resorts to magic to bring him back—with single-minded concentration at needle-point.

The life of her monologue lies in the emotional breathlessness with which Simaetha, helpless in her erotic frustration, reaches for whatever remedy, whatever extremity she can imagine in her passionate need to bring her passion to rest. She doesn't. Her night will be one of unbearable and unrelieved pain.

SIMAETHA

Where are the bay leaves, Thestylis, and the charms?
Bring them all.

And tie a blood-red string of wool around the bowl.
Magic will win me back my lover's heart.
It's twelve days now since Delphis came to me,
Twelve bitter days since he set eyes on me,
Or knocked—o misery!—at my waiting door.
His appetites are dragging him elsewhere.
I'm sure that slave of Aphrodite roams. I'm sure.
At dawn, first thing tomorrow, I will run
To Timagetus' wrestling school, and grab him,
And denounce him, and then drag him back to—Well.
For now, I'll use the charms to bring him back.
I'll chant my song, O Moon, I'll chant it low,
And woo the blood-bathed Hecate, your double,
Who wanders over graves, and frightens dogs,
And terrifies the night. All hail to Hecate!
Stay with me, Queen of death, companion me,
And work black witcheries as strong as Circe's
Or mad Medea's or the vile Avenging Ones."

Turn, magic wheel, and bring my lover home.

First, Thestylis, ignite the grain.
No, pile it, pile it on, you stupid thing!
Are you frightened, or are you making fun of me?
Pile it high, and say, "This pile of barley is his bones."

Turn, magic wheel, and bring my lover home.

Now burn the bay-leaves, burn him in the leaves.
Delphis in flames; he flares, and then dies out.
He's wracked, as he wracks me, as fire wastes his flesh,
Till only a powder, nothing but ash, is left.

Turn, magic wheel, and bring my lover home.

Like this, this image of wax, let Delphis melt,
Let Mindian Delphis melt this hour with love,
And swiftly as this magic wheel turns round,
Let Aphrodite hurl him to my door.

Turn, magic wheel, and bring my lover home.

Now burn the corn-husks, Thestylis.—She comes!
Nothing withstands the power of Artemis.
She's close! The dogs are howling, terrified!

She's at the crossroads! Keep us safe, Thestylis!
Strike the gong!

Turn, magic wheel, and bring my lover home.

The voices of the winds and seas are still,
But no, the voice of my despair is not.
I burn, I burn, for him who left me here
Not wife, not virgin, in my misery.

Turn, magic wheel, and bring my lover home.

Three times I pour, three times I chant, Artemis,
"Whatever man or woman shares his bed,
Let him forget that face as soon or sooner
Than Theseus his Ariadne's love."

Turn, magic wheel, and bring my lover home.

He lost this tassel from his robe. I shred
The fringe, and throw it on the flames.
This Love, this Delphis Love, this leech of leeches
Drains my blood, and sucks my body dry.

Turn, magic wheel, and bring my lover home.

Here, Thestylis, now take these herbs, these ashes.
Smear them on his threshold, spit and say,
"My mistress' heart clings still although you scorn her.
Here's your reward: these ashes are your bones."

Remember, Lady Moon, how my love used to be.
He used to come to me four times a day.
He kept his oil-flask here for the wrestling school.
And has he now forgot? Then by these charms
Let him remember, or by Hecate,
He'll soon be knocking at the gates of hell.

Goodnight, bright Moon, goodnight. It shall be done.
As I intend, so it will come about.
Your journey's done tonight. I stay, and wait,
And nurse my longing. Hope, and bear my pain.

THESEUS...LOVE: Princess Ariadne of Crete fell in love with the hero Theseus and
helped him kill the monster Minotaur. Sailing back together to his native Athens, he

left her asleep on the beach on the island of Naxos and departed without her. MINDI-AN: Delphis is from Myndus, a town on the coast of Asia Minor.

39.

BITINNA IN A JEALOUS RAGE HAS HER LOVER STRIPPED, TIED UP, DRAGGED THROUGH THE STREETS, FORGIVEN, AND PERMANENTLY IMPRISONED IN HER HOUSE (OC)

(FL. 3RD CENT. BC) HERONDAS, *THE JEALOUS WOMAN (MIME NO. 5)*, TR. LEON KATZ

[See No. 38, above] A mime—a man or a woman—sets up in a public square, a wine shop, a well-to-do household, or a theatre, with a box of wigs, hats, make-up, props (no masks), and plays all the parts in a short sketch also called a mime. But how to separate—or can we separate?—the literary mime from the publicly performed one? Knowing nothing about Herondas except that he lived during the third-century BC and possibly in Alexandria, we have only the internal evidence of his mimes to tell us how and whether they were meant to be performed. In the instance of these two mimes (No. 39 and No. 40), the conviction that they were, rather than merely recited, is hard to resist.

Both mimes are concerned with the private world of sexual gratification of upper-middle-class ladies in their middle years. Bitinna, not in her first bloom, is in a rage against her priapic slave-lover, Gastron, who's been wandering. As to punishing him, she's of two minds: whether to destroy him or preserve him; whether to shame him publicly or protect him against public shame. She settles for the lesser revenge of shaming him privately and forever. The two ladies in *A Chat Between Friends* keep their socially friendly style of conversation, but get down to basics: how can I get, one is inquiring of the other, a dildo as satisfactory as yours? The portraits are psychologically precise and knowing; their sociological fallout is eye-opening.

Except for the in-house slave-lover (although the equivalent convenience can be imagined) the women and their world are our contemporaries.

BITINNA

Admit it, Gastron. You're finished with me, aren't you?
You've had enough of me waiting in bed for you every night
with my legs wide open. And now you're sniffing around for
Menon's wife, Amphytaie.

GASTRON

Who's Amphytaie? I never heard of her. Amphytaie?

BITINNA

Liar! ...*Liar!*

GASTRON

No, believe me, Bitinna! I'm entirely yours. My whole body,
my blood, my soul, are nobody's but yours!

BITINNA

And that lying tongue of yours too, between your teeth! That's
mine too.—Kydilla! Call Pyrrhis.

KYDILLA

Pyrrhis! Here!

PYRRHIS

Madam?

BITINNA

Yes, I want you to take this liar here, and tie him up.—Tie him
up, what are you waiting for!—Get the wellrope out of the
well, and tie him up with that.—I'll teach you a lesson,
Gastron, you'll never forget, or I'm no woman. Like a stupid
Phrygian fool, I let you climb into my bed every night as my
honorable, faithful lover. Well, we'll make up for my folly now.
Faithful!—Ah, the rope! Strip him naked, Pyrrhis, now! And
tie his hands and feet together.

GASTRON

Bitinna, my God! No! What are you doing?

BITINNA

I'm reminding you, you liar, of the slave you are. Do you remember? How I saw you the first day they brought you here, and bought you immediately for three minae?—Pyrrhis, you idiot, is that the way to tie him up? Do it again. Pull his elbows behind his back, and tie the rope so tight that if he moves, he'll cut his own flesh.

GASTRON

Bitinna! Love! I cheated on you once, I admit it, just once! After all, I'm a man! How can a man help it, how? I swear to you, if I do it again, you can scratch tattoos all over my body.

BITINNA

Save your breath for Amphytaie when you're rutting with her. And when you're remembering me as the stupid clod on whom you used to feed till you were glutted.—Is he tied tight? Good. Make sure he can't get loose no matter how much he squirms. Now drag him off to Herman the Torturer, and tell him I want him beaten a thousand times across his back, and a thousand times across his front.

GASTRON

Bitinna! Do you want to kill me before I'm even proven guilty?

BITINNA

You confessed! Didn't you say, " I cheated on you?" "Bitinna! Love! I cheated on you! Once!" Ha! Once!

GASTRON

I confessed only to get you to calm down!

BITINNA

Take this, and wrap it around his middle to hide his little wang while you drag him through the agora. And remember! A thousand here!

GASTRON

Ow!!

BITINNA

And a thousand here! And don't take any side-streets for short cuts. Drag him right through the middle of main street, right through the market place. Go!

(After a few moments of watching)
Oh my God, what was I thinking? Kydilla, call them back!—Call them back, quick, before they've gone too far!—Look, they're pulling him along the street like an old sack of meal!—Pyrrhis, he's your friend, don't you remember? You're torturing him dragging him like that! Stop! Stop, or before another five days, Pyrrhis, I'll have your swollen hands and your bloody ankles back in chains! You were shackled in them before, remember? Not that long ago!

Good, bring him in. Keep him tied up. Throw him over there. Now find Kosis, and tell him to come here with his tattoo needles and his ink.—He's going to decorate you, liar, from head to foot in one sitting, while you're tied up and hanging from the roof-beam with a gag in your mouth.

KYDILLA

Madam, please. Can't you forgive him this once? Think of your daughter Batyllis' wedding that's coming soon, and the babies that will come to her after that, and the joy you'll have of them. Remembering that coming joy, madam, can't you find it in your heart to forgive him?

BITINNA

Another word, Kydilla, and I'll throw you out of the house. Forgive him? Forgive this betrayer? The whole world would laugh in my face. No, by Gaia, no! "He's a man," he says. "He can't help being a man!" Good. So now he's going to be even more of a man. Kosis is going to tattoo a message all over his face: *Know thyself!* It will remind him.

KYDILLA

The Gerenia Festival for the Dead is only four days away. Only four days before those holy days! Surely, madam...

All right, all right! I'll let him off this once.—You can thank
Kydilla, liar, that I'm sparing you. For now. She's like a
daughter to me, I love her just like my Batyllis. I raised them
both in these arms. So after the holidays, after we've drunk our
homage to the miserable dead, you can look forward to daily
consolations just like theirs. I tell you, lover, you've licked the
honeypot for the last time.

PHRYGIAN: from the area of Troy. AGORA: a town's central market place.

40.

METRO ADMIRES KORITTO'S NEW DILDO, AND WANTS ANOTHER JUST LIKE IT (OC)

(FL. 3RD CENT. BC) HERONDAS, *A CHAT BETWEEN FRIENDS (MIME NO. 6)*, TR. LEON KATZ

[For explanation, No. 39, above]

KORITTO

Oh, please, Metro, please come in.
Won't you sit down?

METRO

I must ask you,
And you must tell me, Koritto dear.
Who made you your beautiful dildo,
The red leather one with the beautiful stitches?

KORITTO

How did you know...
Where did you see it?

METRO

At Erinna's.

Nossis gave it to Erinna's daughter
The day before yesterday.
Such a lovely gift for a young girl.

KORITTO

But who gave it to Nossis?

METRO

You won't give me away, will you?

KORITTO

I swear by my eyes, Metro!
Silent as the grave.

METRO

Eubele, Bita's wife, gave it to her.
And she promised nobody would ever know.

KORITTO

That woman, I tell you, is the absolute limit.
I hadn't even used it yet myself,
But she begged me for it, so I let her have it.
And now she uses it like something
She found, and even gives it away
As though it's hers to give.
A friend like that is no friend. Not any more.
Imagine! Giving away to Nossis what belongs to me!
Nossis! Gods forgive me for talking so unladylike,
But I wouldn't give that Nossis my worn-out, used-up dildo
Even if I had a thousand more.

METRO

Oh now, Koritto, don't get so upset.
I shouldn't have said anything at all. Ach, I talk too much.
But—listen, Koritto, I'd really love to know—
Who made it? You can tell me, can't you? I'm a friend, right?

So why that look? I'm Metro, remember? I'm your friend.
Darling, you don't have to pretend to me.
You can tell me. Who made the thing? What's his name?

KORITTO

Oh, you poor dear! You, begging like that!
All right, I suppose I'll have to tell you.
Kerdon made it.

METRO

Which Kerdon? I know two Kerdons.
There's the grey-eyed one, the one who lives near Myrtaline.
He couldn't build a pick for a harp.
But there's another one who lives off Main Street
Near Hermadoros' apartment building.
That one used to be a real catch,
But he must be getting on by now.
He used to get it on with Pylaithis
When she was alive, I remember.
I wonder if anybody else remembers her?
Maybe her relatives.

KORITTO

No, it's not the one nor the other, Metro.
This one is a Khian or an Erythreian,
And he's short and bald.
He looks exactly like Prexinos,
But he doesn't talk like him.
He works at home and keeps his door locked
To keep away the tax collectors.
His stitching and his polishing, I tell you,
You'd think Athena made them in heaven,
Not Kerdon here below.
He came by here with two of them,
And I thought my eyes would pop out of my head.
I tell you in confidence, darling, we're alone,
No man was ever hung like those two beauties.
They were long and stiff and smooth as silk,
And the leather straps were as soft as wool.
I tell you, that man is a blessing to womankind.

METRO

Then why didn't you buy both of them?

KORITTO

I tried. I tried everything to get them both.
I even, can you believe it, kissed him,

And stroked his bald head,
And treated him to a couple of drinks,
And called him Kerdon darling,
And blew into his hairy ears.
I did everything, actually, but get into bed with him.

METRO

Well, why didn't you, if that's what he wanted?

KORITTO

I would have, sure, but Eubole was here
Grinding her meal on my millstone
Like she always does, day and night.
Honest to God, she's wearing it out,
And if that miser of a husband of hers
Doesn't give her four obols to get one of her own,
Pretty soon I'll have to get a new one myself.

METRO

Tell me the truth, Koritto,
Who brought him here?

KORITTO

Artemis brought him. Kandas' wife.
She showed him the way to the house.

METRO

Hah! Artemis! Wouldn't you know!
She's always sniffing around things like this—anything sexy.
She's worse than that Thallo.
But if he wouldn't let you have both of them,
Didn't you ask who bought the other one?

KORITTO

Of course I did, but he wouldn't tell.
I'm sure it's somebody he wants to get into bed.

METRO

I'd better be going, Koritto.
I could, maybe, run into Artemis now,
And find out from her when Kerdon's at home.
So wish me luck.

Certain feelings are dancing around inside me now.
You know?

'Bye.

41.

ABROTONON THE SLAVE GIRL INVENTS A SCHEME TO ESTABLISH THE IDENTITY OF A FOUNDLING BABY (YC)

(FL. 3RD CENT. BC) MENANDER, *THE ARBITRATION*, TR. LEON KATZ, ACT III

Abrotonon is a slave-girl who's been hired by a young gentleman, a Charisius, for the last three days, but who oddly enough has never touched her in all that time. But she's just figured out a way to gain her freedom. Follow the ring, she reasons.

The ring was found with an abandoned baby, who's at the moment in the possession of a charcoal burner. But the ring is recognized by Onesimus (Charisius' slave) as belonging to his master. And how, he's been wondering, did it get into the swaddling clothes of this baby? Ah, he reasons, he probably dropped it when, drunk, he raped a young girl at the Tauropolia festival, and she, to get rid of the baby, abandoned it along with some trinkets to help with its support should anyone find it. Surely the baby is my master's and so—

But Abrotonon leaps at the news: give me the ring, and I'll let your master see it on me, and I'll tell him it was I he raped at the Festival and—.

But no—She reconsiders: I was there, at the Festival, months ago when I was still a virgin, and I remember a well-to-do young lady who was raped and even though I didn't see the ring on her then, it could well be that she's the mother of this baby, and your master, Charisius, its father. And if that's so, why not tell him so that—

But no—. She reconsiders: More than likely, in his drunkenness, he lost the ring that night in a bet or gave it to a friend as security, and so possibly the friend was the one who—

So—first, I must find out who the actual father is, then trace that girl. Give me the ring, and I'll test Charisius, pretend I remember his raping me and so on and if I can establish in that way that he's the father, then we'll hunt out the mother.

May the goddess Persuasion be my ally, may I convince him at first that I'm his victim, and then find the real victim, and then my reward—freedom.

The solution, largely through Abrotonon's contribution, eventually falls into place. Conveniently, it's the wife whom Charisius abandoned out of suspicion of her infidelity who is the young woman he raped at the Festival—the ring, the son, and wife are all, happily, his. (And he is, after all, at discovery, burdened by a moment of remorse.)

Menander's is the only example we have of the fourth century BC's Greek middle-class urban comedy that displaced the fifth century's politically, sexually, and ritually oriented Old Comedy of Aristophanes. Its situations, characters, plotting, morality, and tone were to be echoed and sometimes precisely replicated by Western comedy for the next 2,300 years. Abrotonon—the ingenious servant who enjoys the exercise of her ingenuity and who as plot engineer moves the play toward its happy conclusion, remains, after the lovers, the major fixed ingredient of classical comedy in both its male and female variations: the clever female servant (Molière) or the witty running slave (Plautus). Her action in this case is governed presumably by one intent, gaining her freedom. But there's also for her the sheer pleasure of unscrambling the plot's puzzle for the benefit of baby, mother, and father. Not all her successors are so altruistically moved, but even the most sullen of them will share her pride in outsmarting the plot, winning the reward, or at least avoiding punishment.

Abrotonon

Listen, Onesimus, is it the charcoal-man who found the baby
that the woman is nursing in the house? O what a dear, sweet
thing! And this ring was found with him. It's your master's
ring, isn't it? So it must be your master's child. Well, if it really
is, can you bear for it to be brought up as a slave? If you can,
you deserve to die; it would serve you right. He lost the ring at
the Tauropolia festival—ah, when he was drunk. Of course.
And then he stumbled onto these women who were there
making a night of it. The same thing happened where I was,
last year at the Tauropolia, when I was still a virgin. Oh yes, I
was, by Aphrodite! I was hired to play the lute for these
women, and this girl was their friend. I'd know her if I saw her

again—a very handsome girl, and rich, they said. While she was with us, she wandered off, and all of a sudden she came running back, tearing her hair and sobbing. And her beautiful silken cloak, O my god, it was torn to shreds, ruined. Did she have the ring then? She may have, but I didn't see it. But you, if you have any sense, you'll listen to me and tell your master. Why should he hide what happened, if the woman is freeborn? So let's find out who she is.—Oh, no, wait! First we must find the culprit. If I'm not sure who he is, I can't go bearing tales to those ladies. Someone else could have gotten the ring from him, and then lost it—who knows? Or he could have placed it on a bet playing dice, or backed someone else's bet, and lost it that way. A million things can happen at a festival when a man is drunk. Until I'm sure of the culprit, I don't want to look for the girl, or blurt out a single word of all this to anyone.

Look, Onesimus, we can plot this together. Here, I'll take the ring, and go in to him inside. He'll see it on my finger, and he'll ask where I got it. "At the Tauropolia," I'll say, "when I was still a virgin." And everything that happened to her, I'll say happened to me. Most of it I know. And if he's really the one involved, drunk as he is now, he'll give himself away, and blurt it all out even before I do. And I'll back up everything he says. And so as not to make any mistakes, I'll let him speak first. I don't want to be caught lying, so I'll feed him all the platitudes. "Oh, and what a brute you were! So rough, the way you threw me down. And my dress! You were so impetuous! You almost tore it off my back!" That's what I'll say, and we'll be in the house, so I'll pick up the baby, and cry, and kiss it, and then I'll ask the wetnurse where she got it. And finally I'll say, "So you fathered a baby!" I'll say, while I'm flashing the ring. Then if it's true, and it's proven dead to rights that he's the father, we can take our time finding the girl.

Now, if he really thinks I'm the mother, he'll buy me from my pimp and give me my freedom. And you'll have been the cause of my happiness; I'll remember that, Onesimus. And don't you worry, I won't stop looking for the mother just to cut you out of the reward. Why should I? I have no craving for a baby; all I want out of this is my freedom. So—quick, the ring. Hand it over.—Now, dear Goddess Persuasion, stand by me, and make the words I speak in his ear prosper!

TAUROPOLIA FESTIVAL: celebration in Athaca in Artemis' honor. "Tauropolos" means "drawn by bulls" or "hunting bulls."

ROMAN

42.

BACCHIS, GOOD-HEARTED COURTESAN, IS DELIGHTED TO RECONCILE HUSBAND AND WIFE (YC)

(165 BC) TERENCE, *THE MOTHER-IN-LAW*, TR. LEON KATZ, ACT V

Taking a leaf from Menander [see No. 41, above], Terence fit his courtesan Bacchis perfectly into Abrotonon's shoes and accomplished the standard miracle for clever servants in classical comedy who cause misunderstandings to be brushed away and are responsible for perfect reconciliations of husbands and wives. The misunderstanding here is almost identical with the one in Menander's comedy: the husband Pamphilus before marriage had raped his future wife without knowing who she was. Discovering that she had given birth while he was away and before he had slept with her after marriage, he refused to receive her as his wife. But it's of course the ring he had taken from her by force and given to his courtesan Bacchis that eventually produces reconciliation. The ring on Bacchis' finger is recognized as the wife Philumena's, and Pamphilus, reassured, receives his wife back again together with their son.

There is a somewhat questionable morality concerning the husband lurking in this frequently told tale that never disturbed either the Hellenistic Greeks during Menander's time nor republican Romans during Terence's. Whatever uneasiness there may have been was sufficiently mitigated by the comedy's outcome to put it out of mind. And it's the outcome that Bacchis celebrates in her delighted recollection of the play's events as she recalls them to her confidant Parmeno, Pamphilus' slave. The suggestion of Abrotonon's kindness as part of her motive in *The Arbitration*, is exploited to the hilt in Terence's comedy. Terence, known for his comedies' notes of urbanity and civility, celebrates in the courtesan an altruism, a motive beyond gross motive, that lends to her character a measure of dignity beyond the stereotypical characterizations given to her class. Terence's civility is even more remarkably in evidence in his characterization of the mother-in-law of the play's title, whose speech from the play [see No. 43, below] reflects impressively her own altruistic civility.

BACCHIS

Parmeno, imagine! I pay one visit to Pamphilus' wife, and all the blessings in the world rain down on the two of them, and all their troubles gone, wiped out! Suddenly, he has a legitimate child, his very own, that was almost doomed by all the women around them, and by him too. And I gave him back a wife, the wife he never expected to look at or live with again. And I got him out from under the suspicions of his father and her father, they wondering, disgusted, about his decency. And all these blessings came from one little ring I was wearing on my finger. Imagine! Because I remembered how I got it. I remembered that about ten months ago, it was just after dark, when Pamphilus was exhausted and drunk and gasping for breath and he came running to my house, all alone—and with this ring! The sight of him, Parmeno! It frightened me, and I shook him, and I said, "Pamphilus, darling, what happened to you, why are you panting like that, and where did you get that ring?" Because he was holding this little ring between his fingers as though he had just grabbed it from someone, but he made believe he didn't hear me, the way they do when they have something to hide, so I insisted and insisted, and finally he told me the whole story. Drunk as he was, he had this little adventure in the street, the way they do, and she wouldn't let him, but he had his way, and in the struggle, he pulled this ring off her finger. And just now, when I was with his wife Philumena where she's staying with Myrrina, her mother, and when Myrrina saw the ring on my finger, she opened her eyes wide and she said, "Where did you get that ring?" and I told her the whole story, and there was this—oh!—recognition! The ring was Philumena's, so she was the girl and the child is her husband's! Parmeno, I was so happy to be the one who brought them all this good news! I suppose everyone will think because I'm only a courtesan and because Pamphilus was my lover for all that time before, that this was something I wouldn't want or like, and because it's not good for me when marriages, especially this one, are happy. But I tell you, I'll never let feelings like that, especially for the money lost, make me play the greedy one. So long as I had Pamphilus for my lover, I truly loved him. Oh yes. He was free with his money, and he was always charming, always good-humored. No, his getting married wasn't convenient for me, oh no, I admit it, and the way I was with him and loved him, I didn't really deserve that inconvenience, no. But there are advantages and disadvantages in everything, and when so many advantages as there are here come to light, I don't mind putting up with the disadvantages. Oh, no, Parmeno, not at all!

43.

SOSTRATA PLEADS WITH HER SON TO TAKE BACK HIS ESTRANGED WIFE (OC)

(165 BC) TERENCE, *THE MOTHER-IN-LAW*, TR. LEON KATZ, ACT IV

Terence made civilized comedy out of those same plots and texts of Greek New Comedy from which Plautus made raucous—funny, but coarse—comedy. *The Mother-in-Law* covers the same ground as do many of the Greek New Comedy plays, on which Roman comedy is based, but with the telling difference of Terence's humane sensibility. It's evident in the instance of his titular character, Sostrata.

One of Terence's variations on the well-worn story adds to it an additional misunderstanding. Sostrata, Pamphilus' mother, is in the dark about the reason why the young wife has left her husband and gone back to her own mother. She's stayed with Sostrata when her husband went off on a journey, but Philumena began to avoid her mother-in-law, and left her when she could no longer hide her pregnancy. Sostrata, sadly supposing that she is the cause of her daughter-in-law's estrangement, makes her generous offer to her son: she will leave, and move out of the city so that Philumena will return to her husband. Terence's civility is in evidence in his characterization of this mother-in-law, whose desire not to be seen as that "hateful cartoon, the mother-in-law," reflects impressively her own altruistic civility.

SOSTRATA

It hasn't escaped me, my dear son, that you're nursing a bit of resentment toward me. You suspect it was my fault that your wife left you, even though—and I thank you for that—you've been kind enough not to show your resentment. But as I hope to prosper and be blessed in your happiness, for which I earnestly pray, I'm certain I've done nothing to deserve her dislike. You love me, I'm sure of that, and today you've very wonderfully proved it. Your father just told me how you've so loyally favored me over your wife. Now I want to pay back such loyalty, and show you that in my heart, your devotion and love for me has its reward. I've decided, my dear Pamphilius, that the very best thing that I can do for you and your wife, and for my own good name and good conscience, is to remove to the country with your father, so that my remaining here will be no bar to you and your wife, and so that Philumena will have no reason not to return to you. Leaving the city is not the loss to me you may think it is. After so many years, the pleasure of my friends and the delights of the city are, I must admit, somewhat worn out. When I was young, of course they were everything to me; now I can very easily do without them. But what does matter a great deal to me now is that no one, least of all my son, feels that my still being alive is a burden to him, so that he's waiting impatiently for me to die. And now,—well, I may not deserve it, but—I'm disliked. And so it's time, I think, to go; time to get rid of any reasons for unhappiness that I, whether I deserve it or not, have inflicted—to clear myself of that, and to altogether appease your wife. I want, God willing, to spare myself and all of us the burden of that hateful cartoon, the mother-in-law. And so all things being equal, and all things being as you would wish, I want you to do one more great good favor for me. Take back your wife.

44.

MEDEA IN MADNESS SLAYS HER TWO CHILDREN (OT)

(AD 50–65) SENECA, *MEDEA*, TR. LEON KATZ, ACT V

[For the story common to Seneca's and Euripides' *Medea*s, see No. 14, No. 15, No. 16 and No. 17, above] "Dredge up the deepest, darkest forces within your soul," invokes Medea, "and let your crimes make those of the young Medea's seem like love." There's more transpiring in Seneca's Medea, as in Euripides', than a series of battles of motive against motive. In Seneca's version, Medea is not merely balancing "wrong against wrong," but out of the depths of her being, releasing forces that, however "dark" they may be, have lain in wait.

It is the same concept of the unconscious and uncontrollable impulse of *ira*, or wrath, dormant in human behavior that governs Atreus in Seneca's *Thyestes* [see in Men's volumes "Atreus Plans His Gruesome Revenge on His Brother Thyestes"]. There, it comes unbidden; for Medea, it is deliberately evoked. Seneca's Medea is motivated not merely by the need for revenge, but by the need to release the whole inner nature of herself, The Medea that is at one with—in fact, the same as—the witch-goddess Hecate. The release, the joy, even the genuine comfort of uninhibited exhibition of that hidden self—it's a longing that attends the ultimate criminal's realization of his or her ultimate crime. The whole being is suffused with a sense of repletion, a sense of the self's perfect victory.

It is this force that overwhelms Medea's more customary human feelings—her vestige of love for Jason, her genuine mother's love for her children. And it is these obstacles of humane feeling that she labors, eventually successfully, to overcome. Once she has downed her compassion for her children—the last barrier—she is ready for the arrival of her accomplices, the ghostly avengers, who swarm invisibly around her: Megaera, vengeful for her slaughter by Heracles; Medea's own brother, whose "scattered limbs" she herself tossed into the sea; the Furies, the very spirits of revenge. Medea, transmuted, with her brother's ghost holding the sword with the hand with which Medea had struck him, murders her child.

A remarkable conflation: her brother's revenge against her own murder of him, and her own revenge against Jason—both accomplished in a single stroke, as one, in the murder of her child. Then Medea the floodgates of her deepest longing—for crime as crime—opened, she waits with entire satisfaction for the avengers armed against her to arrive. Her murders, she vows, "have just begun," her "time has come...to let the world see" her self-display of her "power," her "pride," her "monstrous strength."

MEDEA

Why do you hesitate, Medea? What holds you back?
Your first success, your murder of his bride,

Is only a taste of pleasures still to come.
Her death is a beginning, not an end.
Or did you murder her because you love him still?
No! Follow your vengeance to the end, steel yourself for that,
Put every thought of honor behind you, and womanly modesty,
And every thought of God or fear of man.
Modest revenge will do for pious souls,
Not yours. Dredge from below, dredge up
The deepest, darkest powers within your soul,
And let your coming crimes
Make those of the young Medea's seem like love.

I became Medea through the strength of crime!
I rejoice! Because through me my brother died,
I rejoice! Because through me his limbs were torn.
Because through me, my father lost the golden fleece,
And Pelias' daughters, moved by me, murdered the king, their father.

And so, for my coming crimes, I bring
Well practiced, bloodied hands. And to do what?
What weapon will I use against this enemy?
I know, and yet do not know. A hidden one,
Still buried deep. It gives no sign. Not yet. Not yet.
In madness, out of wrath, the sign will come,
And it will burn my tongue, and come
Without my bidding, and will say:
If only he had children by this hated bride,
Oh then! Not mine, but hers, Creusa's children,
Would pay the ransom for their father's crimes.
If he had children. But my tongue, without my bidding, says:
He has; they are his bride's, Creusa's.
Once they were ours, once they were his and mine.
But now? Now they, my sons, belong to her.
Through them my hate will find its just revenge.
You who were once my children, now no more,
Will pay the price for your father's crimes.

Vengeance on my children! Gods!
It numbs my heart, and terrifies my soul.
My children's blood! O God, my wretched rage,
My hatred for his bride, for him, are gone,
Are driven out, are vanished with the thought of—
Give me better counsel, rage! My children

Have no guilt, my sons, my sons, are innocent.
What is their crime, what is their transgression?
None!
None but one—Jason is their father.
They're his seed. They bear his guilt.
And I, Medea, bear a greater guilt:
I call his sons, my sons. So let them die!

Tears? Of rage? Or love? You waver?
Your anger dies in love, Medea! Come,
My darling sons, come here, and throw your arms
Around my neck. Here. Close. Safe. Lie here.
Unharmed. In my embrace. Before I go.
I'm driven into exile, darling sons,
I'm driven into solitary flight.
Soon they'll tear you from my bosom,
And you'll weep, lamenting for my kisses,
Weep, but follow after him, and her, his bride.

Then die to Jason, as you're lost to me!—
It's so.—Hate burns again, rage swells, it seizes.
I, I follow, follow, where it leads.
Oh God, if I had sons like Niobe, twice seven sons,
Not two—still, still, it is enough. For vengeance,
For the crimes against my father and my brother,
The crimes with which I sweetened Jason's way.

Ah, now the huge snake hisses, writhing, as they lash
Its skin, its coils! Megaera scourges, and she carries
Him—his scattered limbs—my brother's!
They bring my brother! Yes! He seeks revenge!
They come; oh yes; I see them! Come;
Appalling creatures, come! Surround!
Beside! Behind! Prepare the fires! Light
The bloody torch! I hear your lamentation, brother!
The Furies fling their torches in my eyes!
I grant! I grant their vengeance! Brother,
Force the goddesses to leave me to myself!
My brother! Use this hand that held the sword
Above your head! Hold it!—High!

(Kills one of her sons)
And so. Your soul has found revenge.

What noise? Ah yes. Yes. They come in arms

To kill me. Good. They'll learn
Medea's murders have just begun.
Come. Follow. We'll venture to the roof.
Follow, Nurse. With him—my living son.
I'll take the dead with me.
Your time has come, Medea, the time to show your power,
To let the world see you, your pride, your monster's strength.

NIOBE: mother of fourteen children, for which she thought herself superior to Leto, the mother of Apollo and Artemis. All her offspring were slain by the two gods, and Niobe herself was turned by Zeus into a stone that shed tears in the summer.
MEGAERA: her husband, Heracles, was rendered mad by the gods, when he killed their children.

45.

ANTIGONE REFUSES OEDIPUS' DEMAND THAT SHE ABANDON HIM (YT)

(AD 50–65) SENECA, *THE PHOENICIAN WOMEN*, TR. LEON KATZ, ACT I

A virtuous man, believed Seneca, struggling with misfortune, is such a spectacle as the gods might look on with pleasure. It was a notion Christian tradition was to emulate: God, in Christian belief, is not as happy with the virtuous man who knows no misfortune as with the one who overcomes, with virtue, terrible misfortune. Seneca, in his version of Euripides' *The Phoenician Women*, characterizes Oedipus's daughter Antigone as the champion of that Stoic fortitude which urges her father, not despite of but because of his miseries, to live up to such heroic, blessed resolve.

Three years after his downfall, self-blinded and self-exiled, Oedipus wanders in wild country accompanied only by his daughter Antigone, who alone has remained faithful to him. [See No. 35, above, for Euripides' version of the Oedipus plot in his *The Phoenician Women*]. "Why drag out my life's slow length? Why live?" he asks in the first scene of the play. "Bury in the earth at last this hateful body. You wrong me with kind intent, and think it piety to drag along this dead, unburied father." Blood for blood, he believes, he who had, though inadvertently, killed his father must avenge that crime with his own death. But for Antigone, he has not the least but the greatest of possibilities for redeeming his life. Like Hercules, the icon of Stoic unfortunates, Oedipus clearly has the opportunity now to be looked on by the gods with similar pleasure.

"Leave me, leave me!" Oedipus cries unavailingly. Antigone is—traditionally as well as here—steely fortitude. She closes argument from every side. Leave? She's effectually attached to his hand. Find a rewarding life of her own? Her father is her great and only reward. His wish for himself is not hers? Impossible, his wish is her wish, she has no other. He wishes to die? She will accompany him.

In this opening scene, she succeeds at least in persuading him to return to Thebes to urge his warring sons, Eteocles and Polyneices, to end their combat. Her plea temporarily wins him back to life. (But the extant text of Seneca's play is incomplete; how Oedipus' end is resolved is unknown.)

ANTIGONE

No power on earth, my father, can tear my hand from yours,
And none can ever move me from your side.
Let my brothers fight for who'll be king of Labdacus,
To reign over the splendour of our house.
My kingdom has the greatest of my father's gifts,
Himself, my father's self.
He, my brother, King Eteocles, who rules our city—
Who rules it now—can never take from me
This precious gift, nor can the other,
Polyneices, with his army at our gates.
If Jupiter himself spoke thunder from the sky,
And hurled a lightning bolt to break our bond,
Still my hand would hold your hand;
I would not let it go.
If you forbid my hand, I'll guide you still.
Refuse or give me leave, I'll still direct your steps.
Where to? Say. The level plains? We'll go.
The rugged mountain heights? I'll lead the way.
Whatever path you choose, I'm still your guide.
We'll take together, always, the same road.
Even in death, my father, you will not be alone.
Even your hour of death, we'll face together.
Suppose—let us suppose—we stand before a cliff,
Immense, precipitous. It overlooks
A beautiful expanse of sea. Should we not explore it?
Or there, an overhanging rock, and there,
Like gaping jaws, a wide, wide gash of earth.

We'll go there, yes? And there, a raging torrent choked
With fragments of the falling mountains
Plunging in its wake.
We'll know that torrent, too.
Wherever you wish, I'll go. I do not oppose
Nor urge.

To cut the thread of life,
Is that your wish? If it is death you want,
I'll go before; I'll follow if you live.
But change your mind. Summon your will,
Call up the courage of great Oedipus,
The will, the courage that can master grief.
Conquer your sorrows, and with all your might,
My father, long, again, to live.

LABDACUS: father of Laius and grandfather of Oedipus. "Kingdom of Labdacus" is
Thebes.

46.

JOCASTA, ON HER KNEES BETWEEN HER WARRING SONS, PLEADS FOR PEACE (OT)

(AD 50–65) SENECA, *THE PHOENICIAN WOMEN*,
TR. ELLA I. HARRIS, ACT IV, SC. 1

It is three years since Oedipus blinded himself and went into voluntary exile; three years since his sons, Eteocles and Polyneices, were to
share the Theban throne. But Eteocles, though his year of royal power
is at an end, refuses to give up his reign. Polyneices has come to the
gates of Thebes with seven armies to enforce his rights, and the brothers are confronting one another in hand-to-hand combat on the field.
Jocasta (who in this version has not yet slain herself) rushes to the
battlefield to prevent her sons from murdering one another.

Breathlessly, she approaches them, falls to her knees between
them, and, with desperate anxiety, refuses to end her appeal until they
put down their swords and embrace one another in peace. In the
course of her argument (the text below is less than half of it), she uses
a most telling device of persuasion: before you can thrust your

swords into one another, your swords must pass through me; you must kill me first. The tension of hatred between the sons is held in abeyance by the position in which Jocasta has thrown herself; so long as her appeal finds no fruition, she is immovable. Unhappily, so are her sons. As we know from legend, if not from the missing last pages of Seneca's play, Jocasta's entreaties fail to prevent further bloodshed or the death of her sons.

In her strenuous appeal, she addresses first the two assembled armies, the attackers of the city and its defenders. Having stopped their move toward immediate battle, she has leisure to address her sons: first both at once in an excruciatingly delicate attempt to be seen as perfectly impartial; then Polyneices, the one attacking the city ("Embrace me, my son"); and then Eteocles, its defender ("If peace is odious"). Her long subsequent harangue circles back again and again over her entreaties, but ends (the extant text of the play ends here as well) while Eteocles is refusing to give up his power. The last speech we have is his answer to Jocasta's "Would you give your country, your home, your wife, to the flames?" His reply is, "Sovereignty is well bought at any price."

JOCASTA

Against me turn your weapons and your fires,
Attack me only, valorous youths who come
From Argive cities; and ye warriors fierce,
Who from the Theban citadel descend,
Fall upon me alone. Let friend and foe
Alike attack this womb, which bore these sons—
My husband's brothers. Tear these limbs apart,
Scatter them far and wide. I bore you both.
Do you more quickly lay aside the sword?
And shall I say who fathered you, my sons?
Give me your hands, give them while yet unstained
Till now ye have unwittingly done wrong,
Each crime was fortune's that against us sinned,
This is the first base act brought forth between
Those conscious of their guilt. In my hand lies
Whate'er you will: if holy piety
Be pleasing to you, give your mother peace;
If crime be pleasing, greater is prepared,
A mother stands between you, make an end
Of war or of the hinderer of war.
Whom with alternate prayers and anxious words
Shall I first strive to touch, whom first embrace?

With equal love am I to each one drawn.
One was far off—but if the brother's pact
Should hold, the other soon would be far off.
Shall I then never see the two at once
Except as now?

(She turns to Polyneices.)
Embrace me first, my son,
Who hast endured misfortunes manifold
And labors manifold, and now, foredone
By a long exile, dost at last behold
Thy mother. Nearer draw, within its sheath
Put up thy impious sword, and in the earth
Bury thy spear that trembles, poised to slay.
Thy shield prevents thy breast from meeting mine,
Lay it aside; loose from thy brow the bands
And from its warlike covering free thy head,
That I may see thy face. Where dost thou look?
Dost thou observe thy brother's battle line
With timid glance? I'll hide thee in my arms,
Through me must be the pathway to thy blood.
Why hesitate? Art thou afraid to trust
Thy mother?

(She turns to Eteocles.)
If peace is odious, if thou seekest war,
Thy mother asks thee for a short delay
That she may kiss the son from flight returned,
Whether it be the first kiss or the last.
Listen unarmed while I entreat for peace.
Thou fearest him, he thee? I fear thee both,
But for the sake of each. Why willst thou not
Lay by the sword? Be glad at these delays:
You seek to wage a war in which 'twere best
To be o'ercome. Thy hostile brother's guile
Fearst thou? 'Tis often needful to deceive
Or be oneself deceived, yet is it best
To suffer rather than commit a crime.
Fear not, a treacherous thrust from either side
Thy mother will receive. Do I prevail?
Shall I be envious of thy father's fate?
Have I come hither to prevent a crime,
Or see it nearer?

47.

DEIANIRA, HAVING UNKNOWINGLY CAUSED HERCULES' DEATH, CONDEMNS HERSELF (OT)

(AD 50–65) SENECA, *HERCULES OETAEUS*, TR. LEON KATZ

Deianira, suspecting her husband Hercules was bring the Princess Iole to her home as his concubine, is prepared to kill him. But she remembers: the centaur Nessus, while dying from Hercules' poisoned arrow for attempting to abduct Deianira, had secretly given her a vial of his blood, telling her that if Hercules should ever desire to take a concubine, she could forestall it with the gift of a shirt smeared with Nessus' efficacious blood. The news is brought to her by her son, Hyllus, that Hercules, donning the shirt, screamed with pain; in shedding the clinging shirt, he tore off his own flesh. He was dying of the ravages of her gift. The death of Hercules, the revered hero of the Stoics for his deeds of prowess in ridding the world of evil, registers in heaven too: he is the son of Jupiter with the mortal Alcmene (and at his death, deserving a place in Olympus) and therefore the hated rival of Jupiter's forever jealous wife, Juno.

Deianira, in responding to her inadvertent crime, becomes one in a long line of Western tragic heroines, who out of conviction of their culpability-whether for murder, as here, or for adultery, as is more commom-lacerate themselves with a fury, a self-hate, that exceeds and is intended to exceed, and punishment likely to be visited on them by men or heaven. Whether pagan or Christian, all hostile values by which they are or have been judged are so thoroughly internalized that, when they admit to culpability, they are a far worse inquisitor, judge, and executioner of themselves than any that could be visited on them. It's the mark the guilty one has of residual virtue. Her attempts to exceed sane bounds of punishment for herself become the prime evidence in her own eyes of her redemption and worth. It is a self-valuation confirmed by the very power and violence with which she repeatedly condemns her worthlessness and ineradicable guilt.

DEIANIRA

Why so weak? Why stare in amazement, Deianira? It's done.

Your crime is done. Jupiter is taking back his son, and Juno will face her rival once again—great Hercules. And you? You must atone. Take up the sword, and drive it deep, and swift, into your body. So, it must be done. But is so weak a hand as yours equal to such punishment? Strike with your thunderbolts, O God! Destroy your guilty daughter! And not with any ordinary weapon, but with a bolt like his, like Hercules your son once hurled to kill the Hydra. Destroy me as pollution, as an evil worse than woman's wrath, with such a bolt as once you hurled at flying Phaethon. I, in murdering Hercules, murdered all the world.

But why do I ask for weapons from the gods? The wife of Hercules should be ashamed to beg the gods for death. No, she alone, she with her own hand must grant that gift. Take up the sword, hold it. A sword? Why a sword? Is sword enough to hurl you to your death? A cliff, a high cliff, Oeta, and from there, from Oeta, you will soar to death, where broken rocks will rip you into pieces, and every stone will seize a part of you, and hands, your hands, will hang from jagged rocks, and all the mountain side will reek with Deianira's blood.

One death. One death is nothing. Make it more. Find a weapon, choose a weapon on which to fall. My husband's mighty sword, let it become my couch! Yes, I'll die on this, his vengeful sword.—It is not enough! No, not enough that by my own right hand I suffer death. Nations of the earth, assemble! Fling clouds of rocks and flaming brands at Deianira! Let no hand fail to find its target! I will have my rightful punishment! My hand, this hand, has opened wide the world's great path to crime. See! Cruel kings already rule unchecked. And savage monsters kill without restraint. And sacrificial altars reek with brothers' blood. And I, in killing Hercules, have taken from the world the punisher of kings, of tyrants, beasts and monsters. Wife of mighty Jupiter! I've set myself against the gods! Why do you stay your hand? Why do you spare your lightning bolt? Hurl thunder that you snatch from Jove! I've cheated you of glory, cheated you of honor, when I killed your rival, killed great Hercules. It's well, it's good, it's right that I should die!

HYDRA: the serpent monster with many heads killed by Hercules, who then used its poison on his arrows. PHAETHON: the son of Helios, the Sun-God, who permitted him to drive the chariot of the sun. Unable to control the horses, Phaethon drove so near to Mother Earth that she, in torment, appealed to Jupiter, who killed Phaethon with a thunderbolt and caused the chariot to fall into a river below.

48.

PHAEDRA CONFESSES HER HEART "AFLAME WITH LOVE AND MADNESS" FOR HIPPOLYTUS (OT)

(AD 50–65) SENECA, *PHAEDRA*,
TR. FRANK JUSTUS MILLER, ACT II, SC. 3

"For what can reason do when passion rules, When love, almighty, dominates the soul?" Seneca's Phaedra admits openly to her nurse that "raging passion" is forcing her to take "the path of sin." She is doing so entirely consciously, noting, as she glances backward in her flight from "sane counsel," that sane counsel can no longer matter . Unlike Euripides' Phaedra, Seneca's is done struggling with reason, moral sanity, and self-revulsion. She is obsessed, and the play studies the psychology of her obsession. First to be noted: She is, as she says, fully conscious of her descent into sin; she is its observer as much as its agent. As in his study of Atreus [see in Men's volumes "Atreus Plans His Gruesome Revenge on His Brother Thyestes"], Seneca is separating the province of "wrath" that underlies the unbidden, uncontrollable behavior of the self and the "reason" that can take note of it, but has no power whatever to control it. Phaedra's passion for Hippolytus has the same force and the same overwhelming control over her as does Atreus' hatred for his brother, Thyestes. What does her "wrath," or as Phaedra knows it, "passion," do?

Having fallen in love with her son-in-law Hippolytus, she's immune to her nurse's condemnation of her "vicious [incestuous] lust," to her warnings about Theseus her husband's return, and to her reminder of Hippolytus' hatred of women. She's found a fixed answer to the difficulty of her plight: suicide. To prevent it, her nurse relents and is determined to aid her. But Phaedra, suffering the pain of her intense longing, is declining into quiescence. Seneca describes, in a speech given by the Nurse, the detailed and terrible symptoms of a willfully dying woman. Hippolytus is the nurse's recourse: persuade him, she reasons, to relent from his misogyny. He is not only unrelenting, but imperceptive. Phaedra, seeing him, faints; he raises her up, wonders why she longs to die rather than recover; still holding her in his arms, he urges his stepmother to whisper in his ear why she longs to "sink down into death." In an aside, speaking to herself before venturing to speak to him, Phaedra considers, then ventures—at first, overcoming the difficulty of speaking at all, but then, and suddenly, the floodgates open, and she speaks not only out of desperation, but out of release. She offers to be his slave, she confesses the "flame of love" that torments her, she describes her reverence for Hippolytus, the embodiment of the beauty of his father, Theseus, in his youth, and throwing aside all vestiges of nobility, she begs for his love out of pity.

PHAEDRA

> *(Aside)*
> Come, dare, attempt, fulfill thine own command.
> Speak out, and fearlessly. Who asks in fear
> Suggests a prompt refusal. Even now
> The greater part of my offense is done.
> Too late my present modesty. My love,
> I know, is base; but I persevere,
> Perchance the marriage torch will hide my sin.
> Success makes certain sins respectable.
> Come now, begin.
>
> *(To Hippolytus)*
> Bend lower down thine ear,
> I pray; if any comrade be at hand,
> Let him depart, that we may speak alone.
>
> *(Attendants leave.)*
> My lips refuse a passage to my words:
> 'Tis a great pow'r that urges me to speak,
> A greater holds me silent. O ye gods,
> I call on you to witness: what I wish—
> Light cares find words, but heavy ones are dumb.
> The name
> Of mother is an honorable name,
> And all too powerful; a humbler one
> Befits our love. Call me, Hippolytus,
> Sister or slave, slave rather; I will bear
> All servitude. If thou shouldst bid me go
> Through deepest snows, Mount Pindus' frozen top
> Would give me no annoy, or if through fire
> And hostile battle lines, I would not shrink
> From giving to the ready sword my breast.
> Take back the scepter to my charge consigned,
> Receive me as thy slave; it is not meet

A realm of cities by a woman's hand
Should be defended. Thou who flourishest
In the first bloom of youth, thy father's realm
Govern, O take thy suppliant to thy breast,
Pity the widow and protect the slave.
O lover's trusting hope!
Deceitful love! Have I not said enough!
With prayers I will assail him. Pity me,
Hear my unspoken prayers; I long to speak,
Yet dare not.
My heart is all aflame
With love and madness, fiercest fires burn hot
Within my vitals, hidden in my veins,
As o'er the lofty roof the swift flame plays.
I love the form,
The face that Theseus in his boyhood bore,
When first his cheeks were darkened by a beard,
And he beheld the winding labyrinth
Where dwelt the Theban monster; by a thread
He found his path. How glorious was he then!
A fillet bound his locks, a modest blush
Reddened his tender cheeks, on his soft arms
Were iron muscles. Thy Diana's face,
Or my Apollo's had he, or thine own!
Lo! such he was when he made glad his foe,
Thus proudly did he hold his head; in thee
Shines forth his manly beauty unadorned
But greater; all thy father is in thee,
And yet some part of thy stern mother's look,
A Scythian sternness on thy Grecian face.
If thou with him had crossed the Cretan straits,
For thee my sister would have loosed the thread.
O sister, in whatever part of heaven
Thou shinest, I invoke thee in a cause
Both thine and mine; one house has snatched away
Two sisters, thee the father, me the son.
Lo! fallen at thy feet a suppliant lies,
Child of a kingly race. Unstained I was,
Pure, innocent—'tis thou hast wrought this change.
See, to entreaty I have sunk: this day
Must either end my sorrow or my life.
Oh, pity her who loves thee.

MOUNT PINDUS: mountain range north of the Greek peninsula. SCEPTER TO MY
CHARGE CONSIGNED: as Queen of Troezen, Phaedra was ruling in Theseus' absence.

WINDING LABYRINTH...BY A THREAD: Theseus, after killing the Minotaur, escaped the monster's labyrinth by following the thread provided by Ariadne. FILLET: A narrow band tied round the hair. DIANA: the Greek Artemis; goddess of the hunt, to whom Hippolytus is devoted, to the exclusion of the goddess of love. MY APOLLO: Phaedra's devotion to the physical beauty of the god of many functions. THY STERN MOTHER'S LOOK: Hippolytus was the illegitimate son of Theseus and the Amazon queen Hippolyta (also called Antiope). TWO SISTERS, THEE THE FATHER, ME THE SON: Ariadne, Phaedra's sister, who fell in love with Theseus and aided him in his exploit in the Minotaur's labyrinth, was later abandoned by him.

49.

THE TROJAN WOMEN'S CHORUS DENIES THE EXISTENCE OF AN AFTERLIFE (OT)

(AD 50–65) SENECA, *THE TROJAN WOMEN*,
TR. ELLA I. HARRIS, ACT II, SC. 4

"Whither go we after death? Where lie they who never have been born?" The nihilism of this Chorus of women in Seneca's tragedy goes beyond even Hecuba's devastating outcry in Euripides' *Trojan Women*: "Oh women, I have seen the open hand of God, and in it nothing." Seneca's Chorus abandons all belief in the mythology of the gods in heaven and the dead in Hades, as well as all sense of sentient being, or any being, before or after life. The profound bleakness of this view is not germane to Seneca's Stoicism. It is clearly intended, at least dramatically, to strike a note of defiance against dependence for consolation on any agencies other than mortal ones and against any escape in imagination from the devastation of the human lot .

But the statement, whether expressing any aspect of belief Seneca might conceivably have tolerated, is not only extraordinarily startling, but extraordinarily courageous. It violates first and foremost the very function of his teaching. During the moral corruption and oppressive tyrannies that repeatedly resurrected in the days of the early Empire (particularly during Nero's reign, in which Seneca played a major role), his moral philosophy "offered refuge," says one chronicler, "against the vicissitudes of fortune which he daily beheld." The Chorus in this passage offers no such refuge. The finality of its despair is in a way a total betrayal of the effort of Seneca's moral philosophy to shore up God, reason, and a pervasive Providential equanimity against the moral ruin of his moment. The power of the speech lies in its unmitigating drive in a single direction: toward the shutting off step by step of all intellectual escape from its devastating conclusion.

CHORUS OF TROJAN WOMEN

Is it true, or does an idle story
Make the timid dream that after death,
When the loved one shuts the wearied eyelids,
When the last day's sun has come and gone,
And the funeral urn has hid the ashes,
He shall still live on among the shades?
Does it not avail to bear the dear one
To the grave? Must misery still endure
Longer life beyond? Does not all perish
When the fleeting spirit fades in air
Cloudlike? When the funeral fire
'Neath the body, does no part remain?
Whatsoe'er the rising sun or setting
Sees; whatever ebbing tide or flood
Of the ocean with blue waters washes,
Time with Pegasean flight destroys.
As the sweep of whirling constellations,
As the circling of their king the sun
Speed the ages, as, obliquely turning,
Hecate hastes, so all must seek their fate.
He who touches once the gloomy water
Sacred to the gods, exists no more.
As the sordid smoke from smoldering embers
Swiftly dies, or as a heavy cloud,
That the north wind scatters, ends its being
So the soul that rules us slips away;
After death is nothing; death is nothing
But the last mete of a swift-run race,
Then let eager souls their hopes relinquish,
Fearful find the end of fear. Believe
Eager time and the abyss engulf us;
Death is fatal to the flesh, nor spares
Spirit even; Taenarus, the kingdom
Of the gloomy monarch, and the door
Where sits Cerberus and guards the portal,
Are but empty rumors, senseless names,
Fables vain, like dreams that trouble sleep.

Ask you whither go we after death?
Where they lie who never have been born.

PEGASEAN FLIGHT: swift as the flight of Pegasus, the winged horse. HECATE HASTES: speeding fate. TAENARUS: the kingdom of Hades. CERBERUS: the three-headed dog that guards the gate to the Underworld.

50.

CASSANDRA ENVISIONS PROPHETICALLY THE GRUESOME MURDER OF AGAMEMNON WITHIN THE PALACE (YT)

(AD 50–65) SENECA, *AGAMEMNON*, TR. LEON KATZ, ACT V, SC. 1,

"Stop your tears! No weeping for my plight!" Seneca's Cassandra peremptorily demands of her fellow captives, the Trojan women with whom she arrives at Agamemnon's palace. "I myself shall weep enough for the woes of my own house." This Cassandra is more proud royal princess, uncowed by captivity, and fiercely, patriotically Trojan than mad prophetess. Her first gesture is to throw off the wreath that binds her to the service of Apollo [see No. 4, No. 5 and No. 6, above for Cassandra's tale], which signifies the end of her fear and the last of her subjection to his cruelty. Now, with nothing left of fortune, she is beyond loss and therefore beyond fear (a Senecan prescription for psychological calm, emotional equanimity). When she quickly falls under the spell of prophecy again, she envisions not only the coming murder of Agamemnon, but images of her beloved father, Priam, and royal princes in the Underworld, and prays that the "Stygian darkness" of Hades be lifted for a moment that they might see the retribution that the Fates are about to visit on the enemy Greeks. Recovering from her bout of seer's "madness," she bandies words with the now-arrived Agamemnon and mocks him with forebodings of his coming fate, which he does not understand.

With Agamemnon and the Chorus of women gone, Cassandra, in this passage, stands alone in the dawning light and observes prophetically the crime about to be committed. But her prevision of Agamemnon's murder, instead of terrifying her, gives her cause to revel—she, the enemy Trojan princess, loyal to the city and her father, the Trojan King. The destruction of the Greek victor, laden with the spoils of Troy, redeems for her the destruction of the Trojan city. For her, the destroyers of Agamemnon, Clytemnestra and Aegisthus, are the harbingers of a newly victorious Troy, a Troy soon to recover.

But as she watches (at first, prophetically intuiting the deed to come; and then—as Clytemnestra dresses her husband in the net-like robe—the deed as it is happening) as moment succeeds moment, it's gruesomeness, the increasing horror of its execution causes Clytemnestra not only to "shudder," but at first to be horrified, at last to be sickened at the assassins' savagery. She registers her disgust, when it is over, with—metaphorically—a dismissive shrug: what can you expect, she wonders, from the son of such a one as Thyestes, or from a sister of such a one as Helen?

The greatest, the most telling contrast be tween Aeschylus' Cassandra and Seneca's is, at play's end, in their leave-taking before execution. Aeschylus' heroine [see No. 6, above] confronts the sense—the meaning or non-meaning—of life itself (a "wet sponge" leaves a friendless victim's life unremembered, therefore, nonentity). Seneca's Cassandra is somewhat narrower in her frame of reference. She, the Trojan princess, seized by Clytemnestra's guards to be hustled to her death, plays the proud captive flaunting defiance to the end and leaves with a last sneering taunt, "On you, as well, a 'madness' [the avenging Orestes] is to come."

CASSANDRA

A mighty deed is breeding in this house,
A mighty deed as great as all
Of Troy's ten years of war.
What is it? What?
My soul! You're blest with seer's madness!
We who were conquered on the walls of Troy,
We soon again will be the conquerors.
Soon it will be well with us,
And Troy will rise again.
Great Priam, in your very fall, my father,
You dragged the victor down.
Mycenae's king, King Agamemnon,
Falls today. Your conqueror is doomed.

Prophetic frenzy! The sight is clear,
The mind's eye sees, is there,

Inside the house, and revels, sees,
Within, around, the royal feast.
And no, the image does not cheat
The seer's sight.

The feast is spread within the house.
It's thronged with guests;
A royal banquet like the last in Priam's house.
And Agamemnon's couches gleam
With spoils of Troy, the tables heaped
With stolen Trojan gold and Trojan wine.
And he himself, the giver of the feast,
Wears the royal robes my father wore.

And Clytemnestra whispers softly, "Lord,
Put off the clothing of your enemy,
And wear instead this Mycenean robe,
This mantle woven by your faithful wife."

I shudder! Shudder at the sight!
The sight of him, Aegisthus, paramour,
The exile and adulterer, who'll kill
The rightful husband, rightful king,
His hour of retribution, when Agamemnon's blood
Will mix with Trojan wine,
And Clytemnestra's mantle, deadly robe,
Will be her husband's shroud,
Its treachery embracing him for death.
It shackles both his hands, it binds his head,
And she, her right hand trembling, stabs,
But hasn't driven deep when he,
In midstroke, stands, aghast, and like
A bristling boar entangled in the hunter's net
Rages to be free, and by his struggling
Tightens more and more his bonds,
And rages more and more in vain,
So Agamemnon struggles to throw off
His binding net, but tightens it,
And though his body's more and more enmeshed,
It lunges blindly at his murderers.
But Clytemnestra, maddened, grabs the two-edged axe,
And like the sacrificing priest who measures with his eye
The ox's neck before he strikes the blow,
She aims now here, now there—she has it! Done.
His partly cut-off head hangs by a slender thread.

Blood gushes out and down the headless trunk,
And nearby, severed, lie his groaning lips.

The murderers' pleasure's not yet done,
Aegisthus hacks and mangles
Agamemnon's lifeless corpse,
And Clytemnestra, savage, stabs and stabs.
Aegisthus answers to his kind—
He, after all, is brute Thyestes' son;
And Clytemnestra's close kin to her sister,
The one indifferent to the ruin of Troy.

Ah, see! The Sun, its day's work done,
Is shamed to run its normal way.
In horror, might again run backwards,
Like on the terrible day
When Atreus fed Thyestes his own sons.

ITALIAN RENAISSANCE

51.

POLINESTA BRAGS ABOUT THE TRICK THAT WILL TURN HER DISGUISED LOVER INTO HER HUSBAND (YC)

(1509) LUDOVICO ARIOSTO, *THE PRETENDERS*,
TR. LEON KATZ, ACT I, SC. 1

Intervening between the Roman comedies of Terence and Plautus and the comedies imitating them in the Italian Renaissance, are the tales of Boccaccio's *Decameron* and folk tales as salacious as his. Added to the classical repertory of young men raping respectable women who are or are to become their wives, or stealing slaves from procurers and having to hide or pay for them, or fooling and angering fathers about their sexual exploits, are new variations of these plots and novel schemes for illicit lovers joining one another in bed. These, and episodes similar in spirit, were incorporated into the new comedy. And added to classical comedy's restricted range of female roles (the young lady usually the center of desire, victimization, or both in the Roman plays is rarely actually seen on the stage) is a range of servants and bawds and respectable ladies and lascivious ladies and wives with manners and desires that run a gleeful race to the sinful bottom along with the young libertines and the old lechers. Even the sober intention among the playwrights to respect the rigidities of classical plot structure and the proprieties of verisimilitude is violated as often as observed, and the tone of their comedies hardly emulates the sobriety of Terence's. Characteristically, each character is after one thing and it's low: money or sex, sometimes revenge by way of money or sex, sometimes the game of terrifying fools who are after money or sex—and, most elevated of all—money and marriage, or marriage if it's the only avenue to sex. The untrussed morals of the Italian Renaissance are entirely reflected in its stage comedies.

Take Polinesta. The desirable heroine, generally passive and invisible in the old comedy, is here transformed into a woman as complicit as the lover himself in figuring out ways to meet in bed. This lover, Erostrato, is decidedly intent on marriage but during their enforced time of waiting, he and Polinesta have managed for the past two years to engage in nightly practice for that eventuality. Of course, when they are discovered, her father is overcome with shame, the atmosphere becomes sullenly virtuous and threatening for the lovers but as in all comedy, since the situation as imagined doesn't exist at all, but is itself, like some of the characters, in temporary disguise (the shameful impoverished lover is in fact a well-born, rich young man; the father who's the source of his wealth is discovered to approve of his marriage), there's really no obstacle to the satisfying comic ending and if the truth had been known in the first place, there never was.

POLINESTA

Ah, if only, you say, I had fallen in love with someone more respectable than Dulipo, more respectable than one of my father's servants! But who's to blame, Nurse? Who was it who poured into my ear what a fine, handsome fellow this Dulipo was, how he behaved so like a gentleman, how he loved me to distraction, until finally I fell in love with him myself? It was you! And why were you so anxious for him to win favor with me? Was it your compassion for him, or your greed? He paid you well, did he not, so well that you happily lit his way to my bed that first night, and now you're wondering how, my dear Nurse, I could have been so foolish as to let the affair go this far! It was your own doing! No, don't try to defend yourself, don't make excuses, or I'll mention things I'd much rather not bring up! But there's a secret even you don't know, Nurse dear—and that is—how all this mischief you brought about with your meddling has turned out to be nothing but great, good, and wonderful fortune. You didn't suspect, did you, that I never gave my heart to any Dulipo, or to any servant at all, but to someone much loftier than you can even imagine. That's all I'll tell you now; I won't say another word. I made a solemn promise not to tell.

No, no, I haven't changed my mind at all, its not that. Its just that—well, I would tell you, but only if you swear to absolute secrecy, that you won't give me away by the slightest sign that you know the truth. You see, Dulipo is not a servant at all, he's a Sicilian nobleman, and his real name is Erostrato, the son of one of the richest men in Italy. He came to Ferrara to study, but on the very day he arrived, he saw me on the Via Grande, and at once, he fell in love. Well! He was so infatuated that right from the start he threw away his books and his gown, and decided that he would have only one subject of study— me. And wise young man that he is, to have more access to his subject, he exchanged his clothes and his name with his valet Dulipo, and so Erostrato the scholar became Dulipo the servant, and he devotes himself exclusively to the study of the strategies of love, and his very first trial was to win a place in my father's household. And now Dulipo the servant, with his master's gown and books, is studying at the University to his immense profit and everybody's praise.

So its the real Dulipo, mind you, in disguise as Erostrato, who has asked my father for my hand in marriage, but have no fear, my dear Nurse. We're only pretending, so we can fool that horrible old Dottore who insists on wooing me—me!—to be his wife. Oh Lord, there he is! A perfect vision of a husband, no? Believe me, Nurse, I would rather bury myself for the rest of my days in a nunnery, than put up with that man as a husband for a single night.

52.

ALVIGIA MOANS IN DESPAIR OVER THE INJUSTICE OF HER CRIMINAL MISTRESS' SENTENCE OF DEATH (OC)

(1526) Pietro Aretino, *The Courtezan*, tr. Samuel Putnam, Act II

The Italian sixteenth century, writes one historian, is "in all probability the most riotously colorful and the most colorfully depraved epoch in civilized history." Aretino added considerably to the color of its depravity. He was called "the scourge of Princes" for earning enormous wealth and influence by blackmailing the wealthy and powerful, "playing them into submission with the power of his pen." His comedies broke with the academic tradition of Plautus and Terence. They were written without the weight of either tradition or illusion, but from the repertoire of his accurate knowledge of human lusts, weaknesses, and depravities—his stock in trade—and in the common language of the street, the marketplace, and the brothel.

Aretino left the plot for last. It generally waited until the last scene or so, when the play's initial situation was abruptly terminated. The rest of the play moved nowhere in plot but everywhere in satire. The characters spoke with baldness, with anguish, with glee, with venom—the dialogue taking for granted the seaminess of ordinary life.

A case in point is old Alvigia. She is brought into the play by way of its second plot. Parabolano, one of the Pope's stable of male favorites, is nevertheless violently in love with the married Livia. His groom, Rosso, out of malice, makes him believe she's in love with him as well, and prepares to bring him Alvigia, the procuress "who would corrupt chastity itself," to pretend that she's Livia's beloved nurse. But when they meet to plan, Alvigia is mourning her just-executed mistress, who, for a multitude of crimes, was burned at the stake. Alvigia wonders in her sorrow how such little crimes, some even done with good intentions, could have brought about such malicious punishment: poisoning an old man, drowning an unwanted baby, crippling a young lover. And she remembers gratefully the favors her mistress has willed to her—some useful for her trade, but some valuable in enhancing her battle against the ravages of oncoming age.

ALVIGIA

Oh, my mistress! My mistress! She is on fire. They've set her on fire and she's done nothing. It's only a drop of poison which she gave to her godfather out of love for her godmother, and this is the reason Rome is going to lose such a fine old lady. She threw a little baby girl into the river which a certain lady friend of hers had given birth to, as her habit is. She put some kind of beans on a stair and made a jealous lover break his neck. And so she left me heir to all she has. And what did she leave me? Alembics for distilling herbs grown in the light of the new moon, waters for washing away freckles, ointments for removing spots from the face, an ampula of lover's tears, oil for reviving...I don't want to tell you. Flesh...on the...you understand. Yes. She left me bands for my breasts, which are pendulous, she left me an electuary against pregnancy and childbed; she left me a flask of maiden's wine, which is good for mothers on fast days and is especially good for marchionesses. She left me the rope of one who was wrongly hanged, powder for killing jealous men, incantations for producing madness, prayers for producing sleep and recipes for rejuvenation. She left me also a spirit confined—in a thunder-mug.

What do you mean, ha, ha, big stupid? In a thunder-mug, I tell you, and it is a familiar spirit that knows how to find stolen property and tells you whether your lady friend loves you or not. It is called Il Folletto; and she left me an unguent which carries me above wind and water to the walnut tree of Benevento.

I am in despair, my heart is breaking; it is not a thousand years ago that she was drinking six kinds of wine at the Pavone, always from the decanter and without a thought of any reputation in the world. There never was an old lady who was so healthy an eater and so light a worker. At the butcher's, at the delicatessen keeper's, at the baker's, at the stove, at the fair, at the Ponte Santa Maria, at the Ponte Quattro Capre and at the Ponte Sisto, folks always, always stopped to talk to her, and she was regarded as a Solomon, a Sybil, and a Chronicle by constables, innkeepers, porters, cooks, friars and all the world; and she would stalk like a dragon among the gallows, cutting out the eyes of hanged men, and like a female paladin through the cemeteries, tearing off the claws of the dead on some fine midnight.

And what a conscience was hers! On the eve of Pentecost she would not eat meat. On Christmas eve she fasted on bread and wine, and in Lent, beyond a few fresh eggs, she led the life of a lady hermit. If they had plugged up her ears and made a sign on her forehead, she might have gone on living. So she might, and she might now be wearing the mitre which she wore three years ago on the day of St. Peter Martyr; and she would just as soon ride on the ass as on the cart; and she was not at all concerned with the paintings on the mitre, so the neighbours could not say she did it out of vain glory.

Poor woman, she was the sworn sister of the priests of good wine, God knows. That was another sin of hers. And so it was, the poor woman.

ALEMBICS: vessels, retorts. ampula: a vessel for holding consecrated wine or oil. ELECTUARY: medicine composed of a powder mixed with syrup or honey. THUNDER-MUG: bedside container for defecation. SYBIL: prophetess. PALADIN: heroic champion. MITRE: bishop's official headdress.

53.

TOGNA VILLIFIES HER LAZY, DRUNKEN, HATEFUL HUSBAND (OC)

(1526) PIETRO ARETINO, *THE COURTEZAN*, TR. SAMUEL PUTNAM, ACT V

[Continues No. 52, above] To satisfy the lover's longing and still leave Livia—who has no knowledge of and no part in this plot—out of Parabolano's bed, Alvigia suggests a friend who might substitute in the dark: Togna. Her credentials are impeccable. "The wife of Arcolano the baker," Alvigia explains, "a good sort and a great crony of mine. I will have her come to the house, and we will sneak her in in the dark."

Togna, invited into the scheme, is ready for it. But her husband, at the sight of Alvigia, is suspicious and, pretending to be coming out of the tavern drunk, is himself ready to follow his wife and spy unsuspected. But the occasion of his apparent drunkenness awakens Togna's disgust with marriage, with husband, with her lot, giving Aretino occasion to offer up a marital vignette.

TOGNA

I want to see if that old drunkard has come back yet. I hope he falls and breaks a leg. It's too bad the devil hasn't sense enough to take him when he's snoring away in the tavern. Do I see him coming there? I hope who ever gave me such a husband dies a terrible death. I ought to give him something, and I wouldn't be the first wife who did such a thing as that. There's the big pig now. He looks fresh enough. He's got three sheets in the wind already.

(Arcolano comes in, pretending to be drunk.)

Who bought you the wine you've been drinking? I don't know why I don't choke you. Oh God, why wasn't I born a man? It is a great misfortune to be born a woman, and after all, what are we women good for? To cook, to sew, and to stay locked up in the house all year, and for what? To be beaten and insulted every day, and by whom? By a big drunkard and a lazy dolt like this old sport of mine. Oh poor me, what a lot is ours! If your man is a gambler and loses, it is you who are out of luck; if he has no money, it falls on you; if wine takes him off his pegs, it is you who bear the blame; and they are so jealous they think every fly is making or talking love. And if it wasn't that we have brains enough to make sport of them, we might as well go hang ourselves. It is a great sin that the preacher doesn't put in a word for us with the Lord, for it is not right that one like me should go to hell simply for having a husband like the one God has given me. And if the confessor gives me a penance for what I am doing, I hope I die if I don't say to him, for once: "Would you give a penance to a poor unfortunate woman who has for a husband a brute, a gambler, a tavern-hound, a jealous fool and a dog of a gardener?" But Alvigia must be expecting me. I must go find her.

54.

LENA MAKES THOROUGH ARRANGEMENTS FOR GETTING A MAID OUT OF THE HOUSE, THE YOUNG MAN OUT OF A BARREL, AND HIS MONEY IN HER HANDS BEFORE HE BEDS HER CHARGE, LICINIA (OC)

(1528) LUDOVICO ARIOSTO, *LENA*, TR. LEON KATZ, ACT IV, SC. 8–9

Unlike Aretino [see No. 52 and No. 53, above], Ariosto is awash in plot, following more conscientiously in the path of classical comedy. But he adds to it bits of a slightly different sort of comedy, an extended gallery of brightly imagined, witty, and low tricks out of Boccaccio. He shows the stupid duped by the clever, and the avaricious by the more avaricious. In *Lena,* there's the lavishly exploited trick of the lover hiding in a barrel until the obstacle males are out of the way. But the crux of the joke lies in the demonstration of how much it doesn't work, how it teeters constantly on the edge of disaster. Not only money, but time is of the essence; not only time, but that devil: Chance.

It devolves on Lena, the bawd, to unscramble the tangle of developments—which by Act IV, have left Flavio, the young man, not too remote from his objective. He's been hidden in the barrel, pitched and rolled about, almost tossed out of it, and still not able to get to Licinia's bed. Now with a quick maneuver, Lena must get the maid Menica out of the house before she can get Flavio out of the barrel. As for herself, she must also get the fee out of Flavio with no further shilly-shallying, before he can finally enjoy his sport with Licinia. The barrel has been tossed from one house to another, Lena has overcome one obstacle already (getting rid of Flavio's father Fazio), and now, breathless and tense, she's preparing her final moves.

Lena

At least one bit of good luck—Fazio is out of the house. If he hadn't decided to go out, we'd never have gotten Flavio out of the barrel today. While I was watching it being rolled into the house with Flavio inside, I thought my heart would stop, I was so frightened. If he'd made the slightest move, or sneezed, or coughed, or even sighed, we would have been lost. Thank God that's over. Now, Lena, let's make sure there are no more obstacles. Let's just get him out of there without being seen. I'll send Corbolo to get some clothes to cover him so he'll be decent, and—Ah, but first! I have to get the servant out of Fazio's house, so *she* doesn't spot him crawling out.

(Going to Fazio's front door and calling)
Menica!...Menica!....She's deaf.—Licinia!...Ah, good! Tell Menica to put on her veil and come out here, I want to talk to her....Menica, you heard, come here!

(Menica goes to her.)
Menica darling, there's a favor I want from you, and if you do it, I'll be yours forever. I want you to go now—it's all right, don't worry, supper will be ready, trust me, I'll put the pot on the fire—go to the church, the Santa Maria degli Angeli, and when you're there, facing it, go to the left between the Mosti orchard and the monastery, stay on the right, and when you come to a narrow path, turn to the left, and you'll be at a place called—what's its name?—Marisol. Don't waste a minute, Menica, hurry! ...Ah! yes, what to do there—yes, ask where the wife of Pasquino lives, she's on the third floor on the right, I think. She's the one who teaches the girls to read, her name is Dorotea. Find her, and tell her that Lena sent you, she wants to borrow the spindles you use for silk, she needs them in a hurry. So go, go, Menica, and when you get back, I'll give you a great big length of cloth for a bonnet. And don't worry about the dinner. The meat's washed and ready to be put in the pot.

(Menica leaves.)
The meat's ready all right, but it won't get into the pot until he gives me twenty-five florins. I know all about these hot young lovers. The heat lasts as long as they're yearning, and while they're still yearning and panting, they'd give you their whole fortune and the blood out of their veins. But once they get it, water gets poured over the blaze. The fire's out, and they don't give you the tiniest part of what they swore would be yours. So I'd better get in there, and put a stop to any quick ideas he and the girl may be getting.

(Corbolo comes out.)

Corbolo! Hurry up, and get him some clothes so we can get him out of the house while there's still time! And don't think he'll be getting what he's after until he pays me the twenty-five florins. Till he does, trust me, I'll be watching.

55.

LENA EXECRATES HER HUSBAND FOR MAKING HER A WHORE (oc)

(1528) Ludovico Ariosto, *Lena*, tr. Leon Katz, Act V, Sc. 11

[Continues No. 54, above] Lena's complaint that her lazy husband has given her no choice but to become a whore is compounded by his objection to her stooping so low. Her rage is clear, as is her logic in defending not only her whoredom, but her more recent advance to the status of procuress. She speaks the same justification as does Vittoria in Bruno's *Il Candelaio* [see No. 58, below], on the strategic use of time for a beautiful whore before time runs out. But whereas Vittoria looks at the facts with such pragmatic equanimity, Lena looks at them with bitterness. Once she is forced into her decision, Lena is left with no happy feeling of the consolations of pragmatic good sense, but with contempt from the very man by whom that contempt was most fully earned. There's a moral point of order raised here that is normally suppressed in these comedies, but calculatedly, it goes nowhere. Through a maze of recriminations and blunders, the lovers are finally connected and married off; Lena's private arrangement as the mistress of Flavio's father, Fazio, is happily reconfirmed; and these sufficiently satisfactory endings erase the other question— which is, of course, the moral question involved in Lena's continuing to whore in preparation for her old age.

LENA

And who made me a whore? I became a whore to satisfy your greed. You would have died of hunger if I hadn't labored under a hundred men like a cart-horse to keep you fed. And now after I've worked myself sick like that for you, you complain, you pig, that your wife is a whore? Modest! You want your wife to be more discreet, more modest. Let me tell you about modesty, you old cuckold. If I had slept with all the men you urged on me, I'd have been the busiest prostitute in Ferrara, and better known for being an available whore than all the tarts in the Gambaro. And when you began to worry that the front door was getting overused, you made the disgusting suggestion, you remember? that I keep the back door open too.

And now, worse yet, I'm a procuress. And you're ashamed. Well, well. Why am I stooping now so much lower than whore? Because if I could stay young forever, I could go on keeping you in liquor and food the same way I do now. But I like the way the ants do. They prepare for the winter, and I'm preparing for old age. To stay alive, an old woman has to learn how to earn her living long in advance, because when she's old, she doesn't have time to start all over again from the beginning. And what trade would be easier for me to learn now, and more profitable for me when I'm old? It would be stupid for me to wait until it's too late to begin training. Stupid.

56.

THE MAID GIVES EMILIA'S MOTHER SOUND ADVICE ON TRYING OUT HUSBANDS IN ADVANCE (YC)

(1529) LUDOVICO ARIOSTO, THE NECROMANCER, TR. LEON KATZ, ACT II, SC. 4

Machiavelli was not alone in his unabashed pragmatic amorality, which he spelled out in *The Prince* for ruler's use in the political world, and in his play *Mandragola* [see in Men's volumes "Callimaco Reports on His Perfect Night With Lucrezia" and "Fra Timoteo Persuades Lucrezia That It Is Pious to Commit Adultery"] applied with equal consistency to getting ahead in the private world. Like him, the other comic playwrights of the Italian sixteenth century played the game of amoral paradox, testing with straight faces the practical against the moral, and discovering with Machiavellian consistency that the practical uncontaminated by irrelevant strictures of virtue had all the advantages. In a way, more than in their hunt for ingenious variations on farcical plots, the Italian Renaissance playwrights touched the magic core of true comedy more accurately when they were mining this mock-speculative vein. Testing the abandoned freedom that comes from removing uptight stricture is one of comedy's more authentic practices, and creating a world in which conduct pays no mind to either logic or received values, produces the temporary friendliness of upside-down truth. Remarkably, pushing that subversive angle of vision into the real world outside of comedy has always, in every society, lost its luster, produced something like terror, and following that, with the urgings of moral pretense, something like disgust.

The Maid's advice in this speech, outside the context of comedy, makes her an authentic candidate for that disgust; but while still in the play, she's funny. And, of course, pragmatic. Emilia, married to the personable, rich, and amenable Cintio, is suffering marital misfortune: after fifteen days of wedlock, she's "as much of a virgin as she was before the wedding." Her husband's "lance," she's discovered, is "blunt and feeble." Her mother has just been inside the house commiserating with her; coming out, the mother is greeted by her maid and her maid's pertinent advice.

MAID

Really, madam, no one should think of taking on a husband until they've tried him out. Oh, no, believe me. You wouldn't buy the cheapest spindle in a shop until you've stroked it and turned it around in your hand, and held it up to the light, and inspected it inside and out. And as to husbands, who are a lot more important than spindles, do you think it's enough to look them over a couple of times, and sometimes not even get to see them in a strong light before you say yes? I must tell you, I had a neighbor once, a very smart woman, who took a young man to bed every night for more than a year, and tried him out in every conceivable way, before she decided he was well qualified to be a husband for her daughter. I should—what?—be ashamed of myself? Why should I be ashamed of telling you the truth? If you had done this with Cintio, you wouldn't be in this situation now. What better advice can I give you? You have all the proof you need, since your daughter has had the trial of him all this time. Tell him to go, and take his bad luck with him, and you'll find another husband for Emilia. But do it my way. If you don't care to do it yourself, I have a better suggestion. Let me try him out. I'll be able to tell easily whether he'll be enough of a man for your daughter Emilia.

57.

THE NURSE DESCRIBES THE PARADISE OF MARRIAGE TO THE RELUCTANT STABLEMASTER (OC)

(CA. 1533) PIETRO ARETINO, *THE STABLEMASTER*, TR. GEORGE BULL, ACT I

Papal sodomy was dealt with in euphemisms; the laity's was dealt with more bluntly. Aretino, who cared little for euphemism, centered an entire comedy on a layman's—a stablemaster's—squirming embarrassment under the lash of his duke's humor, who thought up a joke to terrify him. The Duke spreads the news that he's blessing his stablemaster with a wife, and that he's to prepare for his imminent wedding. The Stablemaster has many objections, the chief of which is that he's happy with boys; but the persistence of the rumor makes him tremble. He seeks advice, and advice also comes unbidden. Of the unbidden advisers, his old Nurse, longing as she does, to see her old charge wreathed in happiness, is preeminent. And forthright. She comes straight to the point: give up the boys, and paradise waits.

Her description of the paradise of marriage will be countered later by another advisor who will describe it as hell, and the Stablemaster, resigning himself to the truth of the rumor, is plunged into the hell of of helplessness, awaiting his fate. But the picture his nurse paints to woo him to the pleasures of marriage leaves him cold. And so he remains, not enticed and very much terrified, until the joke unravels: the "bride" he's supposedly forced to marry is the duke's page, Carlo. The joke is over; the Stablemaster is relieved.

For all the sweetness and piety oozing from the Nurse's encomium to marriage, Aretino is hardly urging a defense of it: such a recommendation, at this moment in comedy's history, was understood to be one of the play's more fantastic flights of fancy.

Nurse

Did you crucify Christ? No, but you've done something worse.
You know just what I mean. So now take my advice and marry
her, my son, stop going around with young men and do
something to restore your good name. Grow up and start a
family of your own....and you'll be properly known and
respected by everyone imaginable. You poor little fellow, do
you know what happens when you take a wife? You go to
paradise when you take a wife. Now please listen to me, and
then you can make up your own mind what to do.

This is why getting married is like going to paradise. You
arrive home, and your good wife comes to meet you all
smiling at the top of the stairs. She gives you a good, heartfelt
welcome, helps you off with your coat, and then embraces you
joyfully. As you're all sweaty, she wipes you dry with some
towels which are so soft and snowy that you are soon glowing
comfortably all over. Then having put the wine to cool and
laid the table, and fanned you for a while, she gets you to have
a pee.

What are you laughing at, you great oaf! Once you've had a
pee she sits you down to supper, and when you're nicely
relaxed she whets your appetite with some tasty sauces and tit-
bits that would make your mouth water even in the grave. And
while you're eating in the most agreeable way she keeps
putting in front of you now one dish and now another,
offering you all kinds of tasty morsels and saying: "Eat this
and now this, and if you love me try a little more for my sake."
And all her words are so honeyed and sugared that they
transport you not only to paradise but thousands and
thousands of miles beyond.

After supper, she calls her husband to bed, after he has
swallowed his meal, and before he stretches out she washes his
feet thoroughly in water boiled in bay leaves, sage and
rosemary. As soon as she has trimmed his nails, and cleaned
and dried him very nicely, she helps him to get into bed. Then
she clears the table and tidies the room and after saying her
prayers, she gets in beside him, all affectionately. Next she
embraces her beloved husband, kissing him again and again,
and she says to him: "My heart, my soul, dear hope, my own
flesh and blood, let me be your own little girl, your jewel, your
daughter." And if a man's treated like that, isn't he truly in
paradise?

And what's the point of all these caresses? The point of them all is to make sure that babies are started in a holy and proper way. Anyway, in the morning, your busy wife brings you fresh eggs, and your white shirt, and while she helps you to dress, talking to you sweetly and kissing you, she fusses around you so lovingly that you have the same consolation from her as you would from the angels in paradise.

Imagine now that it's winter time and you have come home wet through, covered in snow and frozen stiff. Your clever wife changes your clothes, thaws you out in no time with a good fire, and as soon as you're warm again, you find the dinner ready. Her hot soup and the other nice things to eat revive you completely. If you happen to be worried about something, she acts very gently and says: "What's the matter? What are you thinking about? Don't upset yourself. God will help us and look after us." So all your sadness turns to joy. And then your babies start to arrive—the little darlings, the little imps! Oh God, what comfort, what sweet tenderness a father feels when his little boy touches his face and his breast with those fond little hands, calling him daddy, my daddy, dear daddy! I've seen men longer in the tooth than you overcome by a don't know what kind of emotion at the sound of that "daddy." But when shall I be able to see you acting like that?

58.

VITTORIA RUMINATES ON THE IMPORTANT AND THE UNIMPORTANT IN A POTENTIAL HUSBAND (YC)

(CA. 1581) GIORDANO BRUNO, *IL CANDELAIO*,
TR. JOHN R. HALE, ACT II, SC. 3

Vittoria, a courtesan professionally known as Porzia, has inflamed Bonifacio—he loves her to distraction. He, the "candle maker" or "bearer," of the title, is the prime of the three prime fools whose undoing makes up the play's three interlocked main plots. He's done everything to win the affection of his "traitress"; she's shown him nothing, but contempt. He is, after all, old, stupid, a miser—in no way love's dream. But now, when her bawd Lucia brings a letter and sonnet from the palpitating man, Vittoria—following the basic pragmatic principles of all the characters of Italian Renaissance comedy who are not bereft of sense—reconsiders. There's a direct connection between her reflections on the strategic use of time for a beautiful whore before time wears out, and the equally cynical reflections of Brecht's whore in *Mahagonny*, whose reflections on the same theme are identical, with the slight difference that Brecht's whore learned this wisdom from her mother; Vittoria, on her own, looks facts in the face.

VITTORIA

Love is painted as a young boy, for two reasons: because he doesn't suit old men, and because he turns weak-willed and fickle men into children. But it's not in either of these ways that love has got at him, because he's no real taste for this sort of sport, and as for his mind, well, no one can take away what's not there. But I'm less concerned with him than with my own affairs. Just like the wise and the foolish virgins, there are among us horses of a different color, foolish ones who love the game for its own sake and don't give a thought to the old age which follows so swiftly that they don't see or even suspect it till all their friends have taken to their heels. When faces wrinkle, purses shut. They are left their own misery to hug, while their lovers nod and pass by on the other side. So we must resolve on using our time well. To linger is to lose. I may wait for time, but time is not going to wait for me. We must make use of others while others still have need of us. Take the beast while it is after you, not when it turns and runs; and if you can't hold onto a bird in a cage, you're not likely to catch one in the air. As for him, though in fact he's got neither a good brain nor a good figure, he's got a handsome purse: the first is his own loss; the second can't hurt me; it's the third I must concentrate on. Wise men are for fools, fools for wise men; if everyone was a lord, there'd be no lords at all, so if every man was as wise as the next, there'd be no sages, and if everyone was foolish, there'd be no madmen. The world is very well as it is. But now, Porzia, to business. It's the charming young thing that must think carefully about old age, or winter will strike in the middle of the harvest. So, how can we pluck the feathers from this bird?

59.

VITTORIA FINDS NOTHING ATTRACTIVE
ABOUT LOVE WITHOUT MONEY (YC)

(CA. 1581) GIORDANO BRUNO, *IL CANDELAIO*,
TR. JOHN R. HALE, ACT IV, SC. 1

[See No. 58, above] A plot's already afoot; Bonifacio is doomed.
Vittoria already has sufficient evidence that no cash will come from
Bonifacio, and so her plan for this night is: his wife will be disguised
as herself—Vittoria—and his assignation will be with her, in the
dark, until she brings unwelcome light. But Vittoria's further reflections on her problem of "loving" old miser Bonifacio are occasioned
not only by his imminent visit, but by her discovery that he's been
trafficking with a "magician" (naturally, a fraud who is duping
Bonifacio with vigor) who's to cast a spell over Vittoria so that she
will actually love him. The thought gives her pause—but only for a
moment. Her answer to the question: can she really be so overtaken
by the spirits of darkness? Is quickly answered: "if [Bonifacio] were
the very god of love," but at the same time either poor or miserly, that
power ends. "Poor, stingy, that's a vile and shameful epithet." But
then, developing her theme, it takes on larger meaning. We honor the
great and pray to the sacred images (for a slew of virtuous benefits
somewhere in the air, like defending the oppressed and succoring the
weak), but we live with and think of living men, "those who piss and
crap," and the benefits to be derived from them, she reasons, have to
be cash down. The respect we have for both the mighty and the men
we live with amounts to one and the same thing: the trappings of the
great and the sacred have to show the splendors of wealth, and the living men have to have it. She's ready, then, for Bonifacio's visit, ready
to show him the effects of his magician's spell: but without money in
hand, none.

So far has Bruno elevated the stereotype of the courtesan in
Vittoria that it is not her values, but the weight of the considerations
behind those values that become the measure of her character. As in
great comic writers as in Shaw, for instance—the quality, not merely
the definition, of the "character" is essentially in the mind that moves
the character. Folly in Bruno's play loves what Vittoria loves—
Bonifacio is miserliness personified—but his grasp for money is

mindless appetite; hers is reason's persuasion. Not to recognize the difference, and to think of Vittoria's motive as mere motive, is to miss an essential nuance of great comedy.

Vittoria

To wait, and wait in vain is a sort of death. If we wait too long, we shall have lost our chance. I don't know if there will be another occasion so fit for this creature to reap what his love deserves. Just as I thought his infatuation would help me to a dowry, I heard that he was trying to cast a spell on me, with a wax image. Could it really happen that the spirits of darkness, working with those of air and water, could make me love someone who isn't lovable in himself? If he were the very god of love, but was poor, or miserly, which comes to the same thing, then he's a cold fish and the world can freeze with him. Yes, surely—poor, stingy: that's a vile and shameful epithet; it can make beauty look ugly, nobility squalid, wisdom petty, and vitality impotent. Who do we respect more than kings, monarchs, emperors? And even these, if they are poor, if they haven't got money in their pockets, are like images stripped after their festival day; no one cares tuppence for them. Holy images and men: it's just the same; we worship statues and paintings, we honor holy names, but we think of men, living men. We live in terms of those who piss and crap, though we direct our prayers and requests to pictures and statues, for it's these that reward the virtuous, exalt the humble, defend the oppressed, free the imprisoned, protect their votaries, strengthen the weak. The king, the emperor; unless he is made into a statue, is nothing. What then of Bonifacio, who wants, as if he was the only man in the world, to be loved for his pretty eyes? How far can folly go? This evening he is looking forward to being happy. And this evening I'm looking forward to him seeing the effect of his spell. But he still hasn't come, this bogey who tries and tries—Ah, but there you are!

ELIZABETHAN
AND JACOBEAN

60.

ZENOCRATE IS TORN BETWEEN
HER LOVE FOR TAMBURLAINE
AND HER HORROR OF HIS
WARRIOR'S SAVAGERY (YT)

(1590) CHRISTOPHER MARLOWE, *TAMBURLAINE, PART ONE*, ACT V, SC. 1

Zenocrate is not so much a character as an emblem of the feminine that populates Heroic Drama from Marlowe's time on. She is essentially that which loves the glory of the battlefield hero, the hero whose essential worth is defined, as Tamburlaine puts it, as "the honor that consists in shedding blood." As person, then, she is an anomaly; as a defining factor in the fictional Heroic code, she is indispensable. For she is Beauty, just as he is Virtue, and the two have so much predicated affinity toward one another that no notice is ever taken of the least psychological nuance in their love. They love.

That Virtue (i.e., Italian *virtu,* or martial valor, prowess) genuflects to Beauty is a given in the Heroic Play tradition, but it does so with qualifications. Male Honor—the code of the battlefield—takes precedence over devotion to Beauty; and when it does not, the hero will accuse himself, as Tamburlaine does after a moment of "unseemly" rapture over "beauty's worthiness," of betraying "my sex,/My discipline of arms and chivalry,/My nature and the terror of my name,/To harbor thoughts effeminate and faint!" No such irresolution can enter into Beauty's devotion: her genuflection is unqualified, her rapturous approval is for the totality of what male "glory" entails— Tamburlaine's battlefield savagery, for example, his ringing brag, his inhuman abuse of victims.

But there can be a limit, as there is for Zenocrate and for many other static Beauties in Heroic Plays, and that limit is reached at a peculiarly threatening moment when either their dormant and half-forgotten older loyalties or dormant humanity is outraged. Zenocrate's moment comes when Tamburlaine attacks her native city, Damascus, the center of her father the Soldan of Egypt's domain. She has already extracted a promise from Tamburlaine before the attack that her father, if not his city, will be unharmed, and she, grateful for his concession, has been reassured. But in Act V, she runs onstage after having witnessed the horror of the storming of the city itself, the dying wounded, the severed limbs lying about, and most affectingly, the innocent young maidens pitted on the spears of Tamburlaine's horsemen. And then, just as horrible, the spectacle of the two royal captives who, out of the misery of their plight, have beaten out their brains against the cage in which Tamburlaine had kept them prisoners.

The terrified evocation of her quandary between shame and horror at her country's plight ("a thousand sorrows to my martyr'd soul") and her unblemished loyalty to its conqueror—the one moment, characteristically, when the Heroic Play's Beauty rises to the semblance of humanity—is in fact the playwright's test: does she withstand the intrusion of human feeling on her votary-like devotion as well as male Virtue withstands the intrusion of the bliss of Beauty on his honor?

She does, and quickly. In a moment, Tamburlaine and her captured father arrive, are swiftly reconciled, and Zenocrate is offered both marriage and the crown of Queen of Persia. Quandary altogether removed, she expresses her contentment. "Else," she concedes, "should I forget myself, my lord." (For further discussion of Tamburlaine, see in Men's volumes Tamburlaine's monologues.)

ZENOCRATE

Wretched Zenocrate, that liv'st to see
Damascus walls dy'd with Egyptian blood,
Thy father's subjects and thy countrymen;
The streets strowed with disseevered joints of men,
And wounded bodies gasping yet for life;
But most accurs'd, to see the sun-bright troop
Of heavenly virgins and unspotted maids,
Whose looks might make the angry god of arms
To break his sword and mildly treat of love,
On horsemen's lances to be hoisted up,
And guiltlessly endure a cruel death.
For every fell and stout Tartarian steed,

That stamp'd on others with their thundering hoofs,
When all their riders charg'd their quivering spears,
Began to check the ground and rein themselves,
Gazing upon the beauty of their looks.
Ah, Tamburlaine, wert thou the cause of this,
That term'st Zenocrate thy dearest love?
Whose lives were dearer to Zenocrate
Than her own life, or aught save thine own love.
But see, another bloody spectacle!
Ah, wretched eyes, the enemies of my heart,
How are ye glutted with these grievous objects,
And tell my soul more tales of bleeding ruth!. . .
Earth, cast up fountains from thy entrails,
And wet thy cheeks for their untimely deaths!
Shake with their weight in sign of fear and grief!
Blush Heaven, that gave them honour at their birth
And let them die a death so barbarous.
Those that are proud of fickle empery
And place their chiefest good in earthly pomp,
Behold the Turk and his great Emperess.
Ah, Tamburlaine my love, sweet Tamburlaine,
That fights for sceptres and for slippery crowns,
Behold the Turk and his great Emperess.
Thou that in conduct of thy happy stars
Sleep'st every night with conquest on thy brows,
And yet would'st shun the wavering turns of war,
In fear and feeling of the like distress,
Behold the Turk and his great Emperess.
Ah, mighty Jove and holy Mahomet,
Pardon my love, O pardon his contempt
Of earthly fortune and respect of pity;
And let not conquest ruthlessly pursu'd
Be equally against his life incens'd
In this great Turk and hapless Emperess.
And pardon me that was not mov'd with ruth
To see them live so long in misery!
Ah, what may chance to thee, Zenocrate?

EMPERY: the status, dignity or dominion of an emperor. RUTH: pity. STROWED:
strewed. TARTARIAN STEED: Tartars were a Mongolian tribe who conquered Central
Asia.

61.

ISABELLA, GRIEVING OVER HER SON'S MURDER, TAKES HER OWN LIFE (OT)

(CA. 1588) THOMAS KYD, *THE SPANISH TRAGEDY*, ACT IV, SC. 2

[For further notes on *The Spanish Tragedy*, see in Men's volumes the monologues of Hieronymo.] Horatio, Isabella's son, was murdered by the two princes who were his rivals for the love of Bel-Imperia. His father, Hieronymo, at the sight of his son hanging from a tree in his garden, runs mad. Although he yearns for revenge, he has yet found no way to execute it, given the power of his adversaries. His wife, Isabella, now follows his agonizing course. More helpless than her husband to find justice for her son's murder, she, mad, rushes into the garden with its fatal tree, and in her distraction, she rends it, tearing off its branches, and shredding their remains. But even more power- ful than her physical act is the rage of her malediction against the cursed tree and its garden-plot, in which her rhetoric rises to the scale of Seneca's impassioned tirades, which Kyd is in fact emulating. Her son's ghost rises in her vision "soliciting with his wounds" for revenge, and she, like Hieronymo himself, condemns her husband's "negligence" in pursuing the deaths of the murderers. "None but I bestir me—to no end!" and in her violent frustration, she condemns herself (her womb) and the now rent and barren tree. And in "sorrow and despair," she stabs herself to death.

Mad? Yes, but not as Hieronymo is mad. Isabella's rage is at the edge of reason, but doesn't overreach it. Her madness, in fact, is emo- tional clarity itself—emotion at the pitch, but not the victim, of sheer frenzy.

(Enter Isabella with a weapon.)

ISABELLA

Tell me no more!—O monstrous homicides!
Since neither piety nor pity moves the king to justice or compassion,
I will revenge myself upon this place,
Where thus they murdered my beloved son.

(She cuts down the arbor.)

Down with these branches and these loathsome boughs
Of this unfortunate and fatal pine!
Down with them, Isabella; rent them up,
And burn the roots from whence the rest is sprung!
I will not leave a root, a stalk, a tree,
A bough, a branch, a blossom, nor a leaf,
No, not an herb within this garden-plot,—
Accursed complot of my misery!
Fruitless forever may this garden be,
Barren the earth, and blissless whosoever
Imagines not to keep it unmanur'd!
An eastern wind, commix'd with noisome airs,
Shall blast the plants and the young saplings;
The earth with serpents shall be pestered,
And passengers, for fear to be infect,
Shall stand aloof, and, looking at it, tell:
"There, murdered, died the son of Isabel."
Ay, here he died, and here I him embrace:
See, where his ghost solicits with his wounds
Reverie on her that should revenge his death.
Hieronymo, make haste to see thy son;
For sorrow and despair hath cited me
To hear Horatio plead with Rhadamanth.
Make haste, Hieronymo, to hold excus'd
Thy negligence in pursuit of their deaths
Whose hateful wrath bereav'd him of his breath.
Ah, nay, thou dost delay their deaths,
Forgives the murderers of thy noble son,
And none but I bestir me—to no end!
And as I curse this tree from further fruit,
So shall my womb be cursed for his sake;
And with this weapon will I wound the breast,
The hapless breast that gave Horatio suck.

(She stabs herself.)

RENT: tore. COMPLOT: conspiracy. COMMIX'D: mixed. RHADAMANTH: judge of the dead in the underworld, praised in life for his justice and wisdom. BEREAV'D: deprived.

62.

MARGARET, BLAMING HERSELF, PLEADS WITH PRINCE EDWARD TO SPARE LACY (YC)

(CA. 1589) ROBERT GREENE, *FRIAR BACON AND FRIAR BUNGAY*, SC. 8

Margaret, the fair country maid of Fressingfield, has sufficiently attracted the hunter "in green" (who happens to be Edward, Prince of Wales) to cause him to direct one of his men, Lacy, the Earl of Lincoln, to woo her for him. Signal mistake. The proxy wooer and the wooed quickly fall in love, and in no time, they stand before Friar Bungay ready for marriage vows. It's white magic that permits Friar Bacon to sit in Oxford with the Prince, and display for him the imminent wedding ceremony in Fressingfield. The Prince, outraged at Lacy's betrayal of his mission of trust, has the ceremony magically halted at long distance, and then storms into Fressingfield ready to execute his vassal Lacy.

Lacy, honorable vassal, is willing to accept the Prince's verdict with submission, but Margaret is not. She pleads that the fault is hers, that she invited Lacy's love. Both then plead their indissoluble bond; both are ready to die, if necessary, together. So impressed is the Prince by their devotion and love that he graciously forgives, renounces his interest in winning Margaret for his paramour, and turns to the more honorable thought of his imminent state marriage to the Princess Elinor.

The play denotes an important moment in early Elizabethan comedy for the definition of love, of the romantic, and of woman. The privilege of love is tested against the privilege of class: it has the authority to fend off, first, the omnipotence of royalty, and then the value to overleap the distance between the lesser, but still courtly nobility of Lacy and the farm-freshness of Margaret. What is the elixir that accomplishes these victories for Love's authority? The elixir is Margaret, that is, the woman. Unconvincing as this portrayal is in relation to Elizabethan social realities, it launches the career of Love in Elizabethan romantic comedy in this form and with this understanding: that woman, for all her required avowal of complete submission to the authority of husband, lover, father, brother, guardian, prince, and God, bears within her being—her external beauty and her soul's inner virtue—the awesome power of purification of male desire. Of the many variants in fiction of the concept and practice of love, that the English tradition opted in one of its strains for this version is a tribute to its determined secularization of an essentially religious notion, and its equally determined watering down of a counter-notion: the worship of woman as virgin in Mary the mother of God, together with the obeisance to woman as monarch in the walled garden of Love in the cult of the Court of Love. The fictive posture of the male in both fantasies is more or less the same—he is a votary on his knees—but the character of the woman is somewhat different in each. The romantic heroine in Elizabethan comedy partakes of both, is a combination of both. Note her characteristics. As a secular Virgin Mary ("secular" makes all the difference), she has a virginal purity that is assumed, and with which she is comfortably casual, and about which she doesn't fret. She is first recognized—as she is in her very first appearance in *Friar Bacon and Friar Bungay*—by that purity, as well as by her ease with it (her good-humored off-putting of Lacy's first attempts at seductive talk and her private recognition of his attractiveness to her—pleasurable but hardly felt as a threat.) As a watered-down version of the reigning Queen in the walled garden of the Court of Love's allegorical Bower of Bliss, she uses an inherent, not an overt, power of command—and here, we must look closely at its manifestation. Once the inherent, untrammeled force and quality of her power of love is felt by the male (by the knight who is worthy or, as the Italian sonneteers put it, by the lover of gentle heart), that force commands, it cows, it automatically demands and receives obeisance. It is the recognition of this authoritative sanctity in the farm girl that brings Prince Edward to surrender his own authority; and it is this same quality that bends Lacy to the lover's kneeling posture before that same farm girl.

But once lover's vows are exchanged, once the maiden professes her love for the man, their roles are instantaneously reversed. Vassal becomes divinity; divinity becomes Vassal. The woman, worshipped a moment ago, falls into an ecstasy of submission, knows pain only in her lover's frown or absence, knows life itself only in his smile. His faults, his waverings, his downright falsehoods merely challenge the strength of her faith and her devotion. The analogy is obvious: he, before her favor, is addressing a surrogate Virgin Mary; she, after submission, dons the harness of servitude to a surrogate Almighty.

But one must understand, too, that unlike the deadly fervor of these avowals and relations in French and Spanish concurrent fictions, the Elizabethan romantic heroine becomes increasingly at ease with these ardors, endures them more and more, partly as game and only partly as deadly fact. In English comedy, there's a gradual easing of the fervors of these roles. The Margarets of this play give place to the Rosalinds, Portias, and Beatrices, romantic ladies who are clear about how far these fraught ardors are merely a game and how much of the game, is really in earnest.

There's a forgivable contradiction in the portrait of Margaret as mere farm girl, and the same Margaret who can spout classical literary reference and hit notes of classical rhetoric as handily as the university wits who were the boon companions of the playwright Greene. We have to suppose that the ardor with which she pleads her cause and Lacy's before the Prince elevates cultural memory.

MARGARET

'T was I, my lord, not Lacy stept awry:
For oft he su'd and courted for yourself,
And still woo'd for the courtier all in green;
But I, whom fancy made but over-fond,
Pleaded myself with looks as if I lov'd;
I fed mine eye with gazing on his face,
And still bewitch'd lov'd Lacy with my looks;
My heart with sighs, mine eyes pleaded with tears,
My face held pity and content at once,
And more I could not cipher-out by signs,
But that I lov'd Lord Lacy with my heart.
Then, worthy Edward, measure with thy mind
If women's favours will not force men fall,
If beauty, and if darts of piercing love,
Is not of force to bury thoughts of friends.
Pardon, my lord: if Jove's great royalty
Sent me such presents as to Danae;
If Phoebus, tired in Latona's webs,
Come courting from the beauty of his lodge;
The dulcet tunes of frolic Mercury,—
Not all the wealth heaven's treasury affords
Should make me leave Lord Lacy or his love.
Brave Prince of Wales, honour'd for royal deeds,
'T were sin to stain fair Venus' courts with blood;
Love's conquests ends, my lord, in courtesy.
Spare Lacy, gentle Edward; let me die,
For so both you and he do cease your loves.
What hopes the prince to gain by Lacy's death?

Why, thinks King Henry's son that Margaret's love
Hangs in the uncertain balance of proud time?
That death shall make a discord of our thoughts?
No, stab the earl, and, 'fore the morning sun
Shall vaunt him thrice over the lofty east,
Margaret will meet her Lacy in the heavens.
And if thy mind be such as fame hath blaz'd,
Then, princely Edward, let us both abide
The fatal resolution of thy rage.
Banish thou fancy and embrace revenge,
And in one tomb knit both our carcasses,
Whose hearts were linked in one perfect love.

SUCH PRESENTS AS TO DANAE: Zeus (Jove) came to Danae as a shower of gold, and she conceived Perseus. PHOEBUS, TIRED IN LATONA'S WEBS...: even if Apollo (Phoebus) came courting down from the heavens wrapped in his mother's (Latona) garments. THE DULCET TUNES OF FROLIC MERCURY: Hermes (Mercury) was the trickster among gods. VENUS' COURTS: home of Venus (the goddess of love). DIS-CORD: division. blaz'd: proclaimed.

63.

ISABELLA, SPURNED BY KING EDWARD FOR GAVESTON, YEARNS TO WIN BACK HER HUSBAND'S LOVE (YT)

(1592) CHRISTOPHER MARLOWE, *EDWARD II*, ACT I, SC. 4

[Further on Gaveston and Edward: see their monologues in Men's volumes.] Remote from characters of mere literary convention like Zenocrate [see No. 60, above], Isabella is a character with an interior life and levels of expression and feeling that takes a long step toward the profoundly complex, articulate, and brilliantly forceful women in later Elizabethan and Jacobean tragedies, women who slip out of easy classification or, for that matter, easy comprehension. Superficially villainesses, they tend to be subjectively powerful egos that demand even more dramatic space than many of the male figures in the same tragedies.

King Edward, infatuated with his lover, Gaveston, openly mocks, and invites his lover to mock, his Queen's humiliation. On her knees, she appeals for redress. But Isabella, in these first words addressed to her lord and husband, already exhibits a doubleness of intent—not for the sake of cunning and duplicity, but for a practical and worthy purpose. The language of entreaty with which she addresses him is one thing; the silent language out of which that entreaty is born is altogether another. That language we hear after Edward is gone. The first, speaking of "the tears shed," the "sighing, breaking heart," the "dear lord," is code. Extrapolated from the artifices of literature, or from the artifices of ceremonial high sentence, it functions in the same way as does legal jargon in a court of law: behind the formality and conventionality of phrasing, judge and lawyers know what they're really talking about, and know what they're really saying. This is a strategy of language that reaches its height in Elizabethan and Jacobean tragedy, where the opacity of conventional words lets slip through for the knowing the real discourse, and for the unknowing, for whom nothing slips through, permanent ignorance.

Marlowe, in Isabella's speech, here and in the remainder of the scene, is only at the beginning of the writing of such "flexible" dialogue. After the coded message to her "dear lord" (which translated: "what I'm asking, husband, is my right") and Edward's blunt, insulting spurning of her, she abandons altogether the storybook language of her sighing heart and spits out privately the sentiment burning inside of her: I would rather have died on the journey from my native France to this miserable English marriage or been strangled by this king on our wedding night than endure this. Then, momentarily surrendering to abandon: I'll wail like a jealous Juno when Jupiter doted on his cup-boy Ganymede; but then, quickly catching herself: foolish response; use policy. Better to "speak him fair," and bring back Gaveston. But then, following *that* policy, nothing is gained. Frustrating quandary.

Guardedly, in the rest of the scene, she talks her way out of this quandary. While the angry lords are openly subscribing to the exile of Gaveston, Isabella, returning to the language of the faithful wife and queen, and urging fealty to their king, manages to persuade the disaffected Mortimer and the others to follow her scheme of pretending Gaveston's rescue from exile to the end of isolating him for assassination later. Between her coded language and her private, whispered conference with Mortimer, she is proof—if tapings of talk had then been possible—against the charge of plotting treason. In the same way, the language she subsequently uses with Mortimer is forever marked by queenly propriety, but, read accurately by him, invites their political and physical union.

ISABELLA

Wherein, my lord, have I deserv'd these words?
Witness the tears that Isabella sheds,
Witness this heart, that, sighing for thee, breaks,
How dear my lord is to poor Isabel.

(Exeunt Edward and Gaveston)
O miserable and distressed queen!
Would, when I left sweet France and was embark'd,
That charming Circes, walking on the waves,
Had chang'd my shape, or at the marriage-day
The cup of Hymen had been full of poison,
Or with those arms that twin'd about my neck
I had been stifled, and not liv'd to see
The king my lord thus to abandon me!
Like frantic Juno will I fill the earth
With ghastly murmur of my sighs and cries:
For never doted Jove on Ganymede
So much as he on cursed Gaveston.
But that will more exasperate his wrath,
I must entreat him. I must speak him fair,
And be a means to call home Gaveston.
And yet he'll ever dote on Gaveston;
And so am I for ever miserable.

CIRCES: witch goddess who changed Odysseus' followers into animals. HYMEN: Greek goddess of marriage.

64.

ABIGAIL, TO ESCAPE HER FATHER THE JEW OF MALTA'S VILLAINY, SEEKS CHRISTIAN REFUGE (YT)

(1592) CHRISTOPHER MARLOWE, *THE JEW OF MALTA*, ACT III, SC. 3

"As for myself," brags Barabas, the Jew of Malta, "I walk abroad o' nights/And kill sick people groaning under walls:/Sometimes I go about and poison wells." This is merely the beginning of the litany of his villainies. Among many more are his using his daughter Abigail, first, to recover his hidden wealth by inducing her to join the order of nuns which had taken over his house and, unknowingly, his treasure. To this task, she applies herself with filial devotion. Then, he instructs her to entrap her two Christian suitors by "show[ing] them favor separately," who were then moved to flights of mutual jealousy enough to kill each other. The murder of the one, Lodowick, the son of the Governor of Malta, was Barabas' stratagem for revenge against the governor; the murder of Mathias, whom Abigail truly loved, was gratuitous and cruelly indifferent to his daughter's desire.

Having merely once pretended to join the order of nuns, Abigail, now having suffered her father's unscrupulous cruelty, determines to convert in earnest. But her rebellion goes just so far: she will convert, but not betray the father's wickedness that is causing her own betrayal. Barabas, of course, is not so scrupulous. To punish her true conversion, he poisons the entire nunnery together with his daughter.

Characteristically, as with Jessica and Shylock, the purity of soul of the daughter bears no relation to the devilish soul of the father. In the fixed conventions of fiction well into the Nineteenth Century, virgin daughters of devils and second sons of lords—the poor and disinherited ones—tend to enjoy the same immunity from their forebears' evils.

ABIGAIL

Hard-hearted father, unkind Barabas!
Was this the pursuit of thy policy!
To make me show them favour severally,
That by my favour they should both be slain?
Admit thou lov'dst not Lodowick for his sire,
Yet Don Mathias ne'er offended thee:
But thou wert set upon extreme revenge,
Because the sire dispossess'd thee once,
And could'st not venge it, but upon his son,
Nor on his son, but by Mathias' means;
Nor on Mathias, but by murdering me.
But I perceive there is no love on earth,
Pity in Jews, nor piety in Turks.

(Enter Friar [Jacomo].)
Welcome, grave friar.

Know, holy sir, I am bold to solicit thee
To get me be admitted for a nun.
Till now were my thoughts frail and unconfirm'd,
And I was chain'd to follies of the world:
But now experience, purchased with grief,
Has made me see the difference of things.
My sinful soul, alas, hath pac'd too long
The fatal labyrinth of misbelief,
Far from the Sun that gives eternal life.
Who taught me this?
The abbess of the house,
Whose zealous admonition I embrace:
O, therefore, Jacomo, let me be one,
Although unworthy, of that sisterhood.
I'll change no more.
That was my father's fault.
Nay, pardon me. *[Aside.]*
O Barabas,
Though thou deservest hardly at my hands,
Yet never shall these lips bewray thy life.

THE SIRE DISPOSSESS'D THEE ONCE: Lodowick's father, the governor of Malta, impounded half of Barabas' wealth to help pay the tribute demanded by the Grand Seignior of Turkey. PIETY IN TURKS: Barabas' Muslim slave Ithimore, who shares his pleasure in villainy.

65.

ALICE ARDEN PLEADS WITH HER ACCOMPLICE AND LOVER NOT TO LOSE HIS TRUST IN HER (YT)

(CA. 1592) ANONYMOUS, *ARDEN OF FEVERSHAM*, ACT III, SC. 5

"This naked tragedy," the anonymous author calls his play, meaning one neither fashionably romantic nor classical nor historical, but a tragedy that reports the raw and gross truth of a sordid domestic murder, or, as the Elizabethans would say, of "a private matter." The freedom the play takes in wallowing in such "naked" truth has considerable implication and value for later Elizabethan and Jacobean tragedies, which can frequently bear to look at characters and their psychology without converting them into romantic fictions and without flinching.

Arden is a vicious, hypocritical landowner whose wife has fallen in love with Mosbie, a tailor. Arden, for the money to be got from it, he "winks at their filthy disorder," and invites "very often Mosbie to lodge at his house," says Holinshed's Chronicle, the unabashed source of the story. The lovers plot to murder Arden, and with the help of henchmen, they try and fail (as happened in fact) several times over before the deed is accomplished. The pair live through their anxieties and fears during these trials and inevitably have a violent falling-out, with Mosbie brutally lashing out at the vulnerable Alice.

But not so vulnerable. An extraordinary and realistically drawn character, Alice is by turns passionately loving, bluntly (almost brutally) honest, cunning, begging, demanding, and skillful at flattery as well as insult—all of which, in calculated sequence, brings her lover around.

Alice's "speech of persuasion" quoted here bears no relation to classical speeches of its kind, in which characters even at the height of passion voice clear, logical, sequential argument [see Euripides' *Electra* in No. 11, above]. Alice follows an alternate strategy: she does not win by rational argument, but by siege. As she follows with close attention the body language of her lover (he is facing away; she is working to turn him round) intuiting his silent emotions and deliberations, she, step by step, manipulates their reversal.

The sequence:

1) Blunt, angry accusation: He's loved her, she's discovered from friends, only for her money.

2) Threat: If he doesn't turn round and look at her and listen to her right now, she'll kill herself.

3) Promise: She'll speak nothing but fair in order to give him no offense, because a "stormy look" of his is her very hell.

4) Proof of idolatry: She'll tear out her Bible's pages and substitute his words as the objects of her worship.

5) Test of progress: She checks on his readiness to turn to her and "look"…"listen"…"speak" (the physical acts that would signify his surrender).

6) Flattering reinforcement of that test: She reminds him of his former prowess in hearing, seeing, and speaking (like the keen sight of the eagle, the quick ear of the hare, the smooth tongue of the orator).

7) Conclusion and conclusive promise: Her "little fault" is as nothing compared to her deserving (for which no justification has been offered). He has reason now to give over his "muddy looks" because she will never again disturb him, presumably by repeating her "little fault."

Not classical reasoning, but the resilience of her psychological acuity that structures Alice's persuasive "argument."

ALICE

Ay, now I see, and too soon find it true,
Which often hath been told me by my friends,
That Mosbie loves me not but for my wealth,
Which too incredulous I ne'er believed.
Nay, hear me speak, Mosbie, a word or two;
I'll bite my tongue if it speak bitterly.
Look on me, Mosbie, or I'll kill myself:
Nothing shall hide me from thy stormy look.
If thou cry war, there is no peace for me;
I will do penance for offending thee,
And burn this prayer-book, where I here use
The holy word that had converted me.
See, Mosbie, I will tear away the leaves,
And all the leaves, and in this golden cover
Shall thy sweet phrases and thy letters dwell;
And thereon will I chiefly meditate,
And hold no other sect but such devotion.
Wilt thou not look? Is all thy love o'erwhelmed?
Wilt thou not hear? What malice stops thine ears?
Why speaks thou not? What silence ties thy tongue?
Thou hast been sighted as the eagle is,
And heard as quickly as the fearful hare,
And spoke as smoothly as an orator,
When I have bid thee hear or see or speak,
And art thou sensible in none of these?
Weigh all thy good turns with this little fault,
And I deserve not Mosbie's muddy looks.
A fence of trouble is not thickened still:
Be clear again, I'll ne'er more trouble thee.

66.

ROSE, BEREFT OF HER LOVER, LACY, PINES FOR NEWS OF HIM IN LONDON (YC)

(1599) THOMAS DEKKER, *THE SHOEMAKERS' HOLIDAY*, ACT II, SC. 1

"Poor citizens must not with courtiers wed," complains Sir Otley, lord mayor of London, to the earl of Lincoln about his nephew Lacy. The very high-born earl of Lincoln echoes the same sentiment, the very one that lay in ruins in the face of love's authority in *Friar Bacon and Friar Bungay* [see No. 62, above]. The lesson of the contented comedies of the 1590s was fairly uniform: the democratizing power of love may be too subversive and too destabilizing of class, but whether or no, there's no countering it. So say these accommodating comedies, like this one, that give the power of nature itself to the authority of love. Its magic becomes the main staple, the main force, that undermines and overturns any obstacles of plot, law, parental will, lover's misunderstandings, and, in effect, any structures, with the extraordinary additional magic of having the unerring ability to put them all back together again. In gentle English comedy, love shows a velvet glove which hides a tenderly maneuvering hand.

The lord mayor's daughter Rose has fallen in love with young Lacy, and because of their difference in status, both their guardians are determined to have none of it. Lacy is sent to France to fight the king's current war, and Rose is immured in the mayor's lodge outside of London, where she has the freedom only of its walled garden in which she may gather flowers and pine. But Lacy secretly stays in London, disguises himself as a shoemaker's apprentice, wins employment in the shoemaker Simon Eyre's establishment, and waits his chance to join his love, Rose. She, in her yearning, weaves garlands in his memory, sends her maid Sybil to get news of him in London. Her innocence, her downright naïveté, sustains her through the trials of her father's foisting suitors on her. In the end, Lacy's actual treason in not joining the king's forces in France is easily forgiven by the king, who pays homage—even kings!—to Lacy's reason for desertion: love.

Unexamined love remains from then until now the solvent that operates with dream-like efficacy on every obstacle confronting lovers in the tradition of romantic comedy. Like the comedies themselves, it has no depth, but it does have a solid, if unearned, authority to remedy any fault, no matter how inbred, or any plot, no matter how tangled. [Further on Rose in No. 66, below.]

(Enter Rose, alone, making a garland.)

ROSE

Here sit thou down upon this flow'ry bank
And make a garland for thy Lacy's head.
These pinks, these roses, and these violets,
These blushing gilliflowers, these marigolds,
The fair embroidery of his coronet,
Carry not half such beauty in their cheeks,
As the sweet countenance of my Lacy doth.
O my most unkind father! O my stars,
Why lower'd you so at my nativity,
To make me love, yet live robb'd of my love?
Here as a thief am I imprisoned
For my dear Lacy's sake within those walls,
Which by my father's cost were builded up
For better purposes. Here must I languish
For him that doth as much lament, I know,
Mine absence, as for him I pine in woe.

(Enter Sybil.)

Sybil, what news at London?
Did Lacy send kind greetings to his love?
Will my love leave me, and go to France?
Get thee to London, and learn perfectly
Whether my Lacy go to France, or no.
Do this, and I will give thee for thy pains
My cambric apron and my Romish gloves,
My purple stockings and a stomacher.
Say, wilt thou do this, Sybil, for my sake?
Do so, good Sybil. Meantime wretched I
Will sit and sigh for his lost company.

GILLIFLOWERS: here, probably, the clove pink. CAMBRIC: cotton or linen fabric. ROMISH: usually, derogatory for Roman Catholic. STOMACHER: for women, worn under a bodice covering the stomach and chest.

67.

JANE, AFTER REPORT OF HER HUSBAND'S DEATH, STILL REFUSES A SUITOR'S ADDRESSES (YC)

(1599) THOMAS DEKKER, *THE SHOEMAKERS' HOLIDAY*, ACT IV, SC. 1

As a character, Jane, like Rose [see No. 66, above], is ratcheted up to observe the same fixed laws of woman's place in romantic fiction: once giving her word to her lover (or, in authorized preciosity, "plighted her troth"), she is sworn to unrelenting commitment and unwavering fidelity. But Jane is doubly sworn: unlike Rose, who's won the love of a nobleman and spends the play trembling in hopes of marriage, Jane is already married to the shoemaker's apprentice, Rafe. Both young women function in the plot as demonstrations of "love put to the ultimate test," but it's possible to see, in the contrast between their different responses, a democratizing bias in romantic love's ideology.

Rose, unaware that her lover is merely testing her, when informed that he is affianced to another, immediately condemns him out of hand, and opting for a nunnery, takes the veil. When he later reassures her that he was only joking, she redeems her vow to him by breaking her vow to the Church—Love, naturally, being taken to be the more pressing commitment of the two. Jane, of a less delicate constitution than Rose, a plebeian in fact married to a plebeian, downright and hard-headed as opposed to plaiting lover's wreaths in her garden, confronted by an even more trying test, succeeds for a time where Rose at once failed. Another suitor, pressing hard for her "troth," is told in no uncertain terms that she's already a married woman, and with bluntness and, at the same time, studied politeness, urges him to put an instant end to his pleading. Pressed further, though she is shown the written proof that her husband is dead, a soldier killed in the campaign in France. But even in the face of this terminal disaster, her fidelity holds firm. Overwhelmed by the news, she responds first by denial, and then, at once: "Though he be dead,/My love for him shall not be buried," and longs for nothing more than to be left alone to nurse her grief. Her anxiety to be rid of her suitor who is now doubly distasteful, produces a single but uncertain solace for him: "If ever I wed man, it shall be you." And the plebeian Jane opts for no alternative to her grief and her enduring fidelity. She eventually succumbs to the fact of her husband's death, takes up with the suitor as the promised successor, until she sees her husband once again, alive.

JANE

Good sir, I do believe you love me well;
For 't is a silly conquest, silly pride,
For one like you—I mean a gentleman—
To boast that by his love-tricks he hath brought
Such and such women to his amorous lure;
I think you do not so, yet many do,
And make it even a very trade to woo.
I could be coy, as many women be,
Feed you with sunshine smiles and wanton looks,
But I detest witchcraft; say that I
Do constantly believe you, constant have—
But yet, good sir, because I will not grieve you
With hopes to taste fruit which will never fall,
In simple truth this is the sum of all:
My husband lives—at least, I hope he lives.
Press'd was he to these bitter wars in France;
Bitter they are to me by wanting him.
I have but one heart, and that heart's his due.
How can I then bestow the same on you?
Whilst he lives, his I live, be it ne'er so poor,
And rather be his wife than a king's whore.
My husband, press'd for France, what was his name?
Rafe Damport.
A letter sent from France?

(She takes the letter.)
A gentleman of place; here he doth write
Their names that have been slain in every fight.
Death's scroll contains my love's name.
Ay me, he's dead!
He's dead! If this be true, my dear heart's slain!
Hence, hence!
That bill is forg'd; 't is sign'd by forgery.
For God's sake, leave me.
'T is now no time for me to think on love.
Though he be dead,
My love to him shall not be buried;
For God's sake, leave me to myself alone.

Yea or no, once more?
Once more I say no;
Once more be gone, I pray; else will I go.
Nay, for God's love, peace!
My sorrows by your presence more increase.
Not that you thus are present, but all grief
Desires to be alone; therefore in brief
Thus much I say, and saying bid adieu:
If ever I wed man, it shall be you.
Urge no more;
My breath, my promise, hath made thee rich.
Death makes me poor.

68.

MAQUERELLE THE BAWD PRESCRIBES NOSTRUMS FOR COURT LADIES (OT)

(CA. 1599–1609) JOHN MARSTON, *THE MALCONTENT*, ACT II, SC. 4

In the debauched atmosphere of the Genoese court, the old panderess Maquerelle has her place. She's already insinuated the young courtier Ferneze's suit so successfully on the Duchess that she willingly turns out her former secret lover, Mendoza, and adopts this new visitor to her bed. Maquerelle is, as the violently satirical Malevole puts it, "an old coal, that hath [already] been fired," who though she "cannot flame herself, yet art able to set a thousand virgins' tapers afire." Like her great Spanish counterpart Celestina [see No. 103, below], her cunning is supported by her considerable art: her bawd's accurate knowledge of the underside of human longing and her pharmaceutical expertise. Here she gives instruction to the two court ladies who attend the duchess, instruction which at this court is worth many times Maquerelle's fees: an afficionado's detailed, sound, and many times tested recipes for manufacturing beauty and, possibly more importantly, the philosophy that requires such care: "for your beauty, let it be your saint…when our beauty fades, good night to us."

(Enter Maquerelle, Emilia, and Bianca
with the posset.)

Even here it is, three curds in three regions individually
distinct, most methodical, according to art compos'd without
any drink. Upon my honour. Will you sit and eat? 'Tis a pretty
pearl; by this pearl (how does 't with me?) thus it is: seven and
thirty yolks of Barbary hens' eggs; eighteen spoonfuls and a
half of the juice of cock-sparrow bones; one ounce, three
drams, four scruples, and one quarter of the syrup of
Ethiopian dates; sweetened with three quarters of a pound of
pure candied Indian eringoes; strewed over with the powder of
pearl of America, amber of Cataia, and lamb-stones of
Muscovia. This it doth,—it purifieth the brood, smootheth the
skin, enliveneth the eye, strengtheneth the veins, mundifieth
the teeth, comforteth the stomach, fortifieth the back, and
quickeneth the wit; that's all.

Have you the art to seem honest? Why, then, eat me of this
posset, quicken your blood, and preserve your beauty. Do you
know Doctor Plaster-face? by this curd, he is the most
exquisite in forging of veins, right'ning of eyes, dying of hair,
sleeking of skins, blushing of cheeks, surphling of breasts,
blanching and bleaching of teeth, that ever made an old lady
gracious by torchlight; by this curd, la.

Cherish anything saving your husband; keep him not too high,
lest he leap the pale: but, for your beauty, let it be your saint;
bequeath two hours to it every morning in your closet. I ha'
been young, and yet, in my conscience, I am not above five-
and-twenty: but, believe me, preserve and use your beauty; for
youth and beauty once gone, we are like beehives without
honey, out-o'-fashion apparel that no man will wear: therefore
use me your beauty. Let men say what they will: they are
ignorant of your wants. The more in years, the more in
perfection they grow; if they lose youth and beauty, they gain
wisdom and discretion: but when our beauty fades, goodnight with us. There cannot be an uglier thing to see than an
old woman: from which, O pruning, pinching, and painting,
deliver all sweet beauties!

CURDS: coagulated milk, used for cheese. BARBARY: from the west and central coast
of northern Africa. DRAM: one-sixteenth ounce. SCRUPLE: one-twenty-fourth ounce.
ETHIOPIAN DATE: the fruit of the date palm, a staple food in northern Africa.
ERINGO: eryngo, the fruit of that plant was formerly candied as a sweetmeat.
STREWED: sprinkled. POWDER OF PEARLS: was believed to increase the strength and
also serve as an aphrodisiac. CATAIA: Cathay-China. LAMB-STONES: the testicles of a

lamb. MUSCOVIA: the region surrounding Moscow. MUNDIFY: to cleanse, clean. POS-SET: spiced hot milk curdled with wine or ale. SURPHLING: to bring color to, to make up.

69.

ANNE FRANKFORD CONFESSES HER GUILT AND PLEADS FOR PUNISHMENT(YT)

(1603) THOMAS HEYWOOD, *A WOMAN KILLED WITH KINDNESS*, ACT IV, SC. 5

There is a very particular psychology underlying motive and act in *A Woman Killed with Kindness* that supports the Puritan morality on which the play's plot is based: the story of the seduction of Anne Frankford, wife of the very worthy Christian gentleman John Frankford, by his trusted guest and employee, Wendoll. Mistress Frankford, at first incensed at Wendoll's proposal, hears with compassion the sufferings of conscience he is enduring and not out of lust but out of that compassion, she succumbs to his pleading. The warning is clear: kindness itself can give the devil his hold; and once that hold is secure, he acts decisively and quickly (grabs a toe, and quickly owns the foot). Mistress Frankford, with a further word of seducer's urging, is, as she feared, "in a labyrinth of sin."

When her husband discovers the lovers *in flagrante delicto*, Mistress Frankford flies from the bedchamber and pronounces at once her own condemnation of her act. As many, many fallen women immured in the punishing didacticism of Western tragedy are to demonstrate for four succeeding centuries, Mistress Frankford bears within her an overwhelming and unforgiving consciousness of sin. The judgment she at once visits on herself is far more punishing that her husband's will be. She assumes she'll be, and justly, spurned like a dog, trod under foot, dragged by the hair, and all this as merely preliminary to being hacked to death by sword. She judges too that she is no longer worthy even to be in her husband's presence, even to look up at his face, and yet—one more request of favor (out of love, unforgivable vanity): for him to leave her face and body without marks of violence.

Mistress Frankford is a model of the abject surrender of right, of value, of privilege, and of self, considered mandatory not only by tragedy's custom, but by its women's subscription. Married as she is to an ideally-conceived Christian husband, she fares a lot better than many of her sisters and daughters in the coming decades. Frankford "kills her with kindness" by granting her the leisure to starve to death in solitude, meditating on her sin and so earning forgiveness from him and from Him.

ANNE

(Enters in her nightgown)
Oh, by what word, what title, or what name,
Shall I entreat your pardon? Pardon! Oh!
I am as far from hoping such sweet grace,
As Lucifer from Heaven. To call you husband—
Oh me, most wretched! I have lost that name;
I am no more your wife…
I would I had no tongue, no ears, no eyes,
No apprehension, no capacity.
When do you spurn me like a dog? When tread me
Under your feet? When drag me by the hair?
Though I deserve a thousand, thousand fold,
More than you can inflict—yet, once my husband,
For womanhood, to which I am a shame,
Though once an ornament—even for His sake,
That hath redeemed our souls, mark not my face,
Nor hack me with your sword; but let me go
Perfect and undeformed to my tomb!
I am not worthy that I should prevail
In the least suit; no, not to speak to you,
Nor look on you, nor to be in your presence;
Yet, as an abject, this one suit I crave—
This granted, I am ready for my grave.

70.

GERTRUDE ARRAYS HERSELF "IN THE FRENCH MODE" FOR HER LOVER (YC)

(1604) MARSTON, CHAPMAN, AND JONSON, *EASTWARD HO!*, ACT I, SC. 2

Like bourgeoisie in any age, the Elizabethan/Jacobean middle class yearned to climb to the class above it and labored to live, spend, and dress accordingly. Gertrude is the daughter of the goldsmith Touchstone, an impressively well-to-do merchant-craftsman, but hardly titled. It's Gertrude's who life to make up for that deficiency by marrying into nobility. Her choice falls on Sir Petronel Flash, a "new-made knight" (of the kind the new-made King James I was being laughed at for creating with a suspect and profligate hand) who has title but nothing else. It's an old story, one that is still repeated well into the twentieth century: she needs title, he needs money. As it turns out, sadly for Gertrude, his need is fulfilled entirely at her expense. He marries her, turns her dowry of land into cash, absconds with the cash and with another woman; and Gertude remains bereft, without money and with useless title (but left to the poetic justice of Ben Jonson, his punishment is worse).

Before that outcome, she is all anticipation, thrill, and practical preparation for her knight's arrival: first, her clothes. While her maid, with the sham-pretentious name of Bettrice, is attending to Gertrude's fashionable pet-monkey, she tears off her "city-cut" (her common "citizen" dress) to get into a costume fitting for a knight's lady with the help of her attending tailor Poldavy.

And when her sister Mildred remonstrates with her for turning her back on "that which hath made you and us," she rounds on her. You, but not I, says Gertrude, can put up with clothes that brand you "citizen"—with that tell-tale linen-cap ("coif"), the coarse woolen ("stammel") petticoat with two ornamental trimmings ("guards"), that gown of ugly, coarse-cloth ("buffin") with the tufted-silk ("tuf-taffety") cape and the velvet lace. But she, Gertrude, is determined to be a titled lady. Of course, a few things of middle class taste will remain tolerable—she enumerates: cherries worth ten shillings a pound, dyeing scarlet black, lining a heavy silk ("grogram") gown with velvet, also fine linens, three-pound socks-all these remain tolerable. But intolerable—the tafetta hats ("pipkins"), heavy-cloth ("durance") petticoats, the silver long-pins ("bodkins") to pin up the hair—these, "I cannot endure!"

And to her sister Mildred's warnings of the folly (standard Elizabethan/Jacobean admonishment for overstepping the boundaries of "place") of yoking "a goldsmith's daughter and a knight," Gertrude is airily condescending. When she's a lady, she assures her, "I'll vouch to call you Sister Mil still." And while the monkey is apparently performing "profanely," the tailor Poldavy is constrained to yank tight the bracing at the top of Gertrude's petticoat with a steel "instrument" to rectify, he explains, "the imperfection of the proportion."

The knight's visit is suddenly upon her, and Gertrude begs for quick, quick final adjustments and then is ready to receive her knight.

(A room in Touchstone's house. Enter Gertrude, Mildred, Bettrice, and Poldavy, a tailor: Poldavy with a fair gown, Scotch farthingale, and French fall in his arms; Gertrude in a French head attire and citizen's gown; Mildred sewing; and Bettrice leading a monkey after her.)

GERTRUDE

For the passion of patience, look if Sir Petronel approach, that sweet, that fine, that delicate, that—for love's sake, tell me if he come. O sister Mil, though my father be a low-capped tradesman, yet I must be a lady; and, I praise God, my mother must call me madam. Does he come? Off with this gown, for shame's sake, off with this gown; let not my knight take me in the city cut in any hand; tear 't, pax on 't—does he come?—tear 't off.

I tell you I cannot endure it, I must be a lady: do you wear your coif with a London licket, your stammel petticoat with two guards, the buffin gown with the tuft-taffety cape, and the velvet lace. I must be a lady, and I will be a lady. I like some humours of the City dames well: to eat cherries only at an angel a pound, good! To dye rich scarlet black, pretty! To line a grogram gown clean through with velvet, tolerable! Their pure linen, their smocks of three pounds a smock, are to be borne withal! But your mincing niceries , taffeta pipkins, durance petticoats, and silver bodkins—God's my life, as I shall be a lady, I cannot endure it! Is he come yet? Lord, what a long knight 't is!

Alas! Poor Mil, when I am a lady, I'll pray for thee yet, i' faith; nay, and I'll vouchsafe to call thee Sister Mil still; for though thou art not like to be a lady as I am, yet sure thou art a creature of God's making, and mayest peradventure to be saved as soon as I—does he come?

Now, lady's my comfort, what a profane ape's here! Tailor, Poldavy, prithee, fit it, fit it: is this a right Scot? Does it clip close, and bear up round? Most edifying tailor! I protest you tailors are most sanctified members, and make many crooked thing go upright. How must I bear my hands? Light, light?

(Enter Sir Petronel.)
Is my knight come? O the Lord, my band! Sister, do my cheeks look well? Give me a little box o' the ear that I may seem to blush; now, now! So, there, there, there! Here he is. O my dearest delight! Lord, Lord, and how does my knight?

FALL: a veil. CITIZEN'S: plain, respectable. ANGEL: gold coin, called originally an Angel Noble. MINCING NICERIES: affectedly nice or elegant. TAFFETA: richly decorated. KNIGHT: night. PERADVENTURE: possibly. SCOT: Scotch farthingale. BAND: a flat or falling collar worn by men or women.

71.

GERTRUDE, NOW IMPOVERISHED, BEGS HER MOTHER TO STEAL A BIT FOR HER FROM HER FATHER (YC)

(1604) MARSTON, CHAPMAN, AND JONSON, *EASTWARD HO!*, ACT V, SC. 1

[See No. 70, above] A boatload of adventurers and absconders are leaving London with their booty and their women for a journey to the paradise of the Virginia colony in America to make their fortunes. They are shipwrecked in a storm before even getting beyond the Thames or away from London. Aboard are Sir Petronel, the new husband of Gertrude, with her cash and his new mistress, and the apprentice Quicksilver, the young man affianced to Gertrude's maid-servant with the aggressively Puritan name of Sindefy. Brought ashore dripping wet and arraigned for a variety of felonies, Sir Petronel and Quicksilver are confined to one of the prisonhouses called the Counter. Gertrude, bereft of fortune and home (her father has forbidden her return to his house, importuning her mockingly to live as a knight's lady in her promised castle) is pining in a London lodging house, and Sindefy, wondering how they are going to live. Gertrude's comeuppance, painful though it is, can't suppress her life of fantasy. It burgeons again, as she anticipates finding a jewel on the road or a pot of gold back of the lodging until her mother arrives, weeping for her daughter's plight. Gertrude has only one real question for mother: "Nay, good mother, can you steal no more money from my father?"

In the end, Gertrude creeps back to her parental haven and, with her father's forgiveness, shares in the general blessing of the comedy's end.

(Gertrude and Sindefy)

Gertrude

Ah, Sin, hast thou ever read i' the chronicle of any lady and
her waiting woman driven to that extremity that we are, Sin?
Nay, weep not, good Sin. Thy miseries are nothing to mine,
Sin; I was more than promised marriage, Sin; I had it, Sin, and
was made a lady, and by a knight, Sin; which is now as good as
no knight, Sin. And I was born in London, which is more than
brought up, Sin; and already forsaken, which is past
likelihood, Sin; and instead of land i' the country, all my
knight's living lies i' the Counter, Sin; there's his castle now!

The knighthood nowadays are nothing like the knighthood of
old time. They rid a-horseback; ours go a-foot. They were
attended by their squires; ours by their lackeys. They went
buckled in their armour; ours muffled in their cloaks. They
traveled wildernesses and deserts; ours dare scarce walk the
streets. They were still prest to engage their honour; ours still
ready to pawn their clothes. They would gallop on at sight of a
monster; ours run away at sight of a sergeant. They would
help poor ladies; ours make poor ladies.

And tell me, what shall we pawn next? Let me see, my jewels

be gone, and my gowns, and my red velvet petticoat that I was married in, and my wedding silk stockings, and all thy best apparel, poor Sin! Good faith, rather than thou shouldest pawn a rag more, I'd lay my ladyship in lavender—if I knew where. You do not scorn my ladyship, though it is in a waistcoat? God's my life, you are a peat indeed! Do I offer to mortgage my ladyship for you and for your avail, and do you turn the lip and the alas to my ladyship? Marry now, I warrant you, I'm sure I remember the time when I would ha' given one thousand pounds (if I had had it) to have been a lady; and I hope I was not bred and born with that appetite alone: some other gentle-born o' the City have the same longing, I trust. And for my part, I would afford 'em a penny'orth; my ladyship is little the worse for the wearing. I would lend it (let me see) for forty pound in hand, Sin—that would apparel us—and ten pounds a year—that would keep me and you, Sin (with our needles)—and we should never need to be beholding to our scurvy parents.

Good lord, that there are no fairies nowadays, Sin! To do miracles, and bring ladies money. Sure if we lay in a cleanly house, they would haunt it, Sin. I'll try. I'll sweep the chamber soon at night, and set a dish of water o' the hearth. A fairy may come, and bring a pearl or a diamond. We do not know, Sin. Or there may be a pot of gold hid o' the backside, if we had tools to dig for it? Why may not we two rise early i' the morning, Sin, afore anybody is up, and find a jewel i' the streets worth a hundred pound? Ha? Or may not some old usurer be drunk overnight, with a bag of money, and leave it behind him on a stall? For God's sake, Sin, let's rise tomorrow by break of day, and see. I protest, la! If I had as much money as an alderman, I would scatter some on't i' th' streets for poor ladies to find, when their knights were laid up.

O here's my mother! Good luck, I hope. Ha' you brought any money, mother? Pray you, mother, your blessing. Nay, sweet mother, do not weep. Nay, dear mother, can you steal no more money from my father? Dry your eyes, and comfort me.

IN LAVENDER: in pawn: she means "I would pawn my title". WAISTCOAT: undergarment. PEAT: bold or saucy young lady. TURN THE LIP AND THE ALAS: Curl the lip and sigh, "alas!" AFFORD 'EM A PENNY'ORTH: sell it cheap.

72.

CRISPINELLA PRONOUNCES ON KISSING (FAUGH!), ON COY VIRTUE (FIE!), ON NAKED NATURE (FINE!), ON MARRIAGE, NEVER (YC)

(1605) JOHN MARSTON, *THE DUTCH COURTESAN*, ACT III, SC. 1

Crispinella is the true antidote to the fantasy heroines of the Romantic Comedy of the 1590s. The first decade of the seventeenth century was heavily shadowed by a deep and stabbing skepticism, to which Marston, like Shakespeare, gave voice, the voice largely emulating that of the great French philosopher Montaigne, whose aphorisms can be heard flowing out of the radically skeptical and radically foul-mouthed Crispinella. The skepticism is Montaigne's, the foul mouth decidedly Marston's, from whose invective against virtuous cant Crispinella inherits her free tongue and shaming bluntness. But like Montaigne, her intent is hardly merely corrosive—far from it—but clarifying. "For my part," she declares, "I consider nature without apparel, without disguising of custom or compliment." And what comes of her staring stark nature in the eye, or as we say, looking facts in the face, is—as Montaigne would have it—a reaching for what is undeniably true and, ultimately, what is good. At the moment, gathered with her sister Beatrice and their old Nurse, the three are soon to be celebrating Beatrice's marriage to Freevill, and the Nurse assumes that Crispinella is bent on attaining that same bliss. Crispinella disabuses her, the negative fact of Husband sharing in her disabuse with the "bliss" of kissing, the "disguisings" of moral clothing, the decency of prohibition, and the necessity of the closed mouth—in general, of the concealed and the unexamined. A rare antidote to the romantic fantasy of femininity in comedy, her voice is to be heard again later in English comedy, but rarely as baldly, bluntly, or as blithely.

CRISPINELLA

Pish, sister Beatrice! prithee read no more; my stomach o' late stands against kissing extremely... By the faith and trust I bear to my face, 'tis grown one of the most unsavory ceremonies. Body o' beauty, 'tis one of the most unpleasing, injurious customs to ladies. Any fellow that has but one nose on his face, and standing collar and skirts also lined with taffety silk, must salute us on the lips as familiarly—Soft skins save us! there was a stub bearded John-a Stile with a ployden's face saluted me last day and stuck his bristle through my lips; I ha' spent ten shillings in pomatum since to skin them again. Marry, if a nobleman or a knight with one lock visit us, though his unclean goose-turd-green teeth ha' the palsy, his nostrils smell worse than a putrified maribone, and his loose beard drops into our bosom, yet we must kiss him with a curtsy. A curse! for my part, I had as lief they would break wind in my lips. Let's ne'er be ashamed to speak what we be not ashamed to think; I dare as boldly speak venery as think venery. Now bashfulness seize you! we pronounce boldly robbery, murder, treason, which deeds must needs be far more loathsome than an act which is so natural, just, and necessary as that of procreation. You shall have an hypocritical vestal virgin speak that with close teeth publicly. For my own part, I consider nature without apparel, without disguising of custom or compliment. I give thoughts words, and words truth, and truth boldness. She whose honest freeness makes it her virtue to speak what she thinks will make it her necessity to think what is good. I love no prohibited things, and yet I would have nothing prohibited by policy but by virtue; for, as in the fashion of time, those books that are called in are most in sale and request, so in nature those actions that are most prohibited are most desired… Fie, fie! Virtue is a free, pleasant, buxom quality. I love a constant countenance well; but this froward, ignorant coyness, sour, austere, lumpish, uncivil privateness, that promises nothing but rough skins and hard stools, ha! Fie on't! Good for nothing but nothing.

Your sermon on how we shall behave to our husbands? Read it to my sister, Nurse, for I assure you I'll ne'er marry. What will I do then? Faith, strive against the flesh. Marry? No, faith; husbands are like lots in the lottery: you may draw forty blanks before you find one that has any prize in him. A husband generally is a careless, domineering thing that grows like coral, which as long as it is under water is soft and tender, but as soon as it has got his branch above the waves is presently hard, stiff, not to be bowed but burst; so when your husband is a suitor and under your choice, Lord, how supple he is, how obsequious, how at your service, sweet lady! Once married, got up his head above, a stiff, crooked, knobby, inflexible, tyrannous creature he grows; then they turn like water: more you would embrace, the less you hold. I'll live my own woman, and if the worst come to the worst, I had rather price a wag than a fool…Virtuous marriage? There is no more affinity betwixt virtue and marriage than betwixt a man and his horse. Indeed, virtue gets up upon marriage sometimes and manageth it in the right way, but marriage is of another piece; for as a horse may be without a man, and a man without a horse, so marriage, you know, is often without virtue, and virtue, I am sure, more oft without marriage. But thy match, sister, by my troth, I think 'twill do well. He's a well-shaped, clean-lipped gentleman, of a handsome but not affected fineness, a good faithful eye, and a well-humored cheek. Would he did not stoop in the shoulders, for thy sake.

STANDING COLLAR: high, straight collar fastened in front. TAFFETY SILK: shiny, soft material. JOHN-A-STYLE: fictitious name for a party (as in, John Doe). PLOYDEN'S FACE: lawyer's face. POMATUM: pomade. LOCK: of hair. MARIBONE: a bone containing edible marrow. VENERY: the gratification of sexual desire. VESTAL VIRGIN: the vestal virgins cared for the sacred flame in the temple of Vesta, Roman goddess of the hearth. BOOKS THAT ARE CALLED IN: censored books. FROWARD: obstinate, willful. WAG: a wit, joker.

73.

LADY POLITIC WOULD-BE VISITS HER GARRULITY ON VOLPONE, AND DRIVES HIM TO DISTRACTION (OC)

(1606) BEN JONSON, *VOLPONE*, ACT III, SC. 5

"The sun, the sea, will sooner both stand still/Than her eternal tongue! Nothing can 'scape it." Lady Politic Would-Be is not only maddeningly garrulous, but also maddeningly learned. The rattle of her tongue takes its cue from Volpone's desperate attempts to shut her up and get rid of her. He sweats and suffers and needs silence? She has an endless prescription for sickness. He protests that he's well? Wellness suggests liberal pursuits—music, painting, discoursing, writing—all of which arts a woman should accomplish. But Volpone has objected that the highest female grace is silence, for which Lady Would-Be needs footnoting and rattles off a catalogue of Italian author candidates for the distinction. That in turn leads to her comparison of the merits among them. His attention is wandering? Philosophy's the cure, and she has advice on how to move reason and judgment to overrule passion.

Lady Would-Be is deeply enshrouded in vanity—her appearance, her clothes, her learning—in a word, her deep self-love, so deep that she hears and absorbs nothing that interrupts, contradicts or displaces her talk. The degree to which she hears nothing but herself is the degree to which she is enthralled to her "humour"—or, to put it another way, her addiction. But in the instance of her visit to Volpone, there's a distinctly practical side to that addiction: she, like all his other visitors, is after a share in his will, to be revealed presumably after his imminent death. She's being duped like all the others, but the particular gift of solicitous gab she's offering to win his favor is calculated to drive him to the death he's only pretending. [For further commentary on *Volpone,* see the monologues of Volpone and Mosca in Men's volumes.]

LADY POLITIC WOULD-BE

(Goes to Volpone's couch)
How does my Volpone!
Believe me, and I
Had the most fearful dream, could I remember 't—
Alas, good soul! the passion of the heart.
Seed-pearl were good now, boil'd with syrup of apples,
Tincture of gold, and coral, citron-pills,
Your elecampane root, myrobalanes—
Burnt silk and amber. You have muscadel
Good i' the house—
I doubt we shall not get
Some English saffron, half a dram would serve;
Your sixteen cloves, a little musk, dried mints;
Bugloss, and barley-meal—
And these appli'd with a right scarlet cloth.
Shall I, sir, make you a poultice?
I have a little studied physic; but now
I'm all for music, save, i' the forenoons,
An hour or two for painting. I would have
A lady, indeed, t' have all letters and arts,
Be able to discourse, to write, to paint,
But principal, as Plato holds, your music
(And so does wise Pythagoras, I take it,)

Is your true rapture: when there is concent
In face, in voice, and clothes: and is, indeed,
Our sex's chiefest ornament.
The poet
As old in time as Plato, and as knowing,
Says, you say, that your highest female grace is silence?
Which o'your poets? Petrarch, or Tasso, or Dante?
Guarini? Ariosto? Aretine?
Cieco di Hadria? I have read them all.
I think I ha' two or three of 'em about me.
Here's *Pastor Fido*—
All our English writers,
I mean such as are happy in th' Italian,
Will deign to steal out of this author, mainly;
Almost as much as from Montagnie:
He has so modern and facile a vein,
Fitting the time, and catching the court-ear!
Your Petrarch is more passionate, yet he,
In days of sonnetting, trusted 'em with much:
Dante is hard, and few can understand him.
But for a desperate wit, there's Aretine;
Only his pictures are a little obscene—
You mark me not.
Alas, your mind's perturb'd.
Why, in such cases, we must cure ourselves,
Make use of our philosophy—
And as we find our passions do rebel,
Encounter 'em with reason, or divert 'em.
By giving scope unto some other humour
Of lesser danger: as, in politic bodies,
There's nothing more doth overwhelm the judgment,
And clouds the understanding, than too much
Settling and fixing, and, as 't were, subsiding
Upon one object. For the incorporating
Of these same outward things, into that part
Which we call mental, leaves some certain faeces
That stop the organs, and, as Plato says,
Assassinates our knowledge.
Come, in faith, I must
Visit you more a days; and make you well:
Laugh and be lusty.
There was but one sole man in all the world
With whom I e'er could sympathize; and he
Would lie you, often, three, four hours together
To hear me speak; and be sometime so rapt,

As he would answer me quite from he purpose,
Like you, and you like him, just. I'll discourse,
An 't but only, sir, to bring you asleep.

ELECAMPANE ROOT: a composite plant with yellow flowers and aromatic leaves and root. MYROBALANES: a dried plum-like fruit from tropical trees, used for dyes and inks. BUGLOSS: a medicinal herb with rough leaves; also, a blue-flowered herb. POULTICE: a soft, moist medicament applied to the body. PYTHAGORAS: a sixth-century Greek philosopher, mathematician, and religious reformer. CONCENT: harmony. PETRARCH, TASSO, DANTE, GUARINI, ARIOSTO, ARETINE: she lists almost all the major Italian Renaissance poets from fourteenth to sixteenth century. CIECO DE HADRIA: a.k.a., Francesco Bello, fl. 15th century. He wrote the romantic poem Mambriano. PASTOR FIDO: pastoral poem by Guarini, published in 1590. MONTAGNIE: Michel de Montaigne (1533–92), French essayist and philosopher.

74.

CELIA TREMBLES, THEN REASONS, THEN IMPLORES, THEN KNEELS IN PRAYER, WITH NO EFFECT ON VOLPONE'S DRIVING LUST (YC)

(1606) BEN JONSON, *VOLPONE*, ACT III, SC. 7

[See in Men's volumes "Volpone Welcomes the Morning Sun and His Gold" and "Volpone Disguised as a Montebank Hawks Quack Remedies."] "To preserve him, no other means but some young woman…lusty and full of juice, to sleep by him," instructs Mosca, Volpone's parasite, to a palpitating Corvino, desperate that the dying Volpone has taken it into his head to recover. And if other petitioners for the inheritance of Volpone's fortune are beforehand, Corvino will be out altogether, and lose the investment he's already made in Volpone's imminent demise. To forestall the possibility of being cut out of the dead man's will, Corvino reasons that the woman to content the revived but tottering Volpone has to be his own wife.

Jonson's snarling study of animal greed in humans reaches a kind of apotheosis in Corvino's determination to prostitute his wife to keep his hand in the supposed dead man's lottery. It's of course a swindle. Corvino is one of a crowd of dupes, but like all dupes, he believes he's found his moment for outmaneuvering fortune and so drags his wife, Celia, to Volpone's bed.

Corvino's wife is not only beautiful, she's virtuous and honest. She, delivered by her husband into Volpone's hands, is terrified. Her terror registers as one of the most frighteningly real depictions of the terror of rape that outdoes most others of this endlessly repeated event in tragedy and later melodrama. As the threat becomes more imminent and her certainty of its fulfillment becomes more over-whelming, Celia appeals to Volpone's common humanity, begs him to recognize the grossness of his act, and calls to whatever vestige of conscience remains in him. If he has no mercy, then let him have rage ("be bountiful and kill me") or, if not that, "flay my face" to destroy the temptation of beauty or rub her body with leprous diseases—anything but the destruction of her "innocence" and "honor," which are all, she swears, she possesses. For Celia, it is not a boast. So betrayed by her husband and so abandoned by him to Volpone's lust, she has in fact no other possession. Finally, she stoops to abject beg-ging, and the cry that follows—the signature moment in this forever-to-be-repeated episode ("Forbear, foul ravisher!")—is eventually to induce, after so many perfunctory repetitions, only comic effect. But in Celia's appeal to Volpone to spare her innocence more than her life, and in Jonson's structuring of its emotional sequence, her cry overwhelmingly carries the power of true conviction.

CELIA

O God, and his good angels! whither, whither,
Is shame fled human breasts? that with such ease,
Men dare put off your honours, and their own?
Is that, which ever was a cause of life,
Now plac'd beneath the basest circumstance,
And modesty an exile made, for money?
Sir!
Some serene blast me, or dire lightning strike
This my offending face!
Good Sir, these things might move a mind affected
With such delights; but I, whose innocence
Is all I can think wealthy, or worth th' enjoying,
And which, once lost, I have nought to lose beyond it,
Cannot be taken with these sensual baits:
If you have conscience—
If you have ears that will be pierc'd—or eyes
That can be open'd—a heart may be touch'd—

Or any part that yet sounds man about you—
If you have touch of holy saints—or heaven—
Do me the grace to let me scape:—if not,
Be bountiful and kill me. You do know,
I am a creature, hither ill betray'd,
By one whose shame I would forget it were:
If you will deign me neither of these graces,
Yet feed your wrath, sir, rather than your lust,
(It is a vice comes nearer manliness,)
And punish that unhappy crime of nature,
Which you miscall my beauty: flay my face,
Or poison it with ointments for seducing
Your blood to this rebellion. Rub these hands
With what may cause an eating leprosy,
E'en to my bones and marrow: anything
That may disfavour me, save in my honour—
And I will kneel to you, pray for you, pay down
A thousand hourly vows, sir, for your health;
Report, and think you virtuous—

       (He seizes her.)
O! just God!
Forbear, foul ravisher!

SERENE: mildew. BAITS: seductions. FLAY: strip off the skin.

75.

NELL, THE CITIZEN'S WIFE, URGES RALPH, HER HUSBAND'S APPRENTICE, ON THE ACTORS TO PLAY THEIR CHIEF ROLE (OC)

(1607) FRANCIS BEAUMONT AND JOHN FLETCHER,
THE KNIGHT OF THE BURNING PESTLE, INDUCTION

Quoting from Men's volumes "Novice Ralph Inspires Bumbling Men to Battle and Glory": "A play is about to begin at Blackfriars. The Prologue is interrupted by a Citizen in the audience who wants not this sort of play but one about London shopkeepers. The Actor explains their play is ready and they have no other. But the Citizens' Wife has a remedy: Ralph, our apprentice, she volunteers, is a fine actor and will play such a play." She has the advantage of the Actors. As was the custom in the private theatres, she, with some of the rest of the audience, is sitting onstage and in an excellent position to interpose her will (and her husband the Grocer's) on the company. She has another advantage as well: she's never been in a theatre before, and so she carries the assurance and authority of perfect ignorance. Once she establishes Ralph's credentials for acting and for the play he'll improvise, she's up on her feet, directing Ralph a bit, requesting appropriate costume for him, desiring "shawms" (reed instruments) to match the dignity of Ralph's imminent performance, and the accompaniment, she insists, of the "waits" (the street musicians familiar to her neighborhood of Southwark) who'll come on the run from across the river to participate in the show. These arrangements subscribed to, she's content to sit down and let the show begin.

Wife

By your leave, gentlemen all; I'm something troublesome. I'm
a stranger here; I was ne'er at one of these plays, as they say,
before; but I should have seen "Jane Shore" once; and my
husband hath promised me any time this twelvemonth, to
carry me to "The Bold Beauchamps," but in truth he did not. I
pray you, bear with me. Husband, husband, for God's sake, let
Ralph play! Beshrew me, if I do not think he will go beyond
them all. I pray you, youth, let him have a suit of reparel!—I'll
be sworn, gentlemen, my husband tells you true. He will act
you sometimes at our house, that all the neighbours cry out
on him; he will fetch you up a couraging part so in the garret,
that we are all as fear'd, I warrant you, that we quake again:
we'll fear our children with him; if they be never so unruly, do
but cry, "Ralph comes, Ralph comes!" to them, and they'll be
as quiet as lambs.—Hold up thy head, Ralph; show the
gentlemen what thou canst do; speak a buffing part; I warrant
you, the gentlemen will accept of it.

Nay, gentlemen, he hath play'd before, my husband says,
Mucedorus, before the wardens of our company. Ay, and he
should have play'd Jeronimo with a shoemaker for a wager. In,
Ralph, in, Ralph; and set out the grocery in their kind, if thou
lov'st me.

(Exit Ralph.)
I warrant, our Ralph will look finely when he's dress'd.
What stately music have you? You have shawms?

No! I'm a thief if my mind did not give me so. Ralph plays a
stately part, and he must needs have shawms. I'll be at the
charge of them myself, rather than we'll be without them. Let's
have the waits of Southwark; they are as rare fellows as any are
in England; and that will fetch them all o'er the water with a
vengeance, as if they were mad. Sit you merry all, gentlemen;
I'm bold to sit amongst you for my ease.

(Citizen and Wife sit down.)
Take you no care for Ralph; he'll discharge himself, I warrant
you. I' faith, gentlemen, I'll give my word for Ralph.

JANE SHORE: probably Heywood's Edward IV. THE BOLD BEAUCHAMPS: a lost play.
MUCEDORUS: anonymous popular play, falsely ascribed to Shakespeare. JERONIMO: in
Kyd's The Spanish Tragedy.

76.

THE DUCHESS, FOREGOING MURDER, DECIDES ON CUCKOLDRY FOR REVENGE (OT)

(1607) CYRIL TOURNEUR, *THE REVENGER'S TRAGEDY*, ACT I, SC. 2

The Duchess' youngest son is brought to trial for the crime of rape.
With a sigh, the Duke—old and "full of confirmed gravity"—con-
signs the young man (her son, not his) to the judgment of the court.
And despite the kneeling protestations of the Duchess herself begging the court to "temper his fault with pity," her son is doomed. For
the Duchess, as painful to bear as the judgment itself is the futile
response of her husband, "an old-cool duke [who proves] to be as
slack in tongue as in performance." A word from him would have
freed her son.

In the world of *The Revenger's Tragedy,* motive is single-minded,
self-serving, unqualifiedly vicious, and uniformly deadly. With moral

restraint suspended, motive seeks instant fulfillment, smooth effi-
ciency, and, beyond its single aim of revenge, the additional fillip of
inflicting very large allotments of pain. The Duchess, at once studying revenge against her husband's indifference, fixes in a breath on a
punishment worse than murder. For a nobleman of such "confirmed
gravity," worse than death is the dishonor of cuckoldry.

With the same dispatch, the Duchess proceeds to accomplish his
dishonor, and ready-to-hand is Spurio, the Duke's own bastard son
toward whom, irrespective of revenge, her thoughts and gestures had
been beckoning. Her wooing of him is direct. With sufficient zeal, she
makes it clear that winning a duchess is no more difficult than winning a city woman; and his finding a motive should be no problem:
revenge for bastardy. Having given the young man both entree and
motive, she leaves satisfied the arrangement will do. As for the young
man, on the Duchess' departure, his rumination is swift: "Adultery is
my nature."

DUCHESS

Was't ever known step-duchess was so mild
And calm as I? Some now would plot his death
With easy doctors, those loose living men
And make his withered Grace fall to his grave
And keep church better.
Some second wife would do this, and dispatch
Her double loathed lord at meat and sleep.
Indeed 'tis true an old man's twice a child,
Mine cannot speak! One of his single words
Would quite have freed my youngest dearest son
From death or durance, and have made him walk
With a bold foot upon the thorny law,
Whose prickles should bow under him; but 't 'as not:
And therefore wedlock faith shall be forgot.
I'll kill him in his forehead, hate there feed—
That wound is deepest though it never bleed;
And here comes he whom my heart points unto,
His bastard son, but my love's true-begot;
Many a wealthy letter have I sent him
Swelled up with jewels, and the timorous man
Is yet but coldly kind;

(Enter Spurio.)
That jewel's mine that quivers in his ear,
Mocking his master's chillness and vain fear—

H'as spied me now.
Your duty on my hand.
Upon my hand sir, troth I think you'd fear
To kiss my hand too if my lip stood there.
Ah! Witness you would not.

(He kisses her.)
'Tis a wonder,
For ceremony has made many fools.
It is as easy way unto a duchess
As to a hatted dame, if her love answer,
But that by timorous honours, pale respects,
Idle degrees of fear, men make their ways
Hard of themselves. What have you thought of me?

Upon my love I mean.

Let it stand firm both in thought and mind
That the duke was thy father: as no doubt then
He bid fair for't, thy injury is the more;
For had he cut thee a right diamond,
Thou had'st been next set in the dukedom's ring,
When his worn self like Age's easy slave
Had dropped out of the collet into the grave.
What wrong can equal this?
Who would not be revenged of such a father,
E'en the worst way? I would thank that sin
That could most injure him, and be in league with it.
Oh what a grief 'tis that a man should live
But once i' the world, and then to live a bastard,
The curse o' the womb, the thief of Nature,
Begot against the seventh commandment,
Half damned in the conception by the justice
Of that unbribed everlasting law.
Who but an eunuch would not sin, his bed
By one false minute disinherited?
Cold still: in vain then must a duchess woo?
I blush to say what I will do.
Sweet comfort, earnest and farewell.

(She kisses him.)
Faith now old duke, my vengeance shall reach high,
I'll arm thy brow with woman's heraldry.

(Exit)

77.

EVADNE REVEALS TO HER NEWLY-WEDDED AMINTOR THAT HE IS THE DUPE AND CUCKOLD OF THE KING (YT)

(CA. 1608–13) FRANCIS BEAUMONT AND JOHN FLETCHER, *THE MAID'S TRAGEDY*, ACT II, SC. 1

Admittedly, this is a "monologue" forged out of a scene of biting dialogue between two who are arguing a case. For one (Amintor), the case is unspeakable, and for the other (Evadne), it is perhaps unfortunate but acceptable, though obviously irreversible. The King, to shield the possibility of his mistress having an unexplained—or too easily explained—offspring, has taken the precaution of wedding her to his obedient knight Amintor. On this, their wedding night, Amintor is in bed, awaiting his bride to join him in matrimonial endeavor. Piecemeal, she doles out the shameful truth: she will not bed with him, who is a husband in name, but a king's cuckold in truth, and he must accommodate his thoughts and behavior to that fact.

The naïve Amintor is the perfect example of knightly virtue and royal fealty, and his response to this news and the tracing of his gradual accommodation to his horrifying situation are as cynically told as story itself. But the focus of this slice of their dialogue is on Evadne and her extraordinary feeling for and use of the power her situation gives her. She may be immoral, as her situation assures her, but as a king's mistress, she's immune from harm. She makes free if unfeeling use of that power in this bedtime showdown with her erstwhile groom and offers him what patience and tolerance she can. But compared to her own impatient tempo, he is terribly slow to understand the plain facts of his situation, and even slower to accommodate his behavior to its implications. This is Hedda Gabler talking to a slower, dimmer Tesman. But Evadne is not under Hedda's constraints of time and place and pressure of middle-class living room custom. She is living in a far freer time and place, the jaded and somewhat effete world of seventeenth-century royal courts, where what is going on in truth has little to do with what the loyal, feudal-coded Amintors imagine is the case. And this difference, between Evadne's knowledge and ease with the court's substratum and Amintor's dazzled allegiance to its pretense, is the informing metaphor of the tragedy as a whole, in which precisely this distinction between the ostensible and the actual rules of the game is in play.

EVADNE

I am not well.
Good my lord, I cannot sleep.
I'll not go to bed.
I have sworn I will not.
Yes, sworn, Amintor; and will swear again,
If you will wish to hear me.
Put off amazement, and with patience mark
What I shall utter, for the oracle
Knows nothing truer: 'tis not for a night
Or two that I forbear thy bed, but ever.

You hear right:
I sooner will find out the beds of snakes,
And with my youthful blood warm their cold flesh,
Letting them curl themselves about my limbs,
Than sleep one night with thee. This is not feigned,
Nor sounds it like the coyness of a bride.

I have sworn before,
And here by all things holy do again,
Never to be acquainted with thy bed!
Is your doubt over now?
When I call back this oath,
The pains of hell environ me!
Do what thou darest to me!
Every ill-sounding word or threatening look
Thou showest me will be revenged at full.

Think'st thou I forbear

To sleep with thee, because I have put on
A maiden's strictness? Look upon these cheeks,
And thou shalt find the hot and rising blood
Unapt for such a vow. No; in this heart
There dwells as much desire and as much will
To put that wished act in practice as ever yet
Was known to woman; and they have been shown
Both. But it was the folly of thy youth
To think this beauty, to what hand soe'er
It shall be called, shall stoop to any second.
I do enjoy the best, and in that height
Have sworn to stand or die: you guess the man.

You dare not strike him.
Why, 'tis the King.
What will you do now?
What did he make this match for, dull Amintor?
Alas, I must have one
To father children, and to bear the name
Of husband to me, that my sin may be
More honorable!
I must have one
To fill thy room again, if thou wert dead;
To cover shame, I took thee; never fear
That I would blaze myself.
Come, let us practice; and, as wantonly
As ever longing bride and bridegroom met
Let's laugh and enter here.
Down all the swellings of my troubled heart!
When we walk thus entwined, let all eyes see
If better lovers ever did agree.

(Exeunt)

FORBEAR: avoid. STRICTNESS: modesty. BLAZE: expose.

78.

ASPATIA BITTERLY EVOKES THE MISERY OF HER BETRAYED LOVE (YT)

(CA. 1608–13) FRANCIS BEAUMONT AND JOHN FLETCHER, *THE MAID'S TRAGEDY*, ACT II, SC. 2

Like *The Spanish Tragedy*'s Hieronymo [see in Men's volumes "Mad Hieronymo Considers: 'What Is a Son?'"], when the tragic figures of Jacobean drama suffer the loss of belief in their one life-ideal, they "lose their moorings altogether, doubt, despair, and so to speak, 'run mad.'" Their way of mourning their loss indeed looks like madness, but it is essentially the craving to reconstitute stability out of derangement. It involves, in effect, a mad-seeming thrust and lunge toward mock discoveries of an ideal original and fantastic, playful gestures that imitate the progress of rediscovering it, but most painfully, a playacting which indulges in uninhibited sightings into and behind words, things, people, meanings, by which they imagine they expose the sham, the pretense, the bad imitations which among common humanity pass for the real thing—sham that mocks the suffering they unremittingly endure. It's a bitter, tormented game they play under the compulsion that, in conscience, they cannot settle for a more common way of mourning, since that way lacks fit.

Aspatia, the maid of the play's title, is one of those so marked and cursed. It was she to whom Aminta was betrothed and swore fidelity, and he unaccountably betrayed his oath to her by marrying Evadne [see No. 77, above]. She is fixed on that sorrow of betrayed love, and pursues it with the monomaniacal commitment of Hieronymo's pursuit of justice for his son's murder.

But unlike Hieronymo, her intent is not to recover from her sorrow, but to know it in its perfection. She becomes the votary of the very idea of sorrow through love's betrayal, and becomes fixed on discovering an instance, in any person, in any thing that exhibits it. Nothing will do but its absolute. Here are her attempts at evoking the perfect image of betrayed love's perfect sorrow.

1) One glance tells her that the young maidens she is with, Antiphola and Olympias, won't do: they're positively blooming. But if they were to "believe all [men] faithful" suffer love and then betrayal, they might qualify. Since they've not been snared yet, Aspatia has

the charity to tell them how to avoid love's imprisonment altogether. Clasp two asps to the bosom, she advises them; "one kiss [of theirs] makes a long peace for all."

2) She finds potential, however, in Olympia's downcast eye and sees a possible comparison of it to Oenone's grief when, in the myth, Trojan Prince Paris abandoned her for Helen. And, she imagines, the addition of one tear would "express fully" Queen Dido's sorrow as she watched Aeneas' fleet departing Carthage. But if the "wench" Queen Dido, had known Aspatia's grief, then she would have deserved the good fortune of a "pitying god" turning her to marble and thus displacing grief altogether.

3) But Aspatia's truest opportunity for imaging grief comes to her when she glances at the tapestry Antiphila is weaving which shows Theseus abandoning Ariadne on the shore of a desert island—the worst of betrayals, after she had saved his life and mission in the cave of the Minotaur. The look of Theseus, she finds, is adequate for a man: his "cozening [deceiving] heart" shows in his "false smile." But there should be an addition to his story: he met, it should say, with shipwreck from a split ship's keel or a "kind rock." It doesn't, because the gods who might have raised a storm are men and therefore as evil as Theseus. She addresses Theseus in the tapestry: "You shall not go so" (i.e., you shall not get off so easily). And she invents—what should have been in the original tale, she claims—a hidden quicksand into which Theseus' ship is heading for his undoing and, waiting for him in the quicksand, the image of Fear itself.

4) Then Aspatia discovers a serious flaw in the tapestry: the image of the abandoned Ariadne is hardly wan and pale enough. She proposes modeling for the portrait herself and so achieving the ultimate portrait of sorrow, the very "monument" of sorrow. And she poses—arms, hair, face thus—and specifies the look of the landscape around her: a "desolation."

5) And finally, the three of them, she instructs, should sit down and study "that point there" (the desolation) and, meditating in "dull silence," gain new souls with the influx of "a sudden sadness." That influx, and those new souls, would be the cap of the sorrow she's pursuing.

ASPATIA

Away, you are not sad! force it no further.
Good gods, how well you look! Such a full colour
Young bashful brides put on: sure, you are new married!

Alas, poor wenches!
Go learn to love first; learn to lose yourselves;
Learn to be flattered, and believe and bless
The double tongue that did it; make a faith
Out of the miracles of ancient lovers,
Such as spake truth and died in 't; and, like me,
Believe all faithful, and be miserable.

Did you ne'er love yet, wenches? Speak, Olympias:
Thou hast an easy temper, fit for stamp.
Never?
Nor you, Antiphila?
Then, my good girls, be more than women, wise;
At least be more than I was; and be sure
You credit anything the light gives life to,
Before a man. Rather believe the sea
Weeps for the ruin'd merchant, when he roars;
Rather, the wind courts but the pregnant sails,
When the strong cordage cracks; rather, the sun
Comes but to kiss the fruit in wealthy autumn,
When all falls blasted. If you needs must love,
(Forc'd by ill fate,) take to your maiden-bosoms
Two dead-cold aspics, and of them make lovers.
They cannot flatter nor forswear; one kiss
Makes a long peace for all. But man—
Oh, that beast man! Come, let's be sad, my girls:
That down-cast of thine eye, Olympias,
Shows a fine sorrow.—Mark, Antiphila;
Just such another was the nymph Oenone's,
When Paris brought home Helen.—Now, a tear;
And then thou art a piece expressing fully
The Carthage queen, when from a cold searock
Full with her sorrow, she tied fast her eyes
To the fair Trojan ships; and, having lost them,
Just as thine does, down stole a tear.—Antiphila,
What would this wench do, if she were Aspatia?
Here she would stand, till some more pitying god
Turn'd her to marble!—'Tis enough, my wench!
Show me the piece of needlework you wrought
Of Ariadne.
Yes, that piece.—
This should be Theseus; h'as a cozening face.—
You meant him for a man?
Why, then, 't is well enough.—Never look back;
You have a full wind and a false heart, Theseus.—

Does not the story say his keel was split,
Or his masts spent, or some kind rock or other
Met with his vessel?
It should ha' been so. Could the gods know this,
And not, of all their number, raise a storm?
But they are all as evil. This false smile
Was well express'd, just such another caught me.—
You shall not go so.
Antiphila, in this place work a quicksand,
And over it a shallow smiling water,
And his ship ploughing it; and then a Fear:
Do that Fear bravely, wench.
'T will not wrong the story.
'T will make the story, wrong'd by wanton poets,
Live long and be believ'd. But where's the lady?
Fie, you have miss'd it here, Antiphila;
You are much mistaken, wench.
These colours are not dull and pale enough
To show a soul so full of misery
As this sad lady's was. Do it by me,
Do it again by me, the lost Aspatia;
And you shall find all true but the wild island.
Suppose I stand upon the sea-beach now,
Mine arms thus, and mine hair blown with the wind,
Wild as that desert; and let all about me
Tell that I am forsaken. Do my face
(If thou had'st ever feeling of a sorrow)
Thus, thus, Antiphila: strive to make me look
Like Sorrow's monument; and the trees about me,
Let them be dry and leafless; let the rocks
Groan with continual surges; and behind me,
Make all a desolation. See, see, wenches,
A miserable life of this poor picture!
I have done. Sit down; and let us
Upon that point fix our eyes, that point there.
Make a dull silence, till you feel a sudden sadness
Give us new souls.

CORDAGE: rigging. ASPICS: asps. DO THAT FEAR BRAVELY: finely. A MISERABLE LIFE: living image.

79.

EVADNE, IN REVENGE FOR HER SEDUCTION, MURDERS THE KING (YT)

(CA. 1608–13) FRANCIS BEAUMONT AND JOHN FLETCHER, *THE MAID'S TRAGEDY*, ACT V, SC. 1

[For Evadne's earlier state, see No. 77, above.] A lustful monarch initiates the action of *The Maid's Tragedy*. It was his seduction of Evadne and his marrying her to his loyal courtier Amintor to provide cover for their affair that bring about the catastrophe. Evadne, not uninitiated in the ways of the court, had at first small objection to the accommodation of husband and royal lover. "I love with my ambition, not with my eyes," she throws at the king in private when he is growing suspicious and jealous of her wifely ease. But it is Evadne's brother Melanthus, a four-square honorable soldier, who on discovering his sister's case, destroys her ease completely.

A tough Evadne, who can sneer at the husband's torment as well as the king's jealousy, is overcome by her brother's soldier's moral outrage that drives her to beg the pardon of her husband and vow murderous revenge on the king. But remarkably, unlike the multitude of quickly softened women sinners whose forthrightness collapses at their conversion and who become indistinguishable from one another in remorse [see Mistress Frankford, No. 69, above], Evadne's way of staring at reality and giving no countenance to posture doesn't desert her even when she is assassinating her royal lover. The conventional rhetoric of morally driven vengeance does not intrude. The same Evadne who spoke so chillingly to her bridegroom [see No. 77, above] and speaks so chillingly to her victim-king does the job at hand—which is to shame, insult, and kill—with neither tears nor lofty sermonizing.

"The conscience of a lost virtue" is a terrible thing, she reasons. But given "the slaughter on [her] honor" she's already undergone, all she can do with it, she further reasons, is to finish out that slaughter by doing this deed. And the spirit in which she will do it? "I am a tiger," she explains to the king, holding a dagger over his tied-up body, "I am anything that knows not pity." And she proves it.

EVADNE

The night grows horrible; and all about me
Like my black purpose.

(Draws a curtain disclosing the King
abed)
O, the conscience
Of a lost virtue, whither wilt thou pull me?
To what things dismal as the depth of hell
Wilt thou provoke me? Let no woman dare
From this hour be disloyal, if her heart be flesh,
If she have blood, and can fear. 'Tis a daring
Above that desperate fool's that left his peace,
And went to sea to fight: 'tis so many sins
An age cannot repent 'em; and so great,
The gods want mercy for. Yet I must through 'em:
I have begun a slaughter on my honor,
And I must end it there.—'A sleeps. O God,
Why give you peace to this untemperate beast,
That hath so long transgressed you? I must kill him,
And I will do it bravely: the mere joy
Tells me, I merit in it. Yet I must not
Thus tamely do it, as he sleeps—that were
To rock him to another world; my vengeance
Shall take him waking, and then lay before him
The number of his wrongs and punishments:
I'll shape his sins like Furies, till I waken
His evil angel, his sick conscience,
And then I'll strike him dead. King, by your leave;

(Ties his arms to the bed.)
I dare not trust your strength; your grace and I
Must grapple upon even terms no more.
So, if he rail me not from my resolution,
I shall be strong enough.—
My lord the King!—My lord!—'A sleeps,
As if he meant to wake no more.—My lord!—
Is he not dead already? Sir! my lord!

O, you sleep soundly, sir!
I am come at length, sir; but how welcome?
Stay, sir, stay;
You are too hot, and I have brought you physic
To temper your high veins.

I know you have a surfeited foul body;
And you must bleed.

           (Draws a dagger.)
Ay, you shall bleed. Lie still; and, if the devil,
Your lust, will give you leave, repent. This steel
Comes to redeem the honor that you stole,
King, my fair name; which nothing but thy death
Can answer to the world.

I am not she; nor bear I in this breast
So much cold spirit to be called a woman:
I am a tiger; I am any thing
That knows not pity. Stir not: if thou dost,
I'll take thee unprepared, thy fears upon thee,
That make thy sins look double, and so send thee
(By my revenge, I will!) to look those torments
Prepared for such black souls.

Gentle? No, I am not:
I am as foul as thou art, and can number
As many such hells here. I was once fair,
Once I was lovely; not a blowing rose
More chastely sweet, till thou, thou, thou, foul canker,
(Stir not) didst poison me. I was a world of virtue,
Till your cursed court and you (hell bless you for't)
With your temptations on temptations
Made me give up mine honor; for which, King,
I am come to kill thee.

I am.
Peace, and hear me.
Stir nothing but your tongue, and that for mercy
To those above us; by whose lights I vow
Those blessed fires that shot to see our sin,
If thy hot soul had substance with thy blood,
I would kill that too; which, being past my steel,
My tongue shall reach. Thou art a shameless villain;
A thing out of the overcharge of nature,
Sent, like a thick cloud, to disperse a plague
Upon weak catching women; such a tyrant,
That for his lust would sell away his subjects,
Ay, all his heaven hereafter!

Thou art my shame! Lie still; there's none about you,

Within your cries; all promises of safety
Are but deluding dreams. Thus, thus, thou foul man,
Thus I begin my vengeance!

(Stabs him)

I do not mean, sir,
To part so fairly with you; we must change
More of these love-tricks yet.
What bloody villain
Provoked this murder?
Thou, thou monster!
Thou kept'st me brave at court, and whored me, King;
Then married me to a young noble gentleman,
And whored me still.
Hell take me, then! This for my lord Amintor.
This for my noble brother! and this stroke
For the most wronged of women!

(Kills him)

Die all our faults together! I forgive thee.

(Exit)

TO LOOK (FOR): i.e., those torments. CANKER: gangrenous sore. BLESSED FIRES THAT
SHOT: meteors. OVERCHARGE: superfluity. CATCHING: susceptible. CHANGE: exchange.

80.

MISTRESS OTTER VIGOROUSLY CONFIRMS FOR HER HUSBAND HIS SERVILE PLACE IN THEIR HOUSEHOLD (OC)

(1609) BEN JONSON, *EPICOENE, OR THE SILENT WOMAN*, ACT III, SC. 1

Mistress Otter is one of the more assured dragon ladies of English comedy—nearly the most assured. She has the social and financial advantage of being the source of money and respectability in her marriage to the rough, not-too-well-to-do "land and sea Captain"

Otter. She has entirely the psychological advantage for effective bludgeoning in her voice, manner, glare, and entire being that brooks neither contest, argument nor interruption.

For the coming festivities of Morose's wedding [see, in Men's monologues: "Morose Interviews a Potentially Silent Wife"], the Captain, hat figuratively in hand, is offering justification with temerity to his spouse for wanting to include the "exhibitions" for which he's famous. "Tom Otter's bull, bear and horse," he ventures, "is known all over England, *in rerum natura.*" Bull-baiting, bear-baiting, and horse shows are not to Mistress Otter's improved taste. He and his suggestion are crushed by his spouse's iron rhetoric.

Mistress Otter

By that light, I'll ha' you chained up with your bull-dogs and bear-dogs, if you be not civil the sooner. I'll send you to kennel, i'faith. You were best bait me with your bull, bear and horse! Never a time that the courtiers or collegiates come to the house, but you make it a Shrove Tuesday! I would have you get your Whitsuntide velvet cap, and your staff i' your hand to entertain 'em; yes in troth, do. Tom Otter's bull, bear and horse is known all over England, *in rerum natura?* 'Fore me, I will *na-ture* 'em over to Paris Garden, and *na-ture* you thither too, if you pronounce 'em again. Is a bear a fit beast, or a bull, to mix in society with great ladies? Think i' your discretion, in any good polity?

By my integrity, I'll send you over to the Bankside, I'll commit you to the Master of the Garden, if I hear but a syllable more. Must my house or my roof be polluted with the scent of bears and bulls, when it is perfumed for great ladies? Is this according to the instrument, when I married you? That I would be princess, and reign in mine own house, and you would be my subject, and obey me? What did you bring me, should make you thus peremptory? Do I allow you your half-crown a day to spend where you will among your gamesters, to vex and torment me at such times as these? Who gives you your maintenance, I pray you? Who allows you your horse meat, and man's meat? Your three suits' of apparel a year? Your four pair of stockings, one silk, three worsted? Your clean linen, your bands and cuffs when I can get you to wear 'em? 'Tis mar'l you ha' 'em on now. Who graces you with courtiers or great personages to speak to you out of their coaches and come home to your house? Were you ever so much as looked

upon by a lord or a lady before I married you, but on the
Easter or Whitsun holidays, and then out at the Banqueting
House window, when Ned Whiting or George Stone were at
the stake? Answer me to that. And did not I take you up from
thence in an old greasy buff-doublet, with points and green
velvet sleeves out at the elbows? You forget this. O, here are
some o' the gallants! Go to, behave yourself distinctly and with
good morality, or I protest, I'll take away your exhibition.

SHROVE TUESDAY, WHITSUNTIDE: holiday occasions for celebration. IN RERUM NATU-
RA: in the nature of things. PARIS GARDEN: a bear-garden on the Bankside in
Southwark. POLITY: government. INSTRUMENT: legal agreement. PEREMPTORY: final,
admitting of no debate. MAR'L: marvel. NED WHITING OR GEORGE STONE: famous
bears that bore their masters' names. OUT AT THE BANQUETING HOUSE WINDOW:
bears were sometimes baited in the courtyard at Whitehall on holidays. DOUBLET: a
close-fitting outer garment worn by men. POINTS: laces holding clothing together.
EXHIBITION: allowance.

81.
VITTORIA RECOUNTS A DREAM
TO INSPIRE BRACHIANO TO
DOUBLE MURDER (YT)

(1609–12) JOHN WEBSTER, *THE WHITE DEVIL*, ACT I, SC. 2

[See Flamineo's, Francisco's, and Brachiano's monologues in Men's
volumes.] Here is the difference between Elizabethan and Jacobean
dialogue and almost all other: in it, there is an ineradicable play of
irony in almost all its conventionalized discourse, slipping in and out
of codified signaling to the intelligent—a smile, a sneer, a curse, a
bribe, or a soothing lie might live underneath its blather—and, lid
off, the shocking, direct dagger-thrust of naked meaning speaking
naked intent. The leap, or sometimes the slide, from one to the other,
gives dramatic roller-coaster tempo to its dialogue which matches
when occasion warrants the roller-coaster flip of the action from one
moment to the next. Even in soliloquy, it is as though a portion of its
words might well be put in quotes, being used as though for ironic reference to the standard notion of them, now being mocked or

shrugged at or even resuscitated for their original, untarnished signification.

It is one of the defining pleasures of this drama, a sophisticated writer's pleasure that lasted about fifty years, not yet born in the 1580's, and a pleasure fading until no longer alive in the 1640's. It is also so uniquely defining a feature of this period of tragic drama, that all attempts at imitation and emulation since, incapable of such a sustained double feat of both believing and not believing in the simple truth of the same words while they are being spoken, have not only failed, but make one wonder how, as in so many Eighteenth Century and later English imitations, the same words can become so pedestrian, stupid and plain boring.

Here they are not. They're informed consistently—certainly and always, in Webster's tragedies—by a certain sardonic risibility that lies just below the surface of the fine talk (when enemies, for example, are talking politely to one another, or a single soul on stage is contending with his own real and deepest desires against formalist pieties to which, in all conscience, he feels no allegiance, but to which, still, he feels he must answer.) Vittoria, for example, can talk in hardly any other way; like the profoundly sneering Flamineo, her brother, a double intelligence in them that knows the self and also knows the corrupt but polished world, speaks, always, with a sort of double rhetoric; one for his/her own delectation, the other for the world to make of it what it can.

Vittoria, lying in the arms of the Duke Brachiano, brought to his lap by brother Flamineo who serves among other functions as pimp for his employer the Duke, she whispering in almost lyric strain the description of her dream with seductive charm and appealing innocence, is affectionately telling him to murder her husband and his wife.

VITTORIA

To pass away the time I'll tell your Grace
A dream I had last night.
A foolish idle dream:
Methought I walked about the mid of night,
Into a church-yard, where a goodly yew-tree
Spread her large root in ground; under that yew,
As I sat sadly leaning on a grave,
Checkered with cross-sticks, there came stealing in
Your Duchess and my husband; one of them
A pick-axe bore, th'other a rusty spade,
And in rough terms they gan to challenge me,

About this yew.
That tree.
This harmless yew.
They told me my intent was to root up
That well-grown yew, and plant i'th'stead of it
A withered blackthorn, and for that they vowed
To bury me alive: my husband straight
With pick-axe gan to dig, and your fell Duchess
With shovel, like a fury, voided out
The earth and scattered bones. Lord, how methought
I trembled, and yet for all this terror
I could not pray.

When to my rescue there arose, methought,
A whirlwind which let fall a massy arm
From that strong plant,
And both were struck dead by that sacred yew
In that base shallow grave that was their due.

CROSS-STICKS: wooden crosses sticking out of the graves; or possibly checkered patterns created by the overhanging branches of willow trees. GAN: began.

82.

VITTORIA SPITS VENOM AT THE VERDICT OF HER CORRUPT JUDGES (YT)

(1609–12) JOHN WEBSTER, *THE WHITE DEVIL*, ACT III, SC. 2

When the double discourse [described in No. 81, above] is put aside and the "lid" is off (as that note suggests), we hear "the shocking, direct dagger-thrust of naked meaning speaking naked intent." Such naked meaning leaps forth from Vittoria's mouth when she is judged criminal by an ecclesiastic-cum-secular court she utterly despises.

Duke Brachiano obliged both Vittoria and himself by arranging for the murder of his wife and Vittoria's husband with a view to their own union. A difficulty arises when the wife's brother, Francisco, Duke of Florence, and the husband's uncle, Cardinal Monticelso (soon to be Pope), knowing the murderers, want revenge. Brachiano, who is out of jurisdiction, cannot be legally put on trial, and Vittoria cannot be directly accused of murder. She is tried and condemned by the two (who are both her accusers and her judges) merely for sexual offense, and condemned to serve sentence in "a house of convertites."

VITTORIA

A house of convertites, what's that?
A house
Of penitent whores!
Do the noblemen in Rome
Erect it for their wives, that I am sent
To lodge there?
I must first have vengeance.
I fain would know if you have your salvation
By patent, that you proceed thus.
A rape, a rape!
Yes, you have ravished Justice,
Forced her to do your pleasure.
Die with these pills in your most cursed maws,
Should bring you health, or while you sit o'th'bench,
Let your own spittle choke you.
That the last day of judgement may so find you,
And leave you the devil you were before,
Instruct me some good horse-leech to speak treason,
For since you cannot take my life for deeds,
Take it for words. O woman's poor revenge
Which dwells but in the tongue; I will not weep,
No I do scorn to call up one poor tear
To fawn on your injustice; bear me hence,
Unto this house of—what's your mitigating title?

Of convertites.

It shall not be a house of convertites.
My mind shall make it honester to me
Than the Pope's palace, and more peaceable
Than thy soul, though thou art a cardinal.
Know this, and let it somewhat raise your spite,
Through darkness diamonds spread their richest light.

(Exit)

HORSE-LEACH: a blood sucker, a cunning rhetorician; in Erasmus, "the rhetoricians of our day who consider themselves as good as gods—if like horse-leaches they can seem to have two tongues." FAWN: to plead favor by servile demeanor.

83.

VITTORIA, ACCUSED BY HER LOVER BRACHIANO OF BETRAYAL, RESPONDS IN TURN WITH VITRIOL (YT)

(1609–12) JOHN WEBSTER, *THE WHITE DEVIL*, ACT IV, SC. 2

Vittoria is serving sentence in "the house of convertites" for the only crime of which she could be accused, sexual transgression with Duke Brachiano. On his visit to her, he greets her bitterly as "a brave great lady,/A stately and advanced whore." He is enraged by a letter from the Duke Francisco, who [see in Men' volumes "Francisco Fashions His Revenge for Isabella's Murder…"] "plans an amusing prologue [to the eventual murder of Brachiano] to have a letter delivered to Vittoria at the house of convertites, with a message of love from himself, the letter to be delivered in Brachiano's presence. The poisoning pang of jealousy is to precede the pain of Brachiano's death by poisoning." But Brachiano's rage stirs Vittoria's and, with her blast of counteraccusation, turns him into the suitor for her calm and then forgiveness. Her rage towers over his and lasts longer, so that he has little choice but to silence her, at long last, with a kiss. It's the demonstration of a lofty pride of self, their peculiar integrity of person, that, at the end of the storm, neither apologizes, and neither offers explanation. The kiss ends all rancor and all confusion; and they proceed immediately to plan Vittoria's escape with Flamineo.

VITTORIA

No matter.
I'll live so now I'll make the world recant
And change her speeches. You did name the Duchess.
Whose death God revenge
On thee, most godless Duke.
What have I gained by thee but infamy?
Thou hast stained the spotless honor of my house,
And frighted thence noble society:
Like those, which sick o' the palsy, and retain
Ill-scenting foxes 'bout them, are still shunn'd
By those of choicer nostrils.
What do you call this house?
Is this your palace? Did not the judge style it

A house of penitent whores? Who sent me to it?
Who hath the honor to advance Vittoria
To this incontinent college? Is't not you?
Is't not your high preferment? Go, but brag
How many ladies you have undone, like me.
Fare you well, sir. Let me hear no more of you.
I had a limb corrupted to an ulcer,
But I have cut it off: and now I'll go
Weeping to heaven on crutches.
For your gifts, I will return them all, and I do wish
That I could make you full executor
To all my sins. O that I could toss myself
Into a grave as quickly: for all thou are worth
I'll not shed one tear more;—I'll burst first.

O thou fool,
Whose greatness hath by much o'ergrown thy wit!
What dar'st thou do that I not dare to suffer,
Excepting to be still thy whore? For that,
In the sea's bottom sooner thou shalt make
A bonfire.

O ye dissembling men!
Am I not low enough?
Ay, ay, your good heart gathers like snowball
Now your affection's cold.
Your dog or hawk should be rewarded better
Than I have been. I'll speak not one word more.

SICK O' THE PALSY...THOSE OF CHOICER NOSTRILS: Foxes, known for their foul odor, were commonly used in the treatment of the palsy, a disease characterized by convulsions or paralysis. PREFERMENT: promotion.

84.

CORNELIA, HAVING WITNESSED THE MURDER OF HER SON, GOES MAD (OT)

(1609–12) JOHN WEBSTER, *THE WHITE DEVIL*, ACT V, SC. 4

Flamineo, in a quarrel with his younger brother Marcello, promised a duel. To accept his challenge, Marcello sent Flamineo his own sword. Their mother, Cornelia, comes to ascertain whether rumor is true and witnesses Flamineo's arrival. In the act of returning Marcello's sword, he greets his brother with, "I have brought your weapon back," and, on the instant, runs him through. Cornelia, driven mad by this horror, is now dressing the body of Marcello in a winding sheet, and in her distraction, fixed in her task, converts the ceremony into detached, emotionally neutral, wonted labor. Hers is akin to the madness depicted in *The Spanish Tragedy*'s Hieronymo. To quote from Men's volumes "Mad Hieronymo Mistakes a Suppliant for His Dead Son": "Madness is reckoned in Elizabethan and Jacobean drama not so much as the derangement of a mind into verbal incoherence...but rather as the madman imagining he is undergoing sudden and successive shifts of scene and circumstance, each experienced with absolute clarity, almost with the swiftness of thought (as in the rapid shifts of subjective time and place in Ophelia's and Lear's scenes of 'madness')." But for Cornelia, her subjective action doesn't undergo shifts of scene and circumstance; it remains in place. Though doing the mournful task she is realistically called on to do, she is nevertheless altogether detached from its immediacy, as though the reality has been supplanted by its resemblance, and so protecting and diminishing the enormity of its actual association. "Alas! Her grief has turned her child again," remarks one of the women assisting her. But it is not the "childishness" that is governing the methodical routine with which Cornelia prepares her son for burial, but emotional distance. It is not her actions, but that determined distancing, that construes her "madness."

We follow the routine of the strewing of flowers; the instructions to replace the withered ones; the precaution of putting a garland on the corpse's head to protect against its being struck by lightning; her distributing flowers to the mourners, including herself; her taking Flamineo to be the newly arrived gravedigger; her spelling out those sure signs of a new corpse's coming; singing her grandmother's song when a funeral bell tolled, a song about the birds that naturally tended dead bodies, the field creatures that covered the unburied bodies with mounds of earth, with a warning about the wolves who dig them up again. Her song concluded, she notes that this particular corpse, because "he died in a quarrel," might not get burial, but counters that, having paid his church taxes, there's no reason why he should not.

The winding sheet sewn, she stares at the wrapped thing and notes—what is true of any corpse—that his whole wealth, "all his store," is contained inside it. Job done, supplies finished, she shuts up shop, and says goodnight to her assistants.

(Cornelia discovered, winding
Marcello's corse.)

CORNELIA

This rosemary is withered, pray get fresh:
I would have these herbs grow up in his grave
When I am dead and rotten. Reach the bays;
I'll tie a garland here about his head:
'Twill keep my boy from lightning. This sheet
I have kept this twenty year, and every day
Hallowed it with my prayers—I did not think
He should have wore it.
O, reach me the flowers.
You're very welcome.
There's rosemary for you and rue for you,
Heart's-ease for you. I pray make much of it.
I have left more for myself.
You are, I take it, the grave-maker. So.
Here's a white hand:
Can blood so soon be washed out? Let me see:
When screech-owls croak upon the chimney tops
And the strange cricket i'th'oven sings and hops,
When yellow spots do on your hands appear,
Be certain then you of a corse shall hear.
Out upon't, how 'tis speckled! H'as handled a toad sure.
Cowslip-water is good for the memory: pray buy me three
ounces of't.
Do you hear, sir? I'll give you a saying which my grandmother
Was wont, when she heard the bell toll, to sing o'er
Unto her lute—

"Call for the robin-red-breast and the wren,
Since o'er shady groves they hover,
And with leaves and flowers do cover
The friendless bodies of unburied men.
Call unto his funeral dole
The ant, the field-mouse, and the mole
To rear him hillocks that shall keep him warm
And (when gay tombs are robbed) sustain no harm,
But keep the wolf far thence that's foe to men,
For with his nails he'll dig them up again."

They would not bury him 'cause he died in a quarrel
But I have an answer for them.
"Let holy church receive him duly
Since he paid the church tithes truly."
His wealth is summed, and this is all his store:
This poor men get and great men get no more.
Now the wares are gone, we may shut up shop.
Bless you all good people.

ROSEMARY: an evergreen shrub, symbol of remembrance. 'TWILL KEEP MY BOY FROM
LIGHTNING: the garland will protect him from lightning. RUE: yellowish-flowered
medicinal herb, symbol of sorrow. HEART'S-EASE: a pansy, symbol of peace of mind.
REACH: to hand. BAY: the European laurel. CORSE: corpse. COWSLIP: the English
primrose, bearing yellow flowers. HILLOCK: small hill. TITHE: a church tax.

85.

MEGRA OUTFACES THE KING'S CONDEMNATION OF HER LASCIVIOUSNESS BY THREATENING IN TURN THE REPUTATION OF HIS DAUGHTER (OT)

(1610) FRANCIS BEAUMONT AND JOHN FLETCHER,
PHILASTER, ACT II, SC. 4

Later in Restoration comedy, a "character" is briefly and bluntly
described at, or at a moment before, entrance, the description frequently dipped in malice. The practice followed the French fashion of
the *caractère*, a genre in its own right, which delineated and exempli-
fied types. Anticipating that subsequent common practice, *Philaster*
favors the character of Megra with just such a preface: "She'll cog
[wheedle, cajole] and lie with a whole army… Her name is common
through the kingdom, and the trophies of her dishonor advanced
beyond Hercules' Pillars. She loves to try the several constitutions of
men's bodies, and, indeed, has destroyed the worth of her own body
by making experiment upon it for the good of the commonwealth."
Megra obliges her description by immediately seducing the Spanish

Prince on his first night in Messina, a traveler who's journeyed for days for the purpose of marriage to the King's daughter, Arethusa. He, after so many days of abstinence, is not at all unwilling, and such a to-do does their assignation make that the King himself, alarmed by report, stands outside his guest's chamber demanding entrance. The Prince stands on his honor, refuses the King entrance, but Megra, though a court lady, not at all abashed by such intrusions—as she says, she's known them before—appears and faces the King. In fact, outfaces him.

He, outraged at her anticipating his daughter's wedlock by engineering so sordid a previous night's fun with the Prince, excoriates, condemns, threatens this "most ill-shrouded rottenness," this "swollen cloud of infection," and much worse, at all of which Megra merely laughs. She has reason to jeer, she imagines, at the monarch; she knows what he does not know, that his chaste daughter is in fact not so chaste in the arms of a beautiful young boy in her entourage, a fact Megra will have no qualms publishing should the King's rhetoric advance to punishment. With so powerful a weapon of blackmail, she can afford to brave the King himself.

The spectacle of a court lady caught *in flagrante delicto* hurling mocking insults at a King is pure Beaumont and Fletcher, whose plot situations can dally at the edge of plain indecency, only to be rescued from their own implication by the saving grace of later revelations. In this case, the beautiful boy turns out to be, not unexpectedly, a young lady in disguise, who is at court, in concealment, not for the favor of Arethusa but for Philaster, the idol of her infatuation. And so potential scandal is blunted, and blackmail loses its teeth. But before that revelation, Megra remains at court, with little to do for the rest of the play, but safe at least from harm.

> MEGRA
>
> Let 'em enter, prince, let 'em enter;
> I am up and ready: I know their business;
> 'T is the poor breaking of a lady's honour
> They hunt so hotly after: let 'em enjoy it.—
> You have your business, gentlemen; I lay here.
> Oh, my lord the king, this is not noble in you
> To make public the weakness of a woman!
> Your hootings and your clamours,
> Your private whispers and your broad fleerings,
> Can no more vex my soul than this base carriage.
> But I have vengeance yet in store for some

Shall, in the most contempt you can have of me,
Be joy and nourishment.
Will I come down?
Yes, to laugh at your worst; but I shall wring you,
If my skill fail me not.

Faith, sir you must pardon me;
I cannot choose but laugh to see you merry.
If you do this, O King! nay, if you dare do it,
By all those gods you swore by, and as many
More of my own, I will have fellows, and such
Fellows in it, as shall make noble mirth!
The princess, your dear daughter, shall stand by me
On walls, and sung in ballads, anything.
Urge me no more; I know her and her haunts,
Her lays, leaps, and outlays, and will discover all;
Nay, will dishonour her. I know the boy
She keeps; a handsome boy, about eighteen;
Know what she does with him, where, and when.
Come, sir, you put me to a woman's madness,
The glory of a fury; and if I do not
Do 't to the height—

What boy is this?
Alas! good-minded prince, you know not these things!
I am loath to reveal 'em. Keep this fault,
As you would keep your health from the hot air
Of the corrupted people, or, by Heaven,
I will not fall alone. What I have known
Shall be as public as a print; all tongues
Shall speak it as they do the language they
Are born in, as free and commonly; I'll set it,
Like a prodigious star, for all to gaze at,
And so high and glowing, that other kingdoms far and foreign
Shall read it there, nay, travel with it, till they find
No tongue to make it more, nor no more people;
And then behold the fall of your fair princess!
I'll go, and get me to my quarter:
For this time I will study to forget you.
Do you study to forget me.

FLEERINGS: jeers, mockings.

86.

DOLL COMMON VIOLENTLY PUTS AN END TO THE QUARREL BETWEEN SUBTLE AND FACE (YC)

(1610) BEN JONSON, *THE ALCHEMIST*, ACT I, SC. 1

"The venter tripartite! All things in common! Without priority!"—Doll Common insisting that she, Captain Face, and their henchman Subtle are all in their story together, none with larger share, none leader. The three commandeered Lovewit's (Face's master's) house while he was absent, converted it into an alchemist's lab and living quarters for themselves, and are doing thriving business with the dupes and gulls who are paying good money to see the "alchemist" Subtle's alembics calcify and rubrify and eventually produce gold.

Who are they? Face is a poor servant "raised," Subtle rails, "from broom, and dust, and wat'ring pots," and turned by Subtle into master cheat. Subtle, counters Face, is "the vomit of all prisons," a "bawd" (procurer), and now too master cheat. And Doll Common, as her name broadcasts, is a trollop used as sexual decoy for the trio's scams.

Two things, at this critical moment, terrify Doll. One is the possibility that the two screaming men will destroy their thriving partnership, and the other that the neighbors of master Lovewit's respectable house will hear and know and condemn. And so she takes charge: she pulls Face's sword out of his hand, breaks Subtle's "glass" (his telescope) that he was using as a weapon, and throttles Subtle until she forces and then peacefully persuades the two to give up their quarrel and shake hands, bringing the wild roarings at the beginning of the scene to calm and peace.

That doll has the grip and authority to quell the two roaring men brings her close to the great "man woman" Moll Cutpurse in *The Roaring Girl* [see No. 87, below] who quells men not only with the power of her words, but with the lash of her sword. Both, from the grunge of city comedy's London, qualify considerably romantic comedy's picture of London's dew-stained virgins.

DOLL

(She catcheth out Face his sword, and

breaks Subtle's glass.)
'Sdeath, you abominable pair of stinkards,
Leave off your barking, and grow one again,
Or, by the light that shines, I'll cut your throats.
I'll not be made a prey unto the marshal
For ne'er a snarling dog-bolt o' you both.
Ha' you together cozen'd all this while,
And all the world, and shall it now be said,
You've made most courteous shift to cozen yourselves?

(To Face) You will accuse him! You will "bring him in
Within the statute!" Who shall take your word?
A whoreson, upstart, apocryphal captain,
Whom not a Puritan in Blackfriars will trust
So much as for a feather: and you, too,

(To Subtle) Will give the cause, forsooth! You will insult,
And claim a primacy in the divisions!
You must be chief! As if you, only, had
The powder to project with, and the work
Were not begun out of equality!
The venter tripartite! All things in common!
Without priority! 'Sdeath! you perpetual curs,
Fall to your couples again, and cozen kindly
And heartily, and lovingly, as you should,
And lose not the beginning of a term,
Or, by this hand, I shall grow factious too,
And take my part, and quit you.
Death on me!
Help me throttle him.

(Seizes Sub by the throat.)
Because o' your fermentation and cibation?
Your Sol and Luna—help me.

(To Face) Will you, sir? Do so then, and quickly: swear.
To leave your faction, sir.
And labour kindly in the common work.
I hope we need no spurs, sir. Do we?
Yes, and work close and friendly.

(They shake hands.)
Why, so, my good baboons! Shall we go make
A sort of sober, scurvy, precise neighbours,

That scarce have smil'd twice sin' the king came in,
A feast of laughter at our follies? Rascals,
Would run themselves from breath, to see me ride,
Or you t' have but a hole to thrust your heads in,
For which you should pay ear-rent? No, agree.
And may Don Provost ride a-feasting long,
In his old velvet jerkin and stain'd scarfs,
My noble sovereign, and worthy general,
Ere we contribute a new crewel garter
To his most worsted worship.

MARSHALL: law officer. DOG-BOLT: scoundrel. COZEN'D: cheated. "BRING HIM IN
WITHIN THE STATUTE!": i.e., get him arrested. APOCRYPHAL: false, spurious. PRIMA-
CY OF THE DIVISIONS: larger share of the booty. PROJECT: in alchemy, to transmute
base metals into gold. VENTER TRIPARTITE: threefold agreement. COUPLES: partnership. TERM: of the law courts. FACTIOUS: partisan, quarrelsome. FERMENTATION AND
CIBATION: processes in alchemy. SOL AND LUNA: sun and moon; here, gold and silver.
PRECISE: puritanical. SHALL WE GO MAKE...LAUGHTER AT OUR FOLLIES: foolish
enough to cause proper citizens to laugh at us, people who haven't laughed since the
coronation of James I. RIDE: to ride in a cart in order to be exhibited as a bawd. HOLE
TO PUT YOUR HEAD IN: i.e., to have your head put in the stocks. PAY EAR-RENT: to have
one's ears cut off (to fit the head through the stocks). DON PROVOST: the hangman.
CREWEL: embroidered.

87.

MOLL THE ROARING GIRL, EXPLAINS SOBERLY TO A SUITOR WHY MARRIAGE IS NOT AND NEVER WILL BE FOR HER (YC)

(1611) THOMAS MIDDLETON AND THOMAS DEKKER, THE ROARING GIRL, ACT II, SC. 2

It's one of the male wastrels in *The Roaring Girl* who sets off the
incredible diatribe—one that sounds as though it might have been
written today—by Moll Cutpurse against the automatic assumptions
of men about women and their automatic predations against them.
Moll, in temper, combines commonsensical equanimity and rage
and, in another context, both man's and woman's sexuality (her double entendre: "I love to lie on both ends o' th' bed"). She's all woman
in her moral commitments and all man in their defense. To call her

merely "virago" misses the point. Not to lift her too far out of Jacobean context, an up-to-date prescriptive definition would be something like: bisexual and uncompromisingly feminist. In her plot function, she combines the solicitude of, say, *Romeo and Juliet*'s Nurse and the practical downrightness—with none of the flaunting indecency and greed—of Rojas' Spanish bawd, Celestina [see No. 103, below].

Moll is large, fat, taciturn until provoked, slow in tread and in arousal, and with a face as close to man's as to woman's. When kindly disposed, and when so confronted, she responds in kind. Take for example her extraordinary interview with the young Sebastian. The young man is pretending to be infatuated with Moll, to be longing to marry her, to move his miserly father, Sir Wengrave, to accept the dowryless young woman he *really* loves in order to rescue the family name from the likes of Moll. Sebastian carries his charade so far as to propose—in his father's hearing—to Moll, pushing his father, he prays, to the brink of desperation. But Moll, thoroughly approving of her fake suitor's genuine courtesy and style in making his offer, gives him her considered answer: it is "no," of course, no marriage for reasons that are both evident on the face of it, and also those that are private to her convictions. She does, for one, "lie on both sides of the bed," she's not exactly cut out for wifely obedience, she is in fact herself "man enough for any woman," and—most importantly—she deplores marriage on principle as a bad bargain for the woman, who must exchange her (maiden) head for a worse "head," the man's, whose head must govern.

That's her response to a gentleman. To a *machismo* pretender [see No. 88, below], she has a very different response. Laxton, a character we're to meet several times over in Restoration comedy, is the *faux* libertine who pretends to a prowess to which he can never aspire. At first sight, he supposes that Moll, with the look of a termagant, is right for his negative appetites, and supposes without second thought that she, a woman after all, must be ready to gratify them. He tosses a purse of money to her and arranges for an assignation. Moll takes the money, agrees to the rendezvous, and is set to castrate his pretensions. She meets with him dressed as a man, is unrecognized by him until she removes her hat—the spectacle of his doxy suddenly enlarged into a man for a moment destabilizes him—and then playing the woman who is equal to sporting in the man's world, she draws her sword and demands that he do the same to avenge, as would a man offered the same derogating insult, her honor.

While flourishing her sword in combat, pressing him to the wall, forcing him to the ground, and disarming him of his weapon, she editorializes the very lesson she's acting out on his trembling frame. The argument is recognizable, its terms and points by now familiar to us. But what is astonishing is that Moll, in the early 1700s, so totally anticipates the politics, angers, thoughts, and resentments for woman's sake, not merely for her own time, but for today.

MOLL

Sir, I am so poor to requite you, you must look for nothing but thanks of me. I have no humour to marry. I love to lie o' both sides o' th' bed myself; and again, o' th' other side, a wife, you know, ought to be obedient, but I fear me I am too headstrong to obey; therefore I'll ne'er go about it. I love you so well, sir, for your good will, I'd be loath you should repent your bargain after, and therefore we'll ne'er come together at first. I have the head now of myself, and am man enough for a woman; marriage is but a chopping and changing, where a maiden loses one head and has a worse i' th' place.

But sleep upon this once more, sir; you may chance shift a mind tomorrow. Be not too hasty to wrong yourself. Never while you live, sir, take a wife running. Many have run out at heels that have done 't. You see, sir, I speak against myself, and if every woman would deal with their suitor so honestly, poor younger brothers would not be so often gulled with old cozening widows that turn o'er all their wealth in trust to some kinsman and make the poor gentleman work hard for a pension.

Think upon this in cold blood, sir; you make as much haste as if you were a-going upon a sturgeon voyage. Take deliberation, sir; never choose a wife as if you were going to Virginia.

COZENING: cheating, lying. sturgeon voyage: a fishing-voyage for sturgeon fish. GOING TO VIRGINIA: the contemporary equivalent of the 1840s American Gold Rush, and had the same consequence for its victims.

88.

MOLL, TAKEN FOR A HARLOT, TEACHES HER SOLICITOR "MANNERS" WITH THE END OF A SWORD (YC)

(1611) THOMAS MIDDLETON AND THOMAS DEKKER, *THE ROARING GIRL*, ACT III, SC. 1

[See No. 87, above.]

(Enter Moll like a man.)

MOLL

(Aside) Oh, here's my gentleman! If they would keep their days as well with their mercers as their hours with their harlots, no bankrupt would give sevenscore pound for a sergeant's place; for, would you know a catchpole rightly derived, the corruption of a citizen is the generation of a sergeant. How his eye hawks for venery! *(To him)* Come, are you ready, sir? Where stands the coach?
You're an old wanton in your eyes, I see that.
Stay!

> *(She puts off her cloak and draws [her sword].)*

Here's the point that I untruss: 't has but one tag, 'twill serve though to tie up a rogue's tongue.
Draw, or I'll serve an execution on thee
Shall lay thee up till doomsday.
To teach thy base thoughts manners. Thou'rt one of those
That thinks each woman thy fond flexible whore.
If she but cast a liberal eye upon thee,
Turn back her head, she's thine; or, amongst company,
By chance drink first to thee, then she's quite gone,
There's no means to help her; nay, for a need,
Wilt swear unto thy credulous fellow lechers
That thou'rt more in favour with a lady
At first sight than her monkey all her lifetime.
How many of our sex by such as thou
Have their good thoughts paid with a blasted name
That never deserved loosely or did trip

223

In path of whoredom beyond cup and lip?
But for the stain of conscience and of soul,
Better had women fall into the hands
Of an act silent than a bragging nothing;
There's no mercy in 't. What durst move you, sir,
To think me whorish?—a name which I'd tear out
From the high German's throat if it lay ledger there
To dispatch privy slanders against me!
In thee I defy all men, their worst hates
And their best flatteries, all their golden witchcrafts
With which they entangle the poor spirits of fools.
Distressed needlewomen and trade-fall'n wives—
Fish that must needs bite or themselves be bitten—
Such hungry things as these may soon be took
With a worm fastened on a golden hook;
Those are the lecher's food, his prey. He watches
For quarrelling wedlocks and poor shifting sisters;
'Tis the best fish he takes. But why, good fisherman,
Am I thought meat for you, that never yet
Had angling rod cast towards me? 'Cause you'll say
I'm given to sport, I'm often merry, jest.
Had mirth no kindred in the world but lust?
Oh, shame take all her friends, then! But howe'er
Thou and the baser world censure my life,
I'll send 'em word by thee, and write so much
Upon thy breast, 'cause thou shalt bear 't in mind.
Tell them 'twere base to yield where I have conquered.
I scorn to prostitute myself to a man,
I that can prostitute a man to me!
And so I greet thee.

(Exit Laxton.)

If I could meet my enemies one by one thus,
I might make pretty shift with 'em in time,
And make 'em know, she that has wit and spirit
May scorn to live beholding to her body for meat,
Or for apparel, like your common dame
That makes shame get her clothes to cover shame.
Base is that mind that kneels unto her body
As if a husband stood in awe on 's wife!
My spirit shall be mistress of this house
As long as I have time in 't.

MERCER: a dealer in silks. GIVE A SEVENSCORE POUND: i.e., give a very large bribe.
CATCHPOLE: a petty officer of justice. THE GENERATION OF: the "making" of. VENERY:

gratification of sexual desire. **UNTRUSS:** undress. **TAG:** loose string. **LEDGER:** recorded. **WEDLOCK:** husbands and wives. **OF THIS HOUSE:** i.e., her body.

89.

LEVIDULCIA, INTENT ON SEDUCING A SERVANT, IS INTERRUPTED (OT)

(1611) Cyril Tourneur, *The Atheist's Tragedy,* Act II, Sc. 5

Levidulcia, a court lady with a runaway sexual appetite, is perversely inflamed while contemplating two young ones at court "one wanting [lacking] desire, the t'other ability." While watching their foot-dragging with contempt, she is stimulated, becomes overripe for a quick encounter, and instantly arranges for one—within an hour—with her highly qualified stepson, Sebastian. But either too impatient for such a long wait, or lest Sebastian forgets, she meanwhile spirits Fresco, a young servant, into her chambers and urges him. He's shy and abashed, and the labor of seduction becomes entirely hers. She labors hard, conceals impatience, becomes increasingly explicit in word and gesture, and while the blushing young man is still holding back, there's a knock at the door.

Quickly, tragedy reverts to farce. Not her husband, as she imagined, but Sebastian, whom she forgot, is at the door. Small consolation: her husband follows; not one but two intruding males must be accounted for; but Levidulcia manages with skill and despatch. Later, farce once again gives way to tragedy. Levidulcia, standing with horror and remorse over the bodies of Sebastian and her husband, does the proper thing: she repents and kills herself.

> *(Enter Levidulcia into her chamber,*
> *accompanied by Fresco.)*

LEVIDULCIA

Th'art welcome into my chamber, Fresco. Prithee shut the door.—Nay, thou mistakest me. Come in and shut it. No matter. I have somewhat to say to thee. What, is not thy mistress towards a husband yet? Ah, she has suitors, but they will not suit her. They will not come off lustily, it seems. Ay,

Fresco, they are not bold enough. Thy mistress is of a lively attractive blood, Fresco, and in troth she's o' my mind for that. A poor spirit is poorer than a poor purse. Give me a fellow that brings not only temptation with him, but has the activity of wit and audacity of spirit to apply every word and gesture of a woman's speech and behaviour to his own desire, and make her believe she's the suitor herself, never give back till he has made her yield to it. Ladies are as courteous as yeomen's wives, and methinks they should be more gentle. Hot diet and soft ease makes 'em, like wax always kept warm, more easy to take impression.—Prithee untie my shoe.—What, art thou shamefaced too? Go roundly to work, man. My leg is not gouty; 'twill endure the feeling, I warrant thee. Come hither, Fresco; thine ear.— 'S dainty, I mistook the place; I missed thine ear and hit thy lip. Ha! My ladyship has made you blush. That shows th' art full o' lusty blood and thou knowest not how to use it. Let me see thy hand. Thou shouldst not be shamefaced by thy hand, Fresco. Here's a brawny flesh and a hairy skin, both signs of an able body. I do not like these phlegmatic, smooth-skinned, soft-fleshed fellows. They are like candied suckets when they begin to perish, which I would always empty my closet of and give 'em my chambermaid.—I have some skill in palmistry; by this line that stands directly against me thou shouldst be near a good fortune, Fresco, if thou hadst the grace to entertain it. No less than the love of a fair lady, if thou dost not lose her with faint-heartedness. Alas, a lady is a great thing. Yet, I am a lady. Am I so great I cannot be compassed? Clasp my waist and try.

(Sebastian knocks within.)

'Uds body, my husband! Faint-hearted fool, I think thou wert begotten between the North Pole and the congealed passage. Now, like an ambitious coward that betrays himself with fearful delay, you must suffer for the treason you never committed. Go, hide thyself behind yond'arras instantly.

(Fresco hides himself. Enter Sebastian.)

Sebastian! What do you here so late?

YEOMEN: here, meaning servant class; generally, independent farmers. CONGEALED: frozen.

226

90.

SEMPRONIA DROPS IN FOR A BIT OF A CHAT WITH HER FRIEND FULVIA (OT)

(1611) BEN JONSON, *CATILINE'S CONSPIRACY*, ACT II, SC. 1

Ben Jonson sees Catiline's as a right-wing conspiracy against Republican Rome, so far to the right, in fact, and so into secret and illegal maneuvering as to constitute plain treason from the start. At the stage to which it's advanced when Sempronia—an old (if she were our contemporary) Beltway hand, once beautiful but now pinched and painted to hold her face in countenance, bonafide patrician, formidable behind-the-scenes political power, learned, sharp and filthy rich—is mustering support for the election of Catiline for the consulship, highest office in the Roman government, an office shared by two people. She's been up all night writing letters (massmailing) for campaign support to potential constituencies, and is heading this morning for a conference with Catiline's wife, Aurelia Orestilla, to update and coordinate plans for controlling the election. On the way, she makes a call on an intimate friend, Fulvia, who however turns down Sempronia's appeal for her to come along. But for all the chit-chat between the two old friends, Sempronia is really stopping by with politics alone in mind.

The political problem is this: an interloper—one of the candidates with no wealth, no tradition, no family to speak of, but with a considerable popular following—is, in a field of otherwise safe nonstarters, Catiline's most formidable opponent: "that talker," Cicero. His appeal to the popular vote is large and threatening, and Sempronia rehearses for Fulvia how each of his candidate plusses doesn't and must not matter: his solid virtue, his brilliant oratory, and his formidable learning in Greek—all signal virtues of the patrician class that a lower caste politician has no right to possess and no right to flaunt. Sempronia is fairly certain that she, with the cooperation of Crassus and Julius Caesar, can undermine the election, but she wants Fulvia to get all her patrician friends—a considerable number—to commit. There's one, surely, that Fulvia can start with: her devoted lover Quintus Curius. When Sempronia hears that Fulvia has already banished him as her lover, she dismisses the news, and when Curius comes to the door, Sempronia invites him in over

Fulvia's strenuous objection and leaves them, she's certain, to cement alliance in the cause. As it happens, Fulvia is a spy for the Cicero faction—from whom Fulvia calculates more reward—and subsequently tricks Curius into revealing Catiline's plot to assassinate Cicero and his entire contingent, and forestalls it.

The entire scene between the two women is a striking departure from the stentorian, classical-rhetorical style of the rest of the play. Nowhere else does Jonson drop into so chatty, so gossipy, so uncorseted a vein: high-born ladies seen in the privacy of the boudoir with their hair down—talking politics, exhanging beauty hints, and dishing. The drive behind Sempronia's intent is somewhat dissipated by the "my darling Fulvia" tone she adopts, but only somewhat.

SEMPRONIA

Fulvia, good wench, how dost thou? I am to see
Aurelia Orestilla: she sent for me.
I came to call thee with me.
I have been writing all this night, Fulvia, and am
So very weary, unto all the tribes,
And centuries, for their voices, to help Catiline
In his election. We shall make him consul,
I hope, amongst us. Crassus, I, and Caesar
Will carry it for him.
He's the chief candidate.
There are competitors,
That talker Cicero.
But Catiline and Antonio will be chosen;
Cicero they will not choose.
It will be cross'd by the nobility.
Nor were it fit. He is but a new fellow,
An inmate here in Rome, as Catiline calls him,
And the patricians should do very ill
To let the consulship be so defiled
As 't would be, if he obtain'd it! a mere upstart,
That has no pedigree, no house, no coat,
No ensigns of a family!
He has, they say, virtue. But
Hang virtue! where there is no blood, 'tis vice,
And in him sauciness. Why should he presume
To be more learned or more eloquent
Than the nobility? or boast any quality
Worthy a nobleman, himself not noble?
Virtue only, at first, made all men noble,
I yield you. It might at first, in Rome's poor age,

When both her kings and consuls held the plough,
Or garden'd well; but now we have no need
To dig, or lose our sweat for't. We have wealth,
Fortune and ease: and then their stock to spend on,
Of name, for virtue; which will bear us out
'Gainst all new comers, and can never fail us,
While the succession stays. And we must glorify
A mushroom! one of yesterday! a fine speaker!
'Cause he has suck'd at Athens! and advance him,
To our own loss! no, Fulvia; there are they
Can speak Greek too, if need were. Caesar and I,
Have sat upon him; so hath Crassus too,
And others. We have all decreed his rest,
For rising farther.

Is this grey powder a good dentifrice?
I have one is whiter,
Yet this smells well.
Fulvia, I pray thee, who comes to thee now,
Which of our great patricians?
Thou hast them all. Faith, when was Quintus Curius,
Thy special servant, here?
Thy idolater, I call him.
How! You forbid him entrance?
Venus forbid!
Your so constant lover! You would have chang'd;
So would I too, I am sure:
He's fresh yet, Fulvia;
Beware how you do tempt me.
Thou'rt a most happy wench, that thus canst make
Use of thy youth and freshness, in the season;
And hast it to make use of.
I am now fain to give to them, and keep music,
And a continual table to invite them.
Eat myself out with usury, and my lord too,
And all my officers, and friends besides,
To procure money for the needful charge
I must be at, to have them; and yet scarce
Can I achieve them so.
That's because I too
Affect young faces only, and smooth chins,
If I'd love beards and bristles,
One with another, as others do, or wrinkles—

(Knocking within)

Who's that?
'Tis Quintus Curius.
I'll leave you, Fulvia,
In faith, I will not stay,
I'll not hinder you.
He will not be kept out, no,
Nor shall not, by my means.
By Castor, I'll tell him, you are awake;
And very well: farewell, Fulvia,
I know my manners. Why do you labour thus,
With action against purpose?—Quintus Curius!
She is, I'faith, here, and in disposition!

(*Exit.*)

91.

DAME PURECRAFT WRESTLES WITH HER DAUGHTER'S DESIRE TO EAT PIG (OC)

(1614) BEN JONSON, *BARTHOLOMEW FAIR*, ACT I, SC. 6

Win-the-Fight, wife of Littlewit and daughter of Dame Purecraft, is with Puritan child and has an abominable craving, on the day of the religiously questionable festivities of Bartholomew Fair, to eat pig. Her craving is inarticulate—"um um"—but her mother and husband interpret rightly that it will not go away. Dame Purecraft struggles valiantly to save her daughter from the temptation, but recognizes that parley is necessary. She calls in the elder, Zeal-of-the-Land Busy, to see what he can do with doctrine, and after zealous conference and continued urging from Dame Purecraft, he resolves on a formula that serves both appetite and scruple: "So it be eaten," he determines, "with a reformed mouth…not gorged in with gluttony or greediness, there's the fear." And they determine to go to the Fair all together, to strengthen resolve and "for our better consolation." Resolve is particularly strengthened when Busy later comes up with an especially cogent argument: "by the public eating of swine's flesh, [we] profess our hate and loathing of Judaism," which enlarges Busy's purpose, with such strength of argument behind it, to "therefore eat, yea, I will eat exceedingly."

Mocking Puritans was the Elizabethan theatre's counterthrust to the Faithful's perpetual invective against it. In *Twelfth Night* Shakespeare's thrust was gentle ("Dost thou think," Sir Toby asks Malvolio, who leans toward rectitude, "because thou art virtuous, there shall be no more cakes and ale?"). Jonson was not so gentle. In his *Alchemist*, the Puritan brethren are given short shrift: they're hypocrites who bend doctrine any which way to justify supporting base alchemy to get gold. In *Bartholomew Fair*, the satire is broad, sustained, and deadly.

PURECRAFT

Look up, sweet Win-the-fight, and suffer not the enemy to enter you at this door; remember that your education has been with the purest. What polluted one was it that named first the unclean beast, pig, to you, child?

O! resist it, Win-the-fight, it is the Tempter, the wicked Tempter; you may know it by the fleshly motion of pig. Be strong against it, and its foul temptations, in these assaults, whereby it broacheth flesh and blood, as it were, on the weaker side; and pray against its carnal provocations, good child, sweet child, pray.

What shall we do? Call our zealous brother Busy hither, for his faithful fortification in this charge of the adversary; child, my dear child, you shall eat pig, be comforted, my sweet child. I mean i' the Fair, if it can be anyway made or found lawful. Where is our brother Busy? Will he not come? Look up, child.

(Enter Busy.)
O Brother Busy! your help here to edify and raise us up in a scruple. My daughter Win-the-fight is visited with a natural disease of woman, called "A longing to eat pig." And I would be satisfied from you, religiously-wise, whether a widow of the sanctified assembly, or a widow's daughter, may commit the act without offence to the weaker sisters. Good Brother Zeal-of-the-land, think to make it as lawful as you can. Truly, I do love my child dearly, and I would not have her miscarry, or hazard her first fruits, if it might be otherwise. Aye, and I'll go with you myself, Win-the-fight, and my brother, Zeal-of-the-land, shall go with us too, for our better consolation.

92.

URSULA, THE PIG-WOMAN, READIES HER BOOTH FOR FAIR-DAY (OC)

(1614) BEN JOHNSON, *BARTHOLOMEW FAIR*, ACT II, SC. 2

There's the fair Queen of the May and the fat Queen of the Fair. Ursula the pig-woman is the Fair's empress, a divinity of flesh, gross, gluttonous, and pungent. She's all body, basking in sweat and stink, fire and fat. She waters the ground "like a great garden-pot" as she goes, replenishes with bottles of ale, comforts with a pipe of tobacco, and presses into a chair that leaves her rump chafed in its confines. And from the chair she bellows instructions to her tapster on shilling the patrons with short change and short measure, and thus is ready for the day's custom, selling roast pig and tapping ale.

But there's more to her trade. There are spaces behind the pigstall for the whores and their custom, and there's sending out and receiving back pickpockets and their takings. Swarming around her stall is the riffraff of the Fair, and the mix of these with the respectable and their holiday desires brings them all to shameful crises and to the same level. Ursula is the reigning spirit of the Fair's folks' cravings, and defines the lower limit of nature in Jonson's moral/allegorical field full of folk.

> *(Enter Ursula from the back part of her booth.)*

URSULA

Fie upon't ! Who would wear out their youth and prime thus in roasting of pigs, that had any cooler vocation? Hell's a kind of cold cellar to't, a very fine vault, o' my conscience! What, Mooncalf! *(To Mooncalf)* My chair, you false faucet you; and my morning's draught, quickly, a bottle of ale to quench me, rascal.—I am all fire and fat, Nightingale; I shall e'en melt away to the first woman, a rib again, I am afraid. I do water the ground in knots as I go, like a great garden-pot; you may follow me by the S's I make. Best take your morning's dew in your belly, Nightingale.

(Mooncalf brings in the chair.)
Come, sir, set it here. Did not I bid you should get this chair let out o' the sides for me, that my hips might play? You'll never think of anything till your dame be rump-galled. 'Tis well, changeling; because it can take in your grasshopper's thighs you care for no more. Now you look as you had been i' the corner o' the booth, fleaing your breech with a candle's end, and set fire o' the Fair. Fill, stote, fill.

Fill again, you unlucky vermin. I shall e'en dwindle away to't, ere the Fair be done you think, now you ha' heated me! A poor vexed thing I am. I feel myself dropping already, as fast as I can; two stone o' suet a day is my proportion. I can but hold life and soul together with this (here's to you, Nightingale) and a whiff of tobacco, at most. Where's my pipe now? Not filled? Thou arrant incubee! How can I hope that ever he'll discharge his place of trust—tapster, a man of reckoning under me—that remembers nothing I say to him?

(Exit Nightingale.)
But look to't, sirrah, you were best; threepence a pipeful I will ha' made of all my whole half-pound of tobacco, and a quarter of a pound of coltsfoot mixed with it too, to itch it out. I that have dealt so long in the fire will not be to seek in smoke, now. Then, six and twenty shillings a barrel I will advance o' my beer, and fifty shillings a hundred o' my bottle-ale; I ha' told you the ways how to raise it. Froth your cans well i' the filling, at length, rogue, and jog your bottles o' the buttock, sirrah, then skink out the first glass, ever, and drink with all companies, though you be sure to be drunk; you'll misreckon the better, and be less ashamed on't. But your true trick, rascal, must be to be ever busy, and mistake away the bottles and cans in haste before they be half drunk off, and never hear anybody call (if they should chance to mark you) till you ha' brought fresh, and be able to forswear 'em. Give me a drink of ale. This must all down for enormity, all, every whit on't.

(One knocks.)
Look who's there, sirrah! Five shillings a pig is my price, at least; if it be a sow-pig, sixpence more; if she be a great-bellied wife, and long for't, sixpence more for that.

MELT…RIB AGAIN: melt to her original size, as Adam's rib. RUMP-GALLED: chafed rump. CHANGELING: child substituted, especially by fairies; here, a mild disparagement. FLEAING…CANDLE'S END: burning out fleas from one's breeches. STOTE: standing still; motionless. STONE: fourteen pounds. SUET: animal fat. INCUBEE: incubus, evil spirit. MAN OF RECKONING: man of distinction; here, one who keeps accounts for the drinks. COLTSFOOT: herb used as an adulterant in tobacco. TO SEEK: at a loss. ADVANCE: raise the price. SKINK: to pour. EVERY WHIT: every bit. GREAT-BEL-LIED WIFE, AND LONG FOR'T: pregnant woman's craving.

93.

THE DUCHESS SEDUCES A WILLING ANTONIO INTO MARRIAGE (YT)

(1614) JOHN WEBSTER, *THE DUCHESS OF MALFI*, ACT I, SC. 3

"Will you hear me?" cries the Duchess to her brothers, who are grimly warning her against a widow's second marriage, "I'll never marry." Her brother the Cardinal gives her promise no credit. "So many widows say;/But commonly that motion lasts no longer than the turning of an hour glass." He proves correct; but she proves courageous. The Duke Ferdinand reinforces his brother's injunction several times over: it is lustful; it will "poison your fame"; its hypocrisy "will come to light." But the Duchess is already determined; she is only waiting for these "terribly good" counselors to go before sending for Antonio, her secretary, whom she will wed in secret ceremony the moment they're gone.

The lying, the secrecy of the wedding ceremony, and the several years of secret marriage that are to follow, are the Duchess' response to her brothers' swearing her to celibacy. In Webster's world, which is largely given over to the casual viciousness of wolves among wolves, among the few weapons left the innocent are precisely lying and secrecy. In the end, of course, the Duchess' secrecy is a very weak bulwark against the most dangerous of wolves, her lycanthropic brother, the Duke Ferdinand [see in Men's volumes "Ferdinand Villifies the Duchess and Her Unseen 'Lover'" and "Ferdinand, the Duchess Dead, Condemns the Murder He Enjoined"], who will pursue her to her death.

Her secretary arrives; her command is peremptory: sit, write! The

Duchess, in the midst of her incredibly rash but nevertheless determined course of action, is direct and clear in her intent: instant wedlock. But that very directness—and here, Webster's study of the Duchess takes on brilliant color—is tempered by a game. Instead of a forthright "I command you to be my husband"—which *is* in fact her demand—she indulges in a sort of whimsical playing-out of a *second* intent: guess what I'm about, and do you follow? He does follow, easily, but is at first barely willing to. The Duchess is, after all, dipping far below her station to dredge up a husband, and Antonio, more attuned at the moment to the injunctions of political propriety than she is, is resisting comprehension. The Duchess patiently, amusedly, but more and more insistently is revealing her *fait accompli,* a proposal that brooks no refusal and no hesitation.

As with all of Webster's characters of signal intelligence, as with Vittoria of *The White Devil* [see No. 27, above], there is a play of irony in her discourse, with its naked meaning and intent lingering just below the surface as she sports a language that on the face of it might pass for propriety and as she relishes at the same time the fact that, when clearly understood, it doesn't.

Decidedly, she has it all her own way. Future husband or no, Antonio is in no position to demur, even if he wanted to, although clearly, he doesn't. The game she permits herself is authorized, so to speak, not only by her gentle love (mentioned only, by the bay, in this scene of instant courtship), but her ease and pleasure in authority. The gentle, loving Duchess is, at bottom, a Duchess, and flaunts, however charmingly, the mettle of her authority.

But once the game of innuendo is done and the marriage is accomplished, she excuses her "great one's" need for roundaboutness in wooing, gradually slips into the far tinier role of wife to her man, and effects to lay her head figuratively in the bosom of her lord.

(Enter Antonio.)

Duchess

I sent for you: sit down;
Take pen and ink, and write. Are you ready?
After these triumphs and this large expense
It's fit, like thrifty husbands, we inquire
What's laid up for to-morrow.

When I said I meant to make inquiry
What's laid up for to-morrow, I did mean

What's laid up yonder for me.
In heaven.
I am making my will (as 't is fit princes should,
In perfect memory), and, I pray, sir, tell me,
Were not one better make it smiling, thus,
Than in deep groans and terrible ghastly looks,
As if the gifts we parted with procur'd
That violent distraction?

If I had a husband now, this care were quit:
But I intend to make you overseer.
One of your eyes is blood-shot; use my ring to 't.
They say 't is very sovereign. 'T was my wedding ring,
And I did vow never to part with it
But to my second husband. I
have parted with it now.
To help your eye-sight.

Sir,
This goodly roof of yours is too low built;
I cannot stand upright in 't nor discourse,
Without I raise it higher. Raise yourself;
Or, if you please my hand to help you: so!

        (Raises him)
So, now the ground's broke,
You may discover what a wealthy mine
I make you lord of, and I must tell you,
If you will know where breathes a complete man
(I speak it without flattery), turn your eyes,
And progress through yourself.
The misery of us that are born great!
We are forc'd to woo, because none dare woo us;
And as a tyrant doubles with his words
And fearfully equivocates, so we
Are forc'd to express our violent passions
In riddles and in dreams, and leave the path
Of simple virtue, which was never made
To seem the thing it is not. Go, go brag
You have left me heartless; mine is in your bosom:
I hope 't will multiply love there. You do tremble:
Make not your heart so dead a piece of flesh,
To fear more than to love me. Sir, be confident:
What is 't distracts you? This is flesh and blood, sir;
'T is not the figure cut in alablaster
Kneels at my husband's tomb. Awake, awake, man!

I do here put off all vain ceremony,
And only do appear to you a young widow
That claims you for her husband, and, like a widow,
I use but half a blush in 't.

And 'cause you shall not come to me in debt,
(Being now my steward) here upon your lips
I sign your *quietus est*. This you should have begg'd now.
I have seen children oft eat sweetmeats thus,
As fearful to devour them too soon.

I have heard lawyers say, a contract in a chamber
Per verba [de] presenti is absolute marriage.

(She and Antonio kneel.)
Bless, heaven, this sacred Gordian which let violence
Never untwine.
What can the church force more?
How can the church build faster?
We now are man and wife, and 't is the church
That must but echo this.—Maid, stand apart:
I now am blind.
I would have you lead your fortune by the hand
Unto your marriage-bed:
(You speak in me this, for we now are one).
We'll only lie and talk together, and plot
T' appease my humorous kindred; and if you please,
Like old tale in *Alexander and Lodowick,*
Lay a naked sword between us, keep us chaste.
O, let me shroud my blushes in your bosom,
Since 't is the treasury of all my secrets!

(Exeunt Duchess and Antonio.)

TRIUMPHS: celebrations. HUSBANDS: economists. PROCUR'D: were the cause of. QUIT: removed. THAN IN DEEP GROANS...THAT VIOLENT DISTRACTION: rather than wait till the deep groans of age seem to come from a violent regret at surrendering one's wealth. VERY SOVEREIGN: an excellent cure. DOUBLES: speaks ambiguously. HEART-LESS...YOUR BOSOM: to which her heart is now transplanted. ALABLASTER: alabaster, used for funeral monuments. QUIETUS EST: (Latin) a terminating of business, a final seal; in this case, a kiss. PER VERBA DE PRESENTI: (Latin) by the word of the witness-es. SACRED GORDIAN: this marriage, like the Gordian knot, too intertwined to be dis-entangled. FASTER: more solidly. MAID, STAND APART: the Duchess' maid, Cariola, who assisted at the now-concluded wedding. HUMOUROUS: hard to please. ALEXAN-DER AND LODOWICK: a ballad version of a medieval romance.

94.

THE DUCHESS CONFRONTS HER ASSASSINATION WITH PERFECT COURAGE AND SUPREME DISDAIN (YT)

(1614) JOHN WEBSTER, *THE DUCHESS OF MALFI*, ACT IV, SC. 2

It's value-as-person that's the appropriate measure of Webster's two tragic heroines, Vittoria and the Duchess of Malfi. And their value can be measured not by summing up their virtuous acts and subtracting the others, but by appraising the qualities that emerge in their manner—not at all in the substance of their behavior, but in its style. Even the stridency of Vittoria is delivered from a height, a wrath that shrivels its objects. For the Duchess, it is not her wrath, but her supreme dignity, or her perfect self-regard, vested in her comfortable assumption of authority [see No. 93, above]. They stand very tall among their kind by an inherent assertion of the self that, in the great critical moments of their action, emerges with palpable power.

For the Duchess, it emerges with extraordinary and very quiet power at the moment of her death. She is to be strangled by Bosola under orders from her brother, the Duke Ferdinand. From the moment of his discovery of the Duchess' marriage [see in Men's volumes "Ferdinand Villifies the Duchess and Her Unseen 'Lover'"], which, for him, is no different from whoredom, he has pursued her with gruesome vindictiveness, imprisoning her in her own castle, and terrorizing her with the show of a dead man's hand, images of a dead Antonio with their dead children, the dance of howling madmen, and finally, Bosola and the executioners arriving with bell, coffin, and strangling cords. Her loyal maid Cariola, with her still, cries to her lady, "Call for help!" The Duchess calms her, "To whom?" They're imprisoned with madmen for neighbors. And she diverts Cariola from her terror with practical instructions concerning her children.

In her colloquy with Bosola, her executioner, she sustains a quiet, practical, bemused curiosity about the procedures to come. She asks about the means, makes little of one death as opposed to another, disappoints him that she exhibits no preference for life as opposed to "meet[ing] most excellent company in the other world." Then she sends a message of gratitude to her brothers for their good gift to her of departure, makes only the request that her body be given to her women for modest disposal, and—to the last—sustains the easy irony with which she characteristically buried hard meanings beneath language of fine, tempered wit.

DUCHESS

Call for help?
To whom? To our next neighbours?
They are mad-folks.
Farewell, Cariola.
In my last will I have not much to give:
A many hungry guests have fed upon me;
Thine will be a poor reversion.
I pray thee, look thou giv'st my little boy
Some syrup for his cold and let the girl
Say her prayers ere she sleep.

(Cariola is forced out by the
Executioners.)
What death? Strangling:
I forgive them:
The apoplexy, catarrh, or cough o' th' lungs,
Would do as much as they do.
Doth death fright me?
Who would be afraid on 't,
Knowing to meet such excellent company
In th' other world?
The manner of death should much afflict.
This cord should terrify.
Not a whit:
What would it pleasure me to have my throat cut
With diamonds? or to be smothered
With cassia? or to be shot to death with pearls?
I know death hath ten thousand several doors
For men to take their exits; and 't is found
They go on such strange geometrical hinges,
You may open them both ways: any way, for heaven-sake,
So I were out of your whispering. Tell my brothers
That I perceive death, now I am well awake,
Best gift is they can give or I can take.
I would fain put off my last woman's-fault:
I'd not be tedious to you.
Dispose my breath how please you; but my body
Bestow upon my women, will you?
Pull, and pull strongly, for your able strength
Must pull down heaven upon me:—
Yet stay; heaven-gates are not so highly arch'd

As princes' palaces; they that enter there
Must go upon their knees

(Kneels)
Come, violent death,
Serve for mandragora to make me sleep!—
Go tell my brothers, when I am laid out,
They then may feed in quiet.

(They strangle her.)

REVERSION: inheritance. CASSIA: cinnamon pods from the cassia tree of southern China.

95.
BEATRICE TAKES CARE ON HER WEDDING NIGHT TO SIMULATE VIRGINITY (YT)

(1622) THOMAS MIDDLETON AND WILLIAM ROWLEY, *THE CHANGELING*, ACT IV, SC. 1

[Further notes on *The Changeling*, in De Flores' monologues in Men's volumes.] Beatrice-Joanna, daughter of the Governor of Alicant, has suffered the misfortune of falling desperately in love with Alsemero after becoming betrothed to Alonzo de Piracquo. The detested servant De Flores, whom she's hired to murder de Piracquo, afterwards claims for recompense not money for flight, but Beatrice herself, as he makes clear to her, his "accomplice."

Beatrice, transformed from willful aristocrat to entrapped victim and mistress of De Flores, prepares for her marriage to Alsemero. She is terrified. Her bridegroom's discovery of her unchastity on their wedding night would mean not merely humiliation, but, according to the unwritten laws of bridegroom's honor, certain death. Nothing so clearly defines the shocking difference between the haughty aristocrat who calculates with amoral indifference the murder of one suitor for marriage with another and the Beatrice in this scene, as she rummages through vials and tomes in Alsemero's "physician's closet," looking frantically for a formula or elixir that could save her loss of virginity from detection.

She finds the solution in the books of remedies she pours through, but the most perfect remedy of all comes to her unexpectedly: her waiting-woman, Diaphanta—a sufficient likeness to herself—to take her place in the bridal bed. What is sufficient to calm the fears of the accomplices for the wedding night, is not sufficient for the long run, and so De Flores later takes the precaution of killing the waiting-woman. The discovery of this and their earlier crime will result ultimately in their deaths.

BEATRICE

This fellow has undone me endlessly;
Never was bride so fearfully distress'd:
The more I think upon th' ensuing night,
And whom I am to cope with in embraces,
One who's ennobled both in blood and mind,
So clear in understanding (that's my plague now)
Before whose judgment will my fault appear
Like malefactors' crimes before tribunals.
There is no hiding on't, the more I dive
Into my own distress. How a wise man
Stands for a great calamity! there's no venturing
Into his bed, what course soe'er I light upon,
Without my shame, which may grow up to danger;
He cannot but in justice strangle me
As I lie by him, as a cheater use me;
'Tis a precious craft to play with a false die
Before a cunning gamester. Here's his closet;
The key left in't, and he abroad i' th' park:
Sure 'twas forgot; I'll be so bold as look in't.

     (Opens closet)
Bless me! A right physician's closet 'tis,
Set round with vials; every one her mark too:
Sure he does practice physic for his own use,
Which may be safely call'd your great man's wisdom.
What manuscript lies here?

(reads) The book of Experiment, called, Secrets in Nature:
So 'tis; 'tis so.
(reads) How to know whether a woman be with child or no:
I hope I am not yet; if he should try though!

Let me see, "folio forty-five," here 'tis,
The leaf tuck'd down upon't, the place suspicious:
(reads) If you would know whether a woman be with child or
not, give her two spoonfuls of the white water in glass C—
Where's that glass C? O yonder, I see't now—
(reads) and if she be with child, she sleeps full twelve hours after;
if not, not:
None of that water comes into my belly;
I'll know you from a hundred; I could break you now,
Or turn you into milk, and so beguile
The master of the mystery; but I'll look to you.
Ha! that which is next is ten times worse:
(reads) How to know whether a woman be a maid or not:
If that should be applied, what would become of me?
Belike he has a strong faith of my purity,
That never yet made proof; but this he calls
(reads) A merry slight, but true experiment: the author Antonius
Mizaldus. Give the party you suspect the quantity of a spoonful
of the water in the glass M, which, upon her that is a maid,
makes three several effects; 'twill make her incontinently gape,
then fall into a sudden sneezing, last into a violent laughing; else,
dull, heavy, and lumpish.
Where had I been?
I fear it, yet 'tis seven hours to bed-time.

                    (Enter Diaphanta.)
(Aside) Seeing that wench now,
A trick comes in my mind; 'tis a nice piece
Gold cannot purchase.
(To Diaphanta) Come hither, wench,
To look my lord.

STANDS FOR: is open to. MARK: label. FOLIO FORTY-FIVE: either page 45 in the folio (volume) or volume 45. SUSPICIOUS: conspicuous (meaning, the passage is under-lined). MASTER OF THE MYSTERY: master of the art or craft (in this case, of drugs). ANTOINE MIZALDUS: (1520–78) author of *Centuriae IX. Memorabilium,* from which the text is quoted. INCONTINENTLY: immediately. PIECE: young woman. LOOK: look for.

96.

ISABELLA PRETENDS MADNESS TO TEST ANTONIO'S LOVE (OT)

(1622) Thomas Middleton and William Rowley, *The Changeling*, Act IV, Sc. 3

In *The Changeling*'s subplot, too old and very jealous Dr. Alibius, in charge of a madhouse, keeps his wife Isabella behind locked doors, his jealousy forbidding her contact with all men, even the madmen. Nevertheless, Isabella manages, with the help of the asylum's keeper, to escape her imprisonment when she hears of the arrival of "the handsomest, discreetest madman," one Antonio. Her curiosity is thoroughly rewarded. Antonio confesses to her that he is pretending to be mad out of love for her and, disguised as a madman, is using the stratagem to win her. For honor's sake, she rejects his overtures, but later, trapped by love herself, she uses the same stratagem to escape her husband's "watchful jealousy" and, at the same time, manages to confess her love to Antonio. The test for this lover's love is to penetrate her disguise; but so far is he from doing so that he's thoroughly repelled by the behavior of this woman whom he takes for a mad and hideous stranger. His revulsion at her disguise is matched by her revulsion at her lover's failure to recognize the love behind disguise, and she quits forever this "quick-sighted lover."

Her ploy of "madness" is done in the proper "English" vein. Quoting from Men's volume, "Mad Hieronymo Mistakes a Suppliant for His Dead Son": "Madness is reckoned in Elizabethan and Jacobean drama not so much as the derangement of a mind into verbal incoherence (as was the practice in Italian *commedia dell'arte*), but rather as the madman imagining he is undergoing successive shifts of scene and circumstance, each experienced with absolute clarity." Isabella undergoes four English-style transitions of scene: 1) She observes Icarus on his fatal flight too close to the sun, his fall into, what should be the ocean, Isabella has converted into the Minotaur's labyrinth, from which Theseus was rescued by Ariadne. Isabella promises to do the same for Icarus, with the "clue" of the thread that marked Theseus' passage safely out of the labyrinth. 2) His having fallen into the ocean after all, he emerges from the waters as a huge sea-figure, possibly Poseidon—the clouds borne on his head, the rainbow worn on his back, the roaring, billowing waves in his belly, which she obligingly offers to suck out, just as she offered to help him out of the labyrinth. Finally, she warns him against harm from pirates. 3) Reverting to the image of Icarus, she asks—as though his journey toward the sun has not yet begun—why he should bother to ride the sun-chariot as high as Mercury is permitted by Jupiter to ride it from time to time, and who has the ability to do so. 4) But intruding on that image, she is Selene (or Phoebe), goddess of the moon protecting Endymion whom she loves, by not having him fall into the waves (as Icarus) at all.

But since Isabella is not mad, but only pretending to be so, there is a message for Antonio in her madness—a promise of love and protection for him, no matter what heights he scales or fails to scale to win her. He doesn't get it.

> *(Enter Isabella [dressed as a*
> *madwoman].)*

ISABELLA

Hey, how he treads the air! Shough, shough, t' other way! he
burns his wings else. Here's wax enough below, Icarus, more
than will be cancelled these eighteen moons. He's down, he's
down! what a terrible fall he had!
Stand up, thou son of Cretan Daedalus,
And let us tread the lower labyrinth;
I'll bring thee to the clue.

Art thou not drown'd?
About thy head I saw a heap of clouds
Wrapp'd, like a Turkish turban; on thy back
A crookt chameleon-colour'd rainbow hung
Like a tiara down unto thy hams.
Let me suck out those billows in thy belly;
Hark, how they roar and rumble in the straits!
Bless thee from the pirates!
Why shouldst thou mount so high as Mercury,
Unless thou hadst reversion of his place?
Stay in the moon with me, Endymion,
And we will rule these wild rebellious waves,
That would have drown'd my love.

You are, as sure as I am, mad.
Have I put on this habit of a frantic,

With love as full of fury, to beguile
The nimble eye of watchful jealousy,
And am I thus rewarded?
No, I have no beauty now,
Nor never had but what was in my garments.
You a quick-sighted lover! Come not near me:
Keep your caparisons, y' are aptly clad;
I came a feigner, to return stark mad.

(Exit.)

REVERSION OF HIS PLACE: the right to inherit his place. CAPARISONS: clothing; here, madly ornamental.

97.

LADY ALLWORTH INSTRUCTS YOUNG ALLWORTH ON PROPER CONDUCT FOR THE WELL-BORN (OC)

(1625) PHILIP MASSINGER, *A NEW WAY TO PAY OLD DEBTS*, ACT I, SC. 2

Rarely is the voice of entrenched "old family" conservatism heard with such precision and such dignity as in Lady Allworth's admonitions to her stepson Tom Allworth about his conduct as a soldier and young nobleman, and to Lord Lovell, her compatriot in the landed aristocracy, about his choice of a wife. Two hundred and fifty years later, the same sermon will be preached in Robertson's *Caste* by the Marchioness to her son going off to fight the Sepoys in India for her country's good [see Vol. 4, No. 233]. In 1625, the sermon is fine-tuned; in 1876, it is coarse parody, so threadbare had the solid bulwarks of the old "land" aristocracy become. Not to get too morbidly precise about English economic history, what is occurring in the seventeenth century is a critical moment in the fundamental battle that was to shape English economic and political life: traditional land wealth versus new money wealth, country seat-and-holdings versus city shop and exchange. *A New Way to Pay Old Debts* is about that fight. Sir Giles Overreach [see in Men's volumes "Overreach Tutors His Daughter in Marital Entrapment"] is the outer limit of money crassness, building his fortune on financial extortion alone. Lady Allworth is the champion of the feudal tradition of wealth as land, won not with the filth of money speculation, but with knightly blood spilled on the battlefield. Lady Allworth's mission is not to confront the Overreaches, but her own class. Her warnings to it, in the instance of her stepson and her lordly co-equal, is not to contaminate its values by low behavior, nor its ranks by low marriage.

Her argument for her son: Lady Allworth visits advice on her stepson not on her own authority but on that of his dead father and her dead husband. The advice is therefore transmitted from the givens of tradition. The advice: in war, the soldier is schooled in the principles of honor, which are perfect daring for country, perfect obedience without demur, and perfect endurance of trials without faltering. Unspoken is the battlefield honor for the young nobleman, which is, as once for the medieval knight, a distinction won by deserving. It is destroyed by "lust and riot," the essential demarcation between nobility and ignobility. The same distinction carries over into friendship: the debauched sullies and contaminates, and here too the lines of demarcation between nobility and ignobility are absolute. Further and most significant is the young scion's choice between the vicious and the honorable. His birth and his wealth signify nothing with respect to honor. He must "elect" to uphold that value which, for Lady Allworth, alone defines his class and kind.

LADY ALLWORTH

How is it with
Your noble master?
I am honour'd in
His favour to me. Does he hold his purpose
For the Low Countries?
And how approve you of his course?
You are yet
Like virgin parchment, capable of any
Inscription, vicious or honourable.
I will not force your will, but leave you free
To your own election.
You had a father,
Bless'd be his memory! that some few hours
Before the will of Heaven took him from me,
Who did commend you, by the dearest ties
Of perfect love between us, to my charge;
And, therefore, what I speak you are bound to hear

With such respect as if he liv'd in me.
He was my husband, and howe'er you are not
Son of my womb, you may be of my love,
Provided you deserve it.
These were your father's words: "If e'er my son
Follow the war, tell him it is a school
Where all the principles tending to honour
Are taught, if truly followed: but for such
As repair thither as a place in which
They do presume they may with license practise
Their lusts and riots, they shall never merit
The noble name of soldiers. To dare boldly
In a fair cause, and for their country's safety
To run upon the cannon's mouth undaunted;
To obey their leaders, and shun mutinies;
To bear with patience the winter's cold
And summer's scorching heat, and not to faint,
When plenty of provision fails, with hunger;
Are the essential parts make up a soldier,
Not swearing, dice, or drinking."
To conclude:
Beware ill company, for often men
Are like to those with whom they do converse;
And, from one man I warn you, and that's Wellborn:
Not 'cause he's poor, that rather claims your pity;
But that he's in his manners so debauch'd,
And hath to vicious courses sold himself.
'Tis true, your father lov'd him, while he was
Worthy the loving; but if he had liv'd
To have seen him as he is, he had cast him off,
As you must do.
You follow me to my chamber, you shall have gold
To furnish you like my son, and still supplied,
As I hear from you.

98.

LADY ALLWORTH ADMONISHES LORD LOVELL ON THE DANGERS OF WEDDING NOBILITY'S "SCARLET" TO SERVANTS' "LONDON BLUE" (oc)

(1625) PHILIP MASSINGER, *A NEW WAY TO PAY OLD DEBTS*, ACT IV, SC. 1

[Continues No. 97, above.] Similarly, Lady Allworth admonishes the true nobleman Lord Lovell about the danger she imagines confronting him. The danger is clear to her: both these men of class have lost their wealth—young Allwell all of it, and Lord Lovell most of it. Having overheard a whispered conversation between Lord Lovell and Overreach, in which it appeared Lovell was assenting to a marriage with Overreach's daughter, Lady Allworth is alarmed. Her sermon most perfectly articulates the illusion with which the old landed aristocracy will insulate itself: it will triumph in the sense of what it is, and refuse to regret or even recognize whatever loss in substance or power it may suffer at the hands of the Overreaches.

Lord Lovell, Lady Allworth imagines, is succumbing to the blandishments of money; he will stoop in marriage to regain his comforts. Her warning is wrapped in a careful distinction: "Eminent blood" lives by and for its honors, for which "riches are a useful servant but a bad master"—good when it is "left to 'em by their ancestors," and bad when "meanly acquired" or added to ancestral fortune when like "common men," the sole object is to acquire "sordid wealth." The "rubbish" of tainted money reveals itself when weighed in the scales against "right"; it cannot abide the trial. Nor can the taint rub off. Beautiful and virtuous and rich as Overreach's daughter Margaret is, none "will ever forget who was her father."

That money is money never occurs to Lady Allworth, although she among these divested lordlings is the only one who still has her fortune, which is large and inherited. Her essential point is that money supports the show of moral value; it can never substitute for it. The demarcation between blooded birth and new fortune is fixed; it can never be diminished or overreached.

Massinger is kinder to aristocratic poverty than is the guardian at

aristocracy's gate, Lady Allworth. The aristocrats' scheme for over-
turning Overreach becomes the play's plot, and—in the permissible
environment of the play's cloudcoocooland plot—title ends up with
all the fortune, and fortune is left with no title even to fortune.

LADY ALLWORTH

Save you, my lord!
Disturb I not your privacy?
I ne'er pressed, my lord,
On other's privacies, yet against my will,
Walking, for health sake, in the gallery
Adjoining to your lodgings, I was made
(So vehement and loud he was) partaker
Of his tempting offers.
'Tis, my lord, a woman's counsel,
But true, and hearty;

(To her woman servant)
Wait in the next room,
But be within call; yet not so near to force me
To whisper my intents.

(To Lord Lovell)
Now, my good lord, if I may use my freedom
As to an honored friend—
I dare then say thus:
As you are noble (howe'er common men
Make sordid wealth the object and sole end
Of their industrious aims) twill not agree
With those of eminent blood (who are engag'd
More to prefer their honors, than to increase
The state left to 'em by their ancestors)
To study large additions to their fortunes
And quite neglect their births: though I must grant
Riches well got to be a useful servant,
But a bad master.
As all wrongs, though thrust into one scale
Slide of themselves off, when right fills the other,
And cannot bide the trial, so all wealth
(I mean if ill acquired), cemented to your honor
By virtuous ways achiev'd, and bravely purchas'd,
Is but as rubbish pour'd into a river
(Howe'er intended to make good the bank)
Rend'ring the water that was pure before

Polluted, and unwholesome. I allow
The heir of Sir Giles Overreach, Margaret,
A maid well qualified, and the richest match
Our north part can make boast of, yet she cannot
With all that she brings with her, fill their mouths
That will never forget who was her father;
Or that my husband Allworth's lands, and Wellborn's
(How wrung from both needs no repetition)
Were real motive, that more work'd your lordship
To join your families, than her form, and virtues;
The sum of all that makes a just man happy
Consists in the well choosing of his wife:
And there, well to discharge it, does require
Equality of years, of birth, of fortune;
For beauty being poor, and not cried up
By birth or wealth, can truly mix with neither.
And wealth, where there's such difference in years,
And fair descent, must make the yoke uneasy:—
Why then, my lord, pretend you marriage to her?

99.

THAMASTA, WHILE PASSIONATELY AVOWING HER LOVE FOR PARTHENOPHIL, DISCOVERS HE IS A WOMAN IN DISGUISE (YT)

(1628) JOHN FORD, *THE LOVER'S MELANCHOLY*, ACT III, SC. 2

"'Tis a fate that overrules our wisdoms," Thamasta complains to her maidservant. "Whilst we strive to live most free, we're caught in our own toils." Love is the fate, not the pleasure, of most of Ford's characters. It's one of the fiercest of the varieties of melancholy ("that commotion of the mind, o'ercharged with fear and sorrow") configured in Burton's *Anatomy of Melancholy*, which served as Ford's Freud.

In *The Lover's Melancholy*, the plot is a tangle of overhearings, misunderstandings and false accusations that throws the principal characters, one after another, into love's gloom. Not the most miserably affected, but affected enough, is Thamasta, the proud, highborn cousin to the Prince and wooed appropriately, by Menaphon, an equally wellborn courtier. But fatefully, her "wisdom" is "overruled" by fate when she falls passionately in love with a "straggler," a nobody, an unknown about the court, whose grace, beauty and address charm and move her. Shame and debasement is what she feels and fears in such an entanglement, and, yet—

Her plight is familiar to Renaissance comedy as well as tragedy, in which women, like Olivia in Shakepeare's *Twelfth Night,* regularly fall in love with women unknowingly, the objects of their love disguised as men for strong plot reasons. The situation gives occasion for the game of unsettled gender identity to be played out, sometimes close to the edge of the forbidden. Thamasta first sends an emissary, her maid Kala, to address her lover for her, which results in each becoming jealous of the other. Putting aside shame, like tortured Phaedra confessing to Hippolytus, Thamasta plans a secret assignation herself.

The scene becomes a study in mutual embarrassment, Thamasta not comprehending how the youth can seem not to catch her drift, then to hold back from her offer of her position and self, and then from her offer to give up all position and follow him into poverty. The youth meanwhile struggles to interrupt the flow of Thamasta's self-revelation. At last, in defense against Thamasta's driving love as well as haughty anger, Parthenophil reveals the truth.

Thamasta's response is complex. Her first thought is to ask at once for concealment of "the errors of my passion." She must, of course, not be found out. But then, the overriding recognition: that even with knowing the truth of Parthenophil's sex, it will be a while before the effect of her love on her "reason" will subside. It will be, as she confesses, a "hard task for me to relinquish my affection." What will abide is her jealousy ("jealous of thy company with any"), not too different from a lingering response in opposite-sex lovers' parturition.

(Note to the actor: A particularly difficult burden is placed on the actor in this monologue, for which apology is here made. Like others, it is spliced out of a dialogue. It's possible to imagine, one supposes, that the youth responds in silence until the critical moment of her revelation. In the original, of course, Parthenophil explains; here, it will be necessary for the recognition to come about by way of Thamasta's sudden realization. This of course violates completely Renaissance convention, in which—no matter how likely such a recognition without visual or verbal evidence might be—it never happened.)

THAMASTA

I expose
The honour of my birth, my fame, my youth,
To hazard of much hard construction,
In seeking an adventure of a parley,
So private, with a stranger: if your thoughts
Censure me not with mercy, you may soon
Conceive I have laid by that modesty
Which should preserve a virtuous name unstained.
I am a princess,
And know no law of slavery; to sue,
Yet be denied!
Thou art unwise, young man,
T' enrage a lioness.
Remember well
Who I am, and what thou art.
Parthenophil, in vain we strive to cross
The destiny that guides us. My great heart
Is stooped so much beneath that wonted pride
That first disguised it, that I now prefer
A miserable life with thee before
All other earthly comforts.

Go where thou wilt,
I'll be an exile with thee; I will learn
To bear all change of fortunes.
For thy love,
Hard-hearted youth, I here renounce all thoughts
Of other hopes, of other entertainments,—
When the proffers
Of other greatness,—
When entreats
Of friends,—
Respect of kindred,—
Loss of fame,—
Shall infringe my vows,
Let heaven,—

The self-same sex—a maid, a virgin!
Are you not mankind, then?
Pray, conceal

The errors of my passion.
It will be
A hard task for my reason to relinquish
The affection which was once devoted thine.
I shall awhile repute thee still the youth
I loved so dearly.
O, the powers
Who do direct our hearts laugh at our follies!
We must not part yet.
I shall henceforth
Be jealous of thy company with any:
My fears are strong and many.

TO HAZARD OF MUCH HARD CONSTRUCTION: to risk being misunderstood. PARLEY: discussion, conference. PROFFERS: offers. INFRINGE: curtail.

100.

PENTHEA, HER LOVE FRUSTRATED, IS BROUGHT TO THE VERGE OF MADNESS (YT)

(1633) JOHN FORD, *THE BROKEN HEART*, ACT IV, SC. 2

"No falsehood equals a broken faith," laments Penthea in her madness. Hers is a tragedy of broken faith initiated by her brother Ithocles, who forced her into marriage with a rich nobleman, Bassanes, although she had been contracted to Orgilus. But Penthea's love for Orgilus was built on passion and faith, so powerful a passion and so absolute a faith that her feeling that the sin was perpetrated by her brother in violating her contract is matched by her feeling that she's guilty of an equal and double sin of her own. That she is married to Bassanes is adultery to her, but that she is married and yet, ineradicably, holds sacred her love for Orgilus, signifies that she is also sinning against the sacred vow of marriage. So impassioned a votary is she of the laws of sanctified behavior in both love and marriage that when Orgilus, returned from abroad, met with her alone, she denounced his very attempt to speak with her, let alone woo or even touch her. And her torment is multiplied by the insane and groundless jealousy of her husband, who keeps her imprisoned in his house.

Three tormenters: her brother (Ithocles), her husband (Bassanes), her lover (Orgilus). Each contributed to her state now that is near to madness, and ironically, each has undergone, woefully late, a total change of heart, as each signifies loudly his repentance for the injury he's done her. They are all present when her women bring her out of her solitude in her prison-home, and are aghast at the mad ravings and the starved condition (she has been starving herself to death) of the woman to whose peace each is now so entirely devoted.

Penthea's madness has been compared to Ophelia's in *Hamlet*, but it differs altogether in a most important respect: Ophelia, like Lear or Hieronymo, translates place and time, and behaves in each shift of place and time in her imagination appropriately to that change. [For description of Hieronymo's madness, see in Men's volumes "Hieronymo Mistakes a Suppliant for His Dead Son."] Penthea is entirely present—entirely here and now—knows and addresses the others as themselves, not as surrogate inventions of her mind. She speaks and acts out her inner life and an inner continuity of reflections that is cued by their presence, but is only tangentially addressed to them. She is, in effect, with them, but remains inside herself.

Her "madness" too differs from Ophelia's and Hieronymo's in another respect. In the passage concerning Hieronymo referred to above, a distinction is made between Jacobean English and Renaissance Italian madness: Italianate is a mad jumble of words, thoughts, and images, signifying a sad (but usually in *commedia dell'arte*, a comic) derangement of mind. English is a swift succession of scenes into which the "mad" one enters, each one signifying a compulsive memory or fabrication that bears directly on the very reasons for the madness. One shows the effects of madness, the other explains it. Penthea's madness is as much Italian as English: disjunctions of words, logic, and images that originate in and suggest her plight, but emerging, lose sense. Only dead turtledoves can mourn their mates; it's a "deceit" (not a conceit) to die while dreaming; her hair, leaden, is pouding her into her grave; since she became a wife, she might have been a mother, but since her father never got her a husband, her babes are now bastards, and anyhow, it's too late for her to marry and have children; our last interview (this to Orgilus) is when I became sane and you became mad; married bachelors wear the congealed blood of cold-hearted lovers as ornaments in their ears; her marriage translates into being widowed and ravished; grief is a friend (to guilty souls like hers) because it leaves no comfort.

Having addressed each of her witnesses—so to speak, aslant—she suddenly, at the end, bursts out with plain truth and blunt feeling, "O my wrack'd honour!" This is her guilty torment, shared by the cruel brother who acted the father's role so basely, and the cruel husband who tormented her with his jealousy. It is their cruelty that left her, in her own judgment, a "strumpet," and since the nobility she had possessed was polluted by this shameful marriage and this betrayed faith, it's just that now she starve herself to death.

Penthea

Sure, if we were all Sirens, we should sing pitifully.
And 't were a comely music, when in parts
One sung another's knell. The turtle sighs
When he hath lost his mate; and yet some say
"A must be dead first." 'T is a fine deceit
To pass away in a dream; indeed, I've slept
With mine eyes open a great while. No falsehood
Equals a broken faith; there's not a hair
Sticks on my head but, like a leaden plummet,
It sinks me to the grave. I must creep thither;
The journey is not long.
Since I was first a wife, I might have been
Mother to many pretty prattling babes.
They would have smil'd when I smil'd, and for certain
I should have cri'd when they cri'd:—truly, brother,
My father would have pick'd me out a husband,
And then my little ones had been no bastards.
But 't is too late for me to marry now,
I am past child-bearing: 't is not my fault.
(To Orgilus) I lov'd you once.
Spare your hand;
Believe me, I'll not hurt it.
Complain not though I wring it hard. I'll kiss it;
O, 't is a fine soft palm!—hark, in thine ear:
Like whom do I look, prithee?—Nay, no whispering.
Goodness! we had been happy; too much happiness
Will make folk proud, they say—but that is he—

(Points at Ithocles)
And yet he paid for 't home; alas, his heart
Is crept into the cabinet of the princess;

We shall have points and bride-laces. Remember,
When we last gather'd roses in the garden,
I found my wits; but truly you lost yours.

(Again pointing at Ithocles)
That's he, and still 't is he.

(To Orgilus)
Let you kiss my hand? Kiss it.—
Alack, alack, his lips be wondrous cold.
Dear soul, h'as lost his colour: have ye seen
A straying heart? All crannies! every drop
Of blood is turned to an amethyst,
Which married bachelors hang in their ears.
Take comfort;
You may live well, and die a good old man.
By yea and nay, an oath not to be broken,
If you had join'd our hands once in the temple,—
'T was since my father died, for had he liv'd,
He would have done 't,—I must have call'd you father.—
O my wrack'd honour! ruin'd by those tyrants,
A cruel brother and a desperate dotage!
There is no peace left for a ravish'd wife,
Widow'd by lawless marriage; to all memory
Penthea's, poor Penthea's name is strumpeted:
But since her blood was season'd by the forfeit
Of noble shame with mixtures of pollution,
Her blood—'t is just—be henceforth never heightened
With taste of sustenance! Starve; let that fullness
Whose pleurisy hath fever'd faith and modesty—
Forgive me; O, I faint!

(Falls into the arms of her Attendants)
Lead me gently. Heavens reward ye.
Griefs are sure friends; they leave without control
Nor cure nor comforts for a leprous soul.

(Exeunt the maids supporting Penthea)

SIRENS: three maidens who dwelled between Circe's isle and Scylla and who, with their seductive song, lured sailors to their death. KNELL: death knell. TURTLE: turtle dove. SPARE YOUR HAND: lend me your hand. HE PAID FOR IT HOME: The price her brother Ithocles paid for his "sin" is paradoxically his falling in love with the Princess Calantha. POINTS AND LACES: souvenirs of (Ithocles' coming) wedding. AMETHYST: a jewel made of crystallized purple or violet quartz. PLEURISY: excess.

101.
KATHERINE CONSIDERS THE FUTURE
IN THE FACE OF WARBECK'S IMPENDING
DEFEAT (YT)

(CA. 1634) JOHN FORD, *PERKIN WARBECK*, ACT V, SC. 1

Perkin Warbeck, pretending to be the son of Richard III, or on occasion the brother of Edward IV, was at first supported by the monarchs of France, the Holy Roman Empire, and Scotland's James IV against England's new monarch, Henry VII. The issue? The new king, having defeated Richard III of York (in the Battle of Bosworth Field, made memorable in Shakespeare's *Richard III*), was in the throes of establishing his authority over the English barons. But it was in the interest of Warbeck's supporters to prevent him from achieving powerful monarchy, even at the cost of upholding the pretensions of Warbeck, although in all likelihood, nobody believed them. Warbeck's rebellion was a wan hope. When the last of his supporters, James IV, lost interest in his cause, Warbeck fled from the battlefield, deserted his men, and surrendered. Henry, feeling no particularly serious threat from so quixotic and weak a pretender, offered him an easy captivity until Warbeck attempted escape, and then, after enduring humiliating public confessions for his iniquity, was hanged. His wife, Katherine, was kindly received by Henry into the royal household, ending rebellion and resentment together.

Ford converts this less than inspiring episode and figure into a tale of unalloyed heroism and virtue. In his version, Warbeck believes in his cause, even in his pretension, and so does his faithful wife, Katherine, a woman of stoic virtue as perfect as her husband's own. And so does her woman attendant, Jane, and her "groom," Dalyell, who have followed their soon-to-be-doomed mistress through voyages and battles with undiminished love and loyalty, just as Katherine herself has followed her beloved, brave, and nobly inspired husband.

A conspiracy of virtues marks these characters in the face of history and likelihood. But Katherine herself, of all of them, seems to have both history and Chronicle Play on her side. Of all of them, she seems likely to have been in fact a paragon, capable of facing the bitter reality of their plight at Exeter even before the final battle is joined, and yet capable of sustaining her complete loyalty and unqualified support of her husband's cause. At the same time—in this passage—she stares facts in the face, and sums up the prospects for a future of defeat. Then she concludes, first, that she must live on charity (nothing being left of her position or estate), and then that she can never return to her native Scotland "in my fallen state," to the Scotland whose king betrayed her husband, and so "left us spectacles to time and pity." Her equal concern is for the plight of her devoted servants, whom she offers the choice of returning to the safety of Scotland. Their loyalty, of course, forbids; they bravely refuse.

KATHERINE

It is decreed, and we must yield to fate,
Whose angry justice, though it threaten ruin,
Contempt, and poverty, is all but trial
Of a weak woman's constancy in suffering.
Here in a stranger's and an enemy's land,
Forsaken and unfurnished of all hopes
But such as wait on misery, I range
To meet affliction wheresoe'er I tread.
My train and pomp of servants is reduced
To one kind gentlewoman and this groom.
Sweet Jane, now whither must we?
Home! I have none.
Fly thou to Scotland; thou has friends will weep
For joy to bid thee welcome; but, O Jane,
My Jane, my friends are desperate of comfort,
As I must be of them; the common charity,
Good people's alms and prayers of the gentle,
Is the revenue must support my state.
As for my native country, since it once
Saw me a princess in the height of greatness
My birth allowed me, here I make a vow
Scotland shall never see me being fallen
Or lessened in my fortunes. Never, Jane,
Never to Scotland will I more return.
Could I be England's queen—a glory, Jane,
I never fawned on—yet the king who gave me
Hath sent me with my husband from his presence,
Delivered us suspected to my husband's nation,
Rendered us spectacles to time and pity.
And is it fit I should return to such
As only listen for our descent
From happiness enjoyed to misery

Expected, though uncertain? Never, never!
Alas, why dost thou weep, and that poor creature
Wipe his wet cheeks too? Let me feel alone
Extremities, who know to give them harbor;
Nor thou nor he has cause. You may live safely.
O dear souls!
Your shares in grief are too-too much!

STRANGER'S AND ENEMY'S LAND: in Cornwall. Henry VII stationed troops at Exeter to meet Warbeck in battle. Katherine was awaiting the outcome near Land's End. THE KING WHO GAVE ME: James IV in Scotland had arranged the marriage of Katherine Gordon to Warbeck. SUSPECTED: imagined to be fraudulent (as pretenders). EXTREMITIES: of fear, sorrow, etc. KNOW TO GIVE THEM HARBOR: know how to accommodate them.

102.
THE DUCHESS DENOUNCES THE IMPIETY AND VILLAINY OF THE CARDINAL (YT)

(1641) JAMES SHIRLEY, THE CARDINAL, ACT II, SC. 3

"Take heed," whispers one nervous lord to another, gossiping in the royal chambers; "the Cardinal holds intelligence with every bird i' the air." "Death to his purple pride," retorts the other lord. "He governs all." It's dangerous to cross the king, they admit, but even more dangerous "if the Cardinal is displeased."

The Cardinal whom Shirley had (not so distantly) in mind was Cardinal Richelieu, who had reached the height of his—as the English and others believed—sinister power in France the very year this play was performed. Imagined as a kind of Henry Kissinger, CIA and death squad in one, he was feared and held in awe for the deviousness of his policy and the ruthlessness of his execution of it. In the more limited arena of a plot of intrigue in the effete London theatre of the last years of England's monarchic reign, and with its diminished audience of essentially Royalist society "tainted by the affectation of purity," the Cardinal's villainy is confined to destroying the marriage and eventually the life of a Duchess who has the passion and the power to contend with his evil, will for will.

On this tinier stage, the Duchess loves Alvarez, but the Cardinal is determined she will marry his nephew Columbo. He's forced on her a contract of marriage with his nephew; the Duchess is relieved to discover the king's appointment of Columbo to the battle front, from which she has every expectation he will not return alive. In her next move, this "noblest frame of beauty that this kingdom ever boasted" (flights of hyperbole familiar to Jacobean drama are outclassed in these dying years of Charles I's reign) treads on danger, or as she puts it, "walks upon the teeth of serpents." Her letter to Columbo bids him give up his claim, to which—but only to test her fidelity—he answers, yes. At once, she begs from the king the right to marry Alvarez; at once, the incensed Cardinal confronts her.

Mutual insult mounts: he accuses her of wantonness, she him of partiality "where [his] blood runs," and seeming not quite "a reverend churchman." Outraged at her "insolence" in opposing him and leaving his church-smooth talk, he blurts out, "Then you dare marry him [Alvarez]?" "Dare!": the word releases the flood of her resentment and hatred of all the Cardinal's actions—not merely those related to her own plight. Going far beyond the limits of their own dispute, the flood of her vituperation covers so much of the ground of resentment against the evil of prelate-politicians that she ends by warning him, in effect: you must either mend your ways, or suffer "the short-hair'd men" (i.e., the Puritan Roundheads), to crowd in and "call for justice". At that moment, the scene inadvertently shifts from fictional Navarre to actual England. It happened as the Duchess warned: in a year, the Roundheads "called for justice," and the bloody Civil War was on.

DUCHESS

Dare!
Let your contracted flame and malice, with
Columbo's rage, higher than that, meet us
When we approach the holy place, clasp'd hand
In hand: we'll break through all your force, and fix
Our sacred vows together there.
I am no dissembling lady!
Would all your actions had no falser lights
About 'em!
The people would not talk, and curse so loud.
You turn the wrong end of the perspective
Upon your crimes, to drive them to a far
And lesser sight; but let your eyes look right,
What giants would your pride and surfeit seem!

How gross your avarice, eating up whole families!
How vast are your corruptions and abuse
Of the king's ear! at which you hang, a pendant,
Not to adorn, but ulcerate, while the honest
Nobility, like pictures in the arras,
Serve only for court ornament. If they speak,
'T is when you set their tongues, which you wind up
Like clocks, to strike at the just hour you please.
Leave, leave, my lord, these usurpations,
And be what you were meant, a man to cure,
Not let in agues to religion:
Look on the church's wounds.
Ambition and scarlet sins, that rob
Her altar of the glory, and leave wounds
Upon her brow; which fetches grief and paleness
Into her cheeks, making her troubled bosom
Pant with her groans, and shroud her holy blushes
Within your reverend purples.

In hope, my lord, you will behold yourself
In a true glass, and see those injust acts
That so deform you, and by timely cure
Prevent a shame, before the short-hair'd men
Do crowd and call for justice; I take leave.

MEET US...HOLY PLACE: meet Alvarez and myself at the marriage altar. PERSPECTIVE: telescope. YOUR EYES LOOK RIGHT: without telescope. ULCERATE: poison. ARRAS: tapestry. AGUES: acute fever, illness. SCARLET SINS: mortal, not merely venial sins. GLASS: mirror. SHORT-HAIRED MEN: the Puritans' haircut was trimmed around a bowl; hence, roundheads.

SIXTEENTH- AND SEVENTEENTH-CENTURY SPANISH

103.

CELESTINA PRAYS TO THE GOD PLUTO TO OPEN THE HEART OF MELIBEA (OT)

(1502) FERNANDO DE ROJAS, *LA CELESTINA*,
TR. JAMES MABBE, AD. ERIC BENTLEY, ACT II

La Celestina, or *The Tragicomedy of Calisto and Melibea*, blended formal literary tradition with the gross realism of the world of conmen, cutthroats, prostitutes, and of preeminently the bawd Celestina, one of world literature's great characters. Prowling through the back alleys and fashionable districts of the city for her predations on the rich, the romantic, the gullible, and the criminal, she hovers like a great cloud over the world of the book, and especially over the destinies of the two doomed lovers, Calisto and Melibea.

A Catholic country's secular literature tended to be less bowed down under the weight of obligatory pieties than its equivalent literature in Europe's Protestant North. In the Renaissance, before the Counter-Reformation as it affected Spain, it had little trouble facing facts, and in *La Celestina,* it faced them wholeheartedly and shrewdly. Its moral judgments were altogether religious, to be sure, but it could look at human desires with unfiltered and in no way idealized vision. Take the lovers Calisto and Melibea, and measure their distance from Shakespeare's Romeo and Juliet.

Calisto is an ardent lover, a gulled voluptuary, a worshiper of beauty, and a fool. In his campaign for the conquest of Melibea, in his agonies of sexual frustration awaiting consummation, he's laughed at, deceived, and cheated not only by the professional Celestina, but by friends and servants as well and as thoroughly. Melibea is a splendidly brought-up and splendidly innocent young lady who—in her early meeting with Calisto, when he reveals to her that in her, he sees the greatness of God who endowed her with so perfect beauty—tells him at once to begone: "My patience cannot endure that a man should presume to speak to me of his delight in illicit love!" He prays, he enlists his friends, and he tears his hair. At last he finds his truest remedy, Celestina, who applies herself to Melibea's case so knowingly that the young girl, at another of their visits, is no longer capable "of dissembling my terrible passion." After reciting in detail the physical symptoms of her painful desire, she confesses to the bawd: "No remedy is as sharp as my pain. Though it touch mine honor, wrong my reputation, rip and break my flesh, do what thou wilt! If I may find ease, I shall liberally reward thee."

But Celestina, on her way to her first visit to Melibea, is not altogether certain of so perfect a triumph, and so arms herself. She enlists the aid of her mentor, her guiding spirit, her source of knowledge and power—the god of the underworld together with his hellish underlings—the very darkest powers human evil can evoke for battle against the powers of virtue. Celestina sees just such an adversary in the chaste Melibea, and she herself—ostensibly no more than a seller of thread, ointments, and powders for the aid of beauty and desire—prays to her infernal mentors to load onto the twist of thread she hopes to sell to Melibea not only their powers but their very selves for the girl's seduction. Still, none of this entirely encompasses the towering potency of Celestina herself; it appears only at the end of her prayer and incantation. She knows herself not merely as the votary of Pluto and his retinue, but as their commander. "I conjure thee again to fulfill my command!" she cries to them after her warning against their not fully serving her demand. Celestina the bawd is on earth what Pluto and his rout are in hell, and her prayer before her campaign against virtue, though only contending in this instance against a virginal girl, is equivalent in scale and import for her to the contest of Lucifer against the Lord.

CELESTINA

(Alone) I conjure thee, thou sad god Pluto, Lord of the Infernal Deep, Emperor of the Damned, Captain General of the Fallen Angels, Prince of those three hellish Furies, Tisiphone, Megaera, and Alecto, Administrator of Styx and Dis with their pitchy lakes and litigious chaos, Maintainer of the flying Harpies with the whole rabblement of frightful Hydras, I, Celestina, thy best-known client, conjure thee by these red letters, by the blood of this bird of night wherewith they are

charactered, by the weight of the names and signs in this paper, by the fell poison of those vipers whence this oil was extracted, wherewith I anoint this thread of yarn, come presently to wrap thyself therein and never thence depart until Melibea shall buy it of me and in such sort be entangled that the more she shall behold it, the more may her heart be wrought to yield to my request! Open her heart and wound her soul with the love of Calisto and in so extreme a manner that, casting off all shame, she may unbosom herself to me! Do this and I am at thy command to do what thou wilt! But, if thou do not do it, thou shalt forthwith have me thy capital foe and professed enemy. I shall strike with light thy sad and darksome dungeons. I shall cruelly accuse thy continual falsehoods. And, lastly, with enchanting terms, I shall curse thy horrible name! I conjure thee again to fulfil my command! Once, twice, thrice! And so, presuming on thy great power, I go to her with my thread of yarn wherein I verily believe I carry thyself enwrapped.

DIS: the Roman equivalent of Tartarus or the Underworld. HARPIES: monstrous birds with heads of young maidens. HYDRA: multiheaded dragon killed by Hercules.

104.

MELIBEA CONFESSES HER SIN TO HER FATHER, BEGS HIS FORGIVENESS, AND LEAPS TO HER DEATH (YT)

(1502) FERNANDO DE ROJAS, *LA CELESTINA*, TR. JAMES MABBE, AD. ERIC BENTLEY, ACT V

[Continues No. 103, above.] The sexual gratification between the lovers leads to terrific flights of poetic ardor, but they are encompassed by an atmosphere of greed, lies, cunning, and cynical contempt by the army of cheats and friends who are profiting from the lovers' secret raptures. From theirs and others—there's a world of procuring and gulling that fills out the landscape against which the young lovers' tale is told.

Their rapture ends in tragedy, as Melibea describes it, in this passage, to her father, who, in utter ignorance of the lovers' secret career in his very house, hears her, and, after her act of, in effect, immolation, offers desperate lamentation:"O my bruised daughter," the play concludes, "why has thou left" why hast thou left me comfortless and all alone in this vale of tears?" Despair and compassion, not judgment by the book. But it's Melibea who takes upon herself the guilt for the death of her beloved, and for the city's uproar and the calamities of the night engendered from the start by Calisto's going to Celestina for help in winning Melibea.

Melibea

No, Father, you shall see the death of your only daughter. Hear the last words that ever I shall speak. I am sure you hear the lamentation throughout the city: the ringing of bells, the scriking and crying of people, the howling and barking of dogs, the noise and clattering of armours. Of all this have I been the cause. Even this day I have clothed the knights of this city in mourning. I have left servants destitute of a master. And because you stand amazed at the sound of my crimes I will open the business unto you. It is now many days, dear father, since a gentleman called Calisto, whom you knew, did pine away for my love. (As for his virtues, they were generally known.) So great was his love-torment that he was driven to reveal his passion to a crafty woman named Celestina, which Celestina drew my secret from my bosom and made the match between us. Overcome with the love of Calisto, I gave him entrance to your house; he scaled your walls with ladders, broke into your garden, and took the flower of my virginity. Almost a month have we lived in this delightful error of love. And when he came last night unto me, e'en just about the time that he should have returned home, as Fortune would have it, the walls being high, the night dark, the ladder light and weak, his servants unacquainted with that kind of service, he going down hastily to see a fray in the street, being in choler, making more haste than good speed, not eyeing well his steps, he set his foot quite beside the rungs, and so fell down. With that unfortunate fall, he pitched upon his head and had his brains dashed in pieces against the stones of the street. Thus did the Destinies cut off his thread, cut off my hope, cut off my glory. What cruelty were it now in me that I should live all the days of my life! His death inviteth mine. Inviteth? Nay, enforceth. It teacheth that I also should fall headlong down that I may imitate him in all things. Calisto, I come! My best-beloved father, I beseech you that our obsequies be solemnized together and that we may both be interred in one tomb. Recommend me to my most dear mother, and inform her of the doleful occasion of my death. I am glad with all my heart that she is not here with you. I sorrow much for myself, more for you, but most for her. God be with you and her. To Him I offer up my soul. Do you cover up this body that now cometh down.

(She throws herself from the tower.)

SCRIKING: from "scrike," to utter a shrill harsh cry.

105.
THE DUCHESS OF AMALFI MANEUVERS A MARRIAGE PACT WITH HER STEWARD ANTONIO (OT)

(1599–1606) LOPE DE VEGA, *THE DUCHESS OF AMALFI'S STEWARD*, TR. CYNTHIA RODRIGUEZ-BODENDYCK, ACT I

The early interview between the Duchess of Amalfi and her steward Antonio, in which she hopes for and is prepared to encourage his proposal of marriage, is given a comic if not farcical turn by Lope's introduction of a *quiproquo*, a fixed (plotted) misunderstanding. *Quiproquo* underlies their fencing with one another about the very reason for their interview, and prevents either from voicing too boldly the simple fact that they're in love and want to step over what is ordinarily the fixed obstacle of rank, and get married. Antonio, *hidalgo*, ("lower" nobility), honest and capable steward of the Duchess though he's proven himself to be, is in his own view, and in the view of the time of the play, hopelessly inferior in class to the elevated status of the Duchess. She, fixed in her love for Antonio, couldn't care less; she's in love. But still conscious of the severe code of honor that plainly forbids such transgressions of rank, at the opening of their interview, she tempers, hints, watches in vain for the hint of a response, becomes increasingly exasperated, but waits. Antonio's problem, apart from his feeling the necessity of smothering his lower-class yearning for the Duchess, is under another constraint. He is supposed to be advancing the suit of Ottavio, the nobleman equal in rank to the Duchess, and feels under obligation to put his own yearning entirely aside and plead for Ottavio. Every hint, therefore, every move toward the subject of marriage, Antonio has been loyally turning in the direction of Ottavio's suit.

When the Duchess has had enough of this, she pushes aside this dance of deliberate misapprehension, and hiding behind a slender veil of decorum, she leaves to write the name of her love on a slip of paper, to be delivered to him by her maid. The paper—as it will invariably do in the nineteenth century's well-made play—adds another *quiproquo* to the list, and at last provokes Antonio to confess his torments and bafflements, and angrily prepare to "go where you never need hear my name."

This, of course, persuades the Duchess that he loves her, and frees her to chastise him gently for not quickly taking opportunity by the forelock, and for waiting for her to play the lover and he the lady; and bluntly assuring him that high rank means nothing to a woman in the face of true love. But restoring the code of honor to its proper niche, she tells him just as bluntly that "my consent must be to proper marriage only," and with that made clear, she immediately passes to the problems awaiting them after so irregular a marriage.

Consequently, from the very beginning of the play, the scope of its interest is set in stone: love, rank, honor, and not for a moment does any other intrude. The struggle of the two lovers is to square accounts at every moment with all three, in each and every one of their decisions tallying on their fingers, so to speak, the precision with which they live up to the codified demands of pure love, duty owing to rank, and absolute honor, all at once and without compromise. In this first excerpt, the Duchess is determined to push the limits of what is owing to rank and honor for the sake of love, but, as the play as a whole manages to do, she deftly and willingly, for the sake of love, obliges the other two limits as well.

DUCHESS

Patience, Antonio, patience.
Nay, although
I begin to suspect from this
that you do love me, Antonio,
you must never treat a noble woman thus.
You see me beside myself;
what could you hope I might say?
Was I wrong to think

that you might love me, too?
If your chance is bald behind,
I must think you are the barber.
Or might my arms be poisoned
that Ottavio must taste them for you?
Should I, without regard
for reason or reputation,
put honeyed words in my mouth,
as if you were the lady?
Speak out. Tell me you love me.
Say you're dying. What, do you weep?
You must know that ladies feel
with women's feelings, Antonio.
Be bold. I know you love me.
Well then, make love to me.
Heaven has granted to men
that they should be always the lords.
She who is highest in rank
is no prince, nor aspires to be,
neither serves her own desires
nor covets liberty.
O, fie on thoughtful men
with their trembling circumspection!
For love there is no circumspection,
No force that can silence it.
Antonio, I do adore you, but be advised
That I cannot and shall not love you in this way.
You may not touch me anywhere that honour
May feel an affront. And yet in secret, look you,
you may become my lord if you are discreet.
My honour shall be yours: I'll pledge it to you.
Antonio, beloved, so that we may shun dishonour,
and more than that, avoid offense to God,
my consent must be to proper marriage only.
And even so, if my brothers should learn of it,
I do believe my life and yours are lost.
We'll find no friends in those two highborn men,
whose deeds all France and Spain, and all the lands
washed by the circling oceans celebrate.
Love can be broken by its cause—that is,
the yearning lovers have to know each other.
Well, when a child appears we'll have no choice.
We'll say you are my husband. But meanwhile,
(if heaven deigns to grant me so much grace)
a blessed, secret joy of one another

is all the consummation I desire.
Ascendant Antonio, from this day forth your star
Shall eclipse rank and degree, and I am yours.

IF YOUR CHANCE IS BALD BEHIND, I MUST THINK YOU ARE THE BARBER: A complicated metaphor: opportunity (chance) must be grabbed by the forelock (in front of
the head). Once opportunity passes, and shows only "a bald [head] behind," the fault
must be the "barber's," the one who shaved the back of the head, leaving no "opportunity" to take hold of.

106.
THE DUCHESS OF AMALFI REVEALS HER MARRIAGE AND SURRENDERS HER RANK (OT)

(1599–1606) LOPE DE VEGA, *THE DUCHESS OF AMALFI'S STEWARD*,
TR. CYNTHIA RODRIGUEZ-BODENDYCK, ACT III

[See No. 105, above] With decision, dignity, and compassion for all
her retainers, the Duchess of Amalfi announces, after eight years of
secret marriage and the secret birth of two children with her secret
spouse, the fact of her marriage and, with the news made public, the
necessity of resigning her title and estate.

But why? She and her husband, Antonio, have calculated their
every move and every decision so that though their love was fulfilled,
they had scrupulously satisfied honor as well by their marriage, and
kept secret that marriage out of regard for the sensibilities of "the
world" and particularly her brothers, by not flaunting their violation
of the duty owing to rank. The question had been carefully post-
poned until, as the Duchess and Antonio had calculated, years of
honorable marriage and the birth of children would act as sufficient
persuasion for the propriety of their alliance. That single miscalcula-
tion brings about their tragedy. For the Duchess' brothers, neither the
sanctity of marriage nor the argument of love can conceivably compensate for the greatest sin of all: class, that is, blood and misalliance.
The question is also at the center of the play's interest, just as it is the
center of the interest of the assembled followers of the Duchess and
Antonio in this scene. She appeals to each one to make their own

judgment of whether to accept the propriety of their misalliance and remain, or reject it and leave their service.

The Duchess explains: she is leaving the young Duke—the son of her first marriage—as head of state; she had banished Antonio years before to avoid suspicion of their alliance; now she is joining him in exile with their children, to live as common citizens. She then dispenses to her servants her largesse and gives them their freedom to choose. But it's a doomed decision. For her brother Julio, the sanctity of rank is absolute, and allows for no casuistical adjustment; he murders the Duchess, Antonio, and their children.

Compared to Webster's Elizabethan play, *The Duchess of Malfi* [see *Duchess of Malfi* entries in Men's volumes, and No. 93 and No. 94, above], the circle of Lope's concerns is relatively tiny, which is of course disappointing to English readers. But the constraints of the love/honor/caste codes in Lope's play operate with such overriding authority that the vaster questions explored in Webster could not conceivably be accommodated to their legalistic punctilio. On the other hand, compared to the atmosphere of nightmare and hallucination in Webster, Lope's tragedy passes, until its very last moment, in thoroughly comforting daylight.

DUCHESS

Why have I come if not
to fulfill a just resolve?
This is the moment at last:
they must learn why I have come.
Attend me now, my friends,
while I make my purpose known;
so that you may understand
why I come here as I do.
The time for silence is over,
and if I was silent so long
it was only to await this day.

You know already, friends,
that the death of the Duke my lord
left me still very young; my estate
had an heir but no government.
I sent, therefore, to Naples
for Signor Antonio, a man
whose mind and person and worth
we and all Italy know.

But as the excellence
of his abundant merit
gave me occasion for it,
I cast my eyes on him.
Let this not appear to you
any novel case in this world,
since you see in the *Triumphs* of Petrarch
the example of how love conquers.
I did not disgrace my honour
by seeking such remedies
as those who recount her deeds
have written of Semiramis.
Before my lord Antonio
So much as laid a finger on me,
I was his wedded wife
and married him in secret.
By him as my husband
have I had these two children.
They have been raised in the mountains,
and the birth of the second one
obliged me to banish from my house
the man who was lord of it.
It is this exile, friends,
that has turned speculation loose:
my weeping eyes are weary,
my years are all undone,
my brothers hold me suspect,
my honour is full of suggestion.
And thus, to make an end,
I have come home today to his house.
Friends, Signor Antonio
is my husband, nor do I wish
for title, estate, or lands,
for revenues, vassals or kingdoms.
I leave my estate with a lord:
the young Duke is now a man
and shall govern his own domain;
the Duke can gird on a sword
with which he can defend you,
provide you with succession
by means of marriage to an equal.
Any who wish to go
will have letters and money provided.
Any who wish to remain
will have a house and my love.

Do not weep, nay, for I
Have put my faith in heaven
That my brothers may be moved
By the blood of theirs that's in me,
By the innocence of these children,
And by the mind and courage
Of my lord Antonio, of whom I,
Being who I am, am not worthy.
I take leave of excellencies.
Now Amalfi has its Duke,
I shall be what Antonio is.
I desire neither lands nor life.
I am his.

(To her maidservant Livia)
I shall marry you to Urbino,
For although I am poor and untended
I have the means for your dowry.
Doristo, you have borne yourself
Like a good and honest man.
Change these garments; I wish you
To accompany me.
And now it is fitting, Antonio,
That we give them other garments.
It is fitting.
Well, let us go, and we'll join
What I bring with what you have,
Since for two that love one another
Wealth is the least concern.
We will set up our little house.
And with you, my forever beloved,
A gown of sacking cloth,
A shirt of sailor's canvas,
Will be cloth of Milan to me,
Will be fine as Flemish cambric.

THE TRIUMPHS OF PETRARCH: allegorical poems by Petrarch (1304–74) that describe the triumphal processions of Love, Chastity, Death, Fame, Time, and Eternity. SEMIRAMIS: legendary Queen of Assyria, based on the real Samuramat, ninth century BC.

107.

CASILDA DESCRIBES THE BLISS OF HER MARRIAGE TO PEDRO (YT)

(CA. 1605–14) LOPE DE VEGA, *PERIBANEZ AND THE COMENDADOR OF OCANA*, TR. JILL BOOTY, ACT I

The peasant Pedro Ibanez and his wife Casilda are happy beyond happiness in the first act of *Peribanez,* from which fact we know that they're doomed to suffer in the second, and find rescue in the third. The patterns of Lope's tales are not novel, but there's infinite charm in their telling, and multiple ironies in their meaning. Pedro, or familiarly, Peribanez, is elevated in rank by the local Comendador, the governor of the village of Ocana, so that he might be sent on a mission elsewhere. This leaves the Comendador free to seduce Pedro's desirable wife, Casilda. For the attempt, though unsuccessful, Peribanez will subsequently murder the Comendador in revenge and after that, by way of Lope's irony, he is acquitted as a member of the nobility, who has the right to seek revenge against other nobility for the restoration of his honor. The Comendador in arranging for his crime had arranged also the lawful weapon for his own punishment.

But as to happiness in the first act: it is unalloyed. Casilda's neighbor is wondering if Peribanez will be angry if Casilda lends her a dress; Casilda can't imagine Pedro being so mean. "Does he love you very much?" asks Inez. It's Casilda's cue for reporting the rapture of the new husband and the new bride, in their every touch, every kiss, every dish (of which Pedro generously shares half with the wife who prepared it, after he has finished his half), every night.

CASILDA

There is not a couple in Ocana more thrilled with each other than we are. We have not been married long, you know! We are still eating the leftovers from the wedding feast. Does he tell me how he loves me? He never says anything else. He makes me so happy that I do not know what I am doing most of the time. As soon as it is dusk and the glowworms come out Pedro comes in from the fields hungry for his supper. I can feel in my bones when he is coming, and I throw down my work and run and open the door. He jumps down off his mule and I run into his arms. We stand there kissing and hugging until the poor old mule becomes impatient and starts to whinny. So then Pedro takes him to the stable and we feed the animals together. Pedro throws the hay in for them and I fetch the oats. He holds the sieve while I help him put it through. Then we both give the oats and bran a good stir around in the manger, and he kisses me again, among the animals. We go back to the house and there is the stew pot calling to us, bubbling up and down and rattling the lid like castanets. The smell of garlic and onions fills the kitchen! I spread a clean tablecloth on the table and serve it up properly. There are no silver plates, of course, but ours are very pretty—from Talavera—with carnations painted on them. He says his stew smells so good the Commander himself could not have better. But he picks out all the best bits and gives them to me! He goes on eating until there is just half left, then he gives the bowl to me and I finish it up. After that, I put a dish of olives on the table, if we have any, and if we have none, then we would just as soon go without. When we have finished we say grace together for what we have received, and go to bed. And when dawn finds us there, we part unwillingly.

108.

MARCELLA PRAYS TO CAESAR TO EMULATE THE MERCY OF THE ELEPHANTS (YT)

(CA.607–08) LOPE DE VEGA, *ACTING IS BELIEVING*, TR. M. MCGAHA, ACT III, SC. 5

With a gracefully turned text, Marcella the actress delivers the prologue for still another play-within-a-play—there's more than one—in *Acting is Believing*. In the whole of Lope de Vega's complex drama, the play Marcella introduces is the most critical play-within-play to be acted before the Roman emperor Diocletian, in which the actor Genesius, while playing the role of Christ, wins Christian faith and, as the familiar legend of St. Genesius had it, is martyred on the spot [see in Men's vols: "Genesius Rehearsing the Part of a Martyr, Wins Christ"]. Not unusually, the prologue has nothing to do with the play that follows, but uses the convention of begging the audience's indulgence—in this case the Emperor's—for what is to follow. What is especially graceful here is the path by which the text arrives at its object: it spells out an example, presumably reported by naturalists, of how elephants gently and kindly protect their weak, small young, which, the prologue begs, might be a model for the Emperor to extend similar indulgence toward the actors. The single intent of the actor doing this monologue should be the same as Marcella's: to woo indulgence.

MARCELLA

Naturalists have written such strange things about the noble elephant that they seem incredible. They tell of one who learned to write, which is amazing and wonderful, since there are many men who have never learned to form letters. They say that he wrote in the sand: "I'm the one who wrote these letters, which may serve as my epitaph and recall my invincible achievement for posterity." They tell about another elephant who was so ashamed because another had shown himself braver than he in battle that he threw himself off a high cliff, where the dolphins wept over his sandy grave. But these are just isolated instances. More generally, two things are said of them which serve my purpose. First, they say that when they have to pass through a flock of simple lambs, they move them out of the way with their trunks so that no one will step on them. Second, when they come to a river, they don't allow the big and small ones to cross over at the same time, for fear that the water level will rise with their bulk and drown the little ones. Hence, they have the little ones cross first, and none of the full-grown ones enters the water till they see that the little ones have reached the other shore safely. Now I see two Caesars before me who have come to this place where, like little lambs, Genesius and his poor and humble flock, who humbly serve you, are passing through. It would be well for you to move us out of the way with your invincible hands, since the whole world owes you homage. And if we must cross so great a sea—no little Po or Tiber—it's up to you to make sure we don't drown. Hence, it is only fitting that we ask your majesty to draw aside and watch us till we reach the other shore in safety, so that none of us may be endangered. Do us this favor, please, for it would be wrong for illustrious men to refuse a reasonable request, especially when it comes from a woman.

PO: a river flowing from the Alps in Northwestern Italy east to the Adriatic. TIBER: a river in central Italy, flowing through Rome into the Mediterranean.

109.

LAURENCIA, RAPED, LASHES OUT AT THE TOWNSMEN FOR NEITHER PROTECTING NOR AVENGING HER (YT)

(1614) LOPE DE VEGA, *FUENTE OVEJUNA*, TR. ROY CAMPBELL, ACT III

At the wedding of Laurencia and Frondoso in the village of Fuente Ovejuna, the Commander of the peasant village bursts in with some of his men, humiliates the groom, abducts the bride, and breaks his staff over the mayor's head. "What slave has ever suffered such injustice?" cries the Alderman at the next day's council of villagers. But the men are at odds: the honor of the village is ruined, but what remedy can they have against the Commander?

On the face of it, there's none. A knight (an *hidalgo*) or nobleman of higher rank can take revenge on another of the same rank with impunity, but it's impossible for a peasant to take revenge against one of higher rank. The men argue: we should send an emissary to the King in Cordoba; we should evacuate the entire village; we should kill the tyrant and die; oh no, no haste, we should tread carefully. And in the midst of this, Laurencia—bleeding, clothes torn, hair disheveled—bursts in on their conference, raging. She's been mocked, abused, raped.

It is the most memorable speech in the play, and one of the most powerful of enraged women's protests in Western drama on the victimization to which they could be reduced, and the incapacity to which they could be condemned. Laurencia, reviling the men of her village—even her own father, the mayor—for doing for doing nothing in the face of the rape of their women, the gratuitous arrest of their fellow villager, the contemptuous treatment by the village's Commander, Don Gomez. And like the women in the historical episode on which Lope de Vega's tale is based, the women who created their own officers and raised their own battle standard, Laurencia threatens to turn the men out of the village altogether, and make Fuente Ovejuna a village of Amazon warriors.

There have been many understandings of Lope's play having to do with precisely formulating his treatment of the dilemma the play's situation raises concerning the concept of honor, and how the solution at play's end accommodates that dilemma to overriding Spanish Counter-Reformation ideas of celestial order, political stability, royal authority, religious fiat, and so on. And the notion, especially adopted in the Soviet Union (where the play was iconic) that it had fundamentally revolutionary meaning, and served as an historic model for the justification of revolution, has been sneered at as totally missing the point. Still, listening to Laurencia's speech, one wonders: is her passion for moral fitness, moral right—so elusive for the underdog in any period—is her rage for action that goes beyond the constraints the men in the village council are deliberating, is the action the village is fired up to undertake because of Laurencia's exhortation—the murder of the Commander and the entire village claiming it did it as one, all guilty or innocent as one—is her fire so entirely modified by the play's ending, in which the King pardons the entire village and takes it under his own rule—is the play's final accommodation to the stability of political authoritarianism sufficiently forgetful of the flame within Laurencia's passion for justice, to douse it, or over and above the smiling satisfaction of that ending, is it unquenched?

(Enter Laurencia, disheveled and torn.)

LAURENCIA

Let me inside! For well I have the right
To enter into council with the men
Since if I cannot vote, at least I can
Scream out aloud. Do any of you know me?
Do you not know Laurencia?
I have come
In such condition, that you well may wonder
Who this is here.
Daughter!
Do not call me
Your daughter!
Why?
For many reasons and of these the weightiest
Is that you neither rescued me from traitors
Nor yet took vengeance on those bestial tyrants

Whom you let kidnap me! I was not yet
Frondoso's, so you can't fob off on him
The duty of avenging me. On you
The duty lies as well. Until the night
When marriage is fulfilled and consummated,
It is the father's duty, not the husband's.
When one has bought a gem, till it's delivered
The buyer does not pay. It is not he
Who has to guard it from the hands of robbers
Till it's been handed over. I was taken
Under your eyes to Fernan Gomez' house.
While you looked on like coward shepherds, letting
The wolf escape uninjured with the sheep.
They set their daggers to my breasts! The vileness
And filth of what they said to me! The threats
They made to tear me limb from limb! The foul
And bestial tricks by which they tried to have me!
Do you not see my hair torn out? These cuts
And bruises and the bleeding flesh that shows
Through my torn rags? You call yourselves true men?
Are you my parents and relations, you
Whose entrails do not burst with grief to see me
Reduced to this despair? You're all tame sheep!
Fuente Ovejuna means the fount where sheep drink—
And now I see the reason! Cowards, give
Me weapons! You are stones and bronze and marble
And tigers—tigers? no! for tigers follow
The stealers of their cubs, and kill the hunters
Before they can escape back to their ships.
No, you are craven rabbits, mice, and hares!
You are not Spaniards but barbarian slaves!
Yes, you are hens to suffer that your women
By brutal force should be enjoyed by others.
Put spindles in your belts. Why wear those swords?
As God lives now, I shall make sure that women
Alone redeem our honour from these tyrants,
And make these traitors bleed! And as for you,
You chickenhearted nancy-boys and sissies,
Spinning-wheel gossips and effeminate cowards,
We will throw stones at you and have you dressed
In petticoats and crinolines and bonnets,
With rouge and powder on your pansy faces!
Now the Comendador's about to hang
Frondoso up alive, to starve and die,
Head downwards from the castle's battlements,

And so he'll soon be doing with you all!
But I am glad of it, you half-men, since
The town will thus be ridded of its women,
And thus become a town of Amazons
Like me, to be the wonder of the age.

110.
THE YOUNG DONA LORENZA CURSES
HER MARRIAGE TO AN OLD AND
JEALOUS HUSBAND (YC)

(1615) MIGUEL DE CERVANTES, *THE JEALOUS OLD MAN*
(*AN INTERLUDE*), TR. WALTER STARKIE

"I'd like to see the old curmudgeon under the sod," Dona Lorenza complains bitterly, "and the man who tied me up with him." Dona Lorenza has reason to complain: she's fifteen, and her husband is seventy. Her salvation has to be, her neighbor Dona Hortigosa explains to her, a young lover. Complain as she will, when Dona Hortigosa lays out a plan to accomplish her salvation, Dona Lorenza demurs—not for pious reasons, but for practical ones: how can he get in, she objects; the windows are barred, there are seven doors leading to her bedroom, and he, the husband, has the key for each.

Cervantes' *entremeses* (short plays performed between acts) of *The Jealous Old Man,* is taken from the large stock of medieval tales of husbands cuckolded by students, friars, wandering minstrels, other husbands, and priests. It was a semi-literate literature that not only Cervantes but Boccaccio, Ariosto, Chaucer, and Molière all relished, copied, or emulated, and was used by all of them for the pleasure of subverting the moral, religious, and romantic codes that otherwise governed the propriety of love and/or marriage tales and plays. The Spanish *entremeses* countered that encoded literature with a large dose of downright, scurrilous realism which unblushingly called spades spades. Dona Lorenza, for example, has little idea of what is so entirely missing from her marriage-captivity, and knows only that she takes no pleasure in wealth, in jewels, in anything her husband lavishes on his imprisoned child-wife. Later in the short play, Dona

Hortigosa manages with a trick—the ingenuity of the trick is always at the heart of these fables—to bring in a lover who provides for Dona Lorenza all her missing information.

Dona Lorenza

It's a wonder, Senora Hortigosa, that my husband didn't lock the door; bad 'cess to him! I declare to God he has driven me daft! This is the first day since I married him that I've had a chance of colloguing with a soul outside the house. I'd like to see the old curmudgeon under the sod, and the man who tied me up with him!
A thousand curses on his money—barring the crosses on the back—to hell with the jewels and all the finery he unloads on me and promises to give me. None of them have done me a pennyworth of good: what use is all that wealth when I'm as poor as a church mouse and famished in the midst of plenty.

I was delivered over to him by one whose word was law, and I as a dutiful girl was quicker to obey than to contradict. But I'm telling you if I had known as much then as I do now, I would have bitten off my tongue rather than say that three-letter word "yes" which will cost me three thousand years' repentance. But I suppose it was all in the cards and had to be, so it's no good crying over spilt milk.

Wealth doesn't mean a thing to me, Senora Hortigosa; I've more jewels than I need, and I'm all confused trying to choose between the different colored dresses in my wardrobe. In this respect I'm as happy as any girl can be, and long live Canizares, say I, for he dresses me up like a doll, and I've more jewels to wear than you would find in a rich silversmith's shop window. If only he wouldn't nail up the windows, lock the doors, watch the house day and night, and drive away tomcats and dogs, simply because they are males, I'd do without his gifts and generosities.

Is he jealous? Well, the other day they tried to sell him a piece of tapestry at a bargain price, but because it had human figures designed on it, he refused to buy it, and he chose another one of foliage pattern which was more expensive and not so attractive. There are seven doors to pass, in addition to the hall door, before one can get to my room, and every one of them has a lock and key. Bless me if I can find where he hides the keys at night. I sleep with him and I've never seen or felt a key on him.

Senora Hortigosa, best for you to be off now; otherwise the old grumbler may find you with me; that would upset all our plans. But if you intend to do anything, do it as soon as you can: I'm so desperate that I've a mind to slip a rope around my neck and make an end for good and all.

COLLOGUING: conversing secretly, gossiping.

111.
THISBE, SCREAMING "FIRE!" SUFFERS THE NIGHTMARE OF HER BETRAYAL BY DON JUAN (YT)

(1630) TIRSO DE MOLINA, THE PLAYBOY OF SEVILLE, TR. WALTER STARKIE, ACT I

"I rejoice /In my soul's freedom," sings Thisbe, a fishermaid, in rapturous self-congratulation, "for I've never yet/Been wounded by the poisoned asp of love." Immune even to the desperate yearnings of the young fisherman Anfriso, she possesses "a tyrant's power to curb his love.../And glory in the flames that sear his heart." Doomed obviously to suffer the same flames, they arrive at once. Don Juan and his lackey Catalinon, after being shipwrecked and nearly drowned, are crawling out of the sea in which Thisbe's rod is fishing. And in no time at all, Don Juan is being succored by her, and she admitting, "Though you're dripping brine, you are afire,/And though all wet, you burn my very soul." Don Juan, using his customary ploy, promises marriage, beds her, and is gone.

Fire and water define the limits of Thisbe's horror and its cure. Her sustained screams of fire and her longing for the dousing of her burning pain find their solace quickly: she casts herself into the curing sea.

THISBE

Fire, O fire! I'm burning, burning!
My cabin's all in flames! Now raise the cry,

My friends! My tears will never quench the fire:
My humble cot has become another Troy.
Fire, oh fire! my shepherds, water, water!
Take pity on me, Love, my heart's ablaze!
For shame, my tiny cot, the squalid scene
Of my own infamy! vile robber's den
That sheltered and abetted all my wrongs.
May blazing stars rain fearsome thunderbolts
To blast and singe your thatched roofs, may the wind
Blow ravenously and fan the writhing flames.
O traitor guest! you have betrayed a woman!
You were a cloud that rose up from the sea
To overwhelm and drown my heart in woe.
Fire, oh fire! Ye shepherds! Water!
Take pity on me, Love, my heart's ablaze.
It was I that always mocked and cheated men,
But always those who cheat are in the end
Themselves deceived, and that cavalier
Seduced me after he had promised marriage,
And he enjoyed me and profaned my bed.
But I lent wings to his foul purposes.
For I gave him the two mares I possessed,
Which carry him far from me in headlong flight.
Oh, follow, follow him. No, let him go.
For in the presence of His Royal Highness,
I'll cry aloud for vengeance. Fire, oh fire!
And water! water! pity my blazing soul.

COT: cottage.

SEVENTEENTH-CENTURY FRENCH

112.

CHIMENE APPEALS TO THE KING TO FURTHER HER REVENGE (YT)

(1638) PIERRE CORNEILLE, *LE CID*, TR. PAUL LANDIS, ACT II, SC. 8

"My father, Sire, is dead; I plead for vengeance." Chimene, at the feet of her king, is pleading for the death of Rodrigue, who challenged her father to a duel and killed him. That Rodrigue is her lover and her love is at one with his has no bearing on her petition; her plea is wholehearted and unqualified.

The code of honor is absolute and brooks no dispute, no questioning [see in Men's volumes "Rodrigue Importunes Chimene to Kill Him for Having Taken Revenge Against Her Father," on the code with respect to Rodrigue]. Both Chimene and her lover are its perfect disciples, and consequently the perfect victims of its inevitable contradiction. To avenge the honor of his father, who was insulted by Chimene's father, Rodrigue was obligated to challenge him and, in their duel, killed him. Chimene, equally so obligated, must kill, or have a champion, or the justice of the King kill Rodrigue. As perfect as their devotion to honor is their love for one another. It is, after all, the perfection of one's honor that is paradoxically the crux of what each one loves. Nevertheless, Chimene, at the feet of the King, pleads without restraint for vengeance against her father's murderer, and pleads as if against her mortal enemy, which, in this respect, Rodrigue is.

But in private argument [in No. 113, below], addressing only her confidante: (almost equivalent in French tragedy to being alone) her anguish is inconsolable. Again and again, she defines her impossible quandary: to forego honor for the sake of love is dishonorable; to forego love for the sake of honor is unbearable. The perfect symmetry of her argument with herself is echoed and reechoed in the symmetry of its rhetoric. Although she concludes with apparent finality—save honor, kill Rodrigue, and die after him—its resolution is not remotely final. Each interview with Rodrigue, in which he argues her case for his own defeat, is met with her anguished refusal to tolerate his sacrifice. As in Men's volumes: "Rodrigue Bids Farewell to Chimene Before Combat": "In the end, two factors mitigate their suffering: the King, whose prerogative allows him to qualify the demands of the code, and time itself, which may overcome the intensity of Chimene's intent." And so the irreconcilability of their dilemma is, possibly questionably, skirted.

CHIMENE

I cry for justice, Sire.
My father, Sire, is dead; my eyes have seen
His blood in great drops flowing from his side,
That blood which has so often saved your walls,
That blood which won so many a battle for you,
That blood, still smoking with the heat of rage;
I saw poured out for other lives than yours.
Unshed amid the thousand risks of war,
Roderick spilled it in your very court.
All weak and pale I hastened to the spot;
I found him lifeless. Pardon, Sire, my grief;
My voice will not recount this tale of death,
The rest is better told with sighs and tears.
I found him lifeless; and to move me more
The blood that issued from his mangled side
Wrote out my duty for me in the dust;
His valor, brought to such a low estate,
Cried out to me and drove me here to you,
That through my voice that dreadful gaping mouth
Might plead its cause to the most just of kings.
Permit not, Sire, such outrage to be done
Under your sway, before your very eyes;
Permit not that the noblest be exposed
So freely to the blows of insolence;
That one rash youth may triumph o'er their glory;
Bathe in their blood and mock their memory.
So brave a warrior, slain and unavenged,
Must cool the ardor of the rest who serve you.
My father, Sire, is dead; I plead for vengeance
More for your sake than for my own relief.
Your loss is great when such a man is killed;

Revenge him with another, blood for blood:
A victim, not for me; but for your crown,
Your person, and your majesty; a victim
I beg of you to show to all the state
The madness of a deed so arrogant.

113.

CHIMENE IS TORN BETWEEN LOVE FOR RODRIGUE AND REVENGE (YT)

(1638) PIERRE CORNEILLE, *LE CID*, TR. PAUL LANDIS, ACT III, SC. 3

[See No. 112, above.]

CHIMENE

At last I am free, at last I may give way,
And let you see the sharpness of my grief;
At last, now, I can give my sad sighs breath,
Open my heart and tell you my distress.
My father is dead, Elvire, and the first sword
Which Roderick ever wielded cut him down.
Weep, weep, my eyes, and drown yourselves in tears!
One half my life has done to death the other,
And by this blow has made me cry for vengeance
For what is gone on what remains to me.
How shall my sorrow ever be appeased
If I may not hate the hand that called it forth?
What may I hope for but eternal torture,
Who punish crime, yet love the criminal?
Love is a word too feeble, I adore him.
My passion wars against my just resentment;
I find my lover in my enemy,
And Roderick, in spite of all my anger,
Does battle with my father in my heart,
Attacks him, drives him, yields, defends himself,
Now strong, now weak, and now at last triumphant:
But in this combat between love and anger,
He wins my heart, but cannot share my soul;
And though my love has power over me,

I do not hesitate to follow duty.
I go unwaveringly where honor leads.
Roderick is dear to me, I mourn his fate:
My heart defends him, but my spirit knows
I am a daughter, and my father's dead.
Ah, cruel chase to which I am compelled!
I seek his death, yet fear to have my wish;
My death will follow his, for which I sue.
My father dead and almost in my arms,
Shall I not hear his blood cry out for vengeance?
And shall my heart, deceived by shameful charms,
Believe my duty paid with futile tears?
Could I be bought by love, however great,
To stifle honor under shameful silence?
Honor demands that I pursue my vengeance;
To save my honor, and end this weariness;
Pursue him, kill him, and die after him.

114.

MADELON DEPLORES THE VULGARITY OF THE UNTUTORED (YC)

(1659) JEAN-BAPTISTE MOLIÈRE, *LES PRECIEUSES RIDICULES*, TR. G. GRAVELEY AND I. MACLEAN, SC. 3

Madelon is explaining to her father the vast difference between the "tender" way of negotiating love and marriage and the unadorned vulgar way. She provides him with a textbook lesson in the strategies of the *carte de tendre*, her knowledge of which comes from her rapt reading of Madame Scudery's novel, *Clelie*. There, she learned that the "map" (or world) of the "tender" is one in which ultimate delicacy of feeling is honored and scrupulously observed. The "map" itself depicts an Arcadia, where the river of Inclination waters the villages of Billets Doux (love letters), Petits Soins (tender cares), etc., allegorizes the stations or stages of love's way and the shoals and harbors of the treacherous journey it must negotiate. The very treacheries offer tests for the endurance of the tender heart.

Western fantasy had been there before. In the medieval *Romance of the Rose*, in the twelfth-century Court of Love, the original cartography of love's allegorical landscape was delineated. What Madelon was reading in Madame Scudery's novel was the updating and downgrading and corruption of those models. Think of medieval Christian knights in servitude for years to their lady, having, at her command, to fight dragons and Muslims, and dragging through assorted psychological/geographical obstacles like the Slough of Despond before they were granted entrance to the Bower of Bliss, and compare those strenuous journeys to Mme. Scudery's itinerary: the lover sighting his love first in church or at a "fateful" meeting; visiting her salon frequentlybut with silent passion; declaring himself at last in a suitable garden not too distant from the main house; suffering first rejection; pursuing still with delicate discretion "the outpourings of his passion;" winning the confession of love torn painfully from her heart; and then together facing hillocks of obstacles met by them with not-entirely-disagreeable complaints and despairs for chapters on end.Clearly, the travails of knighthood are accommodated to the far lesser endurance of the far more court-and-city oriented lady and gentleman of seventeenth century Paris.

Molière's satire has a double objective: it's obviously aimed at the middle-class provincial girl fatuously emulating her betters by adopting one of their more outlandish fashions. But it's obviously also against the fashion itself, which involved not only the cartography of aerated love, but the aerated language of that love. Above, Molière opting, as his moment in French literary controversy directed, for language denuded of pretension.

The play had memorable impact: the fashion of preciosity became ridiculous. But Molière would certainly have been dismayed to discover that the courtship journey outlined in Madame Scudery is fairly precisely preserved in some of the greatest of nineteenth-century novels, such as Jane Austen, Leo Tolstoy, Anthony Trollope, Ivan Turgenev, and Henry James—the lover's first sighting, his stretch of silent passion, his declaration in discreet setting, her murmured confession, the rival, jealousy, misunderstanding, abduction, "and what follows." Mostly, in good sunny weather.

MADELON

Oh, my dear father, what you say is the last word in bourgeois vulgarity. I am positively ashamed to hear you. You really must try to set your ideas to a more fashionable tune. Heavens above! If everyone were like you a novel would soon reach its last page. A nice thing it would be if Cyrus married Mandane in the first chapter, and Aronce was married to Clelie as a matter of course!

My dear father, my cousin will tell you as well as I that marriage should come only after a series of adventures. A suitor, to be agreeable, must express the finest sentiments. He should be a master of the delicacy, tenderness, and passion; and his wooing should run on recognized lines. He should first see the object of his affections in church, or during her afternoon walk, or at some public function; or Fate, in the shape of a relation or friend, may lead him to her home, from whence he departs in a melancholy dream. At first he keeps the loved one in ignorance of his passion, but visits her frequently, and never fails to pose some question about the passion of love to intrigue the wits of the company. At last the day of declaration arrives; which should usually take place in some garden walk, of a short but discreet distance from the rest of the company. Our face instantly blushes scarlet, and with haughty indignation we banish the suitor from our presence. Little by little he finds means to make his peace, accustoms us gradually to the outpourings of his passion, and at last draws from us that confession which it is such an agony to make. After that come adventures; rivals who try to interfere with a settled attachment, the persecution of parents, jealousy caused by mutual misunderstanding, complaints, despair, abduction and what follows. That is how these things are managed in the best style, and if the affair is to be refined they are quite indispensable. But to come point blank to the altar, to reduce one's courtship to the signing of the marriage contract, and literally to start at the wrong end of the novel! Positively, my dear father, nothing could be so vulgar, and the very idea of it nauseates me.

115.

DONA ELVIRE CONTEMPLATES FAIR WARNING FOR HER JEALOUS LOVER (OC)

(1661) JEAN-BAPTISTE MOLIÈRE, *DON GARCIE DE NAVARRE*,
TR. A.R. WALLER, ACT I, SC. 1

Dona Elvire is loved by two men, Don Sylve and the Prince Don Garcie. Both have noble virtues, both have the same high birth. In reason, there is nothing to incline her toward one more than toward the other. But "the shackles of fate," she says, have made her determination for her; her affections have fallen to Don Garcie. But Dona Elvire must deal then with the peculiar characteristic that befalls many of Molière's heroes—their dominant affliction, their ruling passion. For Don Garcie it is famously his jealousy, and Dona Elvire's confidante Elise broaches the danger, and in the same breath provides a happy solution: it is, after all, the case, Elise posits, that it is "by jealousy that a lover's passion can best express itself," and so the more jealous he is, the more one ought to return his love.

At this, the proud and determinedly rational Dona Elvire takes umbrage, puts aside paradox, and considers the question straightforwardly. Even in a lover, she reasons, jealousy is repellent, and she envisions with solemn disgust the life one is doomed to lead with a jealous husband. Nevertheless, Dona Elvire has the capacity to step back from her feelings, and balance arguments objectively for the fitness or unfitness of accepting such a defective lover in marriage. She calculates his qualities, attainments, heroic behavior toward herself (he was her savior), and the prospects of his future service in helping her brother "regain his throne from a perfidious traitor," and weighs these virtues against that one failing, his jealous passion. It is the signature of Dona Elvire's character that the strength of her pride disallows wallowing in and being influenced by feeling alone. In fact, her feeling seems far less engaged than her objective certainty of the demands of her pride in the threat with which she concludes: "If he does not obey me in whatever I command him, it will be in vain for him to aspire to the hand of Dona Elvire." The stiff-necked self-esteem of Dona Elvire remains assured and ungiving in the lovers' seige against one another, until the plot somewhat crudely solves their dilemma. To find gentle humanity in Dona Elvire is a great challenge to the actor.

DONA ELVIRE

Ah! do not bring forward such a strange argument. Jealousy is at all times a hideous thing; nothing can soften its hateful features. The dearer the love is that gives rise to it the more should one feel the blows of the fiend. To see a Prince carried away by it, losing every moment the respect which love inspires between true lovers, and, in the fits of jealousy which sully his mind, quarrel both with what I like and dislike, interpreting my every look as a token of my favour towards some rival! No, no, I am too much insulted by such suspicions. I do not disguise from you that the Prince Don Garcie is dear to my heart; he is able to satisfy the desires of a noble woman. He proved his courage and gave a brave testimony to his love for me in the midst of Leon. He dared for me the gravest dangers, freed me from the toils of cowardly tyrants, and, by enclosing me within these fortified walls, protected me against the horrors of an unworthy alliance. Nor do I deny that I preferred to owe my deliverance to him rather than to another: for a lover's heart, Elise, finds exquisite pleasure in being beholden to the one loved, and the pale flame of our passion burns the brighter when it thinks it can discharge its obligation by bestowing some favour. Indeed, I am glad that by risking his life for me his passion seemed to earn thereby the right of conquest. I rejoice that my peril threw me into his hands. And if the common reports be true and, by the bounty of heaven my brother is brought back to us, I pray most fervently that his arm may aid this brother to regain his throne from a perfidious traitor, and, by the happy issue of a noble enterprise, win my utmost gratitude. But, for all this, if he rouse my anger and fail to purge his passion from its transports of jealousy; if he does not obey me in whatever I command him, it will be in vain for him to aspire to the hand of Dona Elvire: marriage will never unite us, for I abhor ties which would, without question, make life a hell for both of us.

116.

DONA ELVIRA CONDEMNS DON JUAN'S VILLAINY, AND DETERMINES TO BE REVENGED (YC)

(1665) JEAN-BAPTISTE MOLIÈRE, *DON JUAN*,
TR. G. GRAVELEY AND I. MACLEAN, ACT I, SC. 3

[See the four entries in Men's volumes on Don Juan.] "Will you do me the favor to know me, or at least turn your eyes this way?" Dona Elvira asks icily of Don Juan, whose back is insolently turned to her. She asks it as a particular favor she deserves at his hands, she—a convent initiate who fell in love with him; violated her religious vows by escaping the convent and married him; having, after a few days of his enjoying her, been abandoned by him; and now having pursued him, finally tracked him down—finds the whole truth confirmed in an instant of the suspicions she determinedly suppressed while searching for him.

There's a vast difference between the "scorned woman" of seventeenth- and eighteenth-century comedy who is frequently as experienced in the commerce of love as her betrayer, and Dona Elvira, a true innocent who discovers for the first time, and from the single glance of distaste from Don Juan, the whole of the libertine's moral nature. The bedrock of feeling below her condemnation of her seducer is complex: she recognizes not only his hypocrisy, but most remarkably, the pride in herself that forbids the begging and groveling of the abandoned woman for restitution of the love that clearly was never there. It's an extraordinary display of inner dignity: her forestalling the possibility of his denigrating her further by pleading the banal excuses that come freely to the seducer's lips (and which she takes ironic pleasure in anticipating), and her forestalling further the possibility of her taking the usual victim's refuge in a barrage of reproaches. She demands what a man would demand when so betrayed—the restitution of her honor by one means alone, revenge.

DONA ELVIRA

How poorly you defend yourself! A courtier should be more accustomed to such situations. I pity your confusion. Where is your armour of majestic shamelessness? Why don't you swear that your heart is unchanged, that you adore me as much as ever, and that nothing but death can tear you from my side? You should say that you were called away by business so urgent that you had no time to give me even a minute's warning; that, much to your regret, you will be detained here for some time; but that, if I will only go home quietly, I may rest assured that you will follow me as soon as ever your affairs will let you. That you only live in the thought of returning to me, and away from my side you suffer the torments of a body divorced from its soul. That is the defence you ought to make, and not be so tongue-tied as you are. At last I see you as you really are. But, unhappily, the knowledge comes too late; and can only serve to drive me to desperation. But, be sure, your villainy will not remain unpunished. The Heaven you mock will avenge me for your faithlessness.

No, I won't hear a word. Only cowards will stay to hear the story of their shame. For a noble heart, to know is to act. Don't expect me to break out into reproaches. My anger has no breath to waste in empty words. It needs it all for its revenge. I say again, Heaven will punish you, and, if you are not afraid of Heaven, at least beware the anger of the wife you have betrayed.

117.

DONA ELVIRA, RECONCILED TO HEAVEN, PLEADS WITH DON JUAN TO RENOUNCE HIS EVIL (YC)

(1665) JEAN-BAPTISTE MOLIÈRE, *DON JUAN*, TR. G. GRAVELEY AND I. MACLEAN, ACT IV, SC. 6

[See No. 116, above.] It is once again a different Dona Elvira who confronts Don Juan. The innocent religious who left her nun's vows for love of Don Juan, and was then changed in an instant into an avenger, returns now and forgets all thought of revenge as a true and purified religious votary who cares only for the salvation of a sinner's soul. Her love remains, but as "a flame purged of sensuality, a holy affection." Her preachment issues from a wholly generous heart, and she pleads—what she forbid herself to do before—her lasting love for him as persuasion. Predictably, Don Juan's dismissal of her pleading is immediate and out of hand.

(Enter Dona Elvira, veiled.)

DONA ELVIRA

Do not be surprised, Don Juan, to see me again so soon, and in these clothes; but I have urgent reasons for coming, and what I have to say to you will admit of no delay. My anger of this morning is all gone, and I come to you now in a very different frame of mind. I am no longer the Dona Elvira who prayed for your punishment, and whose outraged feelings found an outlet in threats of vengeance. Heaven has banished from my heart all that was unworthy in my love for you; the heady violence of a criminal attachment, the shameful transports of a gross and earthly love. All that remains for you in my heart is a flame purged of sensuality, a holy affection, a pure and disinterested love which, with no thought of self, thinks only of your good.

Moved by this pure and perfect love, I come to bring you a warning from Heaven; to try to draw you back from the precipice, over which you are rushing to destruction. I know the disorders of your life; and the same Heaven which has touched my heart, and opened my eyes to the irregularities of my own behaviour, has inspired me to seek you out, and deliver Its message. Don Juan, the cup of your offences is full. The terrible wrath of God is ready to fall, and there is no escape but by immediate repentance. Perhaps you have only this one day left, to save yourself from the last and greatest of all calamities. I am no longer bound to you by any earthly ties. By God's grace, I have renounced for ever my mad and unruly passions; and, once more in the convent, I ask for no more of life than time to expiate my sins; and, by a severe penance, win pardon for the crimes into which a shameful passion has plunged me. But, lost to the world though I am, it would be a lasting grief to me if one I had loved so dearly became a fearful example of the justice of God; and a joy above all others, if I might only prevail on you to turn aside the deadly blow which threatens you. For pity's sake, Don Juan, as my last request, grant me this sweet satisfaction. With tears I beg you to look to your salvation. If your own self-interest carries no weight with you, at least let my prayers; and spare me the agony of seeing you condemned to everlasting punishment.

I had for you a love past telling. You were dearer to me than anything in the world. There was nothing I would not have done for you. For you I forgot my vows. All I ask in return is that you will live a better life, and save yourself from destruction. Save yourself, Don Juan, I beseech you; if not for your own sake, then for love of me. With my tears I implore you. And if the tears of one you have loved are of no avail, then I conjure you by anything which has the power to move you.

I have given my warning. I have no more to say.

118.

CELIMENE RESPONDS TO THE PRUDE ARSINOE WITH AN ANNIHILATING REPLY (YC)

(1666) JEAN-BAPTISTE MOLIÈRE, *THE MISANTHROPE*, TR. RICHARD WILBUR, ACT III, SC. 5

[On *The Misanthrope* and Celimene, see in Men's volumes "Alceste Condemning Celimene's Falseness, Also Confesses His Love."] The scene is Celimene's Parisian salon, but all the characters in the play are denizens of the court who travel from salon to court and back to salon. In that short journey, they convey the kind of "news" and gossip and politely spoken venom that drives Alceste, the misanthrope of the play's title, to rage.

But his beloved Celimene has no such rage. She basks in city-court ("the world's") duplicities, contributes skillfully to them, and has developed an even more remarkable skill in countering its worst attacks, whether they are whispered or written, or spoken face-to-face with ill-concealed malice. In this scene with Arsinoe, a prude, she demonstrates unearthly skill in countering just such malice. Celimene's reply to Arsinoe is probably the most perfect model of malice-retorting-politely-to-malice in comic literature.

Arsinoe is herself not a negligible master of the form. She is visiting Celimene on an urgent mission: out of friendship, she's come to warn her that she's all but lost her reputation. Her crowd of admirers, her coquettishness, have aroused excessive criticism, which Arsinoe, when she heard such attacks, was quick to counter. But one had to admit, Arsinoe sighs, that some things were hard to excuse—not that she supposes anything is really wrong, but even the shadow of evil causes talk. She begs her friend Celimene to be sensible and take her advice, which is prompted only by concern for her good.

The key to effective malice is solicitousness: a tone that is kindly, deeply forbearing, entirely forgiving. Under its kindly light, diagnostic precision can be killing. In her reply, Celimene mimicks every strategy of Arsinoe's: she is solicitous, forbearing, forgiving, and particularly reassuring of motive—like Arsinoe's, it is in her friend's best interest. But under Celimene's kindly light, Arsinoe's age, looks, desires, losses, unappeal, hypocrisy, sexual frustration, prudishness, and maliciousness are enumerated and illuminated with paralyzing explicitness, and leaves Arsinoe with no option but to turn to Alceste in order to disabuse him of his faith in Celimene and urge him to turn to more virtuous consolation. There, too, she has no solace.

Celimene

Madam, I haven't taken you amiss;
I'm very much obliged to you for this;
And I'll at once discharge the obligation
By telling you about *your* reputation.
You've been so friendly as to let me know
What certain people say of me, and so
I mean to follow your benign example
By offering you a somewhat similar sample.
The other day, I went to an affair
And found some most distinguished people there
Discussing piety, both false and true.
The conversation soon came round to you.
Alas! Your prudery and bustling zeal
Appeared to have a very slight appeal.
Your affectation of a grave demeanour,
Your endless talk of virtue and of honour,
The aptitude of your suspicious mind
For finding sin where there is none to find,
Your towering self-esteem, that pitying face
With which you contemplate the human race,
Your sermonizings and your sharp aspersions
On people's pure and innocent diversions—

All these were mentioned, Madam, and, in fact,
Were roundly and concertedly attacked.
"What good," they said, "are all these outward shows,
When everything belies her pious pose?
She prays incessantly; but then, they say,
She beats her maids and cheats them of their pay;
She shows her zeal in every holy place,
But still she's vain enough to paint her face;
She holds that naked statues are immoral,
But with a naked man she'd have no quarrel."
Of course, I said to everybody there
That they were being viciously unfair;
But still they were disposed to criticize you,
And all agreed that someone should advise you
To leave the morals of the world alone,
And worry rather more about your own.
They felt that one's self-knowledge should be great
Before one thinks of setting others straight;
That one should learn the art of living well
Before one threatens other men with hell,
And that the Church is best equipped, no doubt,
To guide our souls and root our vices out.
Madam, you're too intelligent, I'm sure,
To think my motives anything but pure
In offering you this counsel—which I do
Out of a zealous interest in you.
Indeed, it seems to me
We ought to trade advice more frequently.
One's vision of oneself is so defective
That it would be an excellent corrective.
If you are willing, Madam, let's arrange
Shortly to have another frank exchange
In which we'll tell each other, *entre nous,*
What you've heard tell of me, and I of you.

Madam, I think we either blame or praise
According to our taste and length of days.
There is a time of life for coquetry,
And there's a season, too, for prudery.
When all one's charms are gone, it is, I'm sure,
Good strategy to be devout and pure:
It makes one seem a little less forsaken.
Some day, perhaps, I'll take the road you've taken:
Time brings all things. But I have time aplenty,
And see no cause to be a prude at twenty.

For my part, Madam, I should like to know
Why you abuse me everywhere you go.
Is it my fault, dear lady, that your hand
Is not, alas, in very great demand?
If men admire me, if they pay me court
And daily make me offers of the sort
You'd dearly love to have them make to you,
How can I help it? What would you have me do?
If what you want is lovers, please feel free
To take as many as you can from me.

Oh, please don't feel that you must rush away;
I'd be delighted, Madam, if you'd stay.
However, lest my conversation bore you,
Let me provide some better company for you;
This gentleman, who comes most apropos,
Will please you more than I could do, I know.
Alceste, I have a little note to write
Which simply must go out before tonight;
Please entertain *Madame*; I'm sure that she
Will overlook my incivility.

ENTRE NOUS: (French) between us.

119.

ANDROMACHE DEVISES A DESPERATE PLAN TO SAVE HER SON (YT)

(1667) JEAN RACINE, *ANDROMACHE*,
TR. ROBERT HENDERSON, ACT IV, SC. 1

The manners and customs of Jean Racine's tragic world are as decorous as that of Louis XIV's court, but its emotions are almost savage.
They give no quarter to propriety or reason; feeling either possesses
and conquers, or kills . What is their stability? Feelings have none.
Love becomes hate, and still remains love. Hate, or love, may be
buried and unwilled; but the very act of their burial generates their
eruption. The desire, the passion one feels is itself hated by oneself; it's
an illness, a curse, at the very least, a humiliation one suffers with

pain, even with dread. Most unbearable of all is a love fixed on an ideal, or a sacred vow that one holds to in the face of the onslaught of circumstance, which drains the love itself of all reward.

None of the characters in *Andromache* is immune from one or another of these torments, or from the horrible resolves that grow out of them: Pyrrhus, who loves Andromache, threatens the life of her son if she refuses him; Hermione, who loves Pyrrhus, threatens his life if he betrays her; Orestes, who loves Hermione, threatens Pyrrhus' life as Hermione's unwilling but desiring champion. Andromache is in the most unbearable plight of all: having saved her son Astyanax (in this version) after the fall of Troy, he is again in danger of being murdered by the Greeks, who fear that he will emulate his father Hector's heroism and restore Troy, are determined, by way of preemptive strike, to kill him. Pyrrhus' love for Andromache is fierce, and therefore so is his threat. But her sacred devotion to the dead Hector makes marriage to Pyrrhus an unendurable betrayal.

In this colloquy with her confidante, Cephissa, Andromache makes her determination. She has already won Pyrrhus' sworn oath that he will protect and raise her son, and so she will consent to marry him. Before consummation, she will kill herself, after which, she asks of Cephissa, that her son will live in safety, learn of his father's greatness, but make no attempt to restore Troy.

None of this mutually imprisoned quartet realizes his or her resolution. Pyrrhus is murdered directly after his marriage ceremony, not by a too-slow Orestes, but by the Greek soldiers. Andromache, with the murder of Pyrrhus, has no protection for her son against the Greeks. Hermione, hating and loving Pyrrhus, is cheated of a meaningful vengeance against him as he was killed for the wrong reasons. Lastly, Orestes, violently rejected by a raging Hermione for both his failure to kill Pyrrhus and for allowing him to be killed, goes mad.

ANDROMACHE

It is the last time I shall see my child.
Oh, my dear friend,
With you my soul should never wear a mask.
You have been faithful to me in my trouble,
I hoped you knew me better than to think
That I should ever have so little faith.
And better than to think I could betray
My husband, living still within my heart,
Or that I care not how I vex the dead;

Or that I only think of my own peace.
And would that be the keeping of the promise
That I have often made to Hector's ashes?
And yet, I know that I must save his son.
Pyrrhus has vowed that if he marries me
He will protect him. I may trust his word.
I know him well: he's violent, but true.
He will do more, Cephissa, than his promise.
And also I depend on Greece's anger.
It is her hatred will bestow a father
On Hector's son. But since a victim's needed,
I'll promise Pyrrhus all that's left of life,
And I will bind him to my boy with words
Unspeakable and sacred. After that,
This hand shall, straightway, with a fatal blow,
Cut through the cord of life that's true no longer,
And so I'll keep me free from any stain,
And still give Pyrrhus what is due to him,
Nor fail in paying what I owe my husband
And owe my son, and owe, indeed, myself!
This is the harmless plot my love has made,
Or rather, 'tis the plan of Hector's spirit.
And so, alone, I'll join him and my fathers.
Close you mine eyes.
But I forbid that you should follow me.
I trust my only treasure to your care.
You lived for me; now live for Hector's son.
He is the only keeper of our hopes.
The royal line of Troy will need your care.
Look you to Pyrrhus. See that he keeps faith,
If there be need, then speak to him of me.
Tell him again how I, before I died,
Yielded to him; teach him to prize that bond,
And so to blot his anger from his soul.
Show him, that, since I left my son to him,
I thought him worthy. You must tell my son
Of all his race's heroes; yes, and guide him
To follow in their steps. Tell him their fame;
Not what they were, but rather what they did.
Recount, each day, his father's virtues to him,
And whisper, sometimes, of a mother's love.
But he must never dream that he'll avenge me.
Let him still seek to win his master's friendship.
He'll look upon his birth with modesty,

Though Hector's blood is his; yet he'll remember
Troy lives in him alone. Now, in one day,
I lay down life for him, and hate, and love!

120.

HERMIONE STRUGGLES BETWEEN HER LOVE FOR PYRRHUS AND HER REVENGE (YT)

(1667) Jean Racine, *Andromache*, tr. Robert Henderson, Act V, Sc. 1

[See No. 119, above.] Racine's tragic figures, no matter how profound their emotional torment might be, have the capacity to articulate the character of their suffering rationally, that, sequentially, separating in description one clear and distinct thought and emotion from another. The violence within is not, as in Elizabethan/Jacobean drama, entirely reflected without. The logical, sequential shaping of their discourse separates their clarity of self-understanding from the convulsions of their inner feeling. This separation is the distinctive quality of the discourse of these courtly, aristocratic, tragic figures, whose consciousness of self controls and defines their dignity in suffering.

Not so Hermione. Like other of Racine's characters, she is governed by two contrary emotions at once: her passionate love, her unmitigated hate, and the instability of these emotions, as in other of those characters, is radical. But unlike the others, her discourse tumbles over itself, one emotion impinging so closely on the other that the one almost becomes the other. And her ability to hold to the dignity of those distinctions so tremblingly sustained by the others, fails. And so she appears not only distraught in the Jacobean way, but in relation to Racine's other figures, emotionally vulgar. But something very particular supports this "vulgar" waywardness: images. Unlike almost all of Racine's other characters, Hermione's imagination evokes, not so much a succession of contrary arguments to be considered on the way to forming her resolve, but a succession of contrary images, each of which produces an instantaneous resolve. Each image—the sneering Pyrrhus mocking her; the glorious Pyrrhus winning honor on the Trojan battlefield; the overjoyed Pyrrhus winning Andromache's favor—is at once supplanted by its contrary image, and so generates at once an opposite resolve.

Her situation, of course, explains her emotional frenzies. At Troy, she and Pyrrhus were pledged to one another by their fathers, Menelaus and Achilles, even before they knew one another. Subsequently, Pyrrhus, not professing love but only loyalty to their pledge, brought her to his kingdom to effect their marriage. Now, in Epirus, Hermione hears from his own lips that Andromache "has gained his heart," and he, with guilt and apology, withdraws his pledge to her. But Hermione is now desperately in love with Pyrrhus and, wracked with jealousy, hears not the forthrightness of his explanation but, underlying it, vicious mockery. She answers in kind, with mockery to match what she imagined was his. And inevitably, he responds with the relief of one who discovers, from the "coldness" of her response, that no love whatever had existed between them, and so no guilt or apology need pertain.

So dismissed, so disdained, so throughly misunderstood, Hermione determines on revenge, and enlists an unwilling Orestes to accomplish it by promising the infatuated lover her hand. Awaiting Orestes' return "with Pyrrhus's head," she's at once convulsed with hate and love, vengeance and pity, anxiety for its accomplishment and horror at its instigation.

(Enter Hermione.)

HERMIONE

Where am I? What is this that I have done?
And now,—do what? What frenzies clutch at me?
I wander through these halls, I know not whither.
I am destroyed with grief! I do not know
If I do love or hate him! When he left me,
His eyes,—they seemed to freeze my very soul.
He would not even look as if he pitied.
No, not a moment's tenderness or sorrow!
His heart would never grant one cry to me.
He could not hear my sighing. He was calm
Through all my agony, and all my tears
Could wake no sympathy. And yet I mourn!
To crown its sorrow, this poor heart still throbs
Only for him. The blow will soon be struck.

I tremble at it; I forget revenge.
Indeed I think I almost might forgive him!
No, I shall not call my sentence back.
The traitor dies, since he is dead to me!
He laughs in triumph, and he scorns my anger,
Thinks it a storm that will be spent in tears,
That I am always weak, that I will waver,
That my own hand will shield him from my blows!
I have been kind; he thinks it has no bounds!
And there are other thoughts to fill his mind.
The traitor, in his triumph, does not care
Whether the absent wish him life or death,
And leaves this great perplexity to me!
But one stroke ends it! By Orestes' hand
He meets the death that he might well have looked for,
Which I desire, because he made me wish it!
Then is it I who must pronounce his doom?
He dies because Hermione has loved him?—
He whose great deeds were told and told again,
To give me new delight whene'er I heard them?—
To whom I'd bound my fate, all secretly,
Before they tied us, by that fatal bond?
And have I crossed so many lands and seas,
Coming so far only to dig his grave,
To be his murderer? Before he dies—
What have I done?

121.

HERMIONE CONDEMNS HER AVENGER AGAINST PYRRHUS FOR HIS MURDER (YT)

(1667) JEAN RACINE, *ANDROMACHE*, TR. ROBERT HENDERSON, ACT V, SC. 1

Immediately following Hermione's desperate monologue [in No. 120, above], Cleone, her confidante, brings news of the marriage ceremony of Pyrrhus and Andromache, the joy visible in Pyrrhus, and the uncertainty of Orestes to fulfill his task ("now he listens to his honor, now to love"). Hermione contemptuously dismisses Orestes' indecision as cowardice ("he fears to die, and fears no other thing"). Of Orestes, she says, she's asked merely "that one perjur'd man should die" at little risk to himself, and, she sneers, he refuses! Quickly, she imagines a new scenario: she will accomplish the murder herself ("even by my own death!"), killing Pyrrhus on the marriage altar, and the three, the wedded ones and herself, shall all die together. And at the height of this thrillingly imagined scene, Orestes enters to announce, "It is all over!" He confesses that it was not his arm that accomplished Pyrrhus' murder, but that of the disaffected Greek soldiers. But still, he urges, her purpose is accomplished, and he awaits his promised reward: her promised love.

Instead, horrified at Pyrrhus's death, she rages at Orestes' cowardice for murdering Pyrrhus (which he did not do), at his "treachery" for not countering her demand for vengeance, and—bitter accusation—at his coming to Epirus to claimherself, which was the cause, she accuses, of Pyrrhus turning to Andromache. Orestes, then, she reasons, was the culprit who "made his thoughts turn to her." For the first time, Hermione's "heart" does not "belie whatever words" she speaks. Though her accusations are all false, her meaning, her intent, is altogether at one with "her heart."

HERMIONE

Be still, you traitor! Do not lay this deed—
This crime which brands you coward, at my feet!
Go! Let the Greeks applaud so vile an act!
Go! I disown your cruelty and you,
Who have destroyed the noblest man alive,
On this most fatal day! Was there no pity
To visit your black heart, to stop such murder?
Who made you judge, to sentence him to death?
What was his crime? What right had you to kill him?
Yes, tell me that! Who bade you do it?
I gave the order?
You should not heed a love bereft of reason.
You should have read more deeply in my thoughts!
Did you not see that, while I raved, distracted,
My heart belied whatever words I spoke?
Why, had I meant them, you should have refused
A wish like that, if made a hundred times!
You should have asked again, before you struck,
And still again, or rather, shunned my sight.
You should have let me take my own revenge.

What lured you here? You're hateful to my eyes!
See now what bitter fruit your love has borne!
You bring the ills that follow you, to me.
Your embassy was fatal to us both.
It made his thoughts incline to her—my rival,
For otherwise he might have let me share
His heart again,—at least have played at love!
You go, for I will stay in this Epirus.
Here I renounce my Spartan home and Greece,
Yes, all my kindred! 'Tis enough for me
That they have bred a monster, such as you!

MY SPARTAN HOME AND GREECE: Hermione's mother Helen was a Spartan princess and her father was the Greek king Menelaus.

122.

LAODICE, AFTER MURDERING HER OWN CHILDREN TO MAINTAIN HER THRONE, SUCCUMBS TO, AND FEARS, A COMPROMISING LOVE (OT)

(1668) THOMAS CORNEILLE, *LAODICE*, TR. L. LOCKERT, ACT II

In French neo-classical tragedy, the speaker confesses to her confidante the condition of her own soul as truthfully and openly as though talking to herself. The only distinction between soliloquy and this confessional is the pretense of addressing another. The confidante is by convention as informed about the narrative facts as is the speaker; they're detailed not to inform her of anything new, but to clarify the conditions that logically and inevitably have led to the baffled one's current dilemma. The substance of the speech is characteristically the division between two hostile alternatives; its drama is governed by the variable emotional investment elicited by each of the contending alternatives. The speaker's moral definition—the degree of her seduction by passion, and of her submission to reason, and of her strength of will—is revealed through her emotional perplexity over each of these symmetrical dilemmas.

The dilemma of Laodice, the queen of Cappadocia, is not only symmetrical, it's harrowing. Out of an almost insane lust for the crown, and fear of surrendering it ("[her] burning ardor of …desires which centered all my soul upon the throne"), she poisoned five of her sons, and she commanded the sixth to be taken hostage and murdered. As in Oedipus and other foundling stories, Ariarethes is spared by his intended executioner. Now grown, he, the rightful possessor of the throne, has returned, but to avoid his mother's still lethal intentions, he's in disguise as Orontes.

Inevitably in this world of "romanesque" storytelling [plots derived from the fanciful romances of Scudery and Calpranede. See No. 114, above, and Vol. 4, No. 154], it's Orontes for whom the Queen, unaware that he is her son, has conceived an uncontrollable passion. It does not subvert her reason, but paralyzes her will. It's her hatred of this paralysis on the one hand and her indestructible lust for the throne on the other that have brought her to her dilemma.

Possibly more harrowing than this situation in itself is its follow-up [see No. 123, below]. Laodice, still unaware of his identity, solicits "Orontes" to murder that still troublesome son—himself. There's little charity in the bargain she offers: marriage and the shared throne if he does the crime, but if he does not—now that he knows her plan—death.

LAODICE

Thou knowest I ne'er loved aught except the throne,
And that a vast, insatiable ambition
Made me feel scorn for every other passion.
To slake its thirst, I treated as a weakness
The tender feelings born of natural ties;
And thought the death of five sons was the cost,
I could see naught but the delights of reigning.
My sixth son, who was held at Rome a hostage,
Still caused my jealous heart anxiety.
Fearing that he might some day take the throne
From me, with neither pity nor remorse
I had him carried off, and sought to have
His death appear uncertain still, that thus
The rights which make my daughter queen might be
Held in abeyance, and that I might use
Whatever means I needed to prevent
Her marriage, under the pretense of keeping
The crown for this son. Midst the burning ardor

Of my desires which centered all my soul
Upon the throne, I scarcely can imagine
What abject quality prompts me to seek
A lover in a king of mine own making.
    I feel this shameful, and it irks my pride.
I in my heart call myself weak and vile,
And yet I cannot pluck from out my breast
The sweet thoughts that too charmingly beguile me.
Ever I see Orontes, diligent,
Spirited, loyal, eager to display
By numberless attentions his devotion,
To make my pleasure his sole interest
And comply blindly with whate'er I wish.
I feel myself touched by it, and his deference
So brings my soul into accord with his
That I should now distrust myself if I
Were forced to choose between the throne and him.
    Such feelings, are unworthy, craven, base;
I hate myself for them, but cannot cast them
Out of my heart. It seems that for my shame
The harsh decree of heaven hath made of them
A needful thing for me, and that the love,
Unworthy of a queen, which burns in me,
Is the inevitable penalty
Of my o'erweening pride, and that the wrath
Of heaven hath wished deliberately to kindle
A flame within me at the age when one,
Whate'er one can feel, ought to blush at loving.
Pretexts of policy will cloak my shame;
I can conceal it even from Orontes' eyes,
But I must needs with thee relieve my heart
Of the too heavy burden of its ardor,
That, being with my pride familiar, thou
Canst help me find what hath become of it,
And pity me at least…

123.

LAODICE OFFERS A DEVIL'S BARGAIN TO HER LOVER: JOIN HER IN MURDER AND SHARE HER THRONE (OT)

(1668) THOMAS CORNEILLE, *LAODICE*, TR. L. LOCKERT, ACT III

[See No. 122, above.]

LAODICE

Thou dost not understand me; I must better
Explain myself. I must tell thee all.
Truly, with thee, whose heart is still too tender,
To half explain makes one misunderstood.
Knowing me wholly, thou canst judge of me.
The late king at his death left me six sons.
By different strokes of fate, five of them died.
Perhaps thou'st heard some ugly rumors whispered;
I have disdained their insult and believed
These slanders, while I reigned, not worth my tears.
With my heart charmed by such a brilliant fortune,
I used all means to make it mine more surely.
Carried to Rome as hostage, Ariarathes
Could rob me of it, were he not removed.
I ordered him to be—decreed his death—
But now I see the gods have not allowed it,
That a vile knave betrayed me, and that Rome
And Ariarathes learned my secret aims.
Thou canst from this judge what a son too surely
Convinced of all his mother's pride, can do.
If I would sacrifice his life to reign,
Would he, to reign, in his turn wish to spare me?
He is of mine own blood, a blood too eager
For empire's throne to tremble at the prospect
Of a mere matricide, and if this son
Of mine be not destroyed by me, he soon
Will show himself well versed in mine own lessons.
He must, he must be killed; I have no choice.
'Tis said he comes unguarded with Aquilius.
Do not deceive thyself; though it should be
That crime was odious to him, as to thee,—

That virtue had for him the same attraction,—
With what he knows of me, I would not trust
Myself in his hands. Nay, if I should have
Complete assurance that he would leave the throne
Always in my possession, and would always
Be my submissive subject, I would feel
Still the same ardor to achieve his death.
To make my ordering it just and lawful
'Twould be enough to see that he forgave
My crime, and that I needs would die if he,
Because of noble fears and scruples, did not
Refuse to be as wicked as myself.
Therefore I cannot see him dead too soon.
Though he were but a witness of my shame;
Therefore I always must attempt his life,
I needs must fear his crime or hate his virtue,
And in his blood seek our security,
To save me from the one or to avenge
Myself upon the other. That is all.
Contend no more! Thou must declare thyself
And choose which of these two things thou preferrest.
If to shed blood disturbs thee, gives thee pain,
I know who without qualms will hear a queen,
And for one crime exacted of their fealty,
Will not disdain to rule with me. But ere
I borrow any other arms than thine,
Reflect that one crime oft compels another
And that, when I have told thee my resolve,
Only the throne can he a safe place for thee.

124.

ANGELICA DEFENDS HERSELF AGAINST HER HUSBAND'S ACCUSATIONS OF INFIDELITY (YC)

(1668) JEAN-BAPTISTE MOLIÈRE, *GEORGE DANDIN*,
TR. A.R. WALLER, ACT II, SC. 2

George Dandin's marriage is doubly cursed. He, a mere bourgeois and a rich one, married a young aristocrat and a poor one, but suffers the contempt of her and her aristocratic parents for his low birth. And aristocrat or not, his wife, Angelica, is a coquette—more than a coquette, she is encouraging an affair with her neighbor Clitandre behind her husband's back.

The plot of Molière's farce keeps Angelica in perpetual anticipatory delight and Dandin in perpetual misery. No matter how often he catches her, or her servant Claudine or her lover Clitandre arranging assignations, and no matter how persuasively he is ready to accuse his wife before her parents, the bare-faced lies of the culprits make a mockery of his case. And Dandin, at last losing all credibility before them, must at the end face the prospect of a life of unabating and uncorrectible cuckoldry.

From time to time, Dandin implores his wife to respect him and her marriage vows; always she, counters with arguments sufficiently exculpating for her, but torture for Dandin. But the paradox of the character of Angelica is that although she always argues in total bad faith, her arguments in themselves are entirely sound. These are her arguments: there's little justice in being accused of being attractive to men, and no justice at all in succumbing to the tyranny of the husband who so accuses her. Since she had no voice in the arrangement of her marriage, she feels no obligation "to submit, like a slave" to his will. But there's one demand Angelica makes that has a peculiarly significant and a new ring: her wish "to take the sweet liberties the age permits me." They were sweet indeed and novel: a freedom of acceptable maneuverability that made possible the wife's access to a world, a clique, and a pleasurable acquaintanceship independent of her husband. In the Paris of Louis XIV and later in the eighteenth century throughout the fashionable capitals of Europe, that independence was granted and exploited by women of rank and/or wealth, and put the weapons of marital battle on a new and more equal footing for women. [For the similar plight of Sir Peter Teazle in Sheridan's *The School for Scandal,* see in Men's volumes "Sir Peter Tries to Fathom Why His Wife, Always in the Wrong, Quarrels with Him."] Whatever Angelica's culpabilities as a liar, betrayer, and snob, her reasoning, unlike her behavior, is unanswerable.

ANGELICA

Well, is it my fault? What do you want me to do? Drive them away? for what reason? It does not shock me that people think me handsome, it pleases me. A sensible man is glad to see his wife admired. I do not intend to renounce the world and bury myself alive in a husband. Why should I? Because a man thinks fit to marry me, must everything immediately be at an end for me, must I break off all commerce with the living? This tyranny of the lord and master is a marvelous thing; I think it is excellent in them to wish that we should be dead to all pleasures and live only for them. It is laughable. I do not wish to die so young.

I did not make my vows to you of my own free will, you forced them from me. Did you ask my consent before marriage, or whether I cared for you? On that point you only consulted my father and mother; strictly speaking you married them and therefore you will do well always to complain to them concerning any wrongs you may suffer. I did not tell you to marry me. You took me without consulting my feelings, and I do not pretend to be obliged to submit, like a slave, to your will; I wish to enjoy, by your leave, the few happy days youth has to offer, to take the sweet liberties the age permits me, to see something of the fashionable world, and to taste the pleasure of listening to the pretty things said to me. Prepare yourself for this, as your punishment, and return thanks to Heaven I am not capable of something worse.

125.

THE MAID DORINE TRIES TO REASON WITH ORGON ABOUT HIS INFATUATION WITH TARTUFFE (YC)

(1669) JEAN-BAPTISTE MOLIÈRE, *TARTUFFE*,
TR. A. R. WALLER, ACT II, SC. 2

Dorine has the temerity of almost all the maids in neo-classical comedy. Already exasperated with her master Orgon's infatuation with the religious hypocrite Tartuffe, she's outraged at his latest stupidity, his determination to give his daughter in marriage to that impoverished bigot. Dorine is one of the very few in Orgon's household who has the temerity to stand up to him. He's a man of dearly-held convictions, that is to say, a man of infatuations, which is to say, a man given to monomania, which is to say, a man always and inevitably on the verge of culpability. In Dorine's opinion, he's reached it now, and she takes on the task of undoing the impregnable defenses of those convictions. She won't succeed.

But her argument, which is clearly meant to reflect the celebrated common sense of Molière's own, is illuminating for its own as well as Molière's own degree of bigotry. Her arguments:

1) Wealth has no reason to tolerate mere beggars as sons-in-law.

2) The pious man can have no connection with the gentleman, and for him to claim to be a gentleman is mere vanity.

3) Similarly, the "simplicity of holy life" forbids further connection with "name and lineage," and for the holy man—even though he may have "name and lineage"—should he mention it, is merely boasting.

4) A man who in leading the good life but also has ambition is committing the sin of pride.

5) The continuing virtue of the married woman does not depend on her, but on "the qualities of the husband," and the father who gave her to such a husband is answerable to heaven for the sins she commits.

So it's a question whether the half-truths and non-truths of common sense are any more admirable than the half-truths and non-truths of religious bigotry. Still, admirable or not, they make Dorine's convictions at least as inflexible as Orgon's.

DORINE

Let us talk without becoming angry, Monsieur, I beg. Are you making game of everybody by means of this scheme? Your daughter will never do for a bigot: he has other things to think about. Besides, what good will such an alliance be to you? Why, with all your wealth, do you choose a beggar for a son-in-law? Well, he says he is a gentleman, but this vanity, Monsieur, does not agree well with his piety. He who embraces the simplicity of a holy life should not boast of his name and lineage: the humble ways of goodness have nothing in common with the glare of ambition. Why such pride? But what I say vexes you: let us speak of himself and leave his quality. Can you have the heart to bestow such a daughter as yours upon a man of his stamp? Ought you not to have some regard for propriety and foresee the consequences of this union? You must know the girl's virtue is not safe when she is married against her inclinations, that her living virtuously depends upon the qualities of the husband who is given to her, and that those who have the finger of scorn pointed at them make their wives what we see they are. It is truly no easy task to be faithful to certain husbands; and he who gives his daughter to a man she hates is responsible to heaven for the sins she commits. Consider, then, to what perils your design exposes you.

You could not do better than follow my advice. She? Why, I am sure she will never make anything of him but a fool. I tell you he looks it all over, and his destiny, Monsieur, will be stronger than your daughter's virtue. I only speak for your own good. I will care for you, Monsieur, in spite of yourself.

126.

ELMIRE DEMONSTRATES FOR HER HUSBAND THE INIQUITY OF HIS PROTÉGÉ TARTUFFE (oc)

(1669) JEAN-BAPTISTE MOLIÈRE, *TARTUFFE*,
TR. A.R. WALLER, ACT IV, SC. 5

From entry in Men's volumes "Tartuffe Attempts to Seduce Elmire, the Wife of His Patron": "Molière's *Tartuffe* is the quintessential portrait in Western literature of the man of the cloth as hypocrite. So broad and blatant is his sham piety that, together with his sham poverty, he moves Orgon, a well-to-do bourgeois, to take him into his home as protégé and confessor. No one in Orgon's household but himself and his pious old mother is taken in by Tartuffe… It's Molière's conceit that such a menace is made possible… by two factors: the passion of the dupe to be duped, and the proscriptive weight of religiosity to cow and shut the mouth of the undeceived."

Orgon is planning to give his daughter, who is in love with Valere, in marriage to Tartuffe. Orgon's wife, a model of common sense, has already had one interview with Tartuffe to persuade him to relent from this marriage, when instead, he attempted to seduce her, but was interrupted by the intervention of Orgon's son, Damis. Since there appears to be no way to persuade Orgon of his protégé's iniquity, Elmire determines to demonstrate the fact at a second interview. Orgon will hide under the table, she insists, and see for himself (with the assurance that at her signal—a cough—he will emerge in time to spare Elmire undue trial).

But Elmire must now backtrack; Tartuffe's suspicions are alive. She must persuade him that she is willing, that her first refusal was merely a woman's way of inviting ardor, and that he is free to repeat his proposals. His haste to do so and Orgon's fatuous non-response to his wife's increasingly desperate signals have given to this scene a status in Western comedy shared by very few—the screen scene in *The School for Scandal*, the "contract" scene in *The Way of the World*—possibly a few others.

ELMIRE

Ah! if such a refusal has offended you, how very little you

know a woman's heart, how little you understand what we mean when we defend ourselves so feebly. At such times our modesty always struggles with any tender sentiments we may feel. Whatever reasons we may find for the love which conquers us, there is always a little shame in the avowal of it. We resist at first, but from our manner it can easily be seen our heart surrenders, that our words oppose our wishes for the sake of honour, and that we refuse in such a way as to promise everything. I am making a very free confession to you, to be sure, and I am not sparing woman's modesty; but since these words have at last escaped me, should I have been anxious to restrain Damis, should I, I ask you, have listened to you so long and with so much patience, when you offered me your heart, should I have taken the thing as I did, if the offer of your heart had not given me pleasure? What could you have inferred from such an action when I myself tried to make you renounce the proposed marriage, if it were not that I took an interest in you, and that I should have been grieved if such a marriage had taken place and you had in the least divided that affection which I wanted to be wholly mine?

(She coughs to warn her husband.)
What? Would you proceed so fast and exhaust the kindness of my feelings all at once? I commit myself in making such a tender admission; yet that is not enough for you. Will nothing satisfy you but to push things to their furthest extremity?

Good heavens! How very tyrannical is your love, and in what strange agitation it throws me! What an irresistible power it exercises over the heart, and how violently it clamors for what it desires! What? Is there no avoiding your pursuit? Will you not give me time to breathe? Is it decent to be so very exacting, to insist without quarter on those things which you demand, and by your pressing ardour, thus to take advantage of the weakness which you see is felt for you? How can I comply with your desires without offending that heaven of which you constantly speak?

(After coughing again and striking upon the table)
I have a troublesome cough, it racks me. I very much fear all the liquorice in the world will not do it any good now.

(After coughing again)
Well, I see I must make up my mind to yield: that I must

consent to grant you everything: and that with less than this I
ought not to expect you should be satisfied or convinced. It is
indeed very hard to come to this, and it is greatly against my
will that I venture so far, but since people persist in driving me
to this; since they will not believe anything that is said to
them, and since they wish for more convincing testimony, one
must even resolve upon it and satisfy them. If this gratification
carries any offense in it, so much the worse for those who
force me to this violence; the fault, assuredly, is not mine.

Open the door a little, and pray, look if my husband is not in
that passage. Pray, go out for a moment and look carefully
everywhere outside.

> *(Tartuffe goes out, and Orgon comes out
> from under the table.)*

What? You come out so soon? You make fools of people. Go
back under the table-cloth, it is not time yet; stay to the end to
make sure of things, and do not trust to mere conjectures.

127.

AGRIPPINA PLEADS FOR HER SON NERO'S REVIVED TRUST (OT)

(1669) JEAN RACINE, *BRITANNICUS*,
TR. ROBERT HENDERSON AND P. LANDIS, ACT IV, SC. 2

[For a further note on *Britannicus,* see in Men's volumes "Nero
Recounts His Falling in Love with Junia."] During Nero's reign in
Rome, murder became an act of policy, and winning "influence" a
matter of life and death. Agrippina's appeal in this passage to her son
Nero has that urgency: if she loses influence over him, her life and the
life of those she's supporting are in jeopardy. She herself was a master
of these politic lethal games. The sister of Caligula and the mother of
Nero by her first husband (she murdered her second husband),
Agrippina married the emperor Claudius, her uncle, after the death of
his wife Messalina, and persuaded him to adopt Nero as his heir in

place of his own son Britannicus. After that, she poisoned Claudius and secured the throne for her son.

So much for history. Racine takes much of what followed historically into account and embroiders the sequel. Agrippina, recognizing "the savage nature" and the pride lurking in Nero, a savagery which would inevitably surface, has taken the precaution to "make herself a harbor against the coming storm" by subtly befriending Britannicus' cause, so that "I hold the balance evenly between them." But her influence over her son is rapidly diminishing in favor of Nero's tutor and closest advisor, Burrus, who screens the emperor from visits with his mother. Now she's desperate: Junia, Britannicus' lover, has been abducted by Nero; Agrippina has reason to fear the loss of all control over her son if his violence against Junia and, by implication, against Britannicus goes unchallenged.

Her maneuvering for a meeting with Nero, and the insult of having to do so, have brought her to white-hot rage. But she is nothing if not astute: confronting her son, she is soft in her appeal, slow and precise in her self-justification, generously matter-of-fact in reminding him that he owes his very empire to her sinister efforts on his behalf—but carefully, there is yet no tinge of reproach or accusation. Agrippina, in her pleading for return of his love and faith, demonstrates her skill at diplomacy: her ability to ask for nothing and yet press for everything. It's a long and tortuous battle she describes— the ins and outs of gaining favor; the winning ground against "enemies" with promises of favor, exile, or murder; the winning favor with the populace with gifts and shows in Nero's name, and ultimately, the screening of the murder of Claudius until Nero's support was secured.

"These are my crimes, and this is my reward." Not until her litany of past favors has registered does Agrippina begin, carefully her second litany: her catalogue of affronts at her son's hands. Fact piled on fact, shame on shame, the seething emotion below is strategically controlled until the last of her brief, when she allows the force of her feeling to show less discreetly: "You, too conscious of your perfidy, you dare not come to me and beg forgiveness, you order me [instead] to justify myself."

But her calculated effort comes to nothing. Nero, reading her accurately, answers in the same agreeable vein, and sends her off with protestations of renewed affection and trust. But by that interview, he is thoroughly confirmed in his belief that Britannicus must be murdered so that he will finally be free of "Agrippina's fury."

AGRIPPINA

(Seating herself) Come, Nero, sit beside me. 'Tis my wish
To clear your mind of every false suspicion.
I know not with what crime I have been slandered,
But all that I have done can be explained.
You hold Earth's sceptre now; and yet you know
How far below such eminence you were born.
My fathers, whom Rome placed among the gods,
Had not exalted you without my help.
When Messalina's execution left
The couch of Claudius an open prize,
I sought to triumph over the fair field
Of women who employed his freedmen's aid
Only because I hoped in after years
To give the throne where I should sit to you.
I choked my pride to garner Pallas' favor;
His master, daily cherished in my arms,
By slow degrees drew from his niece's eyes
The love to which I sought to lead his heart.
But kindred blood between us barred our union
As impious incest, nor did Claudius dare
To wed his brother's daughter till the senate,
Subservient to his wish, relaxed the law,
And placed him in my arms, Rome at my feet.
So much for me; for you still nothing gained.
Hard on my steps I made a place for you
Within his household, made you his son-in-law,
Gave you his daughter, whom Silanus loved,
And he, forsaken, marked the fatal day
With his own blood. Still nothing was accomplished.
Could you have guessed that Claudius one day
Had held his son-in-law above his son?
Again I went to Pallas for his help.
On his advice Claudius adopted you;
He called you Nero, and before 'twas time
Wished you to share the power with himself.
Thus it was that thinking on the past,
Men saw my plan already far advanced;
And seeing Britannicus threatened with disgrace,
His father's friends began to murmur. Some
I blinded with fair promises, and exile
Delivered me from those most treacherous;
Claudius himself, grown weary of my plaints,
Sent from his son all those whose constant zeal,

Long loyal to his destiny, could still
Place him upon the pathway to the throne.
I went still further, choosing for my suite
Those only whom I wished to guide his course.
Yet I was careful to appoint for you
Such guardians as Rome held most in honor;
Deaf to intrigues, I trusted only fame;
Recalled from exile and withdrew from war
That very Seneca, that very Burrus,
Who later—Rome then held them honorable.
Tapping the wealth of Claudius meanwhile,
In your own name I gave you lavish gifts.
Presents and shows, invincible attractions,
Won you the people's hearts; the soldiery,
Recalling all their former loyalty,
Favored in you Germanicus, my father.
Claudius, meanwhile, weakened towards his death;
His eyes, long closed, were opened at the end;
He saw his error. Stricken with his fear,
He dropped some words of pity for his son,
And wished, too late, to call his friends together.
But I controlled his bed, his guards, his palace,
And let him vainly waste his tenderness.
I watched him to his latest breath. My care,
Which seemed to minister to his distress,
But hid his son's tears from the dying king.
He died. A thousand shameful rumors spread.
I quickly stopped the news that he had died,
And while in secret Burrus was dispatched
To swear the army to your cause, and you
Were marching to the camp, at my command
The altars smoked through Rome with sacrifices.
Tricked by my deception, all the people
Prayed for the health of a king already dead.
At last, with all the legions sworn to you,
Your power o'er the empire firmly fixed,
I showed them Claudius' body, and the people,
To their astonishment, learned all at once
That Claudius was dead and you were king.

This was what I wanted to confess;
These were my crimes, and this is my reward.
Now that you reap the fruit of all my pains,
In six short months your gratitude is spent;
You feel the burden of respect too heavy,

And scarcely seem to recognize me more.
I have seen how Seneca and Burrus
Stirred you to treachery, and set you lessons,
Till you excelled your teachers in deception;
I have seen young rakes like Senecio
And Otho favored with your confidence
Because they pandered to your every wish;
And when in desperation at your treatment,
I asked some explanation of your acts,
You fled to the sole refuge of an ingrate,
And answered my complaints with fresh affronts.
Today I promised Junia to your brother,
And both were flattered at your mother's choice.
But you—as soon as she was brought to court,
Made her at once the mistress of your heart.
I see your heart has turned against Octavia;
I see you ready, too, to turn her out
From the bed in which I placed her; I see Pallas,
An exile, and Britannicus, a captive.
Finally you destroy my liberty:
Burrus dares to lay his hands upon me,
And you, too conscious of your perfidy,
You dare not come to me and beg forgiveness,
You order me to justify myself.

AGRIPPINA: (AD 16–59), daughter of Germanicus and Agrippina (called the Elder); sister of Caligula, and mother of Nero by her first husband. She was accused of poisoning her second husband in AD 49, and after the death of Claudius' wife Messalina, married him, her uncle. She induced him to adopt her own son Nero as his heir in favor of his own son Brittanicus. In AD 54, she poisoned Claudius and secured the throne for her son. Alarmed at the influence of a freedwoman over Nero, she threatened to support the claims of the rightful heir, Brittanicus, whereupon Nero murdered him, and decided to have his mother murdered as well. MESSALINA: wife of Claudius, murdered by Agrippina, who succeeded her as Claudius' wife. SENECA: (AD 4–65) the Stoic philosopher and playwright, banished to Spain by Messalina, but brought back to Rome by Agrippina to become Nero's tutor; and subsequently advisor, with the military man Burrus, to her son. Later, he was suspected of joining a conspiracy against Nero and, anticipating his sentence, committed suicide. OCTAVIA: daughter of Emperor Claudius and wife of Nero, by whom she was put to death.

128.

AGRIPPINA CONDEMNS NERO'S CRIMES AND FORECASTS HIS FATE (OT)

(1669) Jean Racine, Britannicus,
tr. Robert Henderson and Paul Landis, Act V, Sc. 6

[Continues No. 127, above] Nero, confirmed in his decision to assassinate Britannicus, is nevertheless wavering. The arguments of his mentors, Burrus on the one hand and Narcissus on the other, poise Nero on the edge of decision concerning the murder of his half-brother Britannicus, but he is poised precisely between the two. It's understood but unspoken in the scene that what will govern Nero's decision was foretold: the "savagery" in his nature that Agrippina knew well and so much feared. A single line functions as the hinge of the play: "Come, [Narcissus], let us go and plan what we shall do," when Nero "makes the decision that seals the fate of Britannicus, of Nero and of Rome." The act accomplished, Agrippina confronts her son, this time with neither calculation nor discretion, blurts out her wholehearted condemnation and grim prediction. Burrus, having watched Nero watching the murder, confirms Agrippina's intuition: "If I must explain my sadness, Madam, It is that Nero saw him die unmoved. In his indifferent eyes there was already The look of one inured to crime from birth." One among Agrippina's predictions certain to be fulfilled: her own subsequent murder.

Agrippina

Stop, Nero, I must speak with you.
Britannicus is dead. I heard the cries.
I know his murderer. You! you commanded it!
Go on! You have already gone too far
To turn back now. Your hand, as a beginning,
Is reddened with your brother's blood, and I
Foresee that next your blow will strike your mother.
Deep in your secret heart I know you hate me.
You would be free from gratitude's hard yoke.
But I shall make my death of little use
To your designs. Think not that, dying, I
Shall leave you peaceful. Rome, the sky above,
The very light of day you have from me,

Will keep me everywhere before your eyes.
Regrets will follow you like vengeful furies,
And you will try with fresh atrocities
To set your heart at rest; so fury, feeding
Upon itself, will mark your every day
With some new bloodshed. But I hope at last
That Heaven, weary of your cruelties,
Will add your life to all your other victims;
That after wallowing in their blood and mine,
You'll find yourself compelled to shed your own;
And that your name descend to future times
An insult, to the cruelest of tyrants.
That is the fate my heart predicts for you.
Farewell, you may go now.

129.

ZERBINETTE TELLS HOW A FATHER IS TO BE DUPED OUT OF HIS MONEY, BUT MISTAKENLY TELLS IT TO THE DUPE (YC)

(1671) JEAN-BAPTISTE MOLIÈRE, *LES FOURBERIES DE SCAPIN*,
TR. A.R. WALLER, ACT III, SC. 3

Leander is the son of the well-to-do Geronte. He loves Zerbinette, a supposed gypsy and one of a gypsy band. He must get ransom money from his father to rescue Zerbinette. His father is a miser. How to get around this (two-thousand-year-old, very worn Plautine comic) obstacle? We find out from Zerbinette while she is suffering from an especially helpless, especially lengthy fit of laughter, how the old miser is to be duped out of his money; but unluckily, Zerbinette is sharing the joke, unbeknownst to her, with the old miser.

For Zerbinette's extended *faux pas*, the trick was to be accomplished by the hair-brained genius of the comic valet Scapin, but Zerbinette's telling in her speech below makes Scapin's story and its effect on the old man available and clear. What is exceptionally notable about the speech is the classic challenge to the actor—the equivalent of the coloratura's feat in opera of sustaining a rapid and lengthy cascade of exactly pitched and at the same time continually expressive notes—to sustain an extended punctuation of giggles, snorts, and peals of laughter throughout the telling of her story, while keeping the story itself absolutely clear and the punctuation of its accompanying laughter absolutely believable. Pure aria. It's a feat that belongs very much to the tradition of the actors of *commedia dell'arte;* and it's a feat that, if accomplished, marks the difference between ability and technical mastery.

ZERBINETTE

No, no, sir, it has nothing to do with you; I was laughing to myself at a story I had just heard, the most amusing imaginable. It may be because I am interested in the matter; but I never heard anything so ridiculous as the trick which a son has just played on his father, to squeeze some money out of him. If you want to hear it you will not find it difficult to get it out of me, for I never can keep to myself the tales I hear.

It is an incident that will not long remain secret. Fate decided that I should fall into the hands of a troop of Gypsies, who, wandering from province to province, tell fortunes, and do many other things. On arriving in this town, a young man saw me and fell in love with me. From that moment he dogged my footsteps, at first acting like all other young men, who think they have but to speak, and, at the least word they say, attain their end; but he found a resistance that soon corrected his first thoughts. He told his passion to the people who held me captive, and he found them willing to let him have me for a certain sum. But the trouble of the matter was that my lover was in that condition in which most young men of birth often are, he was somewhat short of money; he has a father, who, although he is rich, is an avaricious boor, the most sorry wretch living. Stay. I wonder if I can remember his name. Ah! Try and help me. Cannot you tell me the name of some one in this town who is known to be a miser of the deepest dye? There is a ron,…ronte in his name. Or,…oronte. No. Ge…Geronte; yes, Geronte, exactly; that is the wretch, I have got it, he is the boor I told you of. Well, to go on with my tale, our people wish to leave this town today; and my lover was going to lose me, because he had no money, if he had not found a helper in his servant in the task of getting it out of his father. I remember perfectly the name of the servant: he is called Scapin; he is a wonderful fellow and deserves all possible praise.

This is the stratagem he used to take in the dupe. Ha, ha, ha, ha. I cannot help laughing heartily whenever I think of it. Ha, ha, ha. He went to find this dog of a miser, ha, ha, ha; and said to him that, in walking along the harbour with his son, he, he, they saw a Turkish galley on which they were invited to go; a young Turk gave them luncheon, ha; and, whilst they were having it, the galley was put out to sea; then the Turk sent the servant Scapin back alone to the shore, in a skiff, with orders to tell his master's father that be would take his son away to Algiers, if be did not immediately send him five hundred crowns. Ha, ha, ha. Behold this wretch, this churl, in acute anguish; the affection he has for his son had a furious combat against his avarice. The five hundred crowns demanded of him were just as though he had had five hundred stabs with a poniard given him. Ha, ha, ha. He could not make up his mind to wrench the sum out of his heartstrings; and the pain it gave him caused him to think of a hundred ridiculous ways to redeem his son. Ha, ha, ha. He wished to send the law officers on the sea after the Turkish galley. Ha, ha, ha. He besought his own valet to offer himself as a substitute for his son, until he had collected the money he did not intend to give. Ha, ha, ha. He gave him four or five old suits to sell, to make up the five hundred crowns, though they were not worth thirty. Ha, ha, ha. The valet gave him to understand, at each attempt, how preposterous his propositions were, and, every time the thing came back to his mind, he wailed out loud: "What the devil was he doing in that galley? Ah! cursed galley! The traitor of a Turk!" In the end, after several attempts at evasion, after having sighed and groaned for ever so long…But you are not laughing at my tale. What do you think of it?

130.

PHILAMINTE EXPLAINS HER PLAN FOR ESTABLISHING AN ACADEMY, COMPLEMENTING PLATO'S (OC)

(1672) Jean-Baptiste Molière, *The Learned Ladies*, tr. H. Baker and J. Miller, Act III, Sc. 2

"These are admirable projects," concludes Philaminte, having put forth the matters to be examined in the learned Academy she and the other women are forming. A hundred years after Molière, in London, they would be called Bluestockings, women who ventured on literary and intellectual accomplishment. They were to be parodied then too, but rarely as scurvily as in Molière's *The Learned Ladies*. Philaminte's project, Molière is careful to point out, is ridiculous on the face of it; she's already seen in her investigations, she says, the man in the moon, and she's committed the Academy to cutting "filthy syllables from the finest words."

On the face of it, *The Learned Ladies* is one of the most offensively patronizing comedies on the subject of women's ambitions toward learning, and it's difficult to discern what deeper levels in it save that face. The pretentious stupidity it attributes to women is so grossly caricatured as to make one wonder how a Parisian salon society already filled with women of intellectual and literary sophistication could countenance Molière's absurdity. The *raisonneur* Clitandre explains the play's comic perspective, and as usual in Molière, the explanation of his middle ground of values is recited plainly, baldly, without the possible mitigation of its being spoken in the vein of good-natured, forgiving fun: "These female doctors are not to my taste. I agree that a woman should have an insight into everything; but I would not have her indulge a monstrous passion, to make herself learned for the sake of being learned; and I love to have her often know, when questions are put to her, how to appear ignorant of things which she knows. In short, I would have her hide her study, and have knowledge without desiring the world should know it." The Pedant was a standard target of Renaissance comedy, and he was laughed at for "citing authors," as Clitandre puts his explanation for his distaste for these women, "speaking bombast words, being constantly learned on the least occasions." But they were satirized for pre-

tending to know what they didn't know, never for the crime Molière
attributes to his learned ladies, of not pretending not to know what
they knew. As with *Les Precieuses Ridicules* [see No. 93, above],
Molière safely pillories his target by displacing it. He gets at a foible of
the upper classes by showing the middle class's aping it. But the
aping, always ridiculous, is not in fact his target; it is the foible itself,
women's pretension toward learning.

Philaminte is the leading spirit, the guiding light, of the Academy
enterprise, though it's not yet launched. She is presiding over a salon,
in which a bad poet, Trissotin, is reading bad verses she thoroughly
admires; in turn, he pays her the compliment of asking her to retali-
ate with her own labor. She demurs, but advertises instead her coming venture.

PHILAMINTE

I myself have done nothing in verse, but I have room to hope
that I may in a little time be able to show you as a friend eight
chapters of the plan of our academy. Plato foolishly forbore
the subject when he writ the treatise of his *Republic*, but I'll
carry the idea, which I have upon paper formed in prose, to
the full effect. For in short I am strangely vexed at the wrong
men do us with regard to wit; and I'll revenge every one of us
of the unworthy class they rank us in, by bounding our talents
to trifling things, and shutting the door of sublime lights
against us. We must get above this shameful condition, and
bravely set our genius at liberty. We would show certain wits
whose pride makes 'em use us with contempt, that women are
likewise furnished with learning; that, like them, they can hold
learned assemblies, regulated in that case by better rules; that
they'll unite there what's separated elsewhere, join fine
language with sublime sciences, discover nature in a thousand
experiments; and upon any questions that may be proposed,
bring in each sect and espouse none.

I long to see our assembly opened, and to signalize ourselves
by some discovery. For my part, without flattering myself, I
have made one already, and have plainly seen men in the
moon.

Morality has charms that my heart is smitten with, and 'twas
formerly the admiration of great geniuses; but I give the
superiority to the Stoics, and I think nothing so fine as their
Wise Man. But the finest project of our academy, which is a

noble enterprise, and with which I'm transported, a design full
of glory, and which will be extolled amongst all the great
geniuses of posterity, is the retrenching of those filthy
syllables, which in the finest words produce scandal; those
eternal jests of the fools of all time; those nauseous
commonplace things of our wretched buffoons; those sources
of a heap of infamous equivocations with which they insult
the modesty of women. These are our admirable projects.

STOICS: the school of philosophy that taught that men should be free from passion
and submit without complaint to unavoidable necessity. THOSE INFAMOUS EQUIVO-
CATIONS...INSULT THE MODESTY OF WOMEN: for which Molière was attacked for his
"suggestive innuendos" in The School for Wives.

131.

PHAEDRA CONFESSES TO OENONE HER PASSION FOR HIPPOLYTUS (OT)

(1677) JEAN RACINE, *PHAEDRA*, TR. ROBERT HENDERSON, ACT I

"It is not love hid in my heart, but Venus in her might seizing her
prey. Justly I fear my sin."

Love in *Phaedra* is involuntary illness; but although it's unbidden
and hostile ("Venus...seizing her prey") it's still the victim's sin. To be
visited by an evil that one hates and yet to bear the blame for it is the
torment of Phaedra. "I hate my life, and hold my love in horror," she
confesses to her nurse Oenone, after confession is wrung out of her.
Even greater than Phaedra's illicit "passion" for her stepson
Hippolytus is her revulsion against herself and against that passion,
and to blot it out, she longs for only two things, silence and death.

Her self-revulsion never leaves her, but the Nurse's invasion into
her silence, and the burst of confessional that's awakened by it, is not
only the beginning of Phaedra's doom, but of the doom that is to
overwhelm everyone. Oenone who cannot bear to witness Phaedra's
physical anguish and unspoken torment, overcomes her sovereign's
determination to go to her death without ever revealing the sin of her
"passion." After so long an effort of repression, when confession
comes—or more accurately, is disgorged—it flows almost gratefully.

And although she is reliving its anguish, Phaedra articulates freely the entire history of her "sin."

She's explaining the oncoming of disease and the invincible ways in which it imprisoned her. Soon after her marriage to Theseus, the first sight of his son Hippolytus chilled and fevered her. Strenuously she lashed about for "remedy" in prayer, altar service, and votive offering, but no effect, since—the hallucinatory effects of her illness—in the very face of Venus, in the very face of Theseus, she saw—and inadvertently prayed to—Hippolytus. Another tactic: banishment; she prevails upon Theseus to exile his son to Troezen. Most disastrous "remedy" of all, since, fatefully, Phaedra was soon sent there too, to remain during Theseus' absence. The final remedy is death, and Phaedra ends her confession by praying that Oenone does not attempt to snatch her away from it, her only possible "remedy."

It's the fatality of Phaedra: the visitation of "sin" and the utter helplessness, and therefore the ineradicable guilt, of the human will to overcome it.

Phaedra

My wound is not a new one. Scarcely had I
Been bound to Theseus by our marriage tie,
With peace and happiness seeming so well secured,
Until at Athens I saw my enemy.
I looked, I first turned pale, then blushed to see him,
And all my soul was in the greatest turmoil;
A mist made dim my sight, and my voice faltered,
And now my blood ran cold, then burned like fire.
In all my fevered body I could feel
Venus, whose fury had pursued so many
Of my sad race. I sought to shun her torments
With fervent vows. I built a shrine for her,
And there, 'mid many victims did I seek
The reason I had lost; but all for nothing.
I found no remedy for pain of love!
I offered incense vainly on her altars,
I called upon her name, and while I called her,
I loved Hippolytus, always before me!
And when I made her altars smoke with victims,
'Twas for a god whose name I dared not utter,—
And still I fled his presence, only to find him—
(The worst of horrors)—in his father's features!
At last I raised revolt against myself,
And stirred my courage up to persecute

The enemy I loved. To banish him
I wore a harsh and jealous step-dame's manner,
And ceaselessly I clamored for his exile,
Till I had torn him from his father's arms!
I breathed once more, Oenone. In his absence
The days passed by less troubled than before—
Innocent days! I hid my bitter grief,
Submitted to my husband, cherished the fruits
Of our most fatal marriage,—and in vain!
Again I saw the one whom I had banished,
Brought here by my own husband, and again
The old wound bled. And now it is not love
Hid in my heart, but Venus in her might
Seizing her prey. Justly I fear my sin!
I hate my life, and hold my love in horror.
I die:—I would have kept my name unsullied,
Burying guilty passion in the grave;
But I have not been able to refuse you;
You weep and pray, and so I tell you all,
And I shall be content, if as I perish,
You do not vex me with unjust reproaches,
Nor vainly try to snatch away from death
The last faint sparks of life, yet lingering!

132.

PHAEDRA CONFESSES TO HIPPOLYTUS HER PASSION FOR HIM AND HER SELF-LOATHING (OT)

(1677) JEAN RACINE, *PHAEDRA*, TR. ROBERT HENDERSON, ACT II

[Continues No. 131, above.] Twice over in the course of *Phaedra*, the ground of circumstance shifts, and Phaedra is confronted by a new "political" situation. Theseus is reported to be dead (just as later he will be reported to be once again alive). With his death, all strategies pertaining to the fact of his living become at once irrelevant. Since the same reshuffling of assumptions will happen again, there is deliberate irony in the shifting facts of external circumstance as opposed to the unalterable fixity of the tragedy's inherent course.

Oenone quickly seizes on the value of the new political situation for Phaedra's salvation. The claim of Phaedra and Theseus' young son to royal succession is in jeopardy; there will be rival claims. As a matter of expediency, then, Phaedra must ally her interests with Hippolytus', and after Theseus' death, she may approach Hippolytus, even confess her love, without guilt. Political astuteness, Oenone urges, may now spare Phaedra's life, her love, and her son's throne.

In her confrontation with Hippolytus, Phaedra, at first trembling lest her inability to conceal her passion betrayed her mission for her son, begins valiantly. But the very logic of her appeal to him to set aside hostility and suspicion between them leads quickly to her helplessly, even abjectly, confessing her love. Hippolytus, outraged, moves to escape ("for very shame I cannot see you longer"), but Phaedra, abandoning all formal distance between them, speaks out: put aside pretense, "you understood me...you could not well mistake."

Freed from all pretense, she protests in every word the depth of her love as well as the depth of her shame and guilt. Then all confession, unrestrained, tumbles out: her love, her self-hatred, and her deliberately instilling hatred of herself in him, as well as confession of her failed intent in confronting him now ("You think this vile confession...is what I meant to say?"). Inevitably, following this betrayal of her ostensible purpose in meeting with him, emerges her deepest purpose: her longing to be "healed." Kill me, she begs, plunge this sword, be the one to punish this abject guilt. And finally, if "you find it shameful to drench your hand in such polluted blood...lend your sword to me." Racine's *Phaedra* is possibly the most radical instance in Western drama of the longing of the self-judged transgressor for self-immolation even though transgressing in thought alone. The context of such intensity of guilt is attributed conventionally to Racine's religious education in the austerities of Jansenism; but beyond those austerities there is the long tradition in Western drama and belief in the propriety, if not sanctity, of just such surrenders for women transgressors into self-annihilation.

[For examples, see No. 58 and No. 59, above.]

PHAEDRA

Ah, prince, you understood me,—
Too well, indeed! For I had said enough.
You could not well mistake. But do not think

That in those moments when I love you most
I do not feel my guilt. No easy yielding
Has helped the poison that infects my mind.
The sorry object of divine revenge,
I am not half so hateful to your sight
As to myself. The gods will bear me witness,—
They who have lit this fire within my veins,—
The gods who take their barbarous delight
In leading some poor mortal heart astray!
Nay, do you not remember, in the past,
How I was not content to fly?—I drove you
Out of the land, so that I might appear
Most odious—and to resist you better
I tried to make you hate me—and in vain!
You hated more, and I loved not the less,
While your misfortunes lent you newer charms
I have been drowned in tears and scorched by fire!
Your own eyes might convince you of the truth
If you could look at me, but for a moment!
What do I say? You think this vile confession
That I have made, is what I meant to say?
I did not dare betray my son. For him
I feared,—and came to beg you not to hate him.
This was the purpose of a heart too full
Of love for you to speak of aught besides.
Take your revenge, and punish me my passion!
Prove yourself worthy of your valiant father,
And rid the world of an offensive monster!
Does Theseus' widow dare to love his son?
Monster indeed! Nay, let her not escape you!
Here is my heart! Here is the place to strike!
It is most eager to absolve itself!
It leaps impatiently to meet your blow!—
Strike deep! Or if, indeed, you find it shameful
To drench your hand in such polluted blood,—
If that be punishment too mild for you,—
Too easy for your hate,—if not your arm,
Then lend your sword to me,—Come! Give it now!

133.

PHAEDRA PLEADS WITH OENONE TO "FORCE HIPPOLYTUS TO LOVE" (OT)

(1677) JEAN RACINE, *PHAEDRA*, TR. ROBERT HENDERSON, ACT III

[Continues No. 132, above] Having given up every vestige of propriety before Hippolytus, Phaedra is, in a perverse way, free. Free, certainly, of the constraints of silence, modesty, and shame, and free to give vent to their opposites: the madness, the frenzy, and the almost savagery of desire that underlay her now abandoned restraint. She wants openly, and wants nothing else, but to capture the love of Hippolytus, and won't allow Oenone to cavil over the means. Her appeal—or more, command—to Oenone now is made up of a scramble of strategies, justifications and opportunities she imagines will capture him. Note the frailty of their sense:

1) His "pride" is only the barrier of innocence and inexperience. Since he was "bred in the forest," he's never yet known women or their love.

2) The barbaric nature of his mother, the Amazonian Queen Hippolyta, was tempered by love; he can be too.

3) His hatred of women? Helpful, since there is no rival.

4) If love doesn't touch him, ambition does. Oenone must offer him the throne, which Phaedra's son has already won by vote in Athens, and any surrender of Phaedra's power he desires. "He shall control both son and mother."

Stoop to anything, Phaedra instructs Oenone, use anything—tears, groans, say even that I'm dying. The guilelessness of her strategy equals, but exactly subverts, the desperation of her need. With Oenone gone on her mission, Phaedra enlists her ultimate accomplice: Venus, to whom she prays to avenge herself as thoroughly on Hippolytus as she has done on Phaedra herself—by visiting on him the same illness, forcing so "obdurate" an enemy of love, to love.

PHAEDRA

I cannot leave him.
That time is past. He knows how I am frenzied,
For I have overstepped my modesty,
And blazoned out my shame before his eyes.
Against my will, hope crept into my heart.

Did you not call my failing powers to me?
Was it not you, yourself, called back my soul
Which fluttered on my lips, and with your counsel
Lent me new life? Who told me I might love him?
This pride that you detest may yield to time.
The rudeness of the forest clings about him,
For he was bred there by the strictest laws.
Love is a word he never knew before.
Perhaps it was surprise that stunned him so;
There was much vehemence in all I said.
Remember that his mother was barbaric—
She was a Scythian, but she learned to love.
He has a bitter hate for all our sex.
Well, then no rival ever rules his heart.
Your counsel comes a little late, Oenone.
Now you must serve my madness, not my reason.
Love cannot find a way into his heart,
So let us take him where he has more feeling.
The lure of power seemed somewhat to touch him.
He could not hide that he was drawn to Athens,—
His vessels' prows were pointed there already,
With sails all set to run before the breeze.
Go, and on my behalf, touch his ambition,—
Dazzle his eyes with prospects of the crown.
The sacred diadem shall grace his brow,—
My highest honor is to set it there,
And he shall have the power I cannot keep.
He'll teach my son how men are ruled.—It may be
That he will deign to be a father to him.
He shall control both son and mother;—try him,-
Try every means to move him, for your words
Should meet more favor than my own could find.
Urge him with groans and tears,—say Phaedra's dying,
Nor blush to speak in pleading terms with him.
My last hope is in you,—do what you will,
I'll sanction it;—the issue is my fate!

(Exit Oenone.)
Venus implacable, thou seest me shamed
And I am sore confounded. Have I not
Been humbled yet enough? Can cruelty
Stretch farther still? Thine arrows have struck home!
It is thy victory! Wouldst gain new triumphs
Then seek an enemy more obdurate,—
Hippolytus neglects thee, braves thine anger.

He never bows his knee before thine altars.
Thy name offends his proud, disdainful hearing.
Our interests are alike,—avenge thyself,
Force him to love!

134.

PHAEDRA STRUGGLES WITH HER GUILT AND JEALOUSY (OT)

(1677) JEAN RACINE, *PHAEDRA*, TR. ROBERT HENDERSON, ACT IV

[Continues No. 133, above] [For notes on Hippolytus and Aricia, see in Men's volumes "Hippolytus Confesses His Long Concealed Love for Aricia."] Suddenly, again, a seismic change in circumstance: Theseus is in fact alive, and returning. With horror, Phaedra recognizes the additional shame of which she is guilty: her open confession of love for Hippolytus, and the worst, most ignoble shame of all should Theseus learn of her adulterous yearning for his son. Once again Oenone rescues Phaedra from her renewed resolve on death, urging a different course. Arguing that "proud Hippolytus" will now rejoice in "that, dying, you should lend his tale [of your guilt] belief," she wins a distraught Phaedra's consent to "dare to accuse him first" that he, not Phaedra, was guilty of attempted seduction. Theseus, enraged on hearing this, condemns his son and calls down on him the curse of Neptune. Phaedra is overwhelmed with remorse, but as she is begging Theseus to spare his son, she learns that "Aricia has his heart and soul,/That he loves only her."

Phaedra, abandoning herself to jealousy, rings all the changes of feeling, of painful speculation, of shame, of self-pity that move her directly to the decision that Aricia must be destroyed, and then almost immediately, she is horrified at the thought, and recognizes that added to her overriding guilt is the lie of hypocrisy. In a bewildering round of self-accusations, she turns all of them against Oenone, who first roused her, after she had "left the light of day," to maneuver for advantage and for life. But Oenone's guilt of and that of Phaedra are intertwined, and her anathema against Oenone has already become anathema against herself. Following Oenone's suicide, it is only a step to her own. Her confession to Theseus of her guilt toward his son comes too late, and even Theseus shares in the universal complicity and in the doom that follows. [See in Men's volumes "Theramenes Reports the Gruesome Death of Hiopplytus."]

PHAEDRA

Aricia found the entrance to his heart!
Now for what other pains am I reserved?
All I have suffered,—ecstasies of passion,
Longings and fears, the horrors of remorse,
The shame of being spurned with contumely,
Were feeble tastes of what is now my torment.
They love each other! By what secret charm
Have they deceived me? When and where and how
Did they contrive to meet? You knew it all,—
And why, then, was I kept from knowing of it?
You never told me of their stolen hours
Of love and of delight. Have they been seen
Talking together often?—did they seek
The forest shadows? Ah, they had full freedom
To be together. Heaven watched their sighs.
They loved,—and never felt that they were guilty.
The morning sun shone always clear for them,
While I,—an outcast from the face of Nature,
Shunned the bright day, and would have hid myself,—
Death the one god whom I dared ask for aid!
I waited for the freedom of the grave.
Oenone, can I bear this happiness
Which so insults me? I would have your pity.
Yes, she must be destroyed. My husband's fury
Against her hated race shall be renewed.
The punishment must be a heavy one.
Her guilt outruns the guilt of all her brothers.
I'll plead with Theseus, in my jealousy,—
What do I say? Oh, have I lost my senses?
Is Phaedra jealous? Will she, then, go begging
For Theseus' help? He lives,—and yet I burn.
For whom? Whose heart is this I claim as mine?
My hair stands up with horror at my words,
And from this time, my guilt has passed all bounds!
Hypocrisy and incest breathe at once
Through all I do. My hands are ripe for murder,
To spill the guiltless blood of innocence.
Do I still live, a wretch, and dare to face

The holy Sun, from whom I have my being?
(to Oenone) What counsels did you give me?
Why would you still pour poison in mine ears?
You have destroyed me. You have brought me back
When I should else have left the light of day.
You made me to forget my solemn duty,
And see Hippolytus, whom I had shunned.
What have you done? Why did those wicked lips
Slander his faultless life with blackest lies?
It may be you have murdered him. By now
The prayer unholy of a heartless father
May have been granted. I will have no words!
Go, monster! Leave me to my sorry fate.
May the just gods repay you properly,
And may your punishment remain forever
To strike with fear, all such as you, who strive
To feed the frailty of the great with cunning,
To push them to the very brink of ruin
To which their feet incline,—to smooth the path
Of guilt. Such flatterers the gods, in anger,
Bestow on kings as their most fatal gift!

(Exit Phaedra)

CONTUMELY: a humiliating insult.

GLOSSARY OF GREEK
AND ROMAN NAMES

Aphrodite: (Greek mythology) goddess of love, daughter of Zeus

Apollo: (Greek mythology) god of the sun, healing, music, and prophecy; patron of the Oracle at Delphi; son of Zeus

Ares: (Greek mythology) god of war, son of Zeus and Hera, sometime paramour of Aphrodite

Argive: a native of ancient Argos; or, any Greek

Artemis: (Greek mythology) virgin goddess of the hunt, also identified with the moon; twin sister of Apollo

Ate: (Greek mythology) Avenger, goddess of rage and mischief; daughter of Eris (Strife) and Zeus. She personifies infatuation, with guilt its cause and evil its consequence.

Athena Pallas: (Greek mythology) warrior goddess, goddess of wisdom, the arts and sciences; patroness of Athens; daughter of Zeus

Bacchus: Roman equivalent of Dionysus

Charon: (Greek mythology) with his boat, he takes the souls of the dead across the river Lethe or Styx to Hades

Cypris: the island of Cyprus (or Cypris). Center for the worship of Aphrodite; hence, "the Cyprian"

Delphi: a town in northern Greece, site of the famous oracular shrine of Apollo (see Pytho)

Demeter: (Greek mythology) goddess of agriculture; sister of Zeus, mother of Persephone

Dionysus: (Greek mythology) god of wine; patron of drama in Athens; son of Zeus

Elysium: (Greek mythology) the equivalent of Heaven

Erynyes: see Furies

Furies: (Greek mythology) spirits of Divine Vengeance, especially transgressions that touch on the basis of human society. They punish violations of filial duty, the claims of kinship, rites of hospitality, murder, perjury, etc., eventually reconciled by Athena to Athenian law

Hades: (Greek mythology) god of the Underworld, where the souls of the dead go; brother of Zeus and Poseidon; also used as a name for the Underworld

Hecate: (Greek mythology) a confusing divinity, identified with the moon, Artemis, and Persephone, and invoked by sorcerers. She is the great sender of visions, of madness, and of sudden terror. Medea was her witch-priestess before falling in love with Jason.

Helios: Apollo

Hera: (Greek mythology) sister and wife of Zeus

Hermes: (Greek mythology) messenger of the gods and guide of souls departing to Hades

Hymen: (Greek mythology) god of marriage

Ilion: Greek name for ancient Troy

Ilium: Greek name for ancient Troy

Jove: see Jupiter

Jupiter: Roman equivalent of Zeus

Lethe: (Greek mythology) the river in Hades, from which the souls of the dead drank and became oblivious to their past lives. Then they were carried across by Charon in his boat.

Neptune: Roman equivalent of Poseidon

Orpheus: (Greek mythology) a Thracian philosopher, poet, and musician, who wins permission by his music to bring his wife back to earth from Hades

Pallas: Athena

Persephone: (Greek mythology) wife of Hades, queen of the underworld, daughter of Demeter

Phoebus: epithet for Apollo meaning purity, light

Phrygian: of Phrygia, an ancient country in Asia Minor, one of whose cities was Troy

Pluto: Roman equivalent of Hades

Poseidon: (Greek mythology) god of the sea; brother of Zeus and Hades

Pytho: ancient name for Delphi, Apollo's seat of prophecy. It is conducted by the prophetess Pythia seated on a tripod over the Oracle proper, which is a cleft in the ground in the innermost sanctuary, from which rose cold vapors that have the power of inducing the ecstasy that induces the priestess to have prophetic vision. Her responses are ambiguous, but though always true, give rise to misinterpretation.

Styx: see Lethe

Tartarus: (Greek mythology) the infernal depths of Hades

Zeus: (Greek mythology) chief of the gods, master of the lightning bolt

BIBLIOGRAPHY OF
MONOLOGUE SOURCES

Aeschylus, *Agamemnon*: Translated by Leon Katz (unpublished); alternate source: Aeschylus, *The Oresteia*. Translated by Ted Hughes. Farrar, Strauss & Giroux, 1999.

———, *Prometheus Bound*: Robert W. Corrigan, ed. *Classical Tragedy, Greek and Roman*. Applause Books, 1990.

Anonymous, *Arden of Feversham*: Martin White, ed. *Arden of Feversham*. New Mermaids, 1982.

Aretino, Pietro, *The Courtezan*: Samuel Putnam, editor and translator. *The Works of Aretino*. Covici-Friede, 1933.

———, *The Stablemaster*: Bruce Penman, ed. *Five Italian Renaissance Comedies*. Penguin, 1978.

Ariosto, Ludovico, *Lena*; *The Necromancer*; *The Pretenders*: Translated by Leon Katz (unpublished); alternate source: Edmond M. Beame and Leonard G. Sbrocchi, editors and translators. *The Comedies of Ariosto*. University of Chicago, 1975.

Aristophanes, *Lysistrata*: Translated by Leon Katz (unpublished); alternate source: Robert W. Corrigan. *Classical Comedy, Greek and Roman*. Applause, 1987. Translated by Donald Sutherland.

———, *Thesmaphoriazusae*: Translated by Leon Katz (unpublished); alternate source: Whitney J. Oates and Eugene O'Neill Jr., ed. *The Complete Greek Drama*. Modern Library, 1938.

Augier, Emile, *Olympe's Marriage*: Stephen S. Stanton, ed. *Camille and Other Plays*. Mermaid Dramabook, 1957.

Baillie, Joanna, *De Monfort*: Mrs. Incbald, ed. *The British Theatre* vol. 24. Longman, Hurst, Rees, Orme, 1808.

Balzac, Honoré de, *The Stepmother*: J. Walker McSpadden, ed. *The Works of Honoré de Balzac*. Avil Publishing, 1901.

Banks, John, *The Unhappy Favorite, or The Earl of Essex*: James Sutherland, ed. *Restoration Tragedies*. Oxford University, 1977.

Beaumont, Francis, and John Fletcher, *The Knight of the Burning Pestle*; *The Maid's Tragedy*: A.H. Nethercourt, Ch. R. Baskervill, and V.B. Heltzel, ed. *Elizabethan and Stuart Plays*. Holt, Rinehart & Winston, 1971.

———, *The Philaster*: C.F. Tucker Brooke and N.B. Paradise, ed. *English Drama 1580–1642*. D.C. Heath & Co., 1933.

Behn, Aphra: *The Feigned Courtesans*; *The Lucky Chance*: Aphra Behn. *The Rover and Other Plays*. Edited by Jane Spencer. Oxford University, 1995.

———, *Sir Patient Fancy*: Katharine M. Rogers, ed. *The Meridian Anthology of Restoration and Eighteen Century Plays by Women*. Meridian Press, 1994.

———, *The Young King*: Montague Summers, ed. *The Works of Aphra Behn*, vol. 2. William Heinemann, 1965.

Boucicault, Dion: *The Corsican Brothers; London Assurance*: A. Parkin, ed. *Selected Plays of Dion Boucicault*. Catholic University of America Press, 1987.

Bruno, Giordano, *Il Candelaio*: Eric Bentley, ed. *The Genius of the Italian Theater*. New American Library, 1964.

Büchner, Georg, *Danton's Death*: Georg Büchner. *Complete Plays and Prose*. Translated by Carl Richard Mueller. Hill & Wang, 1963.

Bulwer, Edward, *Richelieu*: M.R. Booth, ed. *English Plays of the XIX Century*, vol. 1. Clarendon, 1969.

Cervantes, Miguel de, *The Jealous Old Man, an Interlude*: Walter Starkie, editor and translator. *Eight Spanish Plays of the Golden Age*. The Modern Library, 1964.

Chapman, George, John Marston, and Ben Jonson, *Eastward, Ho!*: Brian Gibbons. *Elizabethan and Jacobean Comedies*. E. Benn, 1984.

Cibber, Colley, *The Careless Husband*: George Nettleton, ed. *British Dramatists from Dryden to Sheridan*. Houghton Mifflin Co., 1939.

———, *Love's Last Shift*: Douglas MacMillan and Howard M. Jones, ed. *Plays of the Restoration and Eighteenth Century*. Holt, Rinehart & Winston, 1966.

Coleridge, Samuel Taylor, *Remorse*: Gerald B. Kauvar and Gerald C. Sorensen. *Nineteenth-Century English Verse Drama*. Associated University Presses, 1973.

Colman, George, the Elder, *The Jealous Wife*: George Nettleton and Arthur Case, ed. *British Dramatists from Dryden to Sheridan*. Houghton & Mifflen, 1939.

Congreve, William: *The Double Dealer; The Way of the World*: Eric S. Rump, ed. *Comedies by William Congreve*. Penguin, 1985.

Corneille, Pierre, *Le Cid*: Paul Landis, ed. *Six Plays by Corneille and Racine*. Modern Library, 1931.

Corneille, Thomas, *Laodice*: Lacy Lockert, tr. *The Chief Rivals of Corneille and Racine*. The Vanderbuilt University, 1956.

Coyne, Joseph Stirling, *Did You Ever Send Your Wife to Camberwell?*: Michael R. Booth, ed. *The Lights o' London and Other Victorian Plays*. Clarendon Press, 1995.

Dekker, Thomas, *The Shoemaker's Holiday*: Brian Gibbons. *Elizabethan and Jacobean Comedies*. E. Benn, 1984.

Dryden, John, *All for Love*: James Sutherland, ed. *Restoration Tragedies*. Oxford University, 1977.

Dumas, Alexandre, *fils, Camille*: Stephen S. Stanton, ed. *Camille and Other Plays*. Mermaid Dramabook, 1957.

Dumas, Alexandre, *père, The Tower of Nesle*: Alexandre Dumas. *The Tower of Nesle*. Translated by Adam Gowans. Gowans and Gray, 1906.

Euripides, *Alcestis; Andromache; Electra; Ion; Euripides. Ten Plays by Euripides*. Translated by Moses Hadas and John McLean. Bantam, 1960.

———, *Bacchae; Iphigenia in Aulis*: Translated by Leon Katz (unpublished); alternate source: Euripides. *Ten Plays by Euripides*. Translated by Moses Hadas and John McLean. Bantam, 1960.

———, *Hecuba*: Euripides. *Hecuba*. Translated by Janet Lembke and Kenneth J. Reckford. Oxford University Press, 1991.

———, *Hippolytus*: Euripides. *Ten Plays by Euripides*. Translated by Moses Hadas and John McLean. Bantam, 1960; Dudley Fitts, ed. *Greek Plays in Modern Translation*. Dial Press, 1947.

———, *Medea*: Dudley Fitts, ed. *Greek Plays in Modern Translation*. Dial Press, 1947.

———, *The Phoenician Women*: Translated by Leon Katz (unpublished); alternate source: Whitney J. Oates and Eugene O'Neill, Jr., ed. *The Complete Greek Drama*. Modern Library, 1938. Translated by E.P. Coleridge.

———, *Rhesus*: Translated by Leon Katz (unpublished); alternate source: Whitney J.

Oates and Eugene O'Neill Jr., ed. *The Complete Greek Drama*. Modern Library, 1938.

————, *The Trojan Women*: Jean-Paul Sartre, ad. *Euripides' The Trojan Women*. Vintage Books, 1967. Translated by Ronald Duncan; Euripides. *Ten Plays by Euripides*. Translated by Moses Hadas and John McLean. Bantam, 1960; Gilbert Murray, editor and translator. *Five Plays of Euripides*. Oxford University Press, 1934.

Farquhar, George, *The Beaux' Stratagem*; *The Constant Couple*: George Farquhar. *The Recruiting Officer and Other Plays*. Edited by William Myers. Clarendon, 1995.

Fitzball, Edward, *The Inchcape Bell, or the Dumb Sailor Boy*: Michael R. Booth, ed. *The Lights o' London and Other Victorian Plays*. Clarendon Press, 1995.

Ford, John, *The Broken Heart*; *The Lover's Melancholy*; *Perkin Warbeck*: John Ford. *Five Plays*. Edited by Havelock Ellis. Mermaid Dramabook, 1957.

Gay, John, *The Beggar's Opera*: Douglas MacMillan and Howard M. Jones, ed. *Plays of the Restoration and Eighteenth Century*. Holt, Rinehart & Winston, 1966.

Gilbert, William Schwenck, *Tom Cobb*: Michael R. Booth, ed. *English Plays of the Nineteenth Century*, Vol. IV. Clarendon, 1973.

Greene, Robert, *Friar Bacon and Friar Bungay*: C.F. Tucker Brooke and N.B. Paradise, ed. *English Drama 1580–1642*. D.C. Heath & Co., 1933.

Hazlewood,Colin Henry, *Lady Audley's Secret*: George Rowell, ed. *Nineteenth Century Plays*. Oxford University, 1972.

Herondas, *The Jealous Woman* (Mime #5); *A Chat Between Friends* (Mime #6): Translated by Leon Katz (unpublished); alternate source: *The Mimes of Herondas*. Grey Fox Press, 1981. Translated by Guy Davenport.

Heywood, Thomas, *A Woman Killed with Kindness*: Kathleen E. McLuskie and David Bevington, ed. *Plays on Women*. Manchester University, 1999.

Hugo, Victor, *Mary Tudor*; *The Twin Brothers*: Victor Hugo. *Victor Hugo, Dramas*, vols. 1, 2, and 4. Anonymous translation. Dana Estes and Company, n.d.

————, *Ruy Blas*: Translated by Leon Katz (unpublished); alternate source: Helen A. Gaubert, ed. *Three Plays by Victor Hugo*. Washington Square Press, 1964. Translated by Camilla Crosland.

James, Henry, *The High Bid*: Leon Edel, ed. *The Complete Plays of Henry James*. J.B. Lippincott, 1949.

Jones, Henry Arthur, *The Middleman*: Michael R. Booth, ed. *The Lights o' London and Other Victorian Plays*. Clarendon Press, 1995.

Jonson, Ben, *The Alchemist*; *Bartholomew Fair*; *Epicoene, or the Silent Woman*; *Volpone*: J. Procter, ed. *The Selected Plays of Ben Jonson*. Cambridge University, 1989.

————, *Catiline's Conspiracy*: *The Complete Plays of Ben Jonson*, vol. 2. E.P. Dutton, 1946.

Joyce, James, *Finnegans Wake*: James Joyce. *Finnegans Wake*. Viking, 1939.

Kyd, Thomas, *Spanish Tragedy*: W. Tydemon, ed. *Two Tudor Tragedies*. Penguin, 1992.

Lee, Nathaniel, *The Princess of Cleves*: Michael Cordner and Ronald Clayton, ed. *Four Restoration Marriage Plays*. Clarendon, 1995.

————, *The Rival Queens, or the Death of Alexander the Great*: D. MacMillan and H.M. Jones, ed. *Plays of the Restoration and Eighteenth Century*. Holt, Rinehart and Winston, 1931.

Le Sage, Alain-René, *Turcaret*: *French Comedies of the XVIII Century*. George Routledge & Sons, n.d.

Lessing, Gottfried Ephraim, *Emilia Galotti*: Translated by Leon Katz (unpublished); alternate source: Peter Demetz, ed. *Gottfried Ephraim Lessing, Nathan the Wise*,

Minna von Barnhelm, and Other Plays and Writings. Continuum, 1991. Translated by Anna Johanna Gode von Aesch.

————, *Miss Sara Sampson:* Ernest Bell, editor and translator. *The Dramatic Works of G.E. Lessing,* vol. 1. George Bell & Sons, 1901.

Lewes, George Henry, *The Game of Speculation:* Michael R. Booth, ed. *The Lights o' London and Other Victorian Plays.* Clarendon Press, 1995.

Lillo, George, *Fatal Curiosity:* Wm H. McBurney, ed. *George Lillo, Fatal Curiosity.* University of Nebraska, 1966.

————, *The London Merchant:* Douglas MacMillan and Howard M. Jones, ed. *Plays of the Restoration and Eighteenth Century.* Holt, Rinehart & Winston, 1966.

Marlowe, Christopher, *Edward II; Tamburlaine:* Christopher Marlowe. *Dr. Faustus and Other Plays.* Oxford University, 1995.

————, *The Jew of Malta:* C.F. Tucker Brooke and N.B. Paradise, ed. *English Drama 1580–1642.* D.C. Heath & Co., 1933.

Marston, John, *The Dutch Courtesan:* John Marston. *The Dutch Courtesan.* Edited by M.L. Wine. University of Nebraska, 1965.

————, *The Malcontent:* Brian Gibbons. *Elizabethan and Jacobean Comedies.* E. Benn, 1984.

Marston, J. Westland, *The Patrician's Daughter:* J.O. Bailey, ed. *British Plays of the Nineteenth Century.* Odyssey, 1966.

Massinger, Philip, *A New Way to Pay Old Debts:* A.H. Nethercourt, Ch.R. Baskervill, and V.B. Heltzel, ed. *Stuart Plays.* Holt, Rinehart & Winston, 1971.

Menander, *The Arbitration:* Translated by Leon Katz (unpublished); alternate source: *Menander.* Wm. Heinemann, 1930. Translated by Francis G. Allinson.

Middleton, Thomas, and Thomas Dekker, *The Roaring Girl:* Kathleen E. McLuskie and David Bevington, ed. *Plays on Women.* Manchester University, 1999.

Middleton, Thomas, and William Rowley, *The Changeling:* A.H. Gomme, ed. *Jacobean Tragedies.* Oxford University, 1971.

Molière, *Dom Garcie de Navarre; George Dandin; Les Fourberies de Scapin:* *The Plays of Molière.* vol. 2. Translated by A.R. Waller. John Grant, 1907.

————, *Don Juan; Les Precieuses Ridicules;* Ian Maclean, Molière, *Don Juan and Other Plays,* Oxford University, 1989. Translated by George Gravely and Ian Maclean.

————, *The Learned Ladies:* Molière. *Comedies* vol. 2. Translated by Henry Baker and James Miller. Everyman's Library, 1948.

————, *The Misanthrope:* Molière. *Four Comedies.* Translated by Richard Wilbur. Harcort Brace, 1982,.

————, *Tartuffe:* Molière. *Molière's Tartuffe or The Impostor,* Translated by Christopher Hampton. Faber & Faber, 1984; Molière *The Plays of Molière.* vol. 2. Translated by A.R. Waller. John Grant, 1907.

Molina, Tirso de, *The Playboy of Seville:* Walter Starkie, editor and translator. *Eight Spanish Plays of the Golden Age.* The Modern Library, 1964.

Musset, Alfred de, *The Follies of Marianne: The Complete Writings of Alfred de Musset,* Vols. 3 and 4. National Library Company, 1905.

Otway, Thomas, *Don Carlos; Venice Preserv'd:* Havelock Ellis, ed. *Thomas Otway.* Mermaid Series, 1888.

Pinero, Arthur Wing, *The Second Mrs. Tanqueray:* George Rowell, ed. *Late Victorian Plays 1890–1914.* Oxford University, 1972.

Pix, Mary, *The Innocent Mistress:* Fidelis Morgan. *The Female Wits: Women Playwrights on the London Stage 1660–1720.* Virago, 1981.

Porto-Riche, Georges de, *Francoise' Luck: Four Plays of the Free Theater.* Syewart and Kidd, 1915.

Racine, Jean, *Andromache*; *Brittanicus*; *Phaedra*: Paul Landis, ed. *Six Plays by Corneille and Racine*. Modern Library, 1931.

Robertson, Thomas William, *Caste*: George Rowell, ed. *Nineteenth Century Plays*. Oxford University, 1972.

Rojas, Fernando de, *Celestina*: Eric Bentley, ed. *The Classic Theatre*, Vol. 3. Doubleday/Anchor, 1959.

Rowe, Nicholas, *The Fair Penitent*: Bonamy Dobree, ed. *Five Restoration Tragedies*. Oxford University Press, 1935.

———, *The Tragedy of Jane Shore*: George Nettleton and Arthur Case, ed. *British Dramatists from Dryden to Sheridan*. Houghton & Mifflen, 1939.

Sade, Marquis de, *Oxtiern*: *The Marquis de Sade: The 120 Days of Sodom and Other Writings*. Compiled and translated by Austryn Wainhouse and Richard Seaver. Grove Press, 1966.

———, *Philosophy in the Bedroom*: Marquis de Sade. *Justine, The Philosophy in the Bedroom, and Other Writings*. Translated by Austryn Wainhouse, Richard Seaver. Grove Press, 1966.

Schiller, Friedrich, *Intrigue and Love*: Friedrich Schiller. *Intrigue and Love*. Translated by Charles E. Passage. Ungar, 1971.

———, *Mary Stuart*: Walter Hinderer, ed. *Schiller, Wallenstein and Mary Stuart*. Continuum, 1991.

Seneca, *Agamemnon*; *Hercules Oetaeus*; *The Phoenician Women*: Translated by Leon Katz (unpublished); alternate source: *The Tragedies of Seneca*. Translated by Ella Isabel Harris. Oxford University Press, 1904.

———, *Medea*: Translated by Leon Katz (unpublished); alternate source: Philip Whaley Harsh, ed. *An Anthology of Roman Drama*. Rinehart, 1960.

———, *Phaedra*: Frank Justus Miller, editor and translator. *The Tragedies of Seneca*. University of Chicago, 1907.

———, *The Trojan Women*; *The Phoenician Women*: *The Tragedies of Seneca*. Translated by Ella Isabel Harris. Oxford University Press, 1904.

Shaw, Bernard, *Back to Methuselah*; *Candida*; *Getting Married*; *Heartbreak House*; *Major Barbara*; *Misalliance*; *Mrs. Warren's Profession*; *The Philanderer*; *Pygmalion*; *Saint Joan*: Bernard Shaw. *The Complete Plays*. Paul Hamlyn, 1965.

Shelley, Percy Bysshe, *The Cenci*: Percy Bysshe Shelley. *The Cenci*. Woodstock Books, 1999.

Sheridan, Richard Brinsley, *Pizarro*: John Hampden, ed. *The Plays of R.B. Sheridan*. Thomas Nelson & Sons, n.d.

———, *The Rivals*: Alexander W. Allison, Arthur J. Carr, and Arthur M. Eastman, ed. *Masterpieces of the Drama*. Macmillan, 1957.

———, *The School for Scandal*: Douglas MacMillan and Howard M. Jones, ed. *Plays of the Restoration and Eighteenth Century*. Holt, Rinehart & Winston, 1966.

Shirley, James, *The Cardinal*: C.F. Tucker Brooke and N.B. Paradise, ed. *English Drama 1580–1642*. D.C. Heath & Co., 1933.

Sophocles, *Ajax*; *Electra*: David Grene and Richard Lattimore, ed. *Sophocles*, vol. 2. University of Chicago, 1954.

———, *Antigone*: Sophocles. *Antigone*. Translated by Nicholas Rudall. Ivan R. Dee, 1998; Sophocles. *Oedipus the King and Antigone*. Translated and edited by Peter D. Arnott. Appleton-Century-Croft, 1960; David Grene and Richard Lattimore, ed. *Sophocles*, vol. 1. University of Chicago, 1954.

Steele, Richard, *The Conscious Lovers*; *The Funeral*; *The Tender Husband*: S.S. Kenny, ed. *The Plays of Richard Steele*. Clarendon, 1971.

Tennyson, Alfred, Lord, *Beckett*: Gerald B. Kauvar and Gerald C. Sorensen. *Nineteenth-Century English Verse Drama*. Associated University Presses, 1973.

Terence, *The Mother-in-Law*: Translated by Leon Katz (unpublished); alternate source: George Duckworth, ed. *Complete Roman Drama*. Random House, 1942.

Theocritus, *Idylls*, 2, "The Sorceress": Translated by Leon Katz (unpublished); alternate source: *The Idylls of Theocritus*. Translated by Robert Wells. Carcanet Press, 1988.

Thompson, Benjamin, *The Stranger*: Douglas MacMillan and Howard M. Jones, ed. *Plays of the Restoration and Eighteenth Century*. Holt, Rinehart & Winston, 1966.

Tourneur, Cyril, *The Atheist's Tragedy*: Sir John Churton Collins, ed. *The Plays and Poems of Cyril Tourneur*. New York Books for Libraries Press, 1972.

———, *The Revenger's Tragedy*: Cyril Tourneur. *The Revenger's Tragedy* Edited by Brian Gibbons. The New Mermaids, 1989.

Trotter, Catherine, *Love at a Loss*: Edna L. Steeves, ed. *The Plays of Mary Pix and Catharine Trotter*. Garland, 1982.

Vanbrugh, Sir John, *The Provok'd Wife*: *Twelve Famous Plays of the Restoration and the Eighteenth Century*. Modern Library, 1933.

———, *The Relapse*: D. Davison, ed. *Restoration Comedies*. Oxford University, 1970.

Vega, Lope de, *Acting is Believing*: Lope de Vega. *Acting Is Believing*. Translated by Michael D. McGaha. Trinity University Press, 1986.

———, *The Duchess of Amalfi's Steward*: Lope de Vega. *The Duchess of Amalfi's Steward*. Translated by Cynthia Rodriguez-Bodendyck. Dovehouse Canada, 1985.

———, *Fuente Ovejuna*: Eric Bentley, ed. *The Classic Theatre*, Vol. 3. Doubleday/Anchor, 1959.

———, *Peribanez and the Comendador de Ocana*: Lope de Vega. *Lope de Vega: Five Plays*. Edited by R.D.F. Pring-Mill. Translated by Jill Booty. Mermaid Dramabook, 1961.

Voltaire, *The Prodigal; Zaire*: *The Dramatic Works of Voltaire* vol. 5. E.R. DuMont, 1901.

Webster, John, *The Duchess of Malfi*: A.H. Nethercourt, Ch.R. Baskervill, and V.B. Heltzel, ed. *Stuart Plays*. Holt, Rinehart & Winston, 1971.

———, *The White Devil*: John Webster. *The White Devil*. Edited by Christina Luckyj. W.W. Norton, 1996.

Wilde, Oscar, *An Ideal Husband; Lady Windermere's Fan; Salome; A Woman of No Importance*: *Oscar Wilde, The Complete Works*. Barnes & Noble, 1994.

Wiseman, Jane, *Antiochus the King*: Jane Wiseman. *Antiochus the Great, or The Fatal Relapse*. W. Turner & R. Bassert, 1702.

Wycherley, William, *The Country Wife*: D. Davison, ed. *Restoration Comedies*. Oxford University, 1970.

———, *The Plain Dealer*: B. Gibbons, ed. *Five Restoration Comedies*. Bloch/New Mermaids, 1984.

COPYRIGHT INFORMATION